PSYCHO
CONSEQUEN
AMERICAN CIVIL WAR

PSYCHOLOGICAL CONSEQUENCES OF THE AMERICAN CIVIL WAR

R. Gregory Lande

McFarland & Company, Inc., Publishers

Jefferson, North Carolina

ISBN (print) 978-1-4766-6737-9
ISBN (ebook) 978-1-4766-2694-9

LIBRARY OF CONGRESS CATALOGUING-IN-PUBLICATION DATA

BRITISH LIBRARY CATALOGUING DATA ARE AVAILABLE

Front cover: Image of Camp sentry at Rappahannock Station,
Virginia. Edwin Forbes, artist (Library of Congress)

Printed in the United States of America

*McFarland & Company, Inc., Publishers
Box 611, Jefferson, North Carolina 28640
www.mcfarlandpub.com*

To my family:
my mother, Anne, who modeled compassion;
my father, Maurice, who taught me objectivity;
my wife, Brenda, who tirelessly supports our relationship;
and the radiant light of my life, my son, Galen.

Table of Contents

Preface

Wars do not end with peace. When America's Civil War was over it set the stage for another, more enduring conflict, as a fractured society confronted the lingering psychological consequences that followed four brutal years of deprivation, distrust, and death. The enemy was intangible, lurking in the minds of the war's survivors. Like any great conflict, the battles raged back and forth, as the war-weary country fought the mental demons.

Psychological Consequences of the American Civil War describes the postwar pathos and why, for some, solace lay in Spiritualism, patent medicines, phony physicians, or alcohol and drug abuse. For others, the demons' demands were dangerous, setting loose a crime wave that inundated the nation. Some lapsed into insanity or sought the ultimate escape through suicide.

Taken as a whole, these public pursuits hinted that all was not right in postwar America. In a general sense they suggested that elements of society were broken, with dysphoria and disillusionment dominating.

My inspiration for this book came from the common observation that wars produce ripples and ruptures through societies, effects that last long after the battlefields are quiet. That was certainly the situation as America emerged from the Civil War. Modern societies accept and debate that proposition as a cost of potential conflict. This was not the case during America's Civil War. I ask the reader to imagine a time when infectious diseases were a leading cause of death, antibiotics the stuff of science fiction, religious faith a major moral force, the study of human behavior in its infancy, and the emotional consequences of war rarely discussed.

The combination of these inhibiting factors made the discovery of the psychological factors affecting postwar Americans a challenge. Helping me overcome that hurdle was my training as a physician, which emphasizes a person's medical and social history, constituting as it does a natural part of any

1

patient interaction. My specialization in psychiatry extended that interest, making a person's history a particularly important component in understanding human behavior. Adding to that professional background, my personal experiences in forensic psychiatry and addiction medicine have contributed insights that collectively informed my analysis of the social forces shaping America's postwar period.

Guided by my professional experiences, I searched through a variety of primary source documents such as newspapers, popular periodicals, medical journals, census records, soldiers' letters, and contemporary books. Certainly many other eminent historians have done the same, but *Psychological Consequences of the American Civil War* differs in terms of its scope and analysis. For example, understanding the psychological role of patent medicines is not gleaned through an investigation of the bottle's contents but instead through what was printed on the label.

My research and writing tells only part of the story. This book's publication depended on three others: Brenda Lande, my wife, is an avid lover of books, and, as a librarian, she brought this passion to my aid. I owe a deep debt of gratitude for Brenda's assistance and encouragement. Galen Lande provided critical technological support in keeping the computers humming and, in a more direct role, offered invaluable research suggestions.

Introduction

America was a seething cauldron in the nineteenth century. Long-held customs and beliefs were under attack. An increasingly fractious public discourse eventually aligned along diametrically opposed poles of the compass. The political disputes led to a geographical divide, with the southern states united in their rigid opposition to the northern ones. An implacable hatred, fanned by partisan newspapers and politicians, propelled the nation toward war. Confederate forces in South Carolina launched the first salvo, attacking federal troops stationed at Fort Sumter on April 12, 1861. The fury unleashed that day set in motion decades of mayhem, misery, and malevolence.

As the violence of the civil war spread, it increasingly doused the hot tempers and patriotic fervor that propelled men, their families, and their governments to support the armed conflict. After years of brutal battles, a sagacious General William Tecumseh Sherman captured the core of a pyrrhic victory with his plaintive plea that "I am sick and tired of fighting—its glory is all moonshine; even success the most brilliant is over dead and mangled bodies, with the anguish and lamentations of distant families, appealing to me for sons, husbands, and fathers.... And, so far as I know, all the fighting men of our army want peace; and it is only those who have never heard a shot, never heard the shrieks and groans of the wounded and lacerated (friend or foe), that cry aloud for more blood, more vengeance, more desolation."[1]

Sherman's pensive reflection was not entirely accurate. Citizens safely ensconced far from the frontlines were not entirely immune to the horrors of war. Newspapers and other periodicals of the day regaled readers far from the battlefields with all the gory details, marking the Civil War as America's first armed conflict thoroughly visible in both words and images to noncombatants.[2,3]

America had barely begun the war when reports from Maryland breathlessly declared that "one of the most bloody and well-contested fields known

3

to ancient or modern times" had taken place at Antietam Creek.[4] Newspapers provided readers far removed from the battle with a vicarious opportunity to see the slaughter. A seemingly nonchalant and dispassionate reporter studied the landscape soon after the great battle was over, paying particular attention to the most hotly contested areas:

> The dead and wounded were strewn upon the places indicated, in hideous confusion.... Scattered here and there were groups of blackened corpses.... Mingled with the dead came up to the ear the groans of those in whose breasts there yet remained a spark of vitality, but whose lamp had nearly expired; the hopeful cases, so far as possible, were removed for medical assistance ... the hopeless cases were allowed to remain upon the field. A rebel soldier ... vainly attempted [to] rise; he had received a wound upon the temple from which the brain protruded; he clutched at the air ... and in a moment more the helpless victim fell over upon his face, and was numbered with [the] dead.[5]

Not surprisingly, the steady drumbeat of devastation slowly but surely eroded the war's public support. Worrisome concerns about lagging recruitment surfaced even before news started trickling in from the bloody battlefield at Antietam. A northern newspaper reminded readers, barely nine months after the war began, that "recruiting for the army continues very dull."[6] The navy fared no better, with the number of able-bodied sailors also declining.

Filling the ranks fundamentally depended on two factors: recruitment and retention. Much like bailing water from a sinking ship, efforts at recruitment were hampered as an endless stream of losses kept the military precariously pitched, ever in danger of capsizing. Both were inextricably intertwined, with a military service member's motivation dampened by the emotional cost. As the war dragged on, the price of participation, calculated by factors such as homesickness, illness, injury, and death, was simply too high for too many to accept.

The psychological consequences of war were not a trendy topic in nineteenth-century America. Perhaps the only emotion countenanced, albeit begrudgingly, was homesickness, which by its frequency defied denial. In many cases recognition of homesickness, far from facilitating an empathic approach, invited a withering, morally indignant attack. An Ohio newspaper, no doubt convinced of the destructive influence of homesickness, published a story surely aimed at weak-kneed soldiers and their families: "A lady residing in one of the interior counties of New York had an only son. When the war broke out he volunteered as a private; went to Fortress Monroe; remained there some time; became discontented and home-sick; deserted, and came home in the night. Expecting a warm reception, the wretched youth rushed into the arms of his mother; but instead of returning his caresses, she flung him from her in disgust, exclaiming: 'You are a deserter; you have disgraced the name you bear. I had a thousand times rather see you dead than living thus degraded."[7] In a final flourish, the anonymous reporter concluded the cautionary tale with the disgraced son's subsequent disappearance in Canada. This story, possibly hovering somewhere between fact and fantasy, was a slick piece of propaganda, denouncing a home-sick deserter while at the same time commending the mother's righteous rebuke.

In a letter revealing both the prevalence of homesickness and a soldier's reaction to it, a member of the 21st Ohio Volunteer Infantry stationed at Camp Jefferson, Kentucky, proudly noted that "I have not yet had a single attack of the blues, or suffered from homesickness in the least."[8] His experience was not universally shared. Reminiscing about a winter encampment along the south bank of the Potomac River in 1862, Lieutenant Colonel R.B. Irwin remembered that "nostalgia raged fearfully ... the disease better known as homesickness."[9]

In many respects, homesickness represented an embryonic recognition of the emotional consequences of conflict. For the most part, though, only the most severe behavioral disorders defined by delusional thinking, referred to as insanity in the nineteenth century, earned the moniker of "mental illness."[10] Enlightened physicians of the time fundamentally considered insanity a brain disease, although the exact physical etiology remained elusive. However, home-sickness was variously viewed derisively as a moral weakness, disparaged as an easily simulated fraud, and dismissed by beleaguered military surgeons inun-dated with the genuine illnesses and injuries of war. In spite of the denigration, homesickness was a serious problem demanding attention as it sapped military morale, spread infectiously, and left legions of soldiers unfit to fight.

Homesickness was not confined to the federal forces. A cache of captured official letters contained a Confederate officer's sober assessment that "our troops are utterly demoralized, and heartsick and homesick."[11] Union authorities quickly grasped the propaganda value of the officer's candid disclosure, ensuring its widest publication. Displayed yet again was the bipolar depiction of homesick-ness, on the one hand, as a poignant description of a unit's morale and, on the other, as a moral weakness.

While this seesaw assessment of homesickness was unfolding on the bat-tlefields, another group, tiny though it was, took a singular interest in the curi-ous condition. Collectively, military surgeons focused almost exclusively on the illnesses and injuries that defined their duties. In the midst of this chaos, homesickness received scant consideration, and when it did force its way to the surgeon's attention, it was often met with derision. However, an exception to this response surfaced as some inquisitive surgeons detected a malignant var-iant of homesickness. Physicians adopted the term "nostalgia" in an effort to separate the condition from its benign and more controversial cousin. Military surgeons then started studying serious cases of homesickness, cloaked by a mantle of medical legitimacy.

By at least 1862, newspapers were publishing detailed accounts of nostalgia. In one example, a physician described a case of nostalgia compared in its severity to insanity. According to this account, a soldier recovering from a disabling fever was recuperating in the hospital, but it was not the soldier's physical condition that concerned the doctor. Replacing qualms about the fever's resolution was the soldier's odd behavior. Each day at dawn the soldier would quietly but resolutely pack his small hoard of worldly possessions, announce his departure, and traverse the short path to the nearby wharf. After a moment of despondent gazing, the soldier returned to his bed. The secret unlocking the soldier's behavior was finally revealed: "In his sleep, he talked continuously of wife and child; daytimes he said little, but finally made a confidant of me, and said that 'all night and all day dreamed and thought of home.'"[12] A happy ending, with a cautionary footnote, concluded the doctor's reminiscence. Recognizing the nostalgia, and convinced that without intervention the soldier would commit suicide, the doctor wisely prescribed a medical furlough, confident that his action would spare the army another grievous (and unnecessary) loss.

Most reported cases of nostalgia had dramatically different outcomes, most likely the result of an unsympathetic attitude. A reporter investigating hospital conditions at a general hospital in Nashville, Tennessee, criticized the lack of empathetic care. Leading the list of his numerous examples were cases of homesickness. From the reporter's interviews, he concluded that "homesickness is one of the most frequent, difficult, and annoying complications we have in the treatment of hospital patients."[13]

James A. Mowris, a military surgeon with the 117th Regiment New York Volunteers (Fourth Oneida), recalled a particularly painful case of nostalgia: "The writer has a case vivid in memory, of a boy of eighteen, who had been steadily melting away ... the most approved remedies employed in vain; he became scarcely, a living skeleton."[14] Mowris counted nostalgia among the more serious infirmities afflicting soldiers, given its remorseless downward progression that, if left untreated, ended in death. An enlightened physician aware of the symbiotic relationship between mind and body, Mowris issued a medical furlough for his young patient. As the emaciated soldier was gingerly placed on a homeward-bound boat, many of those remaining behind silently predicted his death. Such was not the case, as the simple but compassionate intervention was remarkably successful, and with the soldier's spirits fully restored, he subsequently returned to duty and completed his enlistment.

Joining the minority of physicians exploring the new frontier bordering on the psychological consequences of war was De Witt C. Peters, an assistant surgeon in charge of Jarvis Hospital in Baltimore, Maryland. Writing to his colleagues in a medical journal in 1863, Peters authored an insightful commentary on nostalgia, replete with recommendations for prevention and treatment.

According to Peters, "the evils of youthful enlistments" was the essential ingredient of nostalgia. With a directness that may have startled his readers, the doctor criticized a war effort that relied on the recruitment of eighteen-year-old soldiers. As he astutely observed, these young men, many from rural environments, were filled with patriotic and romantic visions of war. The hardships of military life, with its endless deprivations, discipline, and deaths, overwhelmed the young recruits' naiveté. Peters considered older men resilient, more accustomed to life's privations and problems. In another interesting comment, Peters credited a young cavalry soldier's relationship with his horse as a protective factor, emphasizing the value of an emotional attachment and the animal's role in bridging the soldier's loss of family support.

Unfortunately for soldiers destined to develop nostalgia, Peters painted a grim picture. In describing the disease's progression, the doctor likened nostalgia to a mild form of insanity: "The symptoms produced by this aberration of the mind, are first, great mental dejection, loss of appetite, indifference to external influences ... as the disease progresses it is attended by hysterical weeping, a dull pain in the head, throbbing of the temporal arteries, anxious expression of the face, watchfulness ... and a general wasting of all the vital powers."[15] In some cases nostalgia could resolve itself, but in other cases the die was cast and the soldier's course inexorably worsened, ending in death.

The treatment regime recommended by Peters was unconventional. Instead of plying the affected man with medications, he suggested rest, exercise, and a nutritious diet. If that approach failed to stem the decline, the last option proposed by Peters was a medical discharge from military service.

Dwindling manpower forced armies on both sides of the conflict to implement compulsory military service. Conscription invited criticism, and the many complaints leveled at its institution included an observation that among drafted men "the longing for discharge in many cases resembled insanity—medically speaking—and that strange malady which shrinks from popular contempt under the scientific name of nostalgia, but is nothing more than homesickness, raged in some regiments like an epidemic."[16]

The intense distaste of military service bred malingering. One of the many problems confronting military surgeons was the imperative need to consider, detect, and defeat malingering. Feigning an illness or injury was an art form, with some soldiers doing their level best to play a convincing role.[17] Homesickness and its lethal cousin nostalgia inspired simulation, a seemingly easy fraud with successful actors yearning for sympathy, modified duties, and even medical discharges. Connecting nostalgia with malingering reinforced a negative view of psychological disorders and probably discouraged a broader inquiry into the emotional consequences of war.

The issue surfaced in an Ohio newspaper less than a year after the war began. In a small insert dripping with derision, the anonymous reporter took aim at the term "nostalgia" as nothing more than a thinly veiled medical excuse for pathetic, homesick soldiers. To reinforce his point, the reporter recalled "a cowardly lieutenant" who demanded a discharge predicated on homesickness. Following a brief examination, the military surgeon confirmed the presence of a mild case of nostalgia and recommended the officer's medical discharge, caustically commenting that the man was totally useless. Even with this ignominious narrative attached to his discharge paperwork, the officer "gladly left the service upon those terms."[18]

Military surgeons seeking advice on detecting deceptions could find many suggestions. In one venerable text, the author recognized the existence of nostalgia but at the same time acknowledged that nostalgia could be faked. Distinguishing between a fraud and the genuine article relied on the fact that malingerers openly, vigorously, and excitedly sought to return home, "while those who are really diseased are taciturn, express themselves obscurely … and are little affected by the consolations which hope or promises offer to them."[19]

Even with a tilt toward disbelief, military surgeons could not ignore the reality of homesickness and nostalgia. At a time when the study of psychological medicine was in its infancy, these emotional byproducts of war found recognition in *The Medical and Surgical History of the War of the Rebellion*, a compilation of official medical records tabulated by reports from military surgeons in the field and doctors in various hospitals. Nostalgia was briefly reviewed in a volume titled *On Certain Diseases Not Heretofore Discussed*.[20]

The Medical and Surgical History of the War of the Rebellion devoted three pages to the subject of nostalgia, attempting to draw a clear distinction between it and homesickness. In the writer's view, both conditions were camp diseases with roots in boredom and inactivity, which, in the absence of mental stimulation (or, perhaps more precisely, mental distraction), left a man's mind sentimentally wandering toward home. Homesickness was both infectious and preventable. Once focused by a pending battle or occupied in garrison by training and healthy sports, the incidence of homesickness receded. Conversely, long stretches of idleness and recreational pursuits consisting of tobacco use, alcohol consumption, and gambling, all favorite and frequent vices, were inevitably associated with a rising tide of homesickness.

Nostalgia was a morbid extension of homesickness, ambiguously considered a consequence of a soldier's temperament. Physicians reported 5,213 cases throughout the war, calculated as 2.34 cases annually per thousand white troops, leaving the author underwhelmed by nostalgia's incidence. Neither the numbers nor the author's conclusion were entirely credible, given the vagaries of diagnosis and, no doubt, a general reluctance to identify the disorder.

In discussing the presumed etiology of nostalgia, the author paid homage to its roots in homesickness before describing its predisposing characteristics. Those considered most susceptible to nostalgia were "young men of feeble will, highly developed imaginative faculties and strong sexual desires, and married men absent for the first time from their families"—a group of contenders that would seem to have generated many more cases than reported. Even narrative accounts of nostalgia left the impression that the affliction was more common. Surgeon Madison Reese wrote in March 1863 that "nostalgia affected a large number of the men," duplicating a similar observation from a month earlier.

Nostalgia surely plagued Confederate soldiers, although scant evidence exists supporting that assumption. In his memoirs, Basil Gildersleeve, a stout defender of the southern cause and a Confederate officer, recalled that "nostalgia, which we are apt to sneer at as a doctor's name for homesickness ... was a power for evil in those days, and some of our finest troops were thinned out by it."[21] Estimating frequency is impossible, but Confederate regulations aimed at reporting the sick and wounded included a category for nostalgia.[22]

Nostalgia was not limited to the battlefields. Its presence among Confederate prisoners of war at Camp Douglas became "one of the most frequent causes of death."[23] Union soldiers fared no better, as news of their imprisonment at Andersonville led a reporter to conclude that among all the horrific privations suffered, "hope deferred which results in homesickness ... cannot long be survived. Nostalgia ... is more fatal than bullets on the field of battle."[24]

Nostalgia's role in reducing recruitment and retention prevented indifference to the condition. Efforts to suppress homesickness relied mostly on a mixture of scorn and stigma, casting the sufferer as feckless, cowardly, and conniving. Promoters hoped this approach would deter dissemination, fearing an uncontainable contagion. As weapons of war, the motivational value of shame and guilt cannot be calculated but might be inferred as a failure given the progression of homesickness to nostalgia, the incidence of malingering, and possibly the prevalence of drunkenness and desertion. A small group of military surgeons and public officials, perhaps seeing the futility of that approach, took a different view of the soldiers' suffering by normalizing homesickness as a common consequence of war. Viewed in this manner, homesickness was stripped of its stigma, permitting enlightened physicians to suggest compassionate interventions.

The fledgling interest in the psychological consequences of war was a reality forced on public officials and military authorities. Efforts to blunt the emotional consequences of war were grounded in another reality—the need to field a fit, fighting force. A moral blanket thrown over homesickness, in an effort to retard its spread, was extended to other behaviors such as drunkenness, depression, and certainly desertion, no matter the reason. Once again, the imperative need to maintain battle-ready units fostered a stern, unbending response from the military and the public. In spite of this, the sheer, unrelenting number of cases sparked curiosity, concern, and debate, resulting in wide-ranging, stimulating discussions that included the emotional consequences of war. The war's conclusion relieved that immediate pressure, exposing in its aftermath a multitude of new social stressors.

Furious forces unleashed by four years of war did not simply fade away when defeated southern soldiers stacked their rifles at Appomattox. Deep-seated resentment, frustration, and anger accompanied the dejected soldiers on their lonely journeys home. For northern soldiers, a hard-won victory softened, but did not entirely dissipate, years of hatred carried like a knapsack through countless battles. Common soldiers bore the brunt of the brutal conflict, dying in droves, hobbled by horrific injuries, and suffering the psychological wounds of war in silence. No one escaped unscathed, with the war wreaking havoc on every segment of society.

With the war's end, hope struggled to reassert itself, vainly endeavoring to mend a broken country's spirit. For a tired nation, reassembled through force and mourning grievous losses, decades would pass before lingering enmities were buried alongside the fallen soldiers. The war changed society in many ways: death was omnipresent, life was cheapened, every disabled soldier served as a reminder of the cost, civility was a casualty, faith in institutions was weakened, and a devil-may-care attitude bubbled just below the surface.

Peace was no antidote for the war's lingering poison. Venom no longer confined to the battlefields flowed into other segments of society, a spill unleashing a lethal toxin of misery, mayhem and malevolence that washed over America. Just a few months after a collective sigh signaled the conflict's end, a new battle began as alarmed citizens, with memories of the war still fresh, were shaken anew by a tsunami of intemperance, suicides, crime, cults, and quacks spreading across the country. Tossed asunder by the social upheaval were established institutions such as religion and organized medicine. The loss of faith and credibility left many people drifting, desperately searching for life's meaning. Some found solace in alternate beliefs like Spiritualism, which failed to deliver on its extravagant promises. Others, less fortunate, were untethered from society, descending into depression, intemperance, and suicide. At the same time, an antisocial trend swept the country as a crime spree, unrivaled in America's young history, touched every nook and cranny in the nation.

The turbulent decades following the Civil War witnessed a fractured and splintered America. A frayed society produced sharp slivers of despair, quixotic searches for consequence, and enduring periods of misery, mayhem, and malevolence. Taken as a whole, the psychological forces unleashed by four years of civil war profoundly shaped American society.

One

Sadness and Suicide

Nothing sickens the soul like a stubborn sadness. With each passing day the despair deepens, dragging the sufferer relentlessly down. Pessimism permeates the whole person. It seems much easier to see this darkness among individuals, but when an entire society is draped in depression every flicker of light is snuffed out. The miserable miasma sneaks in slowly, steadily obscuring isolated acts of desperation. From an observer's standpoint it would be like trying to see a single light from a distant mountaintop. As the number of individuals succumbing grows, a pattern develops that even from a distance becomes discernible.

In America's Civil War each death produced shock waves that flowed from the battlefield to people's homes. Family and friends grieved their losses. Among the battlefield's survivors were legions of maimed soldiers, who collectively forced a social reckoning of the grievous cost of war. The injured soldiers required ongoing medical support and financial assistance, a postwar luxury that eluded many. As the numbers of dead and injured mounted, the ripples from the war grew larger and more powerful, washing over society like a tidal wave. Emotional afflictions spanning the broad chasm between insanity and suicide among surviving soldiers and their families witnessed a dramatic escalation.

The Civil War created seismic shock waves that shook society to its core. Men left behind whatever comforts they had in exchange for the hardships of war. The separation from loved ones was eased a bit by the belief in the cause, the camaraderie forged in battle, and letters from home. In an untold number of cases, however, this was not enough, with the war sapping soldiers' spirits as a reflective reverie conjured up halcyon visions of home. Among this group of self-absorbed soldiers, many simply deserted, gratifying their deep desire despite the consequences. A smaller group, with their allegiances split between home life and military duty, expressed their conflict-laden equipoise through anxiety, dysphoria, and an endless collection of vague physical problems. Military surgeons and commanders labeled the mild, rather ubiquitous form of this malady as homesickness. In some cases, the wistful hunger for home assumed a nearly delusional force combined with a steady descent into a morbid melancholia. Military surgeons recognized this sometimes fatal form of homesickness as nostalgia.

Homesickness and its deadly sibling nostalgia were nettlesome emotional problems. On a sliding scale from the former to the latter, derision gave way to curiosity. Homesickness was ridiculed and nostalgia medically diagnosed. The two conditions were united in the concern they created. Homesickness was infectious and could decimate the soldiers' resolve, leaving entire units brooding and broken.

Nostalgia was everywhere. It made routine appearances in garrisons, on battlefields, in prisoner-of-war camps, and even among civilians lamenting the loss of loved ones. It was so ubiquitous and debilitating that it led one writer of the era to conclude that "the longing for home which superinduces mental depression, cannot long be survived. Nostalgia is the parent of physical ailments … and it is more fatal than bullets on the field of battle."[1] This author identified an important connection concerning nostalgia, impressively linking the mind and body.

The slippery slope starting with homesickness and ending in nostalgia fostered early efforts at wide-scale prevention. In an effort to contain the problem, military leaders, political figures, and newspapers joined forces to combat homesickness. They fought their disunited battle with admonitions, appeals, and accusations. The goal was straightforward—smother homesickness through shame and guilt. It was a crude campaign, but it was perhaps one of the few approaches that could be systematically implemented.

Shaming is one way to shape behavior. Whether the story was true or merely a fabricated piece of propaganda is unknown, but a short newspaper story titled "How a Mother Received Her Son Who Had Deserted" sent a powerful message. Referring to an unnamed "lady residing in one of the interior counties of New York," the reporter noted that the woman's only son had joined the army. The newly minted army private went to Fort Monroe, Virginia, and soon after arrival became disillusioned with military life. Citing homesickness as the immediate precipitant for his actions, the soldier promptly deserted and in due course returned to his mother. All illusions of a warm reception were shattered when she openly expressed her deep disgust: "You are a deserter; you have disgraced the name you bear. I had a thousand times rather see you dead than living thus degraded." Reeling from his mother's hostility, the deserter again retreated, this time to the home of a more sympathetic neighbor. A day later the unnamed soldier fled to Canada, forsaking both home and country.[2]

A more obvious use of homesickness for a purely political advantage unexpectedly fell into the hands of Union troops when they seized a Confederate mailbag. As the soldiers perused the contents, they came across a letter from a regimental officer. In the most despairing language, the letter's author plaintively cried, "We have neither the men nor the means to carry on the war. Our troops are utterly demoralized, and heartsick and homesick." Naturally, the letter was considered a boon to the Union war effort and soon found its way into newspapers across the north. In reality, though, the forlorn assessment of Confederate capabilities, written in 1862, probably spoke more about the author's state of mind.[3]

The bridge that spanned the emotional eddies set in motion by a soldier's departure was supported by letters from home. These letters soothed troubled waters, offering a sort of levee against homesickness. B.F. Taylor admonished newspaper readers, "It pains me to think that more than one man has let life slip out of a grasp too weak to hold it, just because his dearest friends did not send him a prescription once a week—price three cents—a letter from home." To further dramatize his plea, Taylor recalled an incident in which a soldier fighting in the Chickamauga Campaign narrowly escaped death when a bullet's fatal path was thwarted when it struck a bundle of letters in the soldier's shirt pocket.[4]

Dr. Hunt, a military physician, described a particularly touching example of homesickness. The soldier Hunt so vividly recalled was recovering from a bout of fever. His convalescence was remarkable for its progress. The good-natured soldier's recuperation was far enough along that he refused all medications, but the doctor was still concerned about the man's odd behavior. Every morning the soldier would quietly pack his belongings, walk down to the nearby wharf, gaze wistfully at the boats, and then return without a word to his hospital bed. The soldier's sleep unlocked the mystery, for during slumber he babbled incessantly about home. An astute decision to grant the soldier a medical furlough was clearly indicated, for doing otherwise "would have ended, probably, in suicide."[5]

Homesickness often invited rough treatment, usually by subjecting the victim to ridicule. Such treatment presumably hardened the sensitivities of susceptible soldiers. Peer pressure also sought to lessen the fraudulent portrayal of homesickness. An untold number of soldiers tried to capitalize on the presumed sympathy extended to victims of homesickness, apparently quite willing to accept any accompanying barbs.

A clearly self-centered officer in an Ohio regiment approached the unit's military surgeon seeking a medical discharge on the grounds of homesickness. The surgeon reluctantly agreed but at the same time could not resist annotating the officer's discharge with some punishing comments: "Said lieutenant being so sadly affected with the nostalgia, as to be useless in camp and worthless on the field." The short newspaper story about this incident added to the doctor's condemnation by declaring the officer's conduct "cowardly."[6]

Whether homesickness was widely faked or not, the prevailing presumption seemed to favor the possibility. It was, after all, fairly easy to display a downcast mood, maintain a listless manner, and skip a few meals. Authoritative medical texts came to the rescue by offering helpful hints to weed out the fakers: "Pretenders generally express a great desire to revisit their native country, while those who are really diseased and taciturn, express themselves obscurely on the subject of their malady ... and are little affected by the consolations which hope or promises offer to them." Doctors attempting to follow this advice were probably struck by the contradictions.

Military surgeons had the power to grant medical furloughs and, through that dispensation, provided the best treatment for nostalgia. James A. Mowris, a regimental surgeon with the 117th New York Volunteer Infantry, devoted several pages in his memoirs to nostalgia. Mowris considered nostalgia a "social infirmity" that improved simply upon notice of going home. To illustrate the point, the surgeon described "a case vivid in memory, of a boy of eighteen, who had been steadily melting away ... the most approved remedies had been employed in vain; he became scarcely, a living skeleton." The soldier bravely refused the offer of a furlough, but Mowris issued one anyway. It came just in the nick of time. The prostrate, dying soldier was tenderly placed aboard a ship bound for home. Those remaining behind expected his imminent demise, but in fact the visit home lifted the soldier's spirits so much that he returned to his unit and completed his enlistment.[7]

A trip home saved this soldier's life, but surgeons were for the most part parsimonious in handing out such medical furloughs. No doubt, the surgeons fretted that soldiers would not return or would abuse the compassion through malingering, or that commanders would complain about the troop loss. Many surgeons also probably ignored homesickness, given its wide prevalence, or were simply overwhelmed with the illnesses and injuries of war. In some of those cases, homesickness evolved into a morbid melancholy terminating in death.

The most dangerous dimension of a deep depression was suicide. Throughout the Civil War a small group of soldiers and sailors met a different enemy— the demon within. From the limited accounts of these deaths, only a glimpse is revealed of the inner struggles to which these unfortunate souls eventually succumbed.

In nineteenth-century America, the relationship between war and suicide was mostly a matter of conjecture. The closest well-accepted connection was between military-inspired homesickness, nostalgia, and suicide.[8] Even without a precise understanding of etiology, Union army surgeons reported 268 suicides over a 51-month period from June 1861 through August 1865.[9] Regrettably, what were uniformly missing from these reports were details. The scant information reveals, in terms of absolute numbers, that reported suicides peaked from October 1862 through September 1863, March 1864 through August 1864, and just before the war ended. Smoothing out the peaks and valleys produced an average of 5.25 suicides per month. When accounting for variations in Union troop strength, army surgeons documented the most suicides during 1864, the last full year of the war. In an interesting and reliable pattern, suicides occurred most commonly during the spring months.

It seems reasonable to speculate that the early peak increases in military suicides corresponded with periods of combat intensity. The peak in 1864 may have represented the emotional impact of a grueling, grinding, seemingly never-ending war. By this time, too, compulsory military service was firmly in place, as volunteers could not fill the ranks. Private George W. Whetstine, Company C, 33rd Indiana Volunteer Infantry, was no doubt a typical, reluctant member of his unit, having arrived as a consequence of the draft. Whetstine joined his regiment in North Carolina. Fellow troops later commented on the new recruit's "brooding," which they attributed to his unhappiness with military service. His absence at a morning roll call probably prompted some alarm, given his melancholy. A search was immediately launched and Whetstine was soon found, self-strangled by his suspender.[10]

The death of Lieutenant William P. Shear, the quartermaster for the 2nd New York Infantry (Troy) Regiment, surely shocked his fellow officers, friends, and family. A patriotic impulse propelled the young Shear to join the military. His organizational aptitude impressed his superiors, who quickly promoted him to the important quartermaster position. Before joining the army, Shear had lived in Albany, New York, where he ran a successful business, married into a well-respected family, and traveled in the best social circles. Despite his many social advantages and natural leadership talent, however, Shear "began a career of dissipation, which alarmed his friends." The literary allusion was not further defined, but Shear's removal to an infirmary for recovery suggests an overindulgence in liquor. Shear seemed to be on the mend from the mysterious malady, with an imminent discharge planned. Nothing seemed amiss when a hospital attendant brought the officer his morning breakfast. As it turned out, Shear had other plans. Using "a knife with a very small blade," Shear methodically cut his throat. With a conviction that seemed misplaced given the manner of death, the newspaper concluded that "he was laboring under no aberration of mind at the time."[11]

Newspapers chronicled the suicides of military officers, usually in the most cursory manner possible. The death of William C. Crafts, a lieutenant with Company E, 8th New York Cavalry, was no exception. Crafts committed suicide in late August 1863. Aside from that declaration, the newspaper simply left the reader pondering a young officer's seemingly senseless death.[12]

A slightly more embellished story accompanied the death of Frank Williams, an assistant surgeon with the 4th Regiment, New York Heavy Artillery. Chronic inebriation seemed to play a central role in his demise, although his farewell was certainly clear-headed, suggesting that Williams was not under the influence of the intoxicating beverage in the final moments preceding his death. The doctor calmly entered a New York City drugstore, shook hands with the proprietor, and announced his expected death in about "half an hour." With unerring precision, the assistant surgeon's death soon followed his proclamation. Subsequent inquiries revealed that Williams had consumed, for no discernible reason, a fatal dose of morphine.[13]

An enlisted soldier's suicide rarely caught the attention of national newspapers. To reach such prominence, a common soldier's suicide needed an attention-grabbing angle. Even then, they were superficial stories. In one example, a short paragraph described "a strange suicide" that no doubt alarmed a troop of encamped soldiers in 1861. The unnamed soldier committed suicide by "placing the muzzle of the gun under his chin, and pulling the trigger with his foot." His dramatic, impulsive, self-destructive behavior followed an apparent altercation with a superior. The soldier's insubordination was countered by the threat of arrest. What went through the soldier's mind will never be known, but almost immediately after receiving the warning, he shot himself. Making the suicide even more tragic and inexplicable was the soldier's marriage just a few days earlier.[14]

Stephen N. Bottsford's death was a chilling suicide foretelling the grip that depression would hold long after soldiers left the battlefields. Bottsford's parents were deeply concerned about their son's gloomy mood, deepening almost daily after his release from service following the Battle of Manassas. Where homesick soldiers generally found peace and comfort, Bottsford found despair and despondency. The former soldier complained incessantly about a debilitating headache. On the day of his death Bottsford was especially pious, praying fervently for forgiveness. Whatever transgressions Bottsford sought relief from apparently could only be satisfied through suicide. Banishing his mother and brandishing a razor to hold his father at bay, the tormented veteran quickly slashed his throat.[15]

The search for motives sometimes reflected the drama of the moment. The death of President Abraham Lincoln inspired one writer to speculate about the "suicide of a suspected assassin."[16] An obscure paragraph in a southern newspaper dated April 27, 1865, reported events in Washington, D.C., where "a man who made several attempts at different points to pass the outer line of our pickets around the city, was placed in the guard-room at Fort Thayer ... and there deliberately committed suicide." The man's fine clothing and distinguished appearance, along with his suspicious behavior, led the reporter to conclude that "he knew something of the late assassination."

As might be imagined, examples of Confederate suicides are few and far between. It seems that only the most dramatic stories survived in diaries, letters, and autobiographies. Eugene Grissom, later to be the superintendent of the North Carolina Insane Asylum and an influential member of the Association of Medical Superintendents of American Institutions for the Insane, recalled one such event.[17] The memory emblazoned in Grissom's mind occurred while he was recovering from a leg wound in Moore Hospital located in Richmond, Virginia.[18] John Roland, a nineteen-year-old soldier, was admitted to Moore Hospital during Grissom's period of recuperation. The young soldier languished quietly until the fateful day arrived. Edwin Warren, the hospital's chief physician, had the misfortune of triggering Roland's insane behavior. While passing through the hospital ward, the young man attacked Warren with a knife. The slashing soldier continued his rampage, assaulting hospital attendants who came to Warren's rescue. Finally trapped, Roland turned the knife on himself, slit his throat and then jumped to his death through a nearby window.

Such sorrows did not spare Confederate soldiers and, in some instances, were even briefly reported in local newspapers. Lieutenant C.E. Earle, 4th South Carolina Infantry Regiment, leaped from the sixth floor of the Ballard House in Richmond, Virginia. The Ballard House was an imposing downtown structure, and Earle's rash act (and the 100-foot descent) guaranteed a fatal outcome. Earle left behind a will but no reasons for the suicide. Earlier in the day he had complained "of indisposition," and the services of a local physician were summoned. What transpired between the pair is not known, but the doctor was sufficiently alarmed that he "left word for his patient to be watched, as he feared some attempt on his life from his appearance and bearing." Regrettably, the doctor's advice was ignored.[19]

Jumping from a lofty height was not an uncommon way for a soldier to end his life. George Sheridan was a Confederate soldier recovering from an unspecified ailment in a hospital in Richmond, Virginia. For no obvious reason other than apparently "laboring under mental aberration," Sheridan impulsively fled his sickbed. Clad only in his underclothes, the fleet-footed patient made a bee-line for the nearby bridge. Alarmed hospital attendants made an earnest but futile effort to seize Sheridan. As the horrified and helpless attendants watched, their patient hurled himself off the bridge, striking his head in the fatal fall.[20]

An unnamed Confederate soldier, driven to despair by homesickness, committed suicide while confined within the labyrinth of Richmond's Chimb-orazo Hospital. The hospital staff was treating the soldier for "indisposition," which, given his subsequent behavior, might well have been nostalgia, the vir-ulent version of homesickness. Weeks of lingering in the hospital probably led to a festering fear of never returning home. The soldier asked for the one rem-edy that might have cured his malady—a medical furlough. Shortly after receiv-ing word that his request was denied, the soldier cut his throat.[21]

Another suicide felled Captain Jacob L. Clark, 18th Missouri Infantry, who killed himself in a St. Louis Hospital. Clark was wounded at the Battle of Shiloh in April 1862, committing suicide roughly one month later.[22]

A pair of Confederate suicides surely shook the soldiers in the 9th South Carolina Regiment. A soldier identified as "Burgess" was taking his turn guard-ing the provisions in a commissary tent. In what can only be described as a determined and desperate act, the soldier removed one shoe and sock, carefully placed his rifle on his forehead and pulled the trigger with his bare foot. Just a few days earlier another unnamed soldier had dispatched himself, leaving the reporter to philosophize that "men in war become more reckless of their lives, and attempt, through a mistaken notion, to relieve themselves of a burden too heavy to bear."[23]

Thomas P. Butler, a private in Company I of the 7th South Carolina Reg-iment, checked into the Columbian Hotel in Richmond, Virginia, in mid–February 1862. Butler's stay attracted no particular attention until an unknown but surely concerned passerby noticed blood oozing from beneath the door to his room. When the door was forced open the startled witnesses found the occupant dead after "inflicting several wounds on his body and cutting his throat with a Bowie-knife." The hastily convened coroner's inquest soon dis-covered that Butler was a former officer of a Palmetto cavalry unit during the Mexican-American War. Concluding that the death was a suicide, the coroner's eulogy commented on Butler's "commanding presence[;] he was also an accomplished gentleman and ripe scholar." Aside from a fit of insanity, no rea-son could be found accounting for such a savage death.[24]

The vicissitudes in life occasioned by war were tumultuous enough, but the addition of other stressors sometimes led to a lethal brew. Such was the case with Texas Cavalry Lieutenant J.M. Rutledge. The officer vanished from his room at the Globe Hotel in Augusta, Georgia, leaving behind two letters that together hinted at suicide. In one letter Rutledge referred to a bill in the amount of $95.50, which apparently the beleaguered man could not pay. On the reverse side of the letter he scrawled a pitiful request: "will the members of the M. E. Church have me buried?" In the other letter the anguished officer wrote, "How foolish it is for man to deprive himself of that life granted by the Almighty.... In debt, too proud to let strangers know my situation, no resource left but running away or dying.... The die is cast—may God have mercy on me." Even though no body was found, the ominous tone of the letters favored the notion that the soldier had committed suicide.[25]

A far more certain suicide saddened the troops of the Petersburg Cavalry. Captain C. F. Fisher was the Confederate officer in charge of the Petersburg Light Dragoons, which joined the Confederate cause as the 5th Virginia Cavalry. Fisher was a popular officer worried about his men. On May 23, 1861, Captain Fisher was near Suffolk, Virginia. The Civil War was in its infancy, but Fisher was morbidly preoccupied "that his company was in a position to be cut to pieces by the enemy." A dark cloud soon settled over Fisher's mind, casting long shadows over his troops. The soldiers sensed their commander's deepening despondency and urged him to return home. In a sign of their concern, some of his troops accompanied the forlorn Fisher on the journey back. Roughly a mile from their camp, Fisher "drew his pistol and shot himself twice through the body—fell from his horse, ran a short distance, and then shot himself through the head. He never spoke afterwards, dying in a few minutes."[26] The 45-year-old officer left his wife, their children, and the Petersburg community stunned and grieving. Fisher was the first uniformed Petersburg soldier to die—poignantly felled by personal demons.

It can only be imagined what motivated Sergeant W.H. Large, a Confederate soldier under arrest, to commit suicide. The reporter documenting Large's death omitted the crime that the soldier stood accused of, but the manner of his death was too poignant to ignore. Large was traveling with his wife on a train bound for Atlanta. While lying on his wife's lap, the troubled soldier swallowed a fatal dose of poison. His death was not instantaneous, leaving his stricken wife horrified as her husband slowly succumbed to the poison.[27]

Although much smaller than the south's army, the Confederate Navy added a few sailors to the deadly suicide toll. Marion Stevens, a seaman serving on the CSS *Richmond*, suffered the shame of being branded a coward. As the war came to a close in the south, Stevens' undisclosed behavior led to a reduction in rank from lieutenant to private. The former officer's deeply felt disgrace could apparently be erased only through death. With that mindset, Stevens first attempted to cut his throat. Alert seamen aboard the CSS *Richmond* thwarted that attempt, but Stevens was undeterred. He promptly grabbed a pistol, "and putting it against his forehead, discharged it, sending the load through his skull."[28]

The suffering seen by military surgeons on both sides was dreadful and surely scarred many doctors. Not surprisingly, perhaps some chose suicide to silence their mental torment. S. A. Robinson, a Confederate surgeon with the Second Virginia Regiment, narrowly cheated death. Robinson was staying at the American Hotel in Richmond, Virginia. Prior to asking for the bill, suggesting his imminent departure, the surgeon had purchased a knife. The hotel clerk dutifully prepared the bill and brought it to the doctor's room. The door was securely fastened, and, for unknown reasons, this frightened the hotel clerk. A cry for help was quickly answered, and soon the door was forced open. Robinson was grievously wounded with a self-inflicted laceration extending across his throat. The wound was speedily bandaged, surely saving the doctor from an immediate demise.[29] Others were not so lucky.

The death of Dr. Harry Larrantree, a dentist with the 4th Alabama Infantry Regiment, was deemed a dreadful accident. Larrantree was the acting ward master at a college hospital in Lynchburg, Virginia. In an idle moment, freed from the hospital routine, the physician was playing with a "small four barrel revolver." While standing by a fireplace Larrantree rather absentmindedly discharged the weapon. A nearby hospital attendant rebuked the doctor, who responded with the placating comment, "There are no more bullets in it, see?" Driving home his point, the doctor put the gun in his mouth and pulled the trigger. The muffled explosion proved the doctor wrong. A coroner's jury listening to the evidence concluded that Larrantree's death was an accidental suicide.[30]

Sadness and suicide were not confined to soldiers. In some cases the emotional distress stretched from the battlefield all the way back home, dragging family members down into despair. Ann Wood, the 27-year-old wife of a Union army officer, was such a victim. Her husband served with the 3rd South Carolina Regiment (Colored). Mrs. Wood, eagerly anticipating her husband's safe return home following the completion of his tour of duty, found her hopes dashed when he announced his intention to rejoin the war effort. Her husband's pronouncement instantly converted the joyous homecoming into a panic-stricken distress. The distraught woman climbed to the sixth floor of her residence, opened a window, and flung herself out. On her way to oblivion she crashed through a protruding awning before striking the pavement. Alarmed passersby managed to take the mortally injured woman to a nearby hospital, where she later died.[31]

A husband's battlefield death could at best be mourned and shrouded with praise of the soldier's fidelity and faith, but the loss still haunted the survivors, sometimes leaving suicide as the only escape. Lydia Phillipe learned of her husband's fate in a newspaper article detailing the casualties at the Battle of Williamsburg in 1862. The shocking news left the widow "frantic with grief, and ... she made known to several that she had no longer any object worth living for, and was therefore determined to die." Even more unsettling was Mrs. Phillipe's determination to forfeit her young child's life as well. After a failed attempt to drown herself and her five-year-old daughter, the distraught widow made another, more deliberate and successful attempt. She and her little girl were both subsequently found dead in a hotel room, the victims of a fatal opium overdose.[32]

Catherine Kein, the 31-year-old wife of a soldier, had a different reason for killing herself. During her husband's uninterrupted 18-month absence, "it appears that she proved unfaithful in the marriage relation, and her unfortunate condition was the subject of considerable comment throughout the circle of her acquaintance." The rumors and innuendo proved too much, and in an effort to silence her shame, she conceived a plot to commit suicide. Through unknown means, Kein procured a small amount of phosphorus, which she swallowed. Kein's rash act must have been publicly witnessed, since medical aid soon arrived, though unfortunately not quickly enough to save her life.[33]

In some cases reporters seemed to almost romanticize the tragic deaths of young women. The war had barely begun when "a beautiful young lady, belonging to a high and distinguished family," committed suicide. Her anguish was directly related to her husband's relocation to a distant battlefield. The woman was apparently preoccupied by morbid dreams portending his death. A particularly vivid and frightening nightmare left the nineteen-year-old officer's wife shaken and "determined not to survive him." Unable to suppress her inconsolable fear, the woman instead quaffed a fatal dose of morphine. The reporter softened the story by claiming that the dead woman was now "happy with the thought she would soon be joined with the being she loved most on earth."[34]

Young wives, particularly those with children, surely lived under a dark shadow cast by their soldier husbands' potential death. The loss of one's mate also weighed on men's minds, and in some cases the grief-stricken husband sought solace in death. Such was the case with "Capt. Thyssent, C. S. A., of New Orleans." The Confederate officer's wife died unexpectedly following a seemingly minor illness. With his beloved spouse dead, Thyssent, "overwhelmed with grief, blew his brains out that night." In a touching finale to the tragic tale, the husband and wife were buried together.[35]

The war's end silenced the battlefields but not the sounds of despair. The emotional aftermath of the Civil War can be estimated in terms of the misery that infected society. This was a virulent contagion that rapidly spread across America, leaving in its wake a depressed and demoralized segment of the population. It seems reasonable to assume that when the malaise initially took hold its victims tried to shake their despondency loose using the normal methods. When these failed, some individuals no doubt sought solace, distraction or even punishment in less conventional and, at times, frankly antisocial pathways. The bullets and bombs stopped in 1865, but the social shockwaves were just beginning.

The prototypical paths that postbellum people traveled for the palliation of sorrow involved family, friends, and houses of worship. For many, the Civil War fractured the bonds of family and friends, while others no doubt found their faith shattered. Faced with fewer outlets, the blocked emotions, just like an obstructed river, carved new canals. In many cases these new emotional pathways led to suicide and insanity. Military records and census figures provide clues of the destructive swath cut by the Civil War. A deeper dive into the murky waters of a mostly forgotten history shows the vague outlines of a different kind of wreckage—the psychological casualties of a nation at war with itself.

The Union Army had a decisive edge over the Confederacy, with a greater population and a deeper industrial base from which it prosecuted the war. Throughout the war's duration, the Union Army enlisted 2,898,304 men, of whom roughly half served for three years.[36] The subsequent carnage was reflected in 385,245 casualties. Of that total, 318,187 were wounded and 67,058 killed on the battlefields.

The southern states mostly fought a defensive war. Perhaps morale and motivation were also higher in the Confederacy, at least in the beginning. These factors helped the Confederacy initially overcome the north's advantages, though the situation changed during the later years of the war.

Estimating Confederate enlistment numbers and casualties is tricky. The Confederacy simply did not keep exhaustive records. A reasonable guess would be that the Confederacy marshaled 1,300,000 enlistments and that roughly 1,082,119 men served for three years. In terms of the Confederate Army's battle-field losses, a good guess places the number of killed and wounded men around 329,000.

The 1860 census provides some perspective.[37] The total number of persons in the United States, according to this census, was 31,443,321. Of these, 16,060,666, or 51.1 percent, were men. Among the eleven states that left the union, the total population was 9,103,333, leaving the remaining northern states 22,339,988 persons.

In terms of men of military age, the overall 1860 census reported two groups: men from 20 to 40 totaled 5,030,981, while men aged 15–50 totaled

8,068,595. A better figure examined the population of men from disloyal areas, which included portions of Kentucky and Missouri. The loyal states had 3,606,147 men in the 20–40 group, compared to the disloyal states with 825,400. The disloyal areas could count on 1,335,521 men in the 15–50 age group against the loyal areas, which had 5,444,374. The disparities in manpower between the battlefield contestants helps explain the Confederacy's reliance on longer enlistments and a broader age range.

Mortality statistics from the same census tabulated the number and manner of deaths ending on June 1, 1860. The census reported 394,153 deaths, of which men held a slight edge, constituting 207,943 (or 53 percent) of the total. Of the known causes of death in 1860, infectious diseases were the most frequent. Consumption (tuberculosis) led the list, followed by pneumonia, scarlatina (scarlet fever), and typhoid fever.

The 1860 census reported deaths related to alcohol or mental illness. Delirium tremens accounted for the deaths of 518 men and 57 women, insanity 251 men and 201 women, and intemperance 842 men and 89 women. The census reported 993 suicides, of which men accounted for 789, or 79 percent. The most common method for both genders was hanging (men = 250, women = 56). Following that, men most often used a firearm (109), then poison (93). Women who did not resort to hanging chose poison (44) or drowning (31).

In terms of mental morbidity, the 1860 census reported 23,999 insane persons.[38] Idiocy claimed 18,865 victims. The presumed etiology of both maladies recognized familial transmission. "As a general rule, whatever exhausts the power of the brain and nerves, depresses vitality, or debilitates the body, may, through these effects, become the causative agent of insanity." Among the many examples cited by the 1860 census as contributing to insanity were poor physical health, chronic insomnia, alcoholism, and various mental preoccupations and immoralities. The census also singled out America's education system as a factor promoting insanity because of "the early age at which children are placed in school, their confinement often to ill-constructed seats, in imperfectly ventilated rooms, and the burdens which, in the multiplicity of lessons, are thrown upon them, tend to an undue exhaustion of the brain."

The 1860 census likewise noted that 479 men died of murder versus 49 women. Another 428 men and 33 women died from homicide. A much larger group of violent accidental deaths resulted from drowning, burns, falls, firearms, lightning, poison, railroad, strangulation and suffocation. The combined deaths from this group totaled 18,090 persons, of which men accounted for the majority with 12,427, or 69 percent. Of the known causes, drowning was most frequent, followed by burns and then falls.

The war years dramatically changed the morbidity and mortality numbers.

Best estimates would suggest that each side suffered injuries and deaths of around one-third of a million men from causes directly attributable to the battlefields. Since the United States conducts decennial population surveys, the 1870 census was the first postwar census.

The U.S. population grew to 38,558,371 in 1870, increasing over the decade by nearly 23 percent. Men totaled 19,493,565, or 50.6 percent, of the population.[39] In ten years the number of men had declined by about half a percent, a figure representing 192,792 fewer men when based on the total 1870 population.

The decline in the male population could in part reflect the lingering effects of the Civil War. The number of males per females, particularly among adults age 20–44, declined from 107.9 in 1860 to 99.2 in 1870. The same ten-year time period witnessed a decline in children under the age of five from 15.4 percent in 1860 to 14.3 percent in 1870.

The 1870 census recorded mortality statistics for the inclusive period extending from June 1, 1869, through May 31, 1870.[40] During that time 492,263 persons died, of whom 260,673 (53 percent) were men. The eleven former states of the Confederacy contributed 101,412 deaths to the nation's total; men accounted for 52,732, or 52 percent.

The leading causes of adult deaths in 1870 differed from those of the previous decade. Consumption still led the list, followed by pneumonia, enteric fever, and scarlet fever. Diseases of the nervous system, encephalitis and convulsions, closely followed the infectious diseases as causes of death. Accidental deaths claimed 22,740 victims, most commonly resulting from drowning, burns, and falls.

There were 2,057 homicides and 1,345 suicides (the 1870 census did not include a separate category for murder). Men accounted for 1,907 homicides and 1,060 suicides. Among male suicides, hanging was most common, followed by gunshot deaths. Among the 285 women who committed suicide, poisoning was slightly more common than hanging.

The 1870 census also reported the number of insane and the "idiotic." The total number of insane persons was 37,432, with women accounting for 51 percent, or 19,213. The aggregate "idiotic" number was 24,527, of which men constituted 55 percent, or 13,494.

A total of 740 persons died of alcoholism, with exactly half succumbing to delirium tremens and the other half to intemperance. Evidence also suggests that 1,049 persons died from alcohol-related deaths in 1865. In that year, 612 persons died from delirium tremens and the remainder succumbed to the ill effects of intemperance.[41]

From these figures, it becomes apparent that in the ten years between

1860 and 1870 the rate of suicide increased from approximately 30 per 100,000 to 35 per 100,000. The combined rate of homicide and murder increased from 31 per 100,000 to 53 per 100,000. The number of insane increased from 760 per 100,000 to 970 per 100,000. The rate of "idiocy" likewise increased from 599 per 100,000 to 636 per 100,000. The rate of accidental deaths was about 575 per 100,000 in 1860 versus 590 in 1870.

The ten years between 1860 and 1870 witnessed a nominal increase in the rate of suicide, as stated previously, from approximately 30 per 100,000 to 35 per 100,000. As with all morbidity statistics from this era, government officials openly acknowledged "wholesale omissions from the return of deaths in the census."[42] Such omissions stemmed from multiple sources, ranging from the census taker's failure to inquire to the family's forgetfulness. As might be expected, the gathering of suicide data based on a family's willing self-disclosure was fraught with even more opportunities for failure.

Another piece of the puzzle revealing the increase in suicide comes from state tabulations.[43] Massachusetts appears to have been the first state government to track suicides, an exercise initially undertaken in 1843. That first effort failed to include roughly 10 percent of Massachusetts' population. Interestingly, government officials did not report the victims' gender. The data collection improved over time, and by 1850 a state law required medical examiners to report all violent deaths, including suicides. The inclusion of the medical examiner's report unearthed an apparent reporting bias. Local attending physicians completed the death certificates, but later review by the medical examiner uniformly reduced the number of deaths attributed to suicide by 8 percent.

The other northeastern states, with the exception of Maine, also started collecting suicide statistics. Rhode Island reported two suicides in 1853. Connecticut started collecting suicide statistics in 1848, but, along with the early efforts of Vermont and New Hampshire, the information was riddled with too many holes. By the time the Civil War began, however, the data was reliable enough for comparison between the various northern states.

The unmistakable trend line drawn by suicides reported in the northeastern states from 1860 to 1885 was decidedly up. During the Civil War years, from 1860 to 1865, Massachusetts reported 62.9 suicides per million people, followed by Rhode Island's 56.5 and Connecticut's 45.9. In the five-year period immediately following the war's conclusion, the rate of suicides reported by Massachusetts declined slightly to 60.6, followed by increases in Connecticut (54.6) and Rhode Island (83.5). However, the figures from 1871 to 1875 spiked in Massachusetts to 80, in Connecticut to 66.2, and Vermont to 74.9, while Rhode Island reported a decrease to 73.5. The time period from 1876 to 1880 showed a similar pattern, with Massachusetts reporting 81.1 suicides, Connecticut 86.6,

Rhode Island 82.1, and Vermont 86.7. The final five-year period from 1881 to 1885 tabulated 90.9 suicides in Massachusetts, 103.3 in Connecticut, 82.1 in Rhode Island, and 86.7 in Vermont.

In terms of gender, at no time did the rate of male suicides fall below 70 percent of the total, with the average number during the twenty years standing at 77.5 percent. As the national census figures showed, and the individual states confirmed, there was an essentially equal population distribution between men and women. Thus, men were clearly committing suicide more frequently than women.

The suicide victims' ages were recorded best by Massachusetts. A difference, based on gender, showed that women committed suicide in fairly equal proportions throughout their life cycle. Men's deaths, by contrast, were concentrated in the later years, beginning around age 50 and peaking among those over 70.

The northeastern states also calculated monthly suicide rates. April tallied the highest rate of suicides, with 102.8 per 1,000 persons. It seems that the warmest months correlated with a higher number of suicides. As the northern states defrosted from winter, suicides started sharply rising from March (84.7 per 1,000 persons) through August (88.3 per 1,000 persons). The coldest months, particularly January (62.6 per 1,000 persons) and February (59.1 per 1,000 persons), had the lowest numbers.

It seems clear, when examining the national and state statistics, that misery and mayhem increased in the years following the conclusion of America's Civil War. Further evidence bolstering that contention comes from scattered newspaper reports and editorials documenting with alarm a rising rate of suicides. In America's postwar period suicide was a tragedy evoking unequal mixtures of compassion and condemnation—mostly the latter. The deeply moral taint that declared suicide a shameful act led families, friends, and society at large to rationalize, minimize or simply ignore the death. Only a sensational suicide, defined by the manner of death or status of the individual, seemed to justify publicity. This biased reporting shaped public opinion, skewing social perceptions of suicide as a rare act undertaken by irrational, mostly well-to-do individuals.

The "extraordinary suicide" of William J. Grant was a typical example that captured a reporter's attention. Grant was 30 years old and a very recent immigrant from Scotland. Within weeks of his arrival, Grant's fellow lodgers in a New York City boarding home noticed his excessive use of alcohol. Perhaps their gossip or Grant's self-reflection, or a combination of both, motivated him to change his ways. Grant dramatically announced his intention to adopt a temperate lifestyle. Unfortunately, the sudden cessation of alcoholic consumption resulted in a severe case of delirium tremens. The ensuing agitation and hallucinations alarmed the boarding house residents, who quickly procured the services of a nurse. Fearing for the safety of the patient and the other residents, the nurse removed any objects from Grant's room that could become dangerous projectiles. However, the nurse apparently never considered a wall-mounted souvenir war arrow as a threat. As it turned out, that was a tragic oversight. In a moment of suicidal frenzy, Grant plucked the arrow from the wall and drove the instrument of death deep into his heart.[44]

Another theme gracing the pages of newspapers was a suicide following a failed romance. In these superficial stories the woman was often portrayed, directly or through imputation, as the victim of a callous and insensitive man. Such was the short, sad story of Frances E. Thurston, who, presumably persuaded by future promises, ran off with a married man. The doomed affair ended with Thurston swallowing a fatal dose of poison. The coroner's inquest deemed the death a suicide directly attributable to "the abandonment and misusage of Miss Thurston."[45]

Popular publications, sensing a growing trend of suicide, started documenting the data and speculating about the causes. *McClure's Magazine* tackled the subject in a lengthy and fact-laden article examining "The Problems of Suicide."[46] One of the principal findings in the article was the increase in suicide following the war. The article's author, reasoning from the presumably lower rate of suicide during the war years, suggested that warfare actually increased social bonds through a shared focus and sacrifice. Once those connections were severed by peace, the suicide rate started increasing.

The riveting impact of a war now concluded left society rudderless, drifting toward a reflective introversion and anomie. Against this backdrop, brooding intensified, cynicism increased, and social outlets dried up. For an increasing number of individuals, the nihilistic spiral ended in suicide.

Official Union records rarely recorded much detail when a soldier died in the postwar years. George A. Otis, an assistant surgeon in the Union Army, compiled *A Report of Surgical Cases* treated shortly after the Civil War ended.[47] In one small section of the report, Otis described cases of suicide from gunshot wounds. Otis documented one suicide in 1866, three in 1867, two in 1868 and four in 1869. In all but two instances Otis identified the soldier's unit and provided brief details.

The first postwar suicide reported by Otis claimed the life of Private Nelson Lowry, Company D, 2nd Battalion, 16th U.S. Infantry, in 1866. Lowry suffered from "mental depression caused by religious melancholy." In 1867 suicide claimed an unnamed lieutenant; Private Daniel Kaufman, Company E, 7th U.S. Cavalry; and Private David Wilson, Company H, U.S. Infantry. Private George

Kerne, Company K, 21st U.S. Infantry, and Private Otavius E. Daniels committed suicide in 1868. The four suicides in 1869 included Private John Flannery, Company C, 2nd U.S. Infantry; Lieutenant E.P. Colby, 11th U.S. Infantry; Private James L. Cummings, Company F, 1st U.S. Cavalry; and Private Mark E. Richards.

Peter Moffatt, an assistant surgeon, reported "one of the most deliberate attempts at self-destruction ever witnessed" at Fort Gaston, California. The subject of Moffatt's report was an unnamed, melancholy private whose absence from meals raised concerns about his safety. A search soon found the soldier in a secluded area, his head comfortably resting on his coat, and his clothes saturated with dried blood. Moffatt carefully examined the man, discovering deep self-inflicted lacerations in both thighs and arms. A weak pulse denied the soldier's suicide, and with vigorous efforts Moffatt was able to resuscitate the despondent victim.

The startling increase in suicide following the Civil War provoked equal measures of compassion and condemnation. In the latter camp, some newspapers openly concluded that "there is no more distressing feature of the time than the constant increase of suicides all over the country" and consequently urged a harsh approach. The rising rate of suicide, coupled with the trivial incitements, seemed to sever the long-established moral link prohibiting self-destruction. Although not explicitly indicting or even ignoring religion's role in reining in the social epidemic, the newspaper's somewhat caustic suggestion that "our legislators will do well to give it what attention they can spare from other business" certainly placed more faith in government intervention.

In most cases, a confirmed suicide earned no more than a few paragraphs in a local newspaper. The stories usually included a few lines that served to explain the possible precipitant. For example, toward the end of the Civil War, a young widow, the daughter of a prominent soldier, killed herself in the family's cistern. The brief article concluded by noting that the widow's father was recently fined "for horsewhipping a young man who was paying attention to his daughter."[48] The reader is left to infer the cause of the suicide, perhaps an act of anger directed toward a controlling father or the woman's disconsolate reaction to a lost love.

A similar inexplicable death claimed the life of "an honorary member of the 7th Regiment (N.Y.)."[49] To close acquaintances, James Farnam was an amiable man disposed to prolonged bouts of depression. His friends presumed that his downcast state of mind arose from a lack of employment. In any event, Farnam was seemingly enjoying the festivities accompanying the marriage of his sister. Shortly after midnight, however, Farnam discreetly excused himself and retired to his bedroom. A few minutes later Farnam's mother discovered her son draped across his bed, blood streaming from a self-inflicted gunshot through his heart. In this case, the newspaper ascribed no particular motivation to the seemingly senseless act, ignoring the obvious connection between his sister's happy marriage and his broken heart.

Based solely on magazine and newspaper accounts, the public would certainly be forgiven for thinking that women accounted for the majority of completed suicides. In fact, men far outnumbered women in terms of self-destruction. Male suicides generated less sympathy, with newspapers typically ascribing the death to an ardent addiction to alcohol or an embarrassing reversal of fortunes.

The lingering consequences of the recently concluded War Between the States were rarely considered as a suicide risk factor, even when the connection seemed obvious. Irwin A. Denson was a warrant officer in the Union Navy. The brief account of his death hints at unresolved, simmering emotional turmoil by cryptically commenting that Denson "had been for some time in the Hospital, and when released as cured, was very low spirited."[50] With a mind no doubt reeling from wartime recollections, the loss of his wife was a devastating and ultimately destabilizing blow. After months of brooding, Denson finally decided to end his suffering. Without conveying a hint of hopelessness, he borrowed a handgun from a friend and shortly thereafter shot himself in the head. Denson left two suicide notes, one pensively stating, "I have not seen one happy day since I lost my dear wife." The other letter hinted at a long-running bureaucratic struggle: "I wish you would, also, send my discharges to my brother and tell him Mr. Stilman B. Allen ... has got my claims, and if he ever gets anything, give it to the children."

Denson's death obliquely blamed a convoluted disability system that seemed, in some cases, to force Civil War veterans to fight another protracted battle with their own government. Private John Rabus, Company I, 15th Regiment, New York Heavy Artillery, left nothing to the imagination in indicting the federal government. Rabus committed suicide shortly after the war ended. No doubt dispirited and disgusted, he left behind a damning declaration: "I got a disease (palsy) in the service, from the effects of which I was obliged to stop work; in consequence I applied for a pension from the United States Government. Not receiving any support from the Government, this is to inform my friends and acquaintances I have been obliged to kill myself."[51]

Rabus' sad story was not unique. In the weeks immediately preceding his death, two other local soldier suicides rocked the neighborhoods of New York City. An informal review of suicides across the country led one writer to discover "not less than a dozen similar [suicide] cases during the past Winter."[52]

Roughly a year after Rabus died, a nephew of Gideon Welles, President

Lincoln's secretary of the navy, committed suicide.[53] The sad story began when Robert G. Welles, the son of Thaddeus Welles, calmly approached his father in the early evening hours toward the end of December 1866. The older man was perusing a newspaper when Robert unexpectedly produced a pistol. Surely alarmed by the display, Thaddeus asked his son to set the pistol aside. Instead, the distraught son "flung his left arm around his [father's] neck and kissed him, when with the single exclamation, 'Farewell, father!' he sank back into a chair, put the pistol to his head and fired."[54]

Robert Welles lingered for about an hour following the fatal pistol shot. His suicide was a dreadful outcome that occurred shortly after the death of his brother, Samuel. Gideon Welles' recollections of the tragedy alluded to "some habits contracted in the army [that] affected him." Aside from that vague reference, Gideon dwelled mostly on his nephew's distinguished military service as an officer with Company G, 10th United States Regular Infantry. Robert "was in fourteen hard-fought battles, was shot through the leg at Gettysburg, had been promoted to be captain ... and after the War resigned his commission."[55]

One of the events that may have haunted Robert was the battlefield death of Lieutenant William Fisher. The two officers were close friends. In a letter written to William's father, Robert described the circumstances leading to the death of his son at Gettysburg: "Lieut. Fisher seemed cheerful—we talked and laughed, wondering when we should go into the fight. About 3 PM we moved forward.... There we came to the only fence we had in our way—back of this fence was oak timber—It was about six rods further on that Lt. Fisher was shot.... I passed where Lt. Fisher was lying, he looked up—in that look was everything! I had known him long, he was about my own age, and our time in camp had been spent mostly with each other."[56]

The precise factors precipitating Robert Welles' suicide will never be known. Clearly, the death of his brother was a grievous emotional wound from which he never fully recovered. However, Gideon Welles alluded to military "habits" that hobbled Robert. Add to this unresolved remorse over the death of his friend Lieutenant William Fisher, and it seems more than coincidence that Robert Welles resigned his army commission on December 29, 1865, and died almost exactly one year later.[57]

The increase in civilian suicides both during and following the Civil War captured the attention of national newspapers. Frank Leslie's popular publication ran a mournful tally of New York City in 1869 and reported that suicide "is frightfully on the increase in this city."[58] The newspaper bolstered this claim by noting 111 cases of suicide. Men killed themselves with guns, by taking poison, and by hanging. None of the women resorted to guns, instead committing suicide by poisoning or drowning.

The same newspaper revisited the subject three years later.[59] Instead of focusing solely on New York City, the newspaper examined the trend across America. Starting with 1870, "The percentage was 3.06 per thousand. In 1860 it was 3.02 and in 1850 2.01." Men accounted for the majority, with suicide among women predominating during the "romantic period of girlhood." The reporter, in a further effort to explain the upward trend of suicides, remarked on the higher rates in large northern cities as compared to the rural south.

The postwar rise in suicides was not confined to one region. The increasing suicide rate in North Carolina mirrored that of the larger northern states.[60] Six years after the Civil War ended, North Carolina newspapers documented 14 suicides. While this may seem like a small number, it actually doubled the number of suicides stretching back thirty years. With the passage of another decade, the 1880s witnessed a dramatic rise in the number of suicides reported in North Carolina newspapers. The peak year was 1883, with 31 suicides.

Another factor suggesting a rising tide of suicides was connected to the confluence of life insurance and the law.[61] Perhaps the most famous example was the United States Supreme Court case *Life Insurance Company v. Terry*.[62] In the years preceding this particular legal case, a burgeoning spate of suicides challenged the pocketbooks of insurance companies issuing life insurance policies. For the most part, life insurance policies contained explicit language voiding the payout in cases of suicide. Disgruntled beneficiaries increasingly challenged the exception and, when combined with an apparent rise in national suicides, set the stage for acrimonious legal contests.

Shortly after the Civil War ended, on July 22, 1867, the Mutual Life Insurance Company issued a policy to George Terry's wife.[63] Less than two years later Terry committed suicide, violating one of the provisions of his life insurance contract. As best as could be determined, his suicide was linked to an unhappy marriage. The day before his death, Terry purchased a small amount of arsenic, ostensibly to rid his house of rodents. However, he had a more malignant use for the poison and consumed a fatal quantity the next day. Terry's "widow quickly married again, and sued the company for the amount of the policy." The trial was held in Kansas, and the jury found in the claimant's favor. The Mutual Insurance Company appealed the verdict.

The case eventually was argued in the U.S. Supreme Court. One of the central disputes involved Terry's mental state. If Terry was sane at the time that he took his life, the insurance company would prevail, and if Terry was insane, the company could expect the opposite outcome. The U.S. Supreme Court upheld the lower court's decision but at the same time defined a standard for future such cases: "If the death is caused by the voluntary act of the assured, he knowing and intending that his death shall be the result of his act, but when his reasoning faculties are so far impaired that he is not able to understand the moral character, the general nature, consequences and effect of the act he is about to commit, or when he is impelled thereto by an insane impulse ... such death is not" bound by the suicide clause.[64]

The U.S. Supreme Court's affirmation of the link between insanity and suicide belied the unsettled nature of medical opinions on the subject. John P. Gray, a nineteenth-century professor of psychological medicine and jurisprudence and the superintendent of the New York State Lunatic Asylum in Utica, carefully studied suicide.[65] Gray was also the editor of the *American Journal of Psychiatry*, an influential medical publication from which he espoused his strong views.

The rash of suicides following the Civil War probably played a part in Dr. Gray turning his thoughts to the subject.[66] Another reason was the ascendancy of psychological medicine's authority and the resulting need to weigh in on one of life's most puzzling behaviors. To most people of the nineteenth century, suicide was both an immoral act and certainly the product of an unbalanced mind. In preparing the medical response to suicide, Gray commented that "if from youth we are accustomed to read of suicide, in the daily news ... and we grow up accounting it among the ordinary facts of life, we shall have little horror of such death, morally or physically." Gray went further by explicitly tying the increase in suicides to media publicity: "Imitation [from] ... the publication of suicides ... in the newspapers ... has also a great influence in inducing suicide."

Gray indicted more than newspapers. He also cast blame on philosophers and other moralizers "who reduce the question of continuing life to what the individual may deem expediency and comfort." To Gray, trivializing life in such a manner strained the social fabric by ignoring death's impact on survivors. In the final analysis, Gray considered "the majority of cases, committed by persons who are entirely sane." It was most likely an unexpected and paradoxical assumption from a professor of psychological medicine. However, Gray seemed to recognize the importance of social connections. The promotion of self-interest, agnosticism, or moral relativism loosened those ties, potentially opening the door for suicidal acts.

Gray was not alone in concluding that suicide was mostly a sane act. Nor was he alone in connecting the moral decline of nineteenth-century America with the "suicide mania."[67] Oliver H. Palmer, a Civil War general and strong supporter of Abraham Lincoln, left the military in 1863. In the following years Palmer put his law degree to work by building a team of attorneys for the Mutual Life Insurance Company. The spike in life insurance litigation involving suicide led Palmer to take the "opposite ground from those who claim that suicide is always the result of insanity."

Palmer mirrored Dr. Gray's opinion about suicide and found Gray a receptive editor willing to use the bully pulpit of the *American Journal of Psychiatry* to spread their message. From this platform, Palmer authored a lengthy article arguing that suicide was a byproduct of a sane person's rational calculations. His concluding comments focused on the erosion of society: "The barriers to self-destruction seem to be giving way," the consequence of which, Palmer warned, would be "a harvest of suicides that will astonish the world."[68]

The need to deem suicide a sane act was not limited to life insurance companies. Carlos MacDonald, the superintendent of the State Asylum for Insane Criminals in Auburn, New York, went to great lengths in explaining the death of William Barr.[69]

William Barr was a twenty-year-old itinerant street peddler who ran afoul of the law in 1870. Following a conviction for robbery, the young Irishman landed a ten-year sentence at the notorious Sing Sing Prison in New York. His lengthy stint may have addled his brain. Four years into that stretch prison doctors transferred Barr to the State Asylum for Insane Criminals in Auburn. Barr's transfer was based on his "chronic mania and melancholia," a mental state the prison doctors traced to a vice-laden life saturated with alcohol and tobacco.

The receiving doctors at the State Asylum for Insane Criminals did not record any information about Barr's first admission. Years later, when asked to comment on Barr's hospitalization, the same doctors retained a vivid impression of their former patient. Without a shred of doubt, the doctors adamantly insisted that Barr was not insane but instead a "vicious, depraved quick tempered, incorrigible fellow, who was disposed to be quarrelsome on the slightest provocation." The asylum doctors kept their admittedly sane patient for two years.

Barr's two-year asylum sojourn ended with his return to prison. His confinement lasted only six months before aberrant behavior forced his return to the asylum. This time, a no-nonsense superintendent by the name of Carlos MacDonald was in charge. Barr was quickly labeled "an ugly customer and a feigner" and in record time, a mere nine days, was sent back to prison.

Barr's prison homecoming was soon marred by murder. In February 1877, Barr joined a small detail of prisoners tasked with removing snow dropped by a winter storm. The prisoners probably looked forward to the task, if for no other reason than having a chance to go outside the prison walls. Barr exploited the excursion by flirting with the female pedestrians, earning a stern rebuke from the watchful eye of a nearby guard.

What followed was a fateful spar between an indignant prisoner and an insistent jailer. Barr brought the brawl to a sudden, dramatic, and fatal conclusion by bashing the guard's head with his snow shovel. Somewhat surprisingly, the murder generated a good deal of newspaper coverage that tilted in favor of Barr, as newspaper editorials sympathized with the "obviously" insane inmate.

Barr was transferred to a county jail to await trial for the murder. While there, he "began to act in a most foolish, absurd manner. He made irrelevant replies to questions, muttered incoherently to himself, about 'spirits' and 'devils,' destroyed his clothing and bedding ... and [made] demon-like yells." Barr was silenced when a guard turned a water hose on him.

Much to the disgust of MacDonald, Barr's trial counsel entered a plea of insanity. The trial court judge ordered a "commission of medical experts," led by Dr. John P. Gray, to examine the mental state of the prisoner. The commission conducted and completed the inquiry on October 11, 1877, and found Barr sane.

In spite of the commission's ruling, Barr's attorney proceeded with the insanity defense. Four physicians testified for the defense while an equal number, including MacDonald, testified for the prosecution. "During the trial Barr would frequently laugh and 'grin' in a silly manner, or mutter to himself, and make grimaces and queer gestures." All this mattered not one bit to the jury, which promptly pronounced Barr guilty of second-degree murder.

Once again Barr was sent back to prison, during which time he made several unsuccessful attempts to escape. "After this he seemed to realize, for the first time, that every chance of escape was cut off, and that he had nothing in the world to look forward to ... he terminated his earthly existence by hanging himself."

Barr's suicide provoked a mixture of compassion and condemnation. The latter reaction was aimed at MacDonald and his asylum colleagues. The suicide seemed to confirm the ineptitude of self-proclaimed insanity experts who resolutely pronounced Barr sane. MacDonald penned a lengthy response in the *Journal of Insanity* in a clearly defensive effort to rebut the implicit criticism. He ridiculed the defense experts, painted the grimmest possible picture of Barr, and extolled the sagacity of asylum doctors. In a rebuke to the lay public, MacDonald airily lectured, "Doubtless there are still a few individuals in every community who, in spite of the most convincing evidence to the contrary, refuse to believe that suicide is ever the act of a sane mind."

Whether sane or not, the suicide mania absorbed the nation in self-reflection. Battling medical experts, passionate editorials, and courtroom theatrics gripped the nation's attention. While long on drama, the debate was short on facts. For the most part individual suicides garnered little attention. The few that defied this trend ended up in print for extenuating reasons, mostly because the deaths made interesting reading. This skewed the public's perception of suicide, leaving the impression that suicide only afflicted the affluent or deeply troubled person. Doctors arguing otherwise, essentially claiming that suicide was the byproduct of a rational mind, were greeted with skepticism.

Reporters rarely drew a direct line between wartime injuries and subsequent suicides. Perhaps the sheer magnitude of lost limbs and dreadful wounds obscured their vision. The death of Henry Keyes, a young telegraph operator, could probably be traced to two events. Keyes lost an arm during his service as a private with the 12th New Hampshire Volunteer Infantry. Surely weighing further on his mind was the death of a brother in the war. Keyes, in a very methodical way, set about committing suicide by forging a doctor's prescription for arsenic. The disheartened former soldier died after consuming two ounces of the poisonous liquid.[70]

The *New York Herald* reported the suicides of two army officers, one day apart, in the summer of 1865. Major Albert Elfield, a former officer assigned to the 97th U.S. Colored Troops Infantry, committed suicide "by blowing out his brains with a revolver." The newspaper ascribed the reason for the 55-year-old-man's death to insanity. A day later, Lieutenant Arthur W. Thompson died from ingesting a combination of alcohol and laudanum. In the hours preceding his death Thompson had consumed enough alcohol to become visibly intoxicated. Remarking that he felt sick, witnesses recalled Thompson retiring to his room, along with two ounces of laudanum. The soldier's resort to the tincture of opium probably caused no concern since Thompson publicly declared that "he would have one good long sleep." The dose proved fatal, and a coroner's inquest, despite any confusion about his motives, ruled the death a suicide.[71]

One of the more unusual suicides was chronicled by Frederick W. Fout, a Civil War veteran and recipient of the Medal of Honor. Fout tells an unusual story he titled "Red-Headed Reilley." The Red-Headed Reilley was actually the wife of a renegade named Hispeth, who waged a single-handed war against southern sympathizers in Kentucky. A detachment of Confederate infantry soldiers eventually cornered and killed the rogue. His wife, the Red-Headed Reilley, escaped. The 22-year-old woman was about five feet, two inches tall and weighed around 120 pounds. Apparently she could easily pass for the opposite sex and, taking advantage of that distinction, joined an Indiana infantry regiment. She served undetected for three years. Following the end of the war, the Red-Headed Reilley apparently fell on hard times. Still masquerading as a young boy, she approached Fout, no doubt seeking a job. "Two months later [she] was found dead ... having doubtless committed suicide." Fout only learned of the Red-Headed Reilley's true gender after her death.[72]

In the years following the war suicide was a topic of great concern, claiming ever more lives. A number of factors inhibited a search for the cause, such as the prevailing morality of the time, which assigned a significant stigma to the subject. Regardless, it seems clear that the misery and mayhem did not end at Appomattox when the two armies laid down their arms. Quite the contrary occurred as the psychological wounds of the Civil War sowed decades of dysphoria, discontent, and disillusionment.

Two

A Loss of Faith

Death was everywhere during the Civil War. The battlefield carnage left men piled up like cord wood. Hastily dug graves hid the remains, all too often condemning the nameless victims to an eternal indignity. Illness and injury claimed even more men. Vast prisoner-of-war camps removed the threat of a bullet but substituted a slow starvation-fed demise. At the same time, family and friends dreaded a local newspaper's tabulation of combat casualties. Scanning the list for a loved one's name was a ritual rife with emotion, including joy when the search proved fruitless, but leaving the possibility of heartbreak open for another day. Letters from the battlefield, particularly from an unknown author, might also inform the family of a soldier's death. These memorial missives covered the soldier's death with a benevolent blanket.

The daily dance with death was accompanied by a mournful tune. Pessimistic notes composed a somber song, dampening the spirits of a nation. This war-inspired dirge further debased cherished conventions, leaving a disillusioned populace searching for consolation. Fractured families and broken faith created an emotional void desperately seeking serenity. The movements that arose to fill this vacuum were doubly deceitful, promising delight but delivering depression. Postbellum America, in part defined by dysthymia, disillusionment, and loss of faith in established traditions, was fertile ground for the rapid growth of Spiritualism.

In the dawning days of 1860 Spiritualism was just sprouting roots that would soon entangle America. The seeds were planted in Hydesville, New York, when Michael Weekman and his family assumed that they lived alone in a rather unpretentious house.[1] In 1847 a most curious event occurred. It was early evening and the family was just settling in for the night when a loud rap on the front door disturbed the quiet. As might be expected, Weekman opened the door, but, to his surprise, no visitor was awaiting entry. The mysterious knocking continued, but every effort to discover the source left the family frustrated. A few nights later, the Weekmans' eight-year-old daughter awakened from a sound sleep, screaming about an unseen presence touching her body. The frightened mother calmed her child, but many days passed before the young girl would sleep alone in her room. The Weekman family apparently thought little more of the affair and surely made no mention of it when they sold the house in December 1847 to John D. Fox.

The Fox family had barely settled into their new home when its mysterious nature revealed itself. In late March 1848 the family was safely tucked away for the night when a series of loud rappings reverberated throughout the house. The startled occupants diligently searched the house in vain and, failing in their efforts, retired for the night. Over the next several nights the rappings returned, accompanied by the grating sound of moving furniture.

Curiously, Mrs. Fox, far from being distressed at the prospect of living in a haunted house, took a rather dispassionate and analytic approach. Instead of shrinking away, she began sleuthing and, with a determined spirit, "concluded to go to bed early, and not let it disturb us.... I had just laid down. It commenced as usual." At this point, instead of scooping up her young girls and fleeing the house, Mrs. Fox noted a budding relationship: "The girls, who slept in the other bed in the room, heard the noise, and tried to make a similar noise by snapping their fingers.... As fast as she made the noise with her hands or fingers, the sound was followed up in the room.... When she stopped, the sound itself stopped for a short time." The older daughter, more amused than alarmed, demanded of the noise, "Now do just as I do. Count one, two, three, four, etc., striking one hand in the other at the same time." The obliging noise patiently waited until the girl finished her clapping and then, like an echo, repeated the sequence.

By now Mrs. Fox was convinced: the noises were surely animated by an unseen intelligence. In a final test to settle the matter, the matron of the house spoke to the invisible force, asking for the ages of her children. Once again, the unseen presence responded, correctly rapping the children's ages. The amazingly unruffled mother "then asked if it was a spirit? And if it was, to manifest it by two sounds." Two raps confirmed her suspicion and led to an extended dialogue. During the subsequent conversation the male spirit disclosed that it had died after thirty-one years and left a family behind.

Mrs. Fox, perhaps partly motivated by the significance of her discovery and a need to further confirm it, hastily confided the whole affair to a nearby neighbor. Mrs. Redfield was skeptical but nonetheless made the short journey to the Fox home. Shortly after her arrival, Mrs. Redfield proceeded to communicate with the spirit, receiving in return rapping responses that correctly answered specific questions. Mrs. Fox invited four more neighbors that night to witness the startling manifestations, all of whom quickly replaced doubt with acceptance.

Over the next several days the fantastic news of the haunted house quickly spread. Through continued communications it came to light that the spirit was all that remained of an itinerant peddler by the name of Charles Rosma, supposedly murdered and buried in the basement. The sociable ghost apparently found some solace in chatting with the Fox family.

The Rev. Charles Hammond undertook one of the more interesting examinations of the Fox sisters in 1849. Hammond applied for and received an invitation to the Fox family house. The initially skeptical clergyman carefully cataloged his observations over successive visits. Hammond was probably prepared for disappointment, once the young girls made their appearance, the rappings dutifully followed. Over the course of previous encounters the Fox sisters had trained the ghost to signal letters of the alphabet by rapping in response to the girls' slow enunciation of the letters. This was a decided advance in communication that allowed visitors to pose endless questions to the ghost.

Hammond took advantage of the spirit's crude telegraphy on his next visit. The pastor had prepared a detailed interrogation with obscure personal questions, principally chosen to expose any deception. Although the spirit answered most of the questions correctly, Hammond's suspicions lingered. The fair-minded preacher concluded, "However, as the spirit promised to satisfy me by other demonstrations when I came again, I patiently awaited the opportunity."

The Fox sisters welcomed Hammond back, along with six other men, for a third demonstration. All members of the group assembled in the early evening around a table, dimly lit by a candle. Immediately after taking their seats the rappings commenced, in a frequency and intensity never previously experienced. Hammond must have been surprised when he felt the table "next to me move upward—I pressed upon it heavily, but soon it passed out of the reach of us all." Retaining his wits, Hammond carefully surveyed the scene but could detect no props. The spirit returned the table to its former position accompanied by a pounding cacophony. Impressive as this was, the phantom's fantastic feats were just beginning. Hammond was transfixed when "I felt fingers taking hold of a lock of [my] hair ... then a cold, death-like hand was drawn designedly over my face—three gentle raps on my left knee—my right limb forcibly pulled ... myself and chair uplifted ... and several slaps, as with a hand, on the side of my head." Hammond was clearly impressed by the Fox sisters' mediumship and concluded, "It could not, by any possibility, have been done by them, nor even attempted, without detection." The reverend's ratification was indeed a powerful endorsement.

Around this time, Mrs. Leah Fish, an older, widowed daughter of the Fox family, arrived from Rochester, New York, and, having learned of the strange happenings in Hydesville, was determined to satisfy her curiosity.[2] The rappings and other spiritual trappings impressed the older daughter, eventually converting her to the world of Spiritualism. Despite the spirit's conspicuous geniality, Mrs. Fox apparently harbored some lingering concerns for her youngest daughter's safety. Leah's subsequent departure and return to Rochester, New York, offered the perfect solution. Mrs. Fox arranged for both of her other daughters to leave their Hydesville haunted house. As a consequence, fourteen-year-old Margaret and her younger sister Catherine moved roughly thirty miles west to Rochester, New York. Catherine moved in with her older sister Leah while Margaret lived with her brother David.

Out of an abundance of caution, and in an effort to thwart preexisting spirits from surfacing in Rochester, Leah sought and eventually rented a new home.[3] It was a futile step, with the spirit sounds resuming almost immediately. In an ominous turn, the innocent rappings transitioned to the "terrible sound of the pouring of a pail of coagulated blood upon the floor. It was repeated, in quick succession, three times." Naturally this scared Leah, who screamed, with her daughter Elizabeth and Catherine rushing to her side. After a breathless explanation and a few minutes in the company of the two young girls, Leah regained her composure. It was getting late by now, and the family reluctantly retired for the night.

The sleepless spirits resurfaced around midnight. All were awakened by loud thumping and scraping sounds, and it soon became clear that furniture was moving. Catherine and Elizabeth, alarmed by the commotion, anxiously sought the security of Leah's bed. Soon after snuggling next to Leah, a cold, death-like presence settled on Elizabeth's back, sending her into spasms of fear. The young girl had long suffered a painful spinal affliction, and the ghost, by repeatedly targeting this area, seemed sadistically inclined to worsen it. As it turned out, though, the ghost was actually ministering to the child's longstanding disability, and at the conclusion of the treatment it had affected a complete cure. News of the nocturnal visitor ricocheted around the neighborhood, erasing doubt and increasing the numbers of devoted disciples.

The Fox sisters struggled to restrain the public's curiosity. They plaintively pleaded with the spirits to leave, but the ghosts would hear none of it. A Methodist minister resorted to an exorcism, but that, too, failed. Defeated, the girls accepted their destiny and began welcoming visitors for the explicit purpose of speaking with the spirits. The Fox sisters were becoming full-fledged mediums, bridging the gap between life and death.

Efforts to banish the spirits were met with determined resistance. The ghosts became more obnoxious and intrusive, with thunderous rappings and kitchen dishes flying about. Acting on an impulse during a particularly rambunctious manifestation, Leah remembered communicating with the spirits in Hydesville through the alphabet. She immediately made this proposition to her invisible guests, who, in turn, vigorously rapped their approval. With a reliable means of communication now established, the chatty spirits could not be quieted. Throughout the succeeding days and nights the apparitions took every opportunity to connect with their material counterparts. And connect they did, as hundreds of curious citizens descended on the Fox home and, sitting around a kitchen table, held communion with the dearly departed.

The ethereal beings, emboldened by their success in Rochester, soon surfaced in surrounding cities. For unknown reasons, the spirits would only collaborate with certain people. Those in tune with the spirit world could act as liaisons, forging relationships with long-lost relatives. Even so, the sheer number of mediums and spooks could not quell a persistent sense of disquiet as an air of fraud permeated the practice.

Catherine, Margaret, and Leah seemed to be the epicenter of the spiritual force in Rochester. Naturally, this attracted the attention of the community, including large numbers of skeptics. Apparently the spirits grew tired of the disbelief and insisted the Fox sisters openly confront the challengers. The girls demurred, but the apparitions argued, "You all have a duty to perform. We want you to make this matter more public." The Fox sisters stood their ground, and the spirits retaliated. In a threatening message, the spirits made it clear that they would forever leave the sisters alone unless they relented. Neither party budged, and for twelve days the spirits stayed away, only enticed back by Eliab W. Capron, a frequent visitor to the Fox home.

The audacious spirits set forth the terms of the public hearing. Capron was instructed to rent a large meeting room and, along with the Fox sisters, invite a large public assembly. For the nominal fee of twenty-five cents, spectators were introduced to the history of spirit rapping followed by ghostly manifestations. The spirits insisted that a committee of leading Rochester citizens attend the event and, through whatever means they chose, authenticate the apparitions' activities. After much prodding and persuading, the spirits had their way, and in mid–November 1848 a throng of 400 curious and skeptical patrons filled Rochester's Corinthian Hall. At the conclusion of the demonstration, during which loud rappings occurred and obscure questions were answered, the investigating committee reported that "they entirely failed to discover any means by which it could be done."[4]

A series of additional public events followed the first as the Fox sisters willingly communicated with the spirit world while various committees, consisting of eminent citizens, scrutinized the performances. In one case, "a committee of ladies ... took the young women into a room, disrobed them and examined their persons and clothing, to be sure that there was no fixtures about them that could produce the sounds." Finding no such devices, the committee then took the added precaution of binding the girls' ankles. The Fox sisters surely astonished the committee when they summoned the rappings of the spirits, who responded louder than ever. Other committees took their turn at foiling the Fox sisters, but all failed.

Capron, one of the chief architects of the campaign, gushed over the successful expositions. Even though some events got rowdy, with loud and rude denunciations from the audience, on the whole Capron was satisfied. As he later wrote, "From the day the public investigations ended, the excitement increased. It spread, by the press, from one end of the Union to the other.... The promises and predictions of the spirits in regard to the effect of such an investigation were fulfilled to the letter."[5]

The newspapers of America did indeed widely seed Spiritualism. Cynicism dominated many of these reports, with skeptical reporters flavoring many stories with more than a sprinkle of ridicule. But instead of leaving a bitter taste, growing segments of the public feasted at the phantoms' table. The accommodating apparitions responded with a bountiful buffet, with mediums providing such delights as automatic writing, spirit drawings, music ensembles, and, of course, the levitation of people and all manner of objects. Even so, a stubborn majority refused to believe, convinced that fraud was the chief ingredient.

The first inkling of impropriety inconspicuously surfaced in 1851.[6] Mrs. Norman Culver, related through marriage to the Fox family, explained the mysterious phenomena. According to her, a possibly fatigued Catherine had approached her in confidence. The relentless parade of visitors, many of whom came to expose a suspected fraud, surely strained the young girl. Seeking help, or perhaps consolation, Catherine appealed to Mrs. Culver, hoping she would become a medium.

Apparently Mrs. Culver agreed and began a short apprenticeship. Catherine, the teacher, eventually revealed the real showstopper: the secret of the rappings. According to Mrs. Culver, the sounds emanated from the toes. It took a fair amount of practice, but after a week she was able to discreetly produce all manner of rappings with all ten toes. "Catherine told me to warm my feet, or put them in warm water, and it would be easier work to rap."[7] Toe tapping was mysterious enough, but nothing convinced the skeptic more than having the spirits correctly answer obtuse questions. Catherine carefully schooled her pupil on this subject. Success required that the visitor legibly write the question on a piece of paper and then slowly go through the alphabet, patiently awaiting the spirit's confirmatory rapping. Catherine instructed Mrs. Culver to closely "watch the countenance and motions of the person, and that in that way they could nearly always guess right."

The revelations of Mrs. Culver actually did little damage to the Fox family's reputation. Ardent supporters impugned both her motives and her manipulation of an innocent young girl. Instead of sowing doubt, Mrs. Culver only reaped scorn.

The Fox sisters started a trend. In the preceding millennia of human existence death was the closing act of life, an impenetrable curtain, hinting at but never confirming an afterlife. All of that changed as the Fox sisters lifted the curtain on life's last scene. Spiritualism promised an encore. An insatiable public, driven by curiosity, conviction, and controversy, guaranteed a rapt audience, far exceeding the Fox sisters' capacity. Skilled interlocutors who could summon the traditionally reticent spirits arose from all walks of life to meet the demand. As their numbers multiplied, Spiritualism became a force to be reckoned with.

In an effort to cloak their activities in more mystery, and at the same time add a touch of credulity, the newly consecrated channellers adopted imaginative salutations. Not content with being addressed as a spiritualist or medium, members of this group conferred upon themselves dignified descriptions, such as practitioners of "Electrical Psychology, Electro-Biology, Mental Alchemy, Etherology and Magic Eloquence, Neurology, Pathetism, [and] Mesmerism."[8] The consequential characterizations not only added an imposing aura but also stressed the seers' particular skills.

It was impossible to ignore Spiritualism. The abundance of spiritualists and their mysterious manifestations spread from neighborhoods to villages and then to large metropolitan cities. Determined doubters did their best to detect deceit, but most failed. This left the dubious observers still suspicious but lacking incriminating evidence. The skeptics wavered between two possibilities, engaged in a sort of agnosticism that neither accepted nor rejected Spiritualism. The once determined doubters shifted their focus to explaining the supposedly spiritual phenomena, often leaning on scientific theories or, for the traditionally pious, attributing the communications to the sinister Satan.

Among the faithful, spectral anxiety was a favored theory.[9] According to this view, the deceased experienced distress that could only be relieved by reestablishing ties with the material world. By contrast, the ambivalent audience, seeking a more rational explanation, proposed all sorts of pseudoscientific theories to explain the spirit rapping, writing, and roaming. Leading the list were mesmerism and magnetism.

Mesmerism and magnetism were emerging concepts that predated the

Fox sisters by several decades. Both were controversial but fertilized a belief that would later propagate Spiritualism. Mesmerism and magnetism supplied the philosophical and pseudo-scientific nutrients that were essential to the growth of Spiritualism.

Electricity and magnetism were unseen physical forces that attracted a great deal of attention in nineteenth-century America. Eminent scientists, including Benjamin Franklin, designed elegant experiments convincingly demonstrating the properties of these mysterious forces. Through these experiments the invisible nature of such a demonstrable power was proven. A dispassionate science dispatched all doubt and denied a role for magic or mysticism. It was only a matter of time before the credulity extended to electricity and magnetism was exploited for explaining medical mysteries.

Sleepwalking was a medical curiosity. How could a person carry out complex purposeful physical activities, including movement and speech, yet upon awakening have no memory of the events? Somnambulism sparked one of the earliest efforts to explore the scientific border between the brain and the mind. William Hammond, a Civil War surgeon-general, described a typical example of a young woman sleepwalking: "She was walking very slowly and deliberately, her head elevated, her eyes open, her lips unclosed, and her hands hanging loosely by her side.... Without noticing ... she descended the stairs to the parlor.... Taking a match ... and then, turning on the gas, lit it.... I then made several motions as if about to strike her in the face. She made no attempt to ward off the blows."[10] After a series of further experiments, such as tickling her feet and pinching her face, that produced no response, Hammond shook the young woman in a determined effort to awaken her. She succumbed to his shaking and immediately started sobbing, remembering nothing that had occurred during the twenty-minute somnambulistic episode.

It soon became apparent that some individuals could control somnambulism, either spontaneously through self-induction or with the able assistance of a special handler, eventually called a magnetizer. By the late 1840s, magnetizers were attracting throngs of curiosity seekers. They all could thank Franz Anton Mesmer, a Swiss physician, who had first popularized animal magnetism nearly a century earlier.[11] Mesmer and his cohorts believed that a mysterious, invisible substance could be transmitted between animals. According to Mesmer, animal magnetism was an energy force that could be transmitted from one person to another. Some individuals (like Mesmer) apparently had an abundance of animal magnetism, which they soon discovered had the power to cure the lame and heal the sick. It was also entertaining, and magnetizers were not above packing auditoriums, for a modest fee, with their hypnotic demonstrations. In a fitting tribute to this pioneer, magnetism was just as often referred to as mesmerism.

In the years before the fame of the Fox sisters swept across America, cases of spontaneous somnambulism started popping up everywhere. A Connecticut physician recalled a young girl who "frequently fell into fits of somnambulism, in the day time, and manifested some extraordinary powers. She was able to thread a needle … with her eyes closed; she could read a book, upside down, with great fluency … knew what her friends were doing in any part of the room."[12]

The wonders of mesmerism, also known at the time as hypnosis, were boundless. Practitioners proclaimed that "under the influence of this power, the ignorant become wise … a person of no musical taste or cultivation can sing and play with a skill surpassing the most experienced performers."[13] Mesmerized subjects even dazzled audiences with mind-reading demonstrations, a sort of prelude to the coming wonders from spiritualists.

Magnetizers, mesmerizers or hypnotists, by whatever name, often attracted impassioned patrons suffering from chronic illnesses and injuries. Disillusioned with the limits of traditional medicine, and hoping against hope for relief, the magnetizers benefited from and exploited this disenchantment. Recommendations from the rehabilitated were persuasive and, at least in the beginning, encouraged a steady stream of pilgrims.

Experienced magnetizers shared their therapeutic techniques with novices. For best results, the magnetizer would prepare the subject with an internal cleansing by selecting an appropriate combination of a cathartic and an emetic.[14] Warming the feet seemed to be an essential element, and a hot bottle of water served that purpose. The magnetizer would also insist that the room be comfortable and quiet. With the preliminaries out of the way, the magnetizer would then take a seat opposite the patient and stare intently into their eyes while at the same time successively and rhythmically touching the patient from head to knee. After upward of an hour of the soft, soothing touching, the patient would often enter the somnambulist state. The magnetizer could now turn their attention to the person's discomfort. By simply touching the afflicted area, the magnetizer supposedly transferred their magnetic power to the sufferer and, through this process, relieved all sorts of discomforts and disabilities.

Supportive testimonials from grateful patrons fueled the public's interest. Mesmerists worked their magic among the rich and poor, in private homes and public lecture halls. Thomas Capern, the self-anointed "Secretary and Resident Superintendent of the Mesmeric Infirmary," chronicled over 150 cases in which magnetism made the difference. More than half of Capern's cures relieved chronic rheumatism, but that still left room for toothaches, sprains, epilepsy, eye problems, bowel disorders, and all manner of inflammations. One case involved a hard-working laborer who developed intractable back pain. The man sought the services of three physicians, but their ministrations only relieved his pocketbook. With a bit of coaxing, "he was induced to apply to Mr. Capern who made a few passes over the back and he felt more ease.... He is now quite well."[15]

Animal magnetism had its antagonists. Physicians were among the scoffers. The "Medical Profession, as a body ... branded [magnetism's] operators Imposters, and its recipients Dupes. They have reiterated, that any fluid, force or influence ... existed only in the brain" of the practitioners.[16]

A new front in the battle for respectability blindsided the magnetizers when the Fox sisters launched Spiritualism. The mediums ascribed their marvelous manifestations to spectral influences, not some invisible magnetic force. It seems reasonable to conclude that many magnetizers, fearing contamination from the crackpot psychics, sought the sanctuary of scorn.

Aside from lobbing broadsides, the community of magnetic experts invaded the spiritualists' home turf. Mediums could summon ghosts at will, some of whom took apparent delight in acts of mischief like moving tables. This was indeed a test for the mesmerists, challenging the strength of their faith in a magnetic power. In response, the mesmerists conducted numerous public exhibitions demonstrating the same ability to lift tables. To achieve the desired effect, "Let a few persons [from the audience] take their seats around a wooden table and having denuded their fingers of rings, place their hands flat upon the table, until the table exhibits a tremulous motion."[17] As the table rose, each person was instructed to slowly stand, keeping their fingers a few inches above the table's surface. The best results were obtained when a large group of people attempted the levitation, since the mesmerists conceded that not everyone had such an elevating influence.

Among the early female spiritualists, Cora Hatch rivaled the fame and popularity of the Fox sisters. Cora was born in 1840 near Cuba, New York.[18] Her parents were among the avant-garde of the time and, seeking new horizons, attempted to expand a utopian sect. Unfortunately, Cora's flirtations with the spirit world upended her family's lofty plans. While the eleven-year-old girl was innocently sitting under a tree clutching a slate board, she presumably fell asleep; upon awakening, she found the board covered with a lengthy message from a long-departed sister. Following this enchanting event, Cora began her career as a writing medium.

A spirit physician took control of Cora for the next few years and, through his fledgling medium, brought relief to many sufferers. Naturally this employment left little room for school, and Cora's spirit guide soon persuaded the young girl to abandon formal education. Perhaps not surprisingly, "Cora soon aroused the antagonism of the regular physicians" as their waiting rooms emptied.

Cora eventually gave up psychic healing, setting the stage for her real calling. Through the thoughtful tutelage of her spirits, Cora was trained to enchant audiences with her clairvoyance. Spirit rappings and table turnings would not clutter Cora's performances. Instead, she would dazzle her viewers with intellectual radiance. As her fame grew, audiences would select a small committee to propose the most abstruse, difficult philosophical questions that Cora, acting as a medium for the spiritual intelligentsia, would answer.

By 1857, Cora was performing in New York City. A reporter in attendance was struck by the "slender girl, who apparently has not been 17—the advertised age—for more than three or four years. A profusion of sunny ringlets and a fresh, youthful complexion, gives her an almost childish air."[19] As usual, a committee was assembled from the audience at large with the intention of stumping the young woman. Cora was asked, "Did the various races now inhabiting the earth all Spring from a common mundane person?" and "Was Jesus of Nazareth of divine or human origin?" In response, Cora assumed her trademark posture, staring serenely upward with her hands folded across her chest. She dreamily answered the questions in turn, mixing metaphysical and Christian concepts. The potentially explosive question about Jesus was adroitly sidestepped by suggesting that His divinity was the source of His humanity. After concluding, with a soft shake, Cora returned from the spirit world, and another night's performance came to an end.

Interest, entertainment, enlightenment, and a touch of voyeurism drew big crowds. Cora was "a most attractive preacher, being just seventeen, and looking as pretty by daylight as by gaslight ... her hair hangs over her snowy neck in profuse ringlets."[20] Another enraptured commentary gushed about "a pair of bright eyes, a pretty face, a shower of glossy ringlets."[21]

Frank Leslie's Illustrated Newspaper devoted a full column to Cora Hatch. Due reverence was paid to her appearance as "a fair and slender girl, on whose flowing ringlets seventeen summers sit with light and easy grace.... She remains seated with her upraised eyes.... As the questions to be discussed are stated, an indescribable change steals over her face."[22] This change signaled Cora's trance, through which erudite spirits shared their knowledge. Her lengthy learned responses stood in stark contrast to her youthful appearance, leading the newspaper's reporter to claim that she was "the greatest intellectual curiosity of the day."

For whatever reason, western New York seemed to be the epicenter of American Spiritualism. Around the same time that the Fox sisters were demurely cavorting with ghosts, a pair of brothers burst upon the scene in Buffalo, New York. Ira and William Davenport became mediums in 1855 and traveled across the country and into Europe, mixing showmanship, Spiritualism, and squabbling along the way.

Ira Davenport was born in 1839, followed two years later by William.[23] At the age of 16, Ira, no doubt in a playful but portent-laden mood, summoned his family to the dinner table. Perhaps the famous feats of the Fox sisters were the inspiration when he proposed raising the dead. Ira had no sooner taken a seat at the table than it mysteriously rose from the floor. Repeated entreaties to the invisible movers were duly satisfied, with the table rising higher on each occasion. It soon became apparent that both Ira and William could harmonize with the spirit world, jointly conjuring forth a floating violin peacefully plucked by phantoms. These melodious manifestations became a staple feature of the Davenports' performances.

It was 1864, and, with no end in sight, the bitter battles of the Civil War raged on. All the while, the hale and hearty Davenport brothers were at work onstage, encountering nothing more lethal than cynicism. For the most part, audiences were curious, seeking an entertaining diversion, and were polite but skeptical. At the conclusion of the Davenports' show it was not uncommon for attendees, initially firm in their opposition to Spiritualism, to leave with their convictions a bit shaken. Such was the case when the Davenports descended on the Cooper Institute in New York City for a typical performance.

The Davenport brothers' trademark was a specially constructed spirit cabinet. Looking much like an armoire, the cabinet boasted three doors behind which three large adults could sit rather uncomfortably on wooden benches. To ensure no underhanded trickery, the spirit cabinet securely rested on three sawhorses that allowed the audience to see underneath. Musical instruments were placed outside the cabinet on the floor in front of the three doors.

It was inside this piece of furniture that William and Ira both took a seat in front of a "very full and fashionable house" at the Cooper Institute.[24] Past performances had often been marred by rowdy groups, loudly lampooning the performance, but this night's event mercifully lacked the hecklers. A sort of silent solemnity took hold, during which the emcee solicited a volunteer committee. Members of the committee, usually well-known and respected citizens, bolstered the event's authenticity by supervising the brothers' performance.

A fire marshal and a local judge, with a bit of convincing, finally yielded to the insistent audience and agreed to serve as committee members. Their task was to prevent any humbuggery, and the fire marshal, suspecting some electrical force was involved, insisted that the cabinet be shielded from such an influence. The brothers naturally consented, and large glasses were placed beneath the sawhorses supporting the cabinet. Once inside the cabinet, the committee members securely bound the brothers to the wooden benches.

With a sense of mounting tension, the committee members closed the cabinet doors and the house lights dimmed in response. Almost immediately after closing the doors, "a full chorus of instruments playing a jig was heard inside the closet. The doors were hastily opened, and the Davenports had not moved." In a final test to expose the brothers, the committee members placed finely ground flour in their hands. The brothers were once again bound hand and foot and the cabinet doors closed. A trumpet was thrown out of the cabinet, leading the fire marshal and the judge to instantly pounce on the cabinet and fling open the doors. William and Ira stood serenely before the audience, unbound, and not a flake of flour was found inside the cabinet.

Sometimes the Davenports invited a member of the audience to take a seat in the séance cabinet. This spooky suggestion probably scared many prospective participants, but one New York coroner bravely acquiesced. From a sort of macabre viewpoint the coroner was actually an inspired choice, given his daily duties with the dead. Unfortunately, this association apparently won the coroner few friends in the spirit world.

The coroner and the Davenport brothers were, as usual, soundly knotted together in the spirit cabinet. After the doors were closed a loud ruckus arose, accompanied by the shrieks of the coroner. Alarmed committee members swung open the doors, revealing the distressed coroner still securely tied but now adorned with a large tambourine on his head, a violin on one shoulder, and a guitar in his lap. After recovering some composure, the musically festooned man summoned the courage to explain what happened. A reporter in attendance wrote that "while in the box the Coroner had been visited by the spirits of those upon whom he had held inquests. Some of them were malignantly inclined not being satisfied with the verdicts, and they pulled the Doctor's hair and whiskers, tweaked his nose, and one of them more savage than the rest hit him in the head with the bell, which made him cry out." In a final act of vengeance, the spirits humiliated the coroner with the decorative ensemble.[25]

As might be imagined, the Davenport brothers surely sought the assurances of Civil War service members. The brothers scored a significant coup at a packed New York City performance in 1864 when Colonel John B. Woodward and Captain John Faunce banded together as the night's vigilance committee.[26] Woodward was the commanding officer of the 13th Regiment, New York National Guard, in 1863 when the unit was activated in the days just before the Gettysburg campaign.[27] Shortly after leaving the Pennsylvania battlefield, Woodward's regiment was instrumental in fighting a different conflict, this time crushing the draft riots that erupted in New York in the summer of 1863.

Captain Faunce was arguably better known than Woodward. Faunce had previously commanded the USS *Harriet Lane*, the first ship in the fledgling Revenue Cutter Service.[28] Just before the Civil War began, the *Harriet Lane* was patrolling American coastal waters attempting to intercept slave traders, pirates, and other water-borne threats. With the escalation of heated rhetoric on both sides of the Mason-Dixon line, President Lincoln ordered a flotilla to reinforce the beleaguered Fort Sumter in South Carolina. The *Harriet Lane* and the other ships entered the Charleston Harbor with one principal object in mind: stopping any further rebellious southern resistance.

Not long after the Union fleet arrived in Charleston Harbor, a fast-moving ship caught the attention of Captain Faunce. The flagless vessel was clearly making a beeline toward Fort Sumter, posing the very threat the *Harriet Lane* was ordered to stop. Faunce fired a warning shot in the direction of the ship, which quickly hoisted the American flag, a signal the captain of the *Harriet Lane* accepted. Left free to enter the Charleston Harbor, the steamship *Nashville*, as it was later discovered, repaid the hospitality throughout the war as a Confederate blockade runner.

The Davenports' ability to attract such luminaries as Woodward and Faunce was a testament to their showmanship, a blend of entertainment and spiritual faith attracting throngs of disciples and doubters. Which group the two warriors occupied is unknown, but their credibility was unquestioned, making them the perfect Davenport guarantors.

Woodward and Faunce "carefully examined the box and then tied the Brothers in either end of the 'structure,' so they could not move. The lights were then turned down, the three doors closed, and the spirits began." A phantom band immediately struck up a disharmonious tune, an ensemble consisting of a guitar, tambourine, and violin. When the doors of the spirit cabinet were opened, the Davenport brothers were still firmly bound. At this point, Captain Faunce took a seat in the cabinet, juxtaposed between the brothers, and was securely tied. Again the doors were closed and the startled naval officer "felt distinctly several hands passed over his face and body ... stating that there must have been more than three persons inside the box."[29]

The Davenport brothers took their show overseas, traveling to England and beyond, and seemingly summoned foreign spirits with the same facility they were known for in America. Everywhere they traveled, the brothers attracted a mixture of responses ranging from cynicism to certitude. In an effort to allay the concerns of the former group, the brothers allowed a few audience members to inspect the spirit cabinet and devise any plausible ploy they desired to expose trickery. A newspaper marveled that the brothers "courted rather than evaded the strictest investigation, and in doing so have not simply invited the man of business or the conjuror, but the man of science, of the highest culture, and worth, to find out 'the trick.'"[30]

While the Davenport brothers were wowing audiences, the Fox sisters busily pairing phantoms with patrons, and mesmerists mending maladies, Andrew Jackson Davis was communing with a more literary circle of spirits. In partnership with his ghost writers, Davis became a prolific author and philosopher of Spiritualism.

Born in 1826, Andrew Jackson Davis spent his youngest years in eastern New York, principally Hyde Park and Poughkeepsie, roughly 300 miles from the Fox sisters' haunting grounds. His mother died at an early age, leaving his father, a shoemaker, to raise Andrew himself. The privations of poverty left little time or money for education. As such, Davis could barely read and write.

Davis was approaching the later years of adolescence in 1844 when he took up the art of medical magnetism and affected many miraculous cures. His introduction to magnetism came through a chance encounter with an itinerant practitioner traveling through Poughkeepsie in 1843. Davis agreed to be magnetized and quickly descended into a deep trance, during which he read a book with his eyes closed and described distant lands in detail. Over the next few months Davis demonstrated his newfound clairvoyance for the amusement of the people of Poughkeepsie. But after weeks of fanciful frittering and frivolity, Davis was seemingly admonished during a clairvoyant state to henceforth concentrate on curing illnesses and injuries.

The young hypnotist did as he was bid and spent three successful years as a magnetic healer. In spite of this, fate intervened and charted a new course. Davis' extraordinary capacity to enter a trance was a perfect pathway for the phantoms. This sympathetic communion with the spirit world moved him in a new direction. Through repeated runic reveries, Davis started receiving regular dispatches from the spirit world. His partner, William Fishbough, listened patiently as Davis gave voice to the disembodied denizens of the afterworld. Fishbough transcribed the words Davis mouthed over many months, eventually culminating in an 1845 compendium appropriately titled *The Principles of Nature, Her Divine Revelations, and a Voice to Mankind.*[31]

Fishbough gushed with praise in describing his youthful companion: "His features are prominent.... The expression of his countenance is mild, placid, and indicative of a peculiar degree of frankness and benevolence; and from his eyes beams forth a peculiar radiance which we have never witnessed in any other person." The latter trait was no doubt put to service in Davis' various hypnotic demonstrations. Even more persuasive than his penetrating gaze, however, were the powerful words spilling forth through him from the spirits.

Connecting with the spirit world required the right setting. Davis would sit directly opposite the hypnotist, who would perform the magnetic method. In a few minutes, "A sudden convulsion of the muscles, such as is produced by an electric shock, indicates that the subject is duly magnetized, immediately after which his eyes are bandaged.... He then remains speechless for some four or five minutes.... He next assumes a position inclined to the right or to the left.... His mind is now entirely freed from the sphere of the body." According to the magnetist, this dissociated mental state was the precondition through which the spirits connected with their medium.

Messages from the spectral space came slowly. Davis would spend upward of four hours a day receiving a few sentences at a time, a pace that permit the scribe to capture every word. Over the next eleven months, Davis delivered 157 monologues from the spirit world, all carefully transcribed and presented with a flourish as *The Principles of Nature, Her Divine Revelations, and a Voice to Mankind*. As evidence of the book's ethereal influence, Fishbough reminded readers of Davis' essentially illiterate background.

The Principles of Nature, Her Divine Revelations, and a Voice to Mankind was a massive manuscript partitioned into three sections and filling 786 pages. In discussing "The Principles of Nature," the book dwelled on such earthly themes as the irrationality of war, the fundamental flaws in human society, and transcendentalism; it also devoted numerous pages to magnetism, clairvoyance, and somnambulism. In the section titled "Nature's Divine Revelations," the spirits described the cosmos, including the undiscovered eighth and ninth planets in our solar system, the evolution of humanity, and a description of the Second Sphere, where the spirits existed. The immortal transition transpired "when a spirit leaves the human form, and is introduced into this Sphere; it for a moment cannot realize the change, for it is imperceptible. Spirits retain the same bodily form in the spiritual Sphere ... and then they behold and appreciate the change, and the beauties with which they are surrounded." The third and final section, "A Voice to Mankind," identified three universal stratified social classes consisting of the poor, semi-wealthy, and the wealthy, as well as the manner in which they interacted.

Andrew Jackson Davis was the philosopher and pseudo-scientist ceding the entertainment stage to others such as the Fox sisters. They all orbited each other, with Davis bolstering believability and the mediums sponsoring the spectacles. This dynamic duo of deception awaited the sounds of war and the mournful cries to come. Only the most ardent skeptics could pierce the coming fog.

On the eve of the Civil War most Americans considered communication with the dead to be metaphysical mumbo jumbo. Traditional religious views seemed relatively impervious to the newcomers' charms. That would change, perhaps imperceptibly, with each battlefield death. Seemingly senseless slaughters with acres of land littered by dead bodies left wide swaths of despair. Sons would never return home, and wives became widows. Spiritualism beckoned to the bereaved, proudly standing in the emotional wasteland like a seductive siren.

The large, traditional newspapers uniformly scorned the upstart religion, but smaller publications such as the *Banner of Light* and the *Spiritual Magazine* enthusiastically trumpeted Spiritualism. The first edition of the *Spiritual Magazine* presciently proclaimed in January 1860 that "no man or woman has probably ever lived who has not at some time felt a yearning yet once again to hold communion with some loved one whom death has removed from sight."[32] One year later South Carolina seceded, setting the stage for the southern states to replace animosity with annihilation.

The *Banner of Light*, first published in both Boston and New York in 1857, was a weekly publication decidedly sympathetic to Spiritualism.[33] The newspaper billed itself as a "weekly journal of romance, literature [and] general intelligence," which provided such amusement for an annual subscription fee of two dollars.[34] Readers could enjoy such articles as "The Power of Conscience" and "The Age of Virtue." A special feature of the *Banner of Light* was "The Messenger," in which "each message in this department of the Banner we claim was spoken by the spirit whose name it bears.... We hope to show that spirits carry the characteristics of their earth-life to the beyond, and do away with the erroneous idea that they are more than FINITE beings."

The *Banner of Light* provided "The Messenger" as a sort of public service. Séances were held on Brattle Street in Boston every afternoon, except Sunday and Monday, perhaps in an effort not to unduly tax the spirits. Anyone could attend for free, and for those who missed the opportunity the *Banner* obligingly published the phantoms' ponderings. Examples of typical communications before the Civil War included that of Mary White, who spoke from beyond the grave: "Tell my dear mother that I came here.... Oh, everything is so beautiful here, I wouldn't come back if I was the richest person on earth." William Good likewise reassured his survivors, "Fear not; all is well with the lost one."[35]

The *Banner of Light* painted a peaceful picture of the afterlife, a soothing salve for harrowed hearts. But if the *Banner of Light* was the spiritual canvas, then Mrs. J. H. Conant was the artist. Conant, who changed her name through marriage, was born in 1831 as Frances Ann Crowell.[36] Her childhood was marked by a peculiar sensitivity that attracted regular visitations from the spirits, in the form of rappings and visions. As a young woman she married John H. Conant, and together the pair eventually settled in Boston.

Shortly after arriving in their new home, Mrs. Conant fell deathly ill, and all hope for her recovery was lost. A sympathetic neighbor suggested the sick woman seek the services of a psychic medium, which, after a bit of prodding, she did. Mrs. Conant's medium was an adolescent girl who quickly made contact with a prominent, but deceased, physician. This phantom physician apparently had no problem making house calls and, after a brief examination, promised to cure Mrs. Conant. Since money was probably of little use in the immaterial world, the dead doctor demanded a different disbursement: "I will state my terms.... You have some of the finest mediumistic powers that I have ever seen, and the world ought to have the full benefit of them ... and the fee I require in consideration of your case, is that you will give your powers to the world hereafter."[37] After only a moment's reflection, Mrs. Conant accepted the offer. The doctor was true to his word and cured his patient, who in turn honored her part of the bargain.

Mrs. Conant immediately embarked on her new career as a psychic healer and spiritual medium. Acting as a medium for her patron phantom physician, Conant began diagnosing all sorts of diseases. Since many of her clients' cases were considered hopeless after receiving the ministrations of earth-bound doctors, Mrs. Conant's fame steadily grew when her spirit prescriptions proved effective.

Luther Colby and William Berry, the editors of the *Banner of Light*, were enchanted by Mrs. Conant, and soon they began attending séances hosted by the young woman. Mrs. Conant took to advising mostly Berry on matters of business as related to the operation of the *Banner of Light*. However, years later, Berry eventually grew tired of the spirits' counsel, preferring to strike out on his own. The ghosts would have none of this and gravely warned the errant publicist that unless he yielded, any further disagreements would take place in the afterworld. Whether Berry was deterred by the veiled threat is not known. In any event, the editor of the *Banner of Light* took up arms in the Civil War as a Union officer and was killed a few months later at the Battle of Antietam.

Mrs. Conant began holding a series of public séances at the newspaper's Boston office in 1858. The nature of these contacts changed when the Civil War began claiming its victims. "Spirits from both armies who had passed from their bodies amid the roar of battle ... and had not yet been aroused to a consciousness that for them the trials and pains of earth were over, crowded to this avenue of communication." Bereaved family members could scroll "The Messenger" section in the *Banner of Light*, hoping to read a few comforting words from their departed loved ones.

Less than a year after the Civil War began Mrs. Conant started receiving messages from dead soldiers. By now, the fatigue of almost daily psychic communications was taking a toll on Conant, forcing a more reasonable schedule of public séances only on Monday, Tuesday, and Thursday afternoons. Messages from the soldiers ran the gamut from the profane to the prolific delivered by those both illiterate and intellectual.

According to the *Banner of Light*, in January 1862, the dead soldier Bill Sewell took advantage of Mrs. Conant's mediumship to send a message to his brother. Patriotic flames still burned hot in Sewell, who proudly proclaimed, "I'm Union—I want you to remember that! I don't want you to class me with the cursed rebels.... I belonged to the Second Indiana Regiment.... I was killed—killed in a private brush of my own, with a d—d rascal. I ventured a little too far from the quarters and got surprised and killed." Sewell's description of his death may have closed a lingering chapter for his brother, but the spirited soldier went further. Acting as if the window between the two worlds would slam shut forever, Sewell warned his brother to mend his ways. The moralizing former soldier turned temperance crusader urged his sibling to forsake whiskey, glumly recalling that an overindulgence in the liquid spirits had led to his premature battlefield death.[38]

Mrs. Conant referred to her séances as circles, during which Luther Colby and others documented the impromptu spirit conversations. In many cases the spirits seemed bewildered by the connection with a reality they had just departed, while others took the matter in stride. Oliver Plimpton seemed to fall in the latter group, as evidenced by his casual, even amiable, response to Mrs. Conant's psychic summons. Plimpton opened the conversation with a hearty "Well, stranger, how do you do? I'm very well, I thank you." After exchanging social pleasantries, Plimpton expressed a desire to get a message to his wife. The former Union private seemed mostly concerned with describing his death, which took place on a battlefield at Falls Church, Virginia, in 1862. While Mrs. Conant was in a trance, Plimpton told his story: "Our fight took place in the night, and a very dark night it was, too.... We were stationed at Fall's Church, and were ordered to charge, and charge we did, and done it well, too! One thing is certain; I gave up my body in the service of my country." Plimpton concluded with brief reminiscences about his wife Elizabeth and their marriage, as well as a broadside tirade attacking incompetent military surgeons.[39]

The three-day battle at Gettysburg in 1863 claimed around six thousand men from both armies.[40] As news of the losses spread across the country, it seems reasonable to assume that family members sought news of their loved ones. In some cases, the *Banner of Light* provided death notices from soldiers now forever removed from earthly environs. In a sign of equanimity, the psychic medium was just as likely to conjure up Union soldiers as Confederates. Even so, some Confederate soldiers seemingly possessed enough common sense to step rather gingerly into Conant's Boston-based spirit circle. Philip Thompson, a former officer in the 2nd Virginia Cavalry, politely inquired, "What role have you ... concerning communicants that are not of your politics?" Conant generously responded, "We serve all equally." The anxious but now reassured spirit appreciated the opportunity to send a message to a friend in Tennessee. "I wish to inform him of my death ... wounded at Gettysburg, and died shortly after that."[41]

The *Banner of Light* also published short notices from other psychic mediums. Sometimes in the course of conducting a séance a wandering soul would chance upon the event and unburden themselves. Mrs. Lydia H. Nealley came into possession of an important message from a dead soldier and requested the newspaper's support in relaying it to the intended recipients. The *Banner* obliged and reported that George Wright "was killed in the battle of Gettysburg on the third of July ... that he enlisted ... in the Eleventh Mass. Regiment, and he wished to let his friends know that he had passed away."[42]

Ulysses S. Grant assembled 60,000 Union troops in a determined ploy to annihilate Robert E. Lee's much smaller force near Cold Harbor, Virginia, on June 2, 1864. Unbeknownst to Grant, Lee had fortified his defenses. Following an artillery barrage, the Union soldiers attacked and were met by a Confederate hailstorm. The furious southern fusillade felled 7,000 federal soldiers in thirty minutes in one of the bloodiest and most senseless battles of the Civil War.[43] John D. Henry, "a member of the 3d Massachusetts Battery ... was wounded in the fight before Petersburg on the 2d–3d day June, and died the next day." Death did not dampen this soldier's determination. Speaking through Mrs. Conant in hopes of reaching his former battery commander, Henry remarked, "I want him to know ... I'm happy—want 'em to know that I am a soldier still, only in a different way. I'm ready for action on the other side."[44]

The end of the Civil War did not silence the soldier spirits. Bereaved family members could still subscribe to the *Banner of Light* with every hope of seeing a message from the dearly departed. Robert Reidelberg relished the opportunity, arranged through Mrs. Conant's trance, to reach out to his young wife and child. Long after the Battle of Antietam, Reidelberg caught up with the psychic medium in 1865 and related that "I was shot in five or six places before I found it was time for me to lay down me musket and go the spiritland." Reidelberg spent much of the remainder of his time reassuring his wife that no money or other worldly possessions remained, regrettably the result "of [being] robbed from me by the rebs."[45]

It seems unlikely that a Union or Confederate soldier's idle time would have been spent pondering the mysteries of Spiritualism. Yet, given their daily dance with death, their private thoughts surely gravitated toward weighty considerations about their mortality. However, speaking publicly about such matters unnerved fellow soldiers and also ran the risk of branding the speaker as weak or, even worse, a coward. Talking about Spiritualism probably compounded the contempt. For all of these reasons, only skimpy evidence documenting Civil War soldiers' feelings about Spiritualism seems to exist.

In one rare example, the sun had just set when a group of four good-natured soldiers, members of an Illinois regiment camped near Jackson, Tennessee, started talking about Spiritualism. Two of the soldiers seemed willing to consider the notion of an afterlife while the other two were less receptive. The spirited to-and-fro discussion was interrupted by an orderly sergeant, more intent on assigning picket duty than fantasizing about phantoms. In a macabre finale, one of the soldiers suggested that before too many more months passed the argument might be settled.[46]

In another brief reference, John Beatty, an officer with the 3rd Ohio Volunteer Infantry, recalled an incident early in the war. Beatty was making the social rounds with fellow officers when the occult subject became the centerpiece of a lively banter. As Beatty later recalled in his memoirs, "[I] called on Colonel Scribner and wife, where I met also Colonel Griffin and wife; had a long conversation about spiritualism, mesmerism, clairvoyance, and subjects of that ilk."[47] Beatty provided no further insight into the discussion, leaving the reader rudderless in determining the beliefs of the participants.

The Civil War affected every nook and cranny in America. Loud, thumping politics and moving patriotic melodies did their best to drown out the survivors' sorrow. In a dramatic description of the death dirge, "mourners went about the streets, and still the cry of the war-demon was for life, more life."[48] Little wonder, then, that soldiers and their families sought solace from beyond the grave.

Spiritualism stoked skepticism. It was an affront to science and established religions, both of which attacked it with vigor. Believers were often ridiculed and consigned to the loony bin. For all of these reasons, an accurate reckoning of the faithful is impossible. Even so, soldiers' letters and ethereal communiqués through psychic mediums suggest that the seduction of Spiritualism was gaining an ever more passionate audience during the war years and immediately afterward.

Frank Emmett's story was surely inspirational. Like countless other men before him, Emmett responded to a call to arms by joining the 1st New York Volunteers. Through a combination of courage and chance, Emmett steadily progressed from a lowly private to a lieutenant, along the way earning a reputation for having a charmed life. It seemed that no bullet or bayonet could touch the fierce fighter. Years later, the one-armed soldier/writing medium explained his good fortune. Apparently his long-departed father, summoned through a séance, had explained that "if he [Frank] would go to war no bullet which was yet forged, should harm him; no sword could maim him, or fire scorch him for he [his father, in the spirit world] could and would protect him." On hearing this, a shrewd skeptic looked askance at Emmett's empty sleeve. Setting the man's suspicion aside, the former soldier clarified the contradiction. The obvious loss was an unfortunate consequence of an accident while on furlough (his spirit father had only guaranteed safety on the battlefield).[49]

A spirit shield, deflecting the dispatchers of death, defended an untold number of soldiers from the dangers of the battlefield. In other cases, the spirits apparently turned the tide by offering tactical guidance. Edward T. Steele, "Late Sergeant of Co. D, Second R.I. Vols.," offered such an example of the spirit's guidance through the mediumship of Mrs. Emma Hardinge.[50] According to Steele, "On the morning of the second of April, 1865, when attacking the rebel defenses of Petersburg, Virginia.... My spirit friends had warned me of great danger, directed me how to act, and assured me of their ability to protect me.... I was guided rapidly through a tremendous fire ... to a point in the rebels' abattis where a narrow path was left for their pickets to pass through." Several other soldiers joined Steele in the mad dash toward the startled southerners, who, in a panic, were captured.

Spiritualists started springing up everywhere, helping soldiers survive and forlorn families thrive. It seemed every city, suburb, and settlement boasted psychic seers. Some clearly used their gifts to achieve varying degrees of fame and fortune. Others eschewed the limelight while nonetheless achieving it. The Eddy family reigned supreme among the latter group through carefully cloistered conduct, Christ-like suffering, and a ceaseless series of supernatural sensations.

Without knowing more, Henry S. Olcott seemed an unlikely chronicler of the Eddy family's exploits. Olcott was a veteran of the Civil War with an impressive career in combat and later in civic life. His early military adventures were in the signal corps, with General Ambrose Burnside's Annapolis expedition. A newspaper correspondent witnessed the launch of the naval fleet on a cold winter day in early January 1862. With a mixture of pride, patriotism, and propaganda, the reporter gushed, "The harbor of Annapolis for several days has presented a spectacle of activity, which, combined with the enthusiasm of the troops as one regiment after another went on board, is seldom exhibited in the history of any nation."[51] The naval fleet continued south, with skirmishes along the way, and arrived at Fort Monroe on June 9, 1862.[52]

A chance encounter between Burnside and Olcott seemingly shaped the remainder of the latter's military service.[53] While attacking Roanoke Island, the two officers were frustrated when their ship ran aground, an outcome directly traceable to incompetent procurement. Incensed, Olcott offered to expose the scoundrels responsible for supplying the wrong type of ship. Apparently Burnside ignored the offer, preferring to handle the matter himself, and Olcott's passionate denunciation left an indelible mark on the general's mind.

Several months later Olcott landed in a hospital, one of countless victims suffering from malaria and dysentery. Just when his discharge seemed imminent, Olcott received an assignment as a special commissioner of the War Department based in New York. From this perch, possibly motivated by the chance shipboard encounter with Burnside, Olcott was directed to investigate financial misappropriations resulting from all sorts of schemes, scams, and skimming. His detective work was so successful that the navy requested, and the army granted, his transfer. Olcott duplicated his work in the navy. His crowning achievement followed the assassination of President Lincoln. Recognizing his dogged determination and relentless pursuit of the truth, Olcott was chosen to join a select group investigating Lincoln's murder.

Olcott's early adult life was characterized by service as a soldier, detective, and prosecutor—hardly the sort of temperament seemingly receptive to Spiritualism. The seeds might have been planted very early in his life, lay dormant during the arid war years, and were revived when watered by tears of despondency. Olcott had spent his childhood on a farm, and it was here that his mother's brothers revealed the wonders of Spiritualism. Many years later Olcott traced his interest in the occult to these men: "I may almost regard them as my greatest benefactors in this incarnation."[54] The young Olcott was also infatuated with mesmerism and in short order discovered that he had the power. On one occasion he hypnotized a young girl, apparently sparing her the painful ordeal of a dental procedure.

The war years left Olcott no time for spiritual pursuits. But after the war ended Olcott increasingly turned his attention to spiritual issues. Perhaps part of this interest flowed from a sense of despair, driven by divorce, his two children's deaths, and somber wartime memories. In any event, the Eddy family became beneficiaries of Olcott's occult interests.

Visitors to the Eddy family often felt unwelcome, an invective reserved mostly for the legions of skeptics who descended on the homestead. Olcott was among that group, traveling to the remote village of Chittenden, Vermont, to witness firsthand the supposed spectral phenomena. Olcott withheld from the Eddy family his real intention of preparing an investigative report for the *New York Sun*.[55] The former Civil War soldier, now a newspaper correspondent, began his excursion as a confirmed cynic but returned home a convinced convert.

The mysterious manifestations in the isolated Vermont community attracted hundreds of visitors, doubters and disciples alike. Once they gained admission, having run the gauntlet of the Eddy family's peculiar and often gruff reception, the visitor would join a circle promptly convened every night except Sunday at 8 p.m. About thirty minutes prior to entering the séance, guests joined together in a rousing session of singing and dancing. Following this ice-breaker, the guests entered a room that remained locked throughout the day.

Olcott attended and closely observed several séances at the Eddy family home. Upward of twenty other guests joined in. The entire Eddy family possessed psychic powers, but son William was often the medium at the circles. Shortly after the guests were seated, William entered a small specially constructed room, a spirit cabinet, and pulled a dark curtain across the door. A small kerosene lamp left the guests straining to see not only each other but also the spirit cabinet. Almost immediately after William took a seat in the cabinet, "the curtain stirs, is pushed aside, and a form steps out and faces the audience … motionless, appearing in the character of a visitor from beyond the grave."[56] As might be imagined, the former soldier beheld the spectacle with a mixture of surprise and suspicion, with a tilt toward the latter given the absurdity of the whole affair. Over the next hour a parade of phantoms came forth from the cabinet. Each was different in size, gender, clothing, and mannerisms. At the conclusion of the séance, a haggard William Eddy emerged from the cabinet.

Dozens of departed denizens descended during a typical Eddy family séance. Olcott carefully noted each appearance, slowly authenticating the events. Through three séances, during which thirty-two specters materialized (most of whom were recognized by members of the audience), Olcott's mistrust gradually gave way to a grudging acquiescence. In one example, the covert correspondent reported that "among the remarkable tests of identity coming under my notice was the appearance of a young soldier of about twenty years of age, the son of Judge Bacon of St. Johnsbury, Vt., whose death occurred under painful circumstances in the army." Bacon instantly recognized his son, a heartrending homecoming orchestrated through the mediumship of William Eddy.

The final performance Olcott witnessed a few days later brought forth new apparitions and acts.[57] As usual, William Eddy ascended the short, raised dais and entered the spirit cabinet. Soon thereafter a procession of Indians emerged, some tall, some short, and mostly men. The Sun's correspondent learned that in bygone years a brutal winter had nearly decimated a local Indian tribe, a fate some escaped when members of the Eddy family offered a hospitable sanctuary from the inclement weather. Apparently motivated by gratitude, the Indian spirits regularly haunted the house.

Once the Indians fluttered away, the cabinet séance ended. The small audience then retired to another room, forming a more traditional social circle. Naturally the focus of the chatting centered on the recently concluded séance before drifting toward erudite explanations of the powers of magnetism. At this opportune moment William's brother Horatio joined the gathering and generously offered to demonstrate his peculiar abilities. He first tore a page from a newspaper, dried it carefully over the flame from a kerosene lamp, and then repeatedly dragged the paper across his body. It was through this last act that Horatio's magnetism was transferred to the paper. The electrifying performance concluded when Horatio placed the magnetized paper on the wall, where it stuck with a ferocious tenacity, clinging until forcefully removed the following day.

After the Eddy family members retired for the night, the remaining audience members, who included several sensitive souls with psychic pretensions, took over. As might be imagined, they were less successful than their hosts but nonetheless received a respectful reception.

The former special commissioner of the War Department required more proof, even though the materializations were impressive. Olcott was a detective, having learned through this experience to distrust initial impressions. Employing a methodical approach, Olcott was determined to expose the humbug but only succeeded in overcoming his own disbelief.

Perhaps the most logical place to begin an investigation was the séance room, and Olcott took every liberty in doing so. The Eddy home was unpretentious, with a Spartan décor exuding gothic ambiance. Before fame found the farmhouse, the Eddys summoned the spirits on the ground floor. As the curious crowds grew, a larger area was necessary, and the accommodating family added a second-story séance room. It was this room that Olcott carefully studied.

The windows of the séance room towered nearly fourteen feet above the ground.[58] From a previous investigation, Olcott was satisfied that no ladder existed on the Eddys' property, leaving any trickery incapable of reaching the window's lofty heights. Only one door permitted entry into the large séance room. Visitors sat on two long benches, without the aid of back support, and faced the cabinet. A waist-high bannister protected the spirits from overzealous guests who, perhaps in a fit of frenzy, might have dashed toward the cabinet. William Eddy ceremoniously occupied the cabinet as the supernatural forces emerged. It was a small closet, seven feet long, nearly three feet deep, and averaging about six feet of head room. William Eddy took a seat inside after entering through a two-foot-wide door. A curtain drawn across the door obscured the inner chamber. Olcott examined the tiniest detail throughout before finally concluding that no conceivable knavery was concealed by the Eddy family's séance.

Having substantiated the sanctity of the spirit cabinet, Olcott turned his attention to the Eddy family themselves. They were an odd lot with, a dubious family history that supposedly stretched all the way back to Salem, Massachusetts, where a distant ancestress was executed by the good citizens in 1692. From that time forward the succeeding generations of women all seemed to possess varying psychic abilities, but more tolerant societies mostly ignored the heresy. All that changed when Zephaniah Eddy, "a narrow-minded man, strong in his prejudices, a bigoted religionist," married the woman who would eventually direct the Eddy family's transition from hardscrabble farmers to famed seers.[59]

In the early days of their marriage Mrs. Eddy wisely guarded her gift, rarely revealing her clairvoyance. However, after the birth of her first child she seemed to lose control, with spirit rappings, invisible voices, and ethereal friends haunting the house. The psychic energy appeared to grow exponentially with each subsequent child, leaving Mrs. Eddy and her children chatting amiably with sociable ghosts. Zephaniah, meanwhile, was aghast at the goings-on and, with a pious heart, prayed for relief. When that failed, the mortified man adopted a different tack. Harkening back to the seventeenth-century Salem witchcraft mania, Zephaniah relentlessly beat his children in a vain effort to eliminate a satanic influence. This, too, failed, and after Zephaniah's death in 1860, Mrs. Eddy and her children faced no restrictions. Even so, the spirits were not kind to Mrs. Eddy, calling home many of her children. William and Horatio survived unscathed, and they soon ascended to the summit of Spiritualism.

Henry Olcott, initially a stalwart skeptic, concluded his investigation without discovering any evidence of fraud. His testimonial surely left many a reader of the *New York Sun* surprised. Other witnesses would follow, with some confirming Olcott's opinion. Roughly a month after Olcott completed his inquiry, another visitor to the Eddy home described his experience.[60] This particular visitor made the journey from New York and arrived at the isolated Vermont community late in the afternoon. If he was expecting a warm welcome, the family quickly disabused their uninvited guest of such a quaint notion. Almost immediately upon entering the Eddy home, the family members strongly hinted that he was not welcome, but a final decision would await the whims of William and Horatio.

While the visitor patiently awaited his fate, the Eddy family served a plain dinner, and as the evening wore on the visitor whiled away the time by watching the sunset and exchanging pleasantries with the other guests. William and Horatio finally arrived, and the uninvited guest boldly asked the brothers if he could observe a séance. Horatio reluctantly, and perhaps a bit flippantly, replied, "I guess we can get along with you." Having secured a seat at the séance, the uninvited visitor joined about twenty other guests in the specially constructed room. William took his appointed perch in the cabinet, drew the curtain, and the marvelous manifestations began.

The first ghost to appear soon became a regular figure at the Eddy family circles. She called herself Honto, described by the visitor as an "Indian girl.... She is about five feet five inches in height, slender, and very beautiful. Her long black hair hung down her back in two parts, which she threw to the front." Honto danced gracefully about the small stage but alarmed the audience when her partner, a small rat, joined her. In a slightly risqué routine, Honto hiked her skirt above her knees, ostensibly proving she was not some contrived, stick figure. At the conclusion of Honto's performance she faded away, with the audience no doubt oohing and aahing.

After Honto disappeared, William emerged, exhausted, from the cabinet. The night's show was not over yet, as the Eddy family now treated the audience to a dark séance. Horatio was the medium for this spectacle. To ensure no tricks, Horatio's arms and legs were securely bound with rope. It was a dark night, and when the candles were snuffed, the audience was bathed in total darkness. The spirits were emboldened, and perhaps a bit festive, for soon after the room was plunged into the darkness a veritable cacophony erupted, with trumpets blaring, guitars strumming, and accordions bellowing. Following this impromptu concert, the spirits signaled their interest in answering questions from the assembled mortals, after which the séance ended.

Among the incredulous were vocal groups who loudly criticized the Eddy family in particular, and Spiritualism in general, as nothing more than fake mediums seeking money. Although pride did not seem to be a factor, the Eddy family's local performances were free. Such was not the case, however, when William or Horatio traveled to other areas.[61] In one example, an advertisement promised that one member of the Eddy family would arrive in New York City and share the stage with local seers. Entrance to the event cost the prospective attendee 50 cents for general admission, while an additional 25 cents ensured a front-row seat. "The audience was mostly composed of the highly-respectable but fun loving business men who are daily found in" the big city. Even though the patrons expressed no problem with the nominal price, such fees were fodder for Spiritualism's opponents.

Respectable people from all walks of life fell under the spell of Spiritualism. Henry Olcott, a Civil War veteran, lawyer, and well-known government investigator, spent his remaining years on earth testing the claims of spiritualists. The net result was a profound belief in Spiritualism culminating in his enthusiastic support of the embryonic Theosophical Society, a group of like-minded individuals dedicated to understanding the occult sciences.[62]

By the time Olcott investigated Mary Baker Thayer, a Boston-based medium, the former soldier had developed a strategy to detect deception: "It was necessary to become satisfied pretty thoroughly upon several points, for instance; As to Mrs. Thayer's antecedents.... Her personal character.... The strength of her manifestations.... The conditions indispensable to their occurrence, and especially whether they could only be produced in a certain house or room ...[and] whether they were real phenomena, or only exhibitions of charlatanry."[63] With these criteria in mind, Olcott attended both private and public séances conducted by Mary Baker Thayer.

Mary's earliest years bore remarkable parallels with the story of the Eddy family matriarch. Mary's mother was a prophet portending all sorts of mishaps and misfortunes. These surely left an indelible mark on the young girl's mind, such as when her mother accurately predicted a brother's death. In later years, Mary married, settling down to a domestic life in Boston. Her tranquility was disturbed, and her psychic powers revealed, at the moment of her first child's birth. A startled housekeeper was an eyewitness to a remarkable sight when she entered the birthing room and observed the bed (and both occupants) floating several feet above the floor. Again like the Eddys, as more children populated the Thayer family, mysterious rappings and invisible friends became routine affairs.

Mrs. Thayer's husband died early in their marriage, forcing the woman to adopt various trades, such as dressmaking and housekeeping, to support her family. It was through these jobs that Thayer met some of Boston's social elite. At the same time her psychic powers were growing, with seemingly uncontrollable contacts with the spirits resulting in floating furniture, clothing carelessly tossed about, and apparitions knocking (but not appearing) at customers' homes. None of this would seem to recommend a housekeeper, but Thayer's fame spread among the cultured class clamoring for the clairvoyant.

Olcott attended Thayer's private and public séances, applying his probing principles. The medium quickly became known as "a goddess of flowers," attracting fashion-minded phantoms that brought exotic plants and animals.[64] In different rooms and distant sections of the city, whether with a small group or a large public gathering, Thayer reliably conjured up fragrant, fresh flowers, small birds, and even beautiful butterflies. Many guests marveled at the money these items were worth, guessing that the flowers alone would cost a faker hundreds of dollars, well beyond the means of a humble housekeeper. To fully dispel any lingering suspicion, Olcott even placed the woman inside a specially designed bag. With her entire body restricted, the spirits still came and left a bountiful blooming bouquet. Mrs. Thayer passed all of Olcott's tests and earned his unreserved endorsement.

The list of intellectuals who supported Spiritualism was long. Among this elite group were military officers, prominent professionals, giants of the literary world, mainstream ministers, and even politicians. Joining this erudite troop were all sorts of contriving capitalists principally interested in generating phantom profits. These individuals helped spread Spiritualism from western New York to large cities in the northeast and Midwest. Newspapers gladly fanned the flames by accepting advertisements from psychic mediums, magnetic physicians, occult lecturers, and spiritual booksellers, a notable trend throughout the Civil War and for roughly a decade after.[65] The publicity was not uniformly positive, with every step accompanied by controversy, charlatans, and conflicts.

Richard D. Goodwin was a huckster. An obscure note in the *Banner of Light* reported that "Col R.D Goodwin of Kirkwood, MO," contributed one dollar to the "Eddy Persecution Fund" in 1867.[66] Goodwin had good reason to extend sympathetic support to the Eddy family given his own rough receptions.

Colonel Goodwin joined forces with Miss Van Wie by promoting her career as a psychic medium. In that respect he did a poor job. Goodwin suffered slights with an ill humor, much on display when the promoter and his protégé appeared before a generally polite audience in midtown Manhattan during a summer performance in 1866. As he strode on the stage, Goodwin immediately started chastising the audience members for their disbelief in Spiritualism. He continued the onslaught for an hour, alternately rebuking his patrons, reading lengthy biblical passages, and finally consenting to the appointment of a committee to launch the night's charade.

A reporter in attendance described the demure Miss Van Wie as "young, not more than twenty, loosely built, but rather pretty, with mild eyes." Under the penetrating gaze of the two committee members, the young woman took a seat inside a plain wooden box. She was then firmly tied with a long rope, effectively preventing any movement. Once this was done, the committee members closed the doors, securely sealing Miss Van Wie in the wooden tomb. At this point the audience naturally expected the spirits to lend a hand and untie the woman, who would then gracefully emerge from her confinement. In about ten minutes some muffled rattles lightly shook the box. It grew eerily quiet following this brief burst of activity, and as the minutes ticked by the discomfiture of the spectators grew. Some, no doubt sympathizing with the frail young woman and fearing the worst, loudly called upon Colonel Goodwin to open the box. In response, the feckless handler swore at the spirits, demanding they do his bidding. Even with this admonition, nothing happened except for the audience's ever escalating concern for Miss Van Wie.

The two committee members finally succumbed to the audience's apprehensions and opened the spirit cabinet. Poor Miss Van Wie "sat fainting and drooping, limp in her chair.... The cords had been loosened a little at the end ... the medium was really suffering.... Her wrists and arms were shockingly marked and swollen, her fingers were stiffened and she had no control whatever of her limbs."[67] Efforts to restore the girl eventually proved successful, although Colonel Goodwin did not fare as well. An enraged group, no doubt bent on avenging the young woman, menacingly advanced toward Goodwin. Only the active intervention of local police prevented the crowd from gratifying its wishes.

Some of the more influential proponents of Spiritualism never took to the stage, deftly circumventing the corrosive element of entertainment. Their influence came from their prominent positions in the community, a status sometimes achieved through elections, appointments, or other creative endeavors. Such positions, however, did not always protect the spiritualist from public backlash. Such was the situation with Henry Kiddle.

Henry Kiddle was a teacher, following the traditional path expected of an educator in the nineteenth century. At the age of nineteen he became a principal at a small school, launching a career that climaxed with his appointment as the superintendent of public schools in New York City.[68] Along the way, Kiddle authored textbooks such as *A Manual of Astronomy and the Use of the Globes: For Schools and Academies,*[69] *How to Teach*[70] and *Common-school Teaching.*[71]

Kiddle also generated controversy. The superintendent surely did not endear himself to the legions of public school employees when he famously observed that "the teachers in parochial schools were better prepared and superior to teachers in government schools."[72] As crude as this comment seemed, however, it did not lead to his ultimate downfall. It was instead a rather obscure publication that lit the fires of indignation.

Perhaps Kiddle's long-standing interest in astronomy was the inspiration for his ethereal inclinations. Whatever the precipitant was, it exploded forth on an unsuspecting public when Kiddle published *Spiritual Communications.*[73] The author did not admit "to be[ing] a spiritualist.... Remarkable facts have come to his knowledge (he did not seek them; and although naturally incredulous and skeptical ... but a voice—the voice of duty—has sounded for months in his ears, commanding him to make these things known to his fellow men."[74] Kiddle minded the voice, acutely aware of the potential outcry.

If Kiddle had confined his revelations to a narrow exposé describing a curiosity-driven flirtation with Spiritualism, he might have survived as New York's School superintendent. It all began innocently enough when Kiddle's daughter visited a nearby psychic medium. As she entered the medium's lair, an aura sensed by the psychic portended great powers for the young woman. A tingling sensation in her arm was the first sign of things to come. Over the following days Kiddle's daughter was seemingly possessed by the spirits, who would write messages with her corporeal hand. One of the first communications was from an older sister, dead for many years. It was a reassuring message that no doubt fostered both relief and belief.

Much like a whirlpool, each successive spirit communication added momentum that eventually engulfed Kiddle's mind. The superintendent entertained "no supposition other than it is veritably the spirits of the departed who are communicating." Even this admission might not have proved fatal to his career, but Kiddle went much further. Positioning his narrative as a dispassionate but accurate transcription, Kiddle chronicled hundreds of spirit communications. Father and daughter hosted ghosts both eminent and obscure, their hospitality apparently spreading throughout the spirit world. Among the visitors, William Shakespeare, Queen Elizabeth, Lord Byron, Napoleon Bonaparte, and Abraham Lincoln dropped by for a chat. Various clergymen, authors, and sad souls all took a detour from their phantom pursuits to visit with the Kiddle clan.

Kiddle's conceptions just went too far, straining the high standing extended to a man in his social position. Apoplectic newspaper editorials excoriated the superintendent: "He is incompetent, even in his business, and unsound in the operations of his mind.... It may be that he never has had sufficient mental development to distinguish between truth and falsity."[75] The same newspaper, in musing whether the superintendent suffered from mental or physical stress, contemptuously concluded that "Kiddleism" was a species of insanity.[76]

The scandal ended Kiddle's career in public education. The superintendent resigned, clearly seeing the writing on the wall. Less than a year later Kiddle was lecturing large audiences on the merits of Spiritualism.[77] In a predictable paradox, Kiddle's disgrace was interpreted by ardent believers as yet another example of religious persecution.

Popular authors were particularly persuasive regarding the merits of Spiritualism. Their literary success generally garnered more fame than fortune but nonetheless provided a pulpit for persuasion. This group included two of England's greatest writers, William Makepeace Thackeray and Charles Dickens. While neither could be counted as a fervent advocate of Spiritualism, their names nonetheless were often associated with the movement.

Among the pair, William Makepeace Thackeray is the name least likely associated with Spiritualism. He also achieved literary success much later in life than Dickens.[78] Thackeray was born in 1811 and received all the advantages of the best education England could provide. Despite this, he was not an accomplished student and left his studies without earning a degree. Thackeray always tilted toward the artistic, but his talents as a painter were wanting. His marriage was also a source of sadness. A few years after taking their vows, Thackeray's wife suffered a mental breakdown from which she never fully recovered.

Poverty was the taskmaster forcing Thackeray to write. A dissolute, rudderless life combined with severe financial losses left him few choices when faced with the responsibility of caring for his young children. He eked out a bearable existence by writing short stories for various magazines. Thackeray finally made a name for himself with the publication of *Vanity Fair*. Subsequent books, and especially his role as a touring lecturer, helped ensure a comfortable life. He died on Christmas Eve, 1863, inspiring the *Banner of Light* to memorialize his passing by proclaiming, "He had a warm heart, a wholly manly nature, and was a despiser of shams in every form and shape."[79]

The *Banner of Light*'s observation that Thackeray "was a despiser of shams in every form and shape" was a curious comment for an obituary. It probably referred to the author's brief but controversial brush with Spiritualism through none other than Leah Fox.

Leah was the oldest of the three Fox sisters. Around the age of 44 she married for the third time to Daniel Underhill, a man of means and a fervent believer in Spiritualism.[80] Underhill's wealth surely helped spread Spiritualism among his social connections. His prominent position as a New York businessman and his endorsement of Spiritualism surely swayed many naysayers. Leah benefited from this, attracting a steady stream of skeptics to her public séances, including a visit by William Makepeace Thackeray.

The oldest Fox sister vividly recalled Thackeray's attendance. She remembered that "his course of investigation was unlike those of all others. The first visit he made he sat and listened to the sounds; and when his turn came to ask questions, he politely asked me to accept his arm and walk with him." Leah agreed, and during this brief embrace, Thackeray cooed softly about the pressures and persecutions the famous spiritualist suffered. The gratified (and no doubt flattered) psychic reciprocated by offering the author an invitation to a private séance, which he promptly accepted.

Over the course of his attendance at Leah's séances, Thackeray, at least according to her reminiscences, "was thoroughly convinced that no earthly power could make the sounds as he had heard them." Even so, Leah recognized certain timidity in the author and never expected a public declaration of support from him.

While touring in America Thackeray also visited with Daniel Dunglas Home, another well-known spiritualist.[81] D.D. Home, as he was popularly known, was born in Scotland in 1833 and raised by an aunt. Nine years later Home and his aunt immigrated to America, initially settling in Connecticut. During these early years in their new homeland, far from Scotland, Home's quiet, sensitive nature did not make him a favorite among his peers. A slightly older child by the name of Edwin was an exception, and the two boys developed a deeply loyal attachment to each other. The relationship ended when Home moved to Troy, New York.

Home was thirteen years old when his family moved to Troy. Losing all contact with Edwin saddened the impressionable teenager, but subsequent events proved even more distressing. While lying in bed one moonlit night, Home was startled by a dark shadow creeping across his room. A brilliant light revealed the ghostly figure of Edwin. His friend soundlessly pointed toward heaven, a sign that Home interpreted as indicating his friend's recent death. The following morning Home recounted the incident, receiving in return a naturally skeptical reception. Three days later, however, the family received a letter informing them of Edwin's death. This was the first of a lifelong series of visions foretelling future events, including one predicting his mother's death.

About two years after the Fox sisters gained fame from the mysterious rappings haunting their home, D.D. Home reported a similar experience in his bedroom. His aunt was not amused by the noises and attributed the racket to devil work. Despite her pleas to local clergymen and fervent prayers for relief, the rappings intensified over time. Soon furniture was floating in the air, further upsetting Home's aunt. The distressed woman, clearly at her wits' end, issued an ultimatum—either the apparitions or Home had to go. As might be imagined, the mysterious manifestations continued, forcing the young man out of his aunt's house.

At this point, premonitions, miracle cures, rappings, and levitations were attracting a great deal of attention. Home began traveling throughout the northern states performing séances, always without pay, before returning to New York City. In the big city Home regularly met with leading academics, businessmen, and other local luminaries. John Gray, a famous physician, befriended Home and suggested the bright young man forsake the limelight and pursue a medical education. Perhaps Home briefly considered the offer, but his earnestness and skill in performing séances proved more compelling, launching a career that spanned the globe.

Thackeray's convictions were apparently cemented by witnessing the exploits of D.D. Home. Even so, a line from Thackeray's masterpiece *Vanity Fair* seemed to apply when the author "did not give way to any ebullitions" supporting Spiritualism.[82] The best Thackeray could muster, as editor of the popular *Cornhill Magazine*, was permitting the publication of Robert Bell's short article titled "Stranger Than Fiction."[83]

"Stranger Than Fiction" described the manifestations that Bell witnessed in the presence of D.D. Home.[84] In a typical example, a small séance assembled under the mediumship of Home and made contact with the spirit world. Questions by the audience were answered by the usual rappings, tables moved by means of some invisible agency, and musical instruments frolicked about. Bell attended many such performances before declaring the absence of any humbuggery.

The *Cornhill Magazine* was a staid Victorian publication not known for promoting titillating or eccentric articles. "Stranger Than Fiction" jolted many readers, who responded with varying degrees of withering contempt. Thackeray's soft endorsement of the article, "As Editor of this Magazine, I can vouch for the good faith and honorable character of our correspondent," only made matters worse.[85] In responding to his critics, Thackeray pointedly noted, "It is all very well for you, who have probably never seen any spiritual manifestations, to talk as you do; but had you seen what I have witnessed, you would hold a different opinion."[86]

In the years immediately following the Civil War, the literary figure most commonly invoked by spiritualists was none other than the great English author, Charles Dickens. No one could seriously dispute that Dickens had an interest in ghosts. After all, many of the short stories and novels he wrote were riddled with spooks and spirits. Additionally, Dickens was entranced by mesmerism, both as an observer and later as a practitioner. His accommodating wife agreed to be the first person the author hypnotized. Emboldened by his early success, Dickens extended his clinical consultations to family members and friends, effectively relieving their minor maladies.[87]

Charles Dickens' most famous ghost story was undoubtedly the 1843 publication of *A Christmas Carol*.[88] This enormously popular Christmas story was a fanciful (and at times frightful) critique of capitalism conducted at the expense of charity. As the object of scorn, Ebenezer Scrooge was haunted by a series of ghosts, all of whom, it must be admitted, acted more humane than their victim. Scrooge's reformation reinforced the spirit of philanthropy.

A Christmas Carol could claim descent from an impressive pedigree of phantoms.[89] *The Pickwick Papers*, published as a serial over a twenty-month period beginning in 1836, included five ghost stories; among this group, the most interesting was "The Goblins Who Stole a Sexton," which reads like a prequel to *A Christmas Carol*. In *Nicholas Nickleby*, the spectral Genius of Despair and Suicide alternately tempts and torments the book's namesake before being forcefully fended off. Following the publication of *A Christmas Carol*, Dickens turned toward more morose and frankly macabre stories, thoroughly infused with phantasms. Examples included *The Haunted Man and the Ghost's Bargain*, *The Haunted House*, *The Signalman*, and *The Trial for Murder*.

In spite of Dickens' preoccupation with ghosts, a contemporary account described the author as a skeptic. William Howitt, an acknowledged spiritualist, wrote that "Charles Dickens has played with spiritualism as a cat with a mouse ... all his literary life through he has been introducing the marvelous and the ghostly into his novels, and has of late years ... alternately [been] attacking spiritualism, and giving you most accredited instances of it."[90]

In the short story "Well-Authenticated Rappings," Dickens mercilessly poked fun at Spiritualism.[91] Having attended séances, the author was struck by the spirits' odd choice of communication but even more so by their poor grammar.[92] Dickens satirically reflected that "his vulgar notions of the spiritual world, represented by its inhabitants as probably advanced, even beyond the intellectual supremacy of ... New York ... it seemed ... so very unnecessary to call in immaterial Beings to gratify mankind with bad spelling and worse nonsense." In describing the goings-on at one séance, Dickens attributed the visions and voices from a comical Pork Pie spirit to "this precise article of pastry ... the staple of the writer's lunch."

Dickens' harsh treatment of Spiritualism in "Well-Authenticated Rappings" did not dissuade its devotees. The faithful could simply argue, with some credibility, that the author was at least ambivalent. Why else would Dickens spill so much ink on apparitions? His fascination with mesmerism and magic was also well known.[93] Even so, spiritualists simply could not pin him down. This would have to await Dickens' death.

Charles Dickens died in 1870, leaving behind more than speculation about his spiritual inclinations. Toward the end of his life Dickens had turned his literary talents in a different direction, writing the suspenseful thriller *The Mystery of Edwin Drood*.[94] His untimely death left the novel unfinished and readers bewildered. Dickens enthusiasts sought clues from family members and close acquaintances, but none could resolve *The Mystery of Edwin Drood* with conviction. To fill the gap and gratify the public's cravings, several authors supplied their own endings, but none would claim more certainty in achieving Dickens' original intent than Thomas Power James.

Thomas James was rather unceremoniously known as a tramp printer.[95] Members of this group traveled from town to town burdened only with their journeymen skills (which were all that distinguished them from vagrants). For the most part tramp printers were invisible, doing piece work and then moving on. Such was the case in the 1870s when James "arrived with his alleged wife" in the small community of Brattleboro, Vermont. After completing two printing jobs, James, rather uncharacteristically, withdrew from further employment "in order that he might, as the medium for Dickens, complete the unfinished story, the Mystery of Edwin Drood." Once word got out that a local itinerant printer was communicating with the spirit of Charles Dickens and completing his last novel, nothing could suppress the media. Reporters flocked to the village hoping to meet, and no doubt discredit, this rural rube. James steadfastly maintained his anonymity, frustrating their collective efforts, only yielding in the end to a reporter from the *Springfield Daily Union* in Massachusetts.

Perhaps the most puzzling question was how a tramp printer became a writing medium. The *Springfield Daily Union's* correspondent somehow managed to gain James' confidence, forging a bond that eluded other reporters. Over the course of many intimate interviews the reporter learned much about James, including the tramp printer's first exposures to the occult.[96] Roughly ten months before he began consorting with Dickens' spirit, the naïve printer, succumbing to peer pressure, attended a local séance. The performance included the usual rappings and table gyrations, with most of the frenzy aimed at James. Startled by this turn of events, James resisted a reprise, but once again friends persisted in persuading the printer to attend another spiritual gathering.

It was during the second séance that James discovered his spiritual powers. Much like the first encounter, the boisterous spirits seemed to prefer James' company. Partway through the séance the skeptical printer lapsed into a somnambulistic state, secured a nearby pencil and began writing. After returning to himself, James and the astonished assemblage read the note. It was from a child, long since departed but known to one of the group's members. It seemed most unlikely that James had preexisting knowledge of this child, which lent an air of mystery and veracity to the whole affair.

With his newfound calling as a writing medium, James broadened his contacts with the spirits and was soon relaying more and more messages. Apparently his prowess captured the attention of Charles Dickens, who sent a message to James requesting a private meeting. Initially the medium downplayed the author's appeal, but subsequent pleas grew more insistent and James relented. According to James, the first meeting with Dickens' spirit was a lengthy one, during which the author announced his intention of completing *The Mystery of Edwin Drood*. Lacking the corporal means to write, but apparently retaining his mind, the famous author enlisted James as his secretary.

Not surprisingly, Dickens' spirit began the dictation on Christmas Eve.

Surrounded by pencils and paper, James would retreat to a quiet, dimly lit room and await his collaborator. The *Springfield Daily Union* reporter noted with a touch of awe how "at first he wrote only three times a week and only three or four pages at a time, but he since came to write twice a day, and twelve, fifteen, and sometimes twenty pages at a sitting. The hand-writing is not his own, and shows some of the peculiarities of Dickens's hand." James continued this feverish pace for months before finally completing the work and submitting it for publication.

   The Mystery of Edwin Drood: Complete by Charles Dickens was published by James in 1874.[97] The surrogate author claimed no attribution for himself, leaving that honor solely for Dickens. James anticipated some of the furor that would accompany the book's release and addressed the naysayers in the "Medium's Preface." In attacking the spiritual nonbelievers, James railed against a "class of people who regard everything they do or say as perfectly right and proper, and everything other folks do or say as all wrong." In a further effort to allay criticism, the medium reminded prospective readers that he was "an uneducated man," hoping to draw a stark contrast between his paltry skills and the passages published through Dickens' spirit. Despite the controversy generated by the book, sales were fairly robust. The Dickens-James partnership faltered, though, and no further collaborative works appeared, but James did write a few inconsequential dime novels on his own before sinking into obscurity.[98]

   Practitioners like James exploited every opportunity to gain fame through fraud, and every newfangled idea was ripe for the picking, but the greatest harm came from those who preyed on the disillusioned victims of the Civil War, men and women desperately seeking contact and closure with their lost loved ones.

Three

Promising Much and Delivering Little

Spiritualism's growth in the postwar period owed much to its promise of reuniting grieving survivors with their lost loved ones. As Spiritualism's influence expanded, its credibility paradoxically weakened as skeptics and charlatans grew stronger. Imposters took advantage of new inventions and scientific developments to dupe gullible, grief-stricken patrons. Leading the list were cameras, novel and mysterious devices cynically exploited by merchants of deceit. Photography captured not only images but also the imaginations of nineteenth-century Americans eagerly embracing scientific and technological discoveries. Thus photography and cameras were tailor-made for duplicity.

Practical photography was born in France in 1839.[1] Enthusiasts predicted the imminent demise of portrait painters given the relative ease of capturing real scenes. America's Civil War became the first conflict extensively visualized through photographs. Matthew Brady and his associates photographed every aspect of the war, from the common lives of soldiers to their gruesome deaths.[2] Photographs were palpable, poignant and irrefutable evidence. Spiritualists and their enablers saw the possibilities inherent in the new medium, eventually giving rise to picture galleries of ghosts.

Ever eager to enlist science in its cause, the *Spiritual Magazine* in 1862 rushed into print "a new and interesting development" that left the publication gushing over "a new and satisfactory phase of spiritual-manifestations."[3] The source of the excitement was a picture taken by a Boston photographer that supposedly captured a ghost's image. Not surprisingly, the *Spiritual Magazine* celebrated this chance encounter as positive proof that phantoms existed.

For spiritualists, this was a historical event, and the *Spiritual Magazine* honored the occasion with a detailed description of William H. Mumler, who stumbled into spirit photography on October 5, 1862. Mumler was tinkering in his studio, arranging chemicals and adjusting the aperture on his big camera. The next step in the arduous preparation required a test picture, which the photographer supplied by jumping in the front of the camera. It was in the darkroom, as the picture was developed, that Mumler made his discovery. As Mumler later told the story, he was alone in the studio, but the photograph showed two figures: himself and a young girl sitting in a chair. When closely examined, "the outline of the upper portion of the [girl's] body is clearly defined, though dim and shadowy.... Below the waist, the form ... fades away into a dim mist, which simply clouds the lower part of the picture." Mumler claimed the girl's image resembled a long-departed cousin.

Apparently the spirits enjoyed having their pictures taken—at least by Mumler. Following the accidental apparition Mumler could not keep the ghosts out of his studio. A dozen dead individuals subsequently stopped by for a portrait. In each instance ghostly images joined the mortal, always recognizable as some long-lost relative.

Despite the sensational spirit photographs and the assurances of scientific soundness, the *Spiritual Magazine* charted a cautious course: "While we have the fullest confidence in the truth of the circumstantial account ... the very interesting and even startling character of the alleged phenomena, and the intense desire that will be largely felt for its truth leads us to withhold for the present anything like entire credence."

It took a mere month for the *Spiritual Magazine* to bestow its blessing. A sister publication, the *Herald of Progress*, which was owned by the medium Andrew Jackson Davis, supplied the proof sought by so many spiritualists.[4] Davis arranged for William Guay, an established photographer, in Boston to visit Mumler.[5]

Mumler allowed Guay free rein in his studio. Acting like an auditor, Guay "went through the whole of the operation of selecting, cleaning, preparing, coating, silvering, and putting into the shield, the glass upon which Mr. M. proposed that a spirit form and mine should be imparted, never taking off my eyes, and not allowing Mr. M. to touch the glass until it had gone through the whole of the operation." In short, Guay monitored and controlled all the steps required to take and develop a photograph. Much to Guay's surprise, a spirit image emerged on the photographic plate. Several subsequent tests, with the inspector meticulously scrutinizing the camera and Mumler's every movement, produced the same results. Guay was astonished and, in reporting his findings to Davis' *Herald of Progress*, earnestly declared, "I have been obliged to endorse its legitimacy."

News of Mumler's phantom photographs naturally excited local interest, and his studio soon became a popular haunt for both spirits and the earthbound hoping for portraits graced by the gossamer ghosts. The photographer did not disappoint his customers. Portrait after portrait, often conducted under the closest supervision, delighted Mumler's clientele.

In some cases the filmy figures were not immediately recognizable, but after some reflection and circulation among friends and family members, each spirit was eventually identified. At a time when family pictures were uncommon, Mumler's spirit photographs were treasured as the only images of a lifeless loved one. The happy families surely deemed deceit a distant probability. After all, how could a photographer add a person's picture where none previously existed? The naysayers were stumped, and Mumler's reputation flourished.

Over the course of the next five years Mumler pursued his strange business. Passersby no doubt marveled at the goings-on in the fashionable Broadway studio in New York City. Time after time the photographer granted skeptics a free run of his work space, all of whom suspected duplicity but left in dismay. Mumler also married during this time, not surprisingly choosing a woman who wholeheartedly supported his work.

In February 1869 a local newspaper reporter, with two witnesses, in tow descended on Mumler's studio.[6] The trio was determined to learn more about Mumler's spirit photography. Among the group was a highly skilled photographer who "prepared the sensitive plate himself from the naked glass. Sitting down before the camera, he waited the usual time, and then with his own hands 'developed' the negative." Staring back from the photographic plate were two faces: the photographer and a floating, flimsy figure bearing the likeness of a bearded gentleman.

Still cynical, the reporter volunteered for the next photograph. Before assuming his position in front of the camera, he dogged Mumler's every step, no doubt hoping to discover the trick. Mumler's first effort was spoiled when the glass plate shattered. While sitting for the second shot the reporter quietly remembered his father, long since laid to rest. When the plate was developed a hazy male profile emerged alongside the reporter. After carefully examining the photograph, the astonished newsman confessed its startling similarity to his father. However, even in the face of this evidence, the reporter's incredulity only permitted a cautious interpretation: "if there is any trick used, he [the reporter] does not know what it is.... The whole thing is a marvel any way, and deserves to be investigated by scientific men."

Two months later Mumler was hauled into court. His fairy tale was now tattered and torn by allegations of fraud. His descent from grace followed an investigation sanctioned by New York City's mayor, Abraham Hall, and conducted by Joseph Tooker.[7] Tooker had begun his inquiry by visiting William

Silver's photographic gallery at 630 Broadway. Mumler maintained his studio upstairs while Silver greeted potential customers.

The mayor's agent openly professed a deep disbelief in spirit photography but, given his mission, sought to conceal this fact from Silver. Tooker was not wholly successful in suppressing his unfriendliness, but Silver persisted with his sales pitch. Not too far into the discussion, the subject of money came up, with Tooker protesting the ten-dollar fee. After a bit of wrangling, Silver relented and accepted a deposit of two and a half dollars.

Tooker climbed the stairs leading to Mumler's studio and was greeted by the photographer. After a brief exchange of pleasantries, Mumler must have detected his client's aloofness, leading to another somewhat feverish sales pitch. Tooker finally positioned himself in front of the camera and then awaited the results. When the photograph was presented to the mayor's investigator, Mumler anxiously asked if Tooker recognized the faint shape of the man's face. Tooker replied in the negative. Mumler then suggested that Tooker think about the picture for a few days, certain that he would eventually put a name to the face. Upon his return, Tooker paid an additional eight dollars, secured the remaining pictures, and promptly brought charges against the photographer for "deceiving the public by representing that his shadowy pictures are taken by supernatural means." Mumler responded to Tooker's allegations by demanding a public trial.

Mumler was tripped up by another photographer, P.V. Hickey.[8] Hickey was dubbed an expert in the craft by the local newspapers, but it was his curiosity that launched the investigation into Mumler's spirit photographs. Hickey purchased a set of spirit photos, taken in the usual manner, and paid the customary ten-dollar fee. Incensed by the expense and suspecting fraud, the aggrieved photographer brought his complaints to the mayor's office. Tooker followed up the investigation that led to Silver and Mumler appearing before a magistrate judge. At the initial hearing before the judge, two witnesses, both prominent photographers, testified against Mumler. Following this testimony, the judge "held the accused for examination, and remanded [him] for want of bail."

The sages of Spiritualism were in a quandary. Spirit photography was an exciting new development that could tilt the opinions of many. However, an overly eager embrace might disappoint and damage the movement's reputation. In pondering the possibilities at a New York spiritualist conference, the members pored over several ghost photos. Only one member apparently expressed grave doubts, but that was sufficient to enlist, at a subsequent meeting, the services of an expert photographer. C.B. Boyle proposed what he believed would be an infallible test, and the members promptly formed a committee intent on adopting the approach. The duly designated delegation made the necessary travel arrangements and soon arrived at Mumler's studio. Mumler listened patiently as the committee set forth the terms of the test. Haggling followed over the price and details, with no agreement reached. The spiritualists left and, upon returning home, crafted a befuddled resolution: "that Mr. Mumler's treatment of the Committee does not prove ... the truth or falsity of spirit photography."[9]

If those in the mayor's office expected Mumler to wilt in the face of a criminal prosecution, they were probably surprised. An entourage of attorneys, defense witnesses, and gawkers greeted the presiding judge on the trial's opening day.[10] After some procedural squabbling between the litigators, the judge set the date for the evidentiary phase of the trial. Mumler's two defense lawyers titillated the assembled onlookers by declaring "that they proposed to prove that there is no trick, fraud or deception in what are called spirit pictures."

One reporter's absurd comments chronicled the first day of Mumler's trial. Shamelessly sensationalistic, the anonymous journalist proclaimed that "in all the annals of criminal jurisprudence—and they comprise an array of crimes of almost every description—there has seldom, if ever, been recorded a case analogous to that now pending."[11] Brushing aside all manner of felonious behavior, this particular alleged swindle—a mere misdemeanor—had grown to gargantuan proportions.

Judge Dowling's gavel signaled the start of the trial. Facing the judge were the prosecutor Elbridge Gerry; defense attorneys J.T. Townsend, A.E. Baker and Mr. Day; and numerous witnesses sympathetic to the accused's case.[12] Mumler was strangely tranquil, almost disinterested.

Joseph Tooker testified first, giving a faithful account of his investigation. The defense countered with a slew of witnesses. William Sleed, an experienced photographer, started the onslaught, methodically describing his personal examination of Mumler's work. Sleed testified that "he was utterly unable to discover how the thing had been done." Another photographer not far removed from Mumler's studio had a similar experience and drew the same conclusion. Several satisfied customers lent their support next.

The most interesting witnesses were a judge and a magazine correspondent. John W. Edmonds, a former New York Supreme Court judge, surely received a respectful reception. Edmonds was a well-known spiritualist, with his former judicial role bolstering his believability. His presence was probably more valuable to the defense than the substance of his testimony. After all, the judge had only known about Mumler for a short time. Edmonds' role was to support Spiritualism and, by extension, lend credence to spirit photography. While not directly endorsing Mumler, Edmonds unequivocally testified, "I believe that the camera can take a photograph of a spirit, and I believe also that spirits have materiality ... enough to be visible."

Perhaps the most convincing witness Mumler brought forth was James Gilmore, an author who had previously submitted an investigative report about spirit photography to *Harper's Weekly*. With Mumler's full cooperation, Gilmore sat for three successive pictures. In all but the last a dim figure joined the principal subject. Gilmore could not recognize the apparitions. Remaining resolute, and certainly unconvinced, the author took one additional step, which proved to be the most important part of his testimony: "I afterward called on Mr. Rockwood, another photographer, who told me that he could produce spectral figures by natural means; he tried it in various ways, but I always detected some trickery."

The first day of Mumler's trial ended with at least a technical victory for the accused. Even though the prosecution claimed an elaborate swindle, no witness had been produced who unreservedly fingered the fraud. As the day came to a close, the mystery remained unsolved.

Mumler could not count on a sympathetic press. As the trial unfolded, newspaper reporters and editorial writers variously lambasted and lampooned the whole notion of spirit photography. Such universal condemnation stood in stark contrast to the daily front-page treatment that this trifling topic received. A northern newspaper dripping with damnation declared that "men and women with soft places in their heads, will continue to run after follies of this sort, and ... if judges and bankers are weak enough to believe in ghosts, there will always be Mumlers to take their pictures."[13]

The second day of Mumler's trial opened with as much public interest as the first.[14] Once again the courtroom was packed mostly with sympathetic Mumler supporters. A reporter observing the scene cast a jaundiced eye on the women attendees: "Some of these were staid, matronly-looking females ... others, again, were elderly maidens.... Judging from the appearance of some of these, it would not require the intervention of preternatural means in order to make ghosts of them while they still maintain their corporeal natures."

A steady parade of defense witnesses testified for most of the second day. Each recollected experiencing varying degrees of doubt when they first approached the spirits' favorite photographer, but with each exposure they came to believe in the truth of Mumler's photos. One witness was so entranced with an astral body–like image resembling his wife that he gave Mumler a ten-dollar tip. In response to all of this testimony, Elbridge Gerry, the prosecutor, rather ineffectually cross-examined the defense witnesses. Most of his attack was a poorly aimed fusillade against Spiritualism, presumably in an effort to undermine Mumler's raison d'être.

Two days of testimony seemed to soften some cynics. Sardonic repartee was replaced with reluctant circumspection. When the trial began it seemed inconceivable that Mumler would prevail, but the prosecution's fumbling left many questioning the probable outcome. In some cases editorials started bowing to the possibility that Mumler would leave the courtroom vindicated: "Our impression is, that the result of this trial will be practically nil.... If he be acquitted, it will be in many minds a simple case of 'not proven.'"[15] Even though the verdict was days away, the heady hopes of dealing a major blow to spirit photography were fading.

The third day of Mumler's trial was greeted with the same interest and enthusiasm.[16] Over the course of the day's testimony, Gerry sought to rally sentiment in the prosecution's favor with a parade of both amateur and professional photographers. Each witness droned on in depth about the endless tricks that could produce a phony image. Some of these methods were interesting and even clever. Charles Hull supported his expensive hobby in photography with the proceeds from his soap manufacturing business. Hull described a dozen tricks that could fool anyone, even the most zealous onlooker. Among the deceptions were double exposures, surreptitiously placing a positive image in front of the photographic plate, and, perhaps most ingeniously, "putting a microscopic negative in the lens; it need not be more than a quarter of an inch in diameter." Another prosecution witness was Oscar Mason, the secretary of the Photographic Branch of the American Institute, who mostly echoed Hull's testimony.

Gerry's strategy at this point seemed rather straightforward: a respected coterie of photographers would testify in mind-numbing detail, leaving no listener with a grain of doubt that a spirit photograph could be anything but faked. However, after the last witness had testified and Judge Dowling brought the day's proceedings to a close, the prosecutor had little reason to feel confident. Despite the witnesses' verbal volleys, there was simply no evidence linking Mumler with any of the suggested photographic tricks.

After a slow start, the courtroom once again filled to capacity as Judge Dowling convened the fourth day of the trial.[17] It was yet another chance for the prosecutor to bludgeon the believers in spirit photography by exposing the endless tricks of the trade. In an interesting twist, and merciful relief from the photographers' technical talk, the next witness who bombastically testified was Phineas T. Barnum. The master showman and huckster extraordinaire seemed an odd choice as a witness. Barnum had never met Mumler but was familiar with his spirit photography. Sensing an opportunity to exploit interest in ghost photos, Barnum sought and received a small gallery of pictures from Mumler. Working from little more than his own disbelief, Barnum branded Mumler's work a humbug.

Barnum bantered good naturedly with his antagonist when cross-examined by the opposing counsel. Mumler's attorney could scarcely refrain from mentioning some of Barnum's great hoaxes. Spectators laughed aloud when Barnum defended his woolly horse and mermaid exhibits. Barnum was finally forced to admit, again amusing his audience, that "I never told lies but I may have given the facts a little drapery sometimes."

There was a small stir as the day's testimony wound down.[18] At the behest of the prosecution, a physician from Blackwell's Insane Asylum was prepared to testify that Judge Edmonds' belief in ghosts was nothing more than a hallucination. With a collegial deference, Dowling prevented this witness from maligning Edmonds by obliquely challenging his sanity. The incendiary testimony was thus snuffed out, with the prosecutor meekly submitting to Dowling's judgment.

Harper's Weekly, the widely read "Journal of Civilization," devoted an entire front page to the curiosities of the Mumler trial.[19] What made this coverage unique were the nine finely detailed engravings that illustrated spirit photography. Most of the images were credited to Mumler, but the journal included one faked spirit photograph so readers could examine the pictures side-by-side. By doing so, the journal tried to strike a neutral tone by declaring, "We shall not attempt to give an expression to our own opinions but simply to follow the developments." That sentiment was carried throughout. As the reader turned the pages of this particular issue, a ghost story ominously titled the "Face of Horror" offered a moment's entertainment. Those who continued to the back page surely chuckled at the cartoon displayed there: a corpulent gentleman complying with his fiancée's desire for a photograph serendipitously entered Mumler's studio, but when Mumler returned with the photograph, it bore the faint but recognizable faces of the man's five former wives.

It seemed that everyone in America waited for Judge Dowling's verdict. Mumler had been hauled into court accused of bilking customers out of hard-earned money in exchange for fraudulent photos. Over the course of four days of evidence, Gerry attacked Spiritualism, brought forth eminent experts debunking spirit photography, and even provided moments of levity with P.T. Barnum's grand eloquence. The rebuttal from Mumler's trio of litigators was a spirited defense. Passionate patrons and sober skeptics wreaked havoc on the prosecution's case.

Judge Dowling's verdict vindicated Mumler, boosted Spiritualism, and indirectly endorsed deceit. The outcome was not unexpected, since "the proof against him [Mumler] amounted to nothing, since it failed to show that he had used any trick or artifice to produce the ghost pictures."[20]

After the dust settled, the recriminations and rationalizations started.

Some seized on Mumler's closing comments to Judge Dowling. A surely elated defendant, confident and poised, reasserted the legitimacy of his work, accurately reflecting that "the best evidence of mechanical agency that could have been offered would have been his own camera with which he has operated so many years." Perhaps it was the prosecution's swagger, poor preparation, or flippancy that led to a failure to examine Mumler's photographic equipment. It was a striking blunder that left Gerry open to reproach.

Gerry's courtroom failure surely left the skeptics in Spiritualism somewhat disheartened. To them, Spiritualism was a dangerous belief that scorned science and challenged conventional religions. The only solace nonbelievers could find was the conviction that the verdict was a draw, leaving spirit photography in limbo. Spiritualists, however, rejoiced, with the *Banner of Light* sparing no hyperbole in declaring Mumler's trial "a direct triumph for the cause of Spiritualism."[21]

Mumler, meanwhile, traded the darkroom for the stage lights of the lecture circuit, a perfect perch from which the former spirit photographer could embellish his psychic credentials. Tracing his life history from early childhood forward, Mumler recalled seeing spirits when barely out of diapers, possessing prodigious talents as a teenager, and finally becoming a conduit for supernatural snapshots. Mumler presented each event as evidence of his spiritual evolution. Later audiences were delighted when Mumler promised that "he w[ould] graphically illustrate ... spirit-pictures, life size, by aid of magnesium light."[22]

Success breeds imitation, and Mumler's experience encouraged other spirit photographers. Among this group was A.D. Willis of Crawfordsville, Indiana.[23] Willis was a self-taught commercial photographer with a fairly successful business. His receipts provided a comfortable life for his wife and child. Roughly three months after Mumler's exoneration, Willis was developing a picture that piqued his curiosity. A pale, misty image was captured on the photographic plate alongside that of the paying customer. The presence of the eerie figure left Willis, a devout Christian, suspecting a satanic influence. Despite pious supplications, every subsequent photograph was blemished in a similar fashion. Willis finally succumbed, "producing a great many very fine spirit pictures. His rooms are constantly thronged with persons who are anxious to obtain the likeness of some dear friend." Only a few ended up recognizing the ghosts in their pictures, though this did not deter the faithful.

California was soon infected with the phenomenal photos.[24] In 1871, Los Angeles city marshal Francis Baker visited the Wolfenstien Gallery. The proprietor encouraged Baker to sit for a picture, which he obligingly agreed to do. Unfortunately, the first photograph was imperfect, forcing the city marshal to repeat the exercise. After developing the second plate, the photographer ran excitedly out of the darkroom, breathlessly asking if Baker was a spiritualist. The marshal answered in the affirmative and was presented with a photograph bearing the ghost-like image of his former boss, languidly lying near his protégé. It was well known in Los Angeles that Baker's late boss had been murdered, adding even more mystery to these spectral developments.

As news of the spirit photograph spread around town, wave upon wave of stinging ridicule left the gallery a local laughingstock. The owner hit back, challenging the unbelievers with an encore. A small group of disinterested witnesses, including another photographer, supervised the sitting for another picture. After carefully examining the equipment and ensuring that there were no adulterants on the plate, another picture was taken. To the utter amazement of all assembled, the picture once again captured an even clearer image of the late city marshal.

Spirit photographers were emboldened after Mumler's trial. The ever faithful *Banner of Light*, Spiritualism's loudest trumpet, proclaimed loudly that "the evidence in favor of the genuineness of spirit photography in the celebrated Mumler trial compelled the wise court to admit the claim of its supporters."[25] The court offered no such assurances, but the newspaper's slanted interpretation surely lifted the fortunes of the ghost makers. Perhaps the most brazen effort involved a photographer selling a Bible illustrated with spirit pictures of Abraham, Moses, and other pious prophets.[26]

Mumler capitalized on his celebrity status, though not very effectively. Competition dented his chances, along with some fading of the fad. Even so, Mumler greeted the first new year following his acquittal with an advertisement in the *Banner of Light*.[27] Clearly motivated by the prospects of increasing his business, Mumler reminded "those at a distance who desire to have a spirit photograph taken that it is not actually necessary for them to be present." Later ads prominently displayed the photographer's name and, for 25 cents, promised a generic ghost picture along with instructions for a personal sitting.[28] The notices grew distinctly less ostentatious by 1874, consisting of little more than Mumler consenting, "for a brief period, to devote a portion of his time to spirit-photography."[29]

Mumler's spirit photography reached its summit in 1875. Beginning in January of that year and extending through spring, the *Banner of Light* chronicled "The Personal Experiences of William Mumler in Spirit Photography" through seven installments. Mumler wrote each piece, beginning the journey with a touch of bitterness and victimization by declaring that "the history of all pioneers of new truths is relatively the same, and happy is the man who is not chosen one to meet the prejudices of a skeptical world.... I was condemned as a trickster, branded as a fraud."[30]

Mumler indignantly asserted his authenticity through either monumental hubris or unassailable self-conviction bordering on the delusional. He haughtily dismissed further discussion after "having presented sufficient evidence to show that spirit forms appear upon the negative.... I will now proceed to ... prove that these forms are actual likenesses of those who have passed to spirit-life." His proof in almost every instance consisted of testimonials taken from happy customers who witnessed no tricks and unhesitatingly identified their spirit images.[31]

A few other arguments were borrowed from the burgeoning scientific discoveries of the time. Mumler insisted that spirits, like electricity, could be visible under certain conditions. In a somewhat odd metaphor, the spirit photographer reasoned that electricity, "by employing a medium, in the shape of a vacuum tube ... is made visible to the human eye." In a similar manner, a psychic medium could attract otherwise invisible and shy spirits to sit for a picture.[32]

The famous spirit photographer reached the zenith of his career with the *Banner of Light* articles. A somewhat chastened Mumler cherished his "experience as an instrument in the hands of the dwellers in the invisible world" and suggested that any remaining naysayers should seek further confirmation from his legions of satisfied customers.[33]

Part of Mumler's stellar reputation came from a covey of celebrities. The cultured classes occupied by doctors, lawyers, theologians, artists, and politicians were among the elite that frequented Mumler's studio. In some cases a patron's prominence required discretion—even disguises. Such was the case when a Mrs. Tyndall visited Mumler's studio for the express purpose of obtaining a spirit photograph. She was securely hidden behind a dark veil that gave no hint of her true identity. Mumler took the picture as requested and, upon development, immediately recognized the ghostly image as President Lincoln. Upon further inquiry, Mumler was satisfied that Mrs. Tyndall was in reality Lincoln's widow.[34]

Mumler later elaborated on his encounter with Mrs. Lincoln. According to Mumler, his wife, who was a medium, entered a trance-like state just as Lincoln's widow was examining the spirit photograph. Acting as a channel between the two worlds, Mumler's wife gave voice to the disembodied spirit of President Lincoln. A long, touching talk followed, after which Mrs. Lincoln wept tears of joy and grief at this unexpected reunion.[35]

Mumler's photograph of an ethereal President Lincoln, standing serenely behind his wife and tenderly caressing her shoulders, amplified the whispers about past séances at the White House. Mrs. Lincoln's elaborate deceptions and disguises in Mumler's studio more than hint at Spiritualism's general disrepute. Apparently not even scandal and scorn could dissuade the grieving woman from seeking otherworldly comfort, leaving the deceivers-in-chief claiming yet another despondent, vulnerable soul.

The seeds of the Lincolns' fascination with Spiritualism appear to have been sown shortly after his election. However, gauging the true extent of their interest and involvement is difficult. The cloistered walls of the White House shielded the occupants from public scrutiny, and loyal associates would not harm the president's reputation. But Spiritualism was a growing force during Lincoln's life, and the president and his wife were surely aware of the social trend. The most detailed descriptions of the Lincolns' supposed interest in Spiritualism come from the personal recollections of mediums. The evidence is loosely grouped into exposés of séances at the White House, clandestine encounters with mediums, and metapsychic meetings after President Lincoln's death.

Rumors of mysterious activities at the White House swirled faintly in the early years of the Lincoln presidency. As might be imagined, Lincoln and his surrogates dismissed the idle innuendo. Suspicions were not entirely snuffed out, as wisps of proof persisted. If Lincoln needed any confirmation of the damage that could come from embracing Spiritualism, the foreign press supplied it.

Seemingly sycophantic American newspapers, literally taking a page from their English brethren, republished stories mocking Lincoln's supposed interest in Spiritualism.[36] A London newspaper satirized Lincoln's White House by spoofing Spiritualism, an amusing piece of fluff that obliquely impugned the president. According to the poisoned pen, "President Lincoln had another spiritual séance last night in reference to the war.... A circle having been formed ... the presence of a spirit was announced in a succession of raps which the President ... called the Devil's Tattoo." The spirits were supposedly offended by Lincoln's characterization and signaled their displeasure by briskly rattling the table. Soothed by an apology, the spirits proceeded to play musical instruments. In swift succession, notable persons of the past such as Benjamin Franklin, Socrates, and Archimedes stopped by for a brief visit, with the latter advising the president on matters of military strategy. The final rap came from the British tabloid, which harshly noted, "The séance then concluded, and the company went to liquor up."

It seems unlikely that the British newspapers invented Lincoln's spiritual proclivities. In fact, scattered stories in American newspapers fueled the speculations. A rather matter-of-fact story seemed to take it for granted that Lincoln was at least a dubious devotee of Spiritualism.[37] According to this report, Judge Edmonds was frequently invited to the White House. In addition, "A noted 'medium' of New York City, is frequently sent for, and has interviews with the president.... This, we have excellent authority for saying, is strictly true." During these ethereal tête-à-têtes, former occupants of the White House held political and military counsel with Lincoln. Fortunately, Mr. Lincoln "frequently remark[ed] that the communications from the other world are often delusive."

John F. Whitney claimed firsthand knowledge of Lincoln's interest in Spiritualism.[38] Whitney interviewed the president toward the end of the war, "and his remarks indicated that he was a believer; and he referred to séances at which he had been present." Among the mediums who came to the White House, John B. Conklin proudly claimed at least forty séances conducted under his personal auspices. After Lincoln's death, his widow spent a week at Whitney's home in Florida and reaffirmed Conklin's presidential presence. In another similarly obscure story, an unnamed reporter claimed "that a medium named Colchester ... was always sent for by Mr. Lincoln."[39]

The political perils associated with Spiritualism surfaced almost immediately after Lincoln was elected president. In a thinly veiled effort to embarrass the new president, the *Cleveland Plain Dealer* printed a piece "which the timid feared and the antagonistic hoped would greatly prejudice the cause of the popular Republican leader by associating his name with spiritualism."[40]

What stirred the imagination of the newspaper was the psychic medium John Conklin's claim that Lincoln had attended séances in New York City.[41] Conklin specifically recalled Lincoln's unique physiognomy, his quiet demeanor, and a particular encounter with the future president. With respect to the latter, Conklin recalled a rather severe-looking man who closely questioned him at a séance. Apparently satisfied with the answers derived from the spirit world, the man then asked about the health of a friend. Since only the dead communicated at a séance, the man whom Conklin later identified as Lincoln was taken aback. Just a few days earlier Lincoln's friend had been alive, though ill. According to Conklin, Lincoln later received a telegraph confirming his friend's death.

President Lincoln did not refute the story in the *Cleveland Plain Dealer*. When offered the opportunity to address Conklin's claims, Lincoln allegedly replied, "This article does not begin to tell the wonderful things I have witnessed."[42] Such an admission fueled early speculations that Lincoln was a spiritualist.

Halfway through the Civil War, Lincoln issued his famous Emancipation Proclamation, which righted a wrong too long ignored. As might be expected, the proclamation was greeted with debate throughout the country. Spiritualists, though, warmly embraced Lincoln's decision, with a pretentious endorsement tainted by claims of a psychic intervention.

Among the main instigators connecting Spiritualism with the Emancipation Proclamation was Colonel Simon P. Kase. Even though most references to the man included the military title, lengthy obituaries made no mention of military service.[43] Without battlefield exploits, Kase's memorials concentrated on his industrial and spiritual contributions.[44] In the former category belonged several Pennsylvania railroads that Kase had built. Before that, he was involved in iron manufacturing around Danville, Pennsylvania. However, it was Kase's fervent interest in the occult and unabashed championing of Spiritualism that led to his fame.

Colonel Kase was an impressive character. A newspaper described him as "a large man, with a broad, smooth-shaven face, and with the bristling manners and a general facial resemblance to P.T. Barnum."[45] The newspaper's allusion to P.T. Barnum, the nineteenth–century's master manipulator and circus showman, was probably not accidental. Although Kase was, by any measure, a successful businessman, his fondness for phantoms challenged his credulity.

Described in later years as a friend of Lincoln, Kase's first encounter with the president involved as much serendipity as Spiritualism. His recollection of the events was memorialized in pamphlets, the contents of which circulated widely in newspapers. Kase would spend the remainder of his long life insisting "that President Lincoln was induced, by the knowledge received through Spiritualism, to issue his Proclamation of Emancipation. My knowledge on that subject is extensive."[46]

Kase's odyssey began innocently enough. He arrived in Washington, D.C., in 1862, intent on furthering certain aspects of his Pennsylvania railroad empire. The railroad man took a leisurely stroll near the White House, casually idling away an afternoon shortly after his arrival. He passed a former boarding house that had provided lodging for a previous trip to the nation's capital. As he walked by, he noticed the name H. Conkling prominently displayed on the front door. Kase recognized the moniker as belonging to a well-known writing medium. At the same time that Kase read the name, a disembodied voice insisted he enter the house.

The colonel could not resist the entreaty. Exhibiting no particular concern or curiosity about what other people might consider a mental aberration, Kase did as the voice bid. Possibly primed by spirits, Conkling received his visitor with anxious expectation. Kase had no sooner entered the room than the medium handed him a letter with a plea to personally deliver it to President Lincoln. Wary of the request, Kase politely but firmly declined. The railroad man was on the verge of leaving when once again a voice from nowhere advised otherwise. Kase capitulated and, with Conkling in tow, made his way to the White House.

Kase and Conkling covered the short distance to the White House, requested an audience with the president, and were awarded such after a short wait. Conkling remained behind, allowing Kase to meet privately with Lincoln. For the next half hour the pair amiably discussed politics, after which Kase handed Conkling's letter to the president. Lincoln read the brief memo, which succinctly stated, "I have been sent from the City of New York by spiritual influences, to confer with you pertaining to the interests of the nation. I cannot return until I have an interview. Please appoint the time." After reading the letter twice, Lincoln apparently accepted the offer and instructed Kase to so inform Conkling.

Up to this point Kase had neglected his real reason for visiting Washington, D.C. Over the course of the following month the railroad baron returned to promoting his business interests. This proved successful, and with his mission complete, Kase was probably making plans to return home when once again the spirits intervened.

As Kase later recalled, he was chatting with a friend when an elderly woman approached and thrust a card at the puzzled man. It was an invitation to a séance hosted by Mrs. Laurie, a local spiritualist. Without a moment's hesitation Kase accepted the offer, traveling to the woman's place of business, which was located in one of the more fashionable neighborhoods surrounding the capital. Upon entering Laurie's home, Kase was thunderstruck when President Lincoln and his wife warmly greeted him.

After recovering from the shock, Kase took a seat and witnessed a most unusual exchange. With her eyes closed and her steps measured, a young girl, a trance medium, approached the president and began a lengthy lecture. What followed was a sagacious sermon condemning slavery. The young medium, ostensibly voicing the spirit world's viewpoint, declared, "The world is universally in bondage," and it was Lincoln's duty to relieve this sad state of affairs. In exchange for freeing the slaves, the medium assured the president "that from the time of the issuing of the emancipation proclamation there would be no reverses to the Union armies."

According to Kase, Lincoln was completely enraptured by the young girl. After recovering her normal senses, the girl left the room, but the night's festivities were not over. The spirits were now in a playful mood and began playing a piano. All the guests watched in amazement as the bewitched piano began dancing to its own tune.

Kase returned for an encore performance a few nights later and once again was joined by the president. In a familiar routine, the young trance medium lectured and the piano danced. Less than a month later, President Lincoln signed an executive order publicizing the Emancipation Proclamation. Spiritualists made their own proclamation, convinced that their efforts had changed the course of history.

Stories of Lincoln's supposed Spiritualism continued to surface after his death. Based on these limited and problematic sources, it would again appear that private séances began at least as early as 1862.[47] Among the alleged attendees at one séance, besides the president and his wife, was Major General Daniel E. Sickles. Just a few years before, in 1859, Sickles had murdered his wife's paramour.[48] It was a blatant crime, and the subsequent trial attracted national attention, particularly after Sickles' attorneys successfully argued temporary insanity. Attendance at a séance seemed to fit with Sickles' colorful and controversial life.

Without a doubt the most detailed description of White House séances was written by Nettie Colburn Maynard in a coyly titled book, *Was Abraham Lincoln a Spiritualist?*[49] In a lengthy preface, the publisher at first struck a tone supporting the book's contention that Lincoln's White House was a hotbed of Spiritualism but concluded with a more politically sensitive position that "a decision whether Abraham Lincoln was, or was not a Spiritualist, must be … the judgment of the individual reader."

Maynard's exposé received generous billing in the *Banner of Light*. Prominent advertisements promised readers that "this book will be found peculiar, curious, startling!"[50] At the time of publication, Nettie was bedridden with chronic rheumatism and forced to lean on her husband for assistance in memorializing the events of her life. She began her chronicle by revisiting her youth and describing spiritual influences that molded her mind.[51]

Nettie was first introduced to the mysterious world beyond in 1855. At the time her family resided in Hartford, Connecticut, and made the chance acquaintance of a traveling mystic by the name of Thomas Cook. The young man was invited into the Maynards' home and entertained the family with floating tables and spirit rappings. Perhaps the night's amusements would have gone no further were it not for Cook's declaration that Nettie possessed strong magnetic abilities. Surely flattered by such attention, Nettie soon discovered that she did indeed have special powers as a trance medium. As neighbors learned of the young girl's ability to communicate with the dead, her popularity grew, along with her abilities. Just months after her anointment as a seer, Nettie was hosting increasingly large audiences, during which the enchanted girl funneled thoughts from receptive spirits. Over the next three years the charming enchantress toured throughout New England.

Nettie was lecturing in Albany, New York, when the Civil War began. Her father and brother answered the call to arms and, on the eve of their departure, attended a comforting séance with Nettie presiding. Shortly after the men marched off to war, Nettie received an invitation to hold a public séance in Baltimore, Maryland. Initially reluctant to accept the offer, Nettie relented when she learned of her brother's ill health, a decision that eventually brought her to Lincoln's White House.

Nettie's brother was prostrate, bedridden with an undisclosed ailment in Alexandria, Virginia. Her beleaguered sibling beseeched Nettie for assistance, somehow assuming the young girl could intercede with military authorities and obtain a coveted furlough. Alarmed by the tone of her brother's appeal and fearing the worst, Nettie began a most extraordinary campaign to free her brother from the uncaring clutches of the army.

Although the distance between Baltimore and Alexandria was not great, wartime security forced the girl to run a gauntlet of checkpoints. Undaunted by the hazards of traveling alone and confronting military encampments, Nettie single-mindedly sought a medical furlough for her brother. As might be imagined, the request was met with generous doses of ridicule and rejection from military surgeons. It seems the physicians lacked the conviction of her brother's imminent demise that haunted Nettie.

Nettie was determined to get a medical furlough. Frequent visits with her brother and (in her eyes) his deteriorating condition galvanized her. With her steps repeatedly blocked by military doctors and unit commanders, Nettie finagled an interview with Assistant Secretary of War John Tucker. For whatever reason, Tucker was sympathetic to the girl's plight. Taking a sheet of paper from his desk, the assistant secretary penned a letter to a subordinate official. He then directed Nettie to meet with this person. Doing as she was directed, Nettie proceeded at once to the official's office but was flustered by the hustle and bustle. When she finally found her man, the nervous girl made a poor case. The exasperated bureaucrat was downright inflamed when Nettie remembered Tucker's letter and demurely presented it. Scanning the letter quickly, the officer dismissed its contents and curtly asked her to leave.

Discouraged but not dissuaded, Nettie appealed again to Tucker. After another meeting in his office, the outlook brightened and Nettie finally obtained the coveted furlough. With a sense of triumph Nettie delivered the valuable document to her brother. The grateful recipient immediately set about exercising his new freedom, making plans to return home to Connecticut. In what Nettie would later call divine intervention, her brother lost the precious paper, the apparent victim of a pickpocket.

Nettie did not neglect her spirit friends throughout the furlough ordeal. In fact, she was residing at the home of Mrs. Cranston Laurie, a well-known Washington, D.C., medium. The two became fast friends, with the young girl seeking the protection and guidance of her older mentor. It was apparently through Laurie's intervention that Nettie first came to the White House. It was long rumored that Laurie's abilities as a medium were valued at the White House, apparently more so by Mrs. Lincoln. Using her special relationship, Laurie arranged for a meeting with the president so Nettie could plead her case to the highest authority in the land.

Writing years later after that memorable encounter, Nettie recalled that "Mrs. Lincoln noticed my swollen eyes and inflamed cheeks, and inquired kindly the cause. Mrs. Laurie briefly explained. She quickly reassured me, saying 'Don't worry any more about it. Your brother shall have another furlough, if Mr. Lincoln has to give it himself.'"[52] The grateful girl responded by succumbing to a spirit's influence, and for the next hour she expounded on matters of state that left a deep impression on her listeners. According to Nettie, Mrs. Lincoln exclaimed, "This young lady must not leave Washington. I feel she must stay here, and Mr. Lincoln must hear what we have heard."

Shortly after Nettie's brother returned home, Mrs. Laurie received a note from Mrs. Lincoln requesting the presence of the two mediums. Naturally flattered by the offer, both women proceeded at once to the White House, where Mrs. Lincoln graciously met the pair. The president joined the group moments later, and, as Nettie later recalled, he dropped "his hand upon my head, he said, in a humorous tone, 'So this is our "little Nettie" is it, that we have heard so much about?'" Lincoln then engaged the young girl in some social banter before the suggestion was made to form a spiritual circle. According to Nettie's later account, the president agreed but needed instruction on the process. Shortly after the participants joined hands, Nettie succumbed to the control of the spirits and for a full hour channeled their concerns. Although Nettie never remembered what transpired during her trances, she later learned that she had touched on the forthcoming Emancipation Proclamation. The spirits insisted that Lincoln should not "delay its enforcement as a law beyond the opening of the year; and he was assured that it was to be the crowning event of his administration and life." At the conclusion of the séance, Lincoln thanked Nettie and praised her spiritual gifts.

Nettie's second visit with the president took place in Mrs. Laurie's Georgetown residence and was the same séance Colonel Kase so vividly recalled. It was a rather glum ghost that took control of Nettie that night and warned Lincoln that his troops were drained and dispirited. According to the spirit messenger, reversing course required that the president and his family visit the soldiers in the field. Only this personal touch would lift the discontent that had settled over the army. Shortly thereafter a local newspaper, unaware of the séance, announced the president's impending plan to visit the Army of the Potomac at Fort Monroe, Virginia, seemingly acceding to the spirit's request.

It seems that most other newspapers took scant notice of this trip. The sudden venture apparently caught the press off guard, only leaving space for speculation—and not always favorable to the president. In an apparent reference to the trip, a northern newspaper openly questioned why "Mr. Lincoln has deserted his proper duties at Washington, and under the pretense of being commander-in-chief has gone to Fortress Monroe."[53] Nettie's later rendition of the affair was far more favorable, reporting that Lincoln received an enthusiastic reception from war-weary soldiers.[54]

Throughout the remainder of the Civil War Nettie remained in Washington, D.C. She hobnobbed with politicians and military leaders and held additional séances at the White House. On one specific occasion the president summoned Nettie directly. She obliged as usual and was soon ushered into the presence of Lincoln and two unnamed military officers. The president asked Nettie if she could summon the spirits, at which point the young girl became entranced. As she later recalled, "One hour later I became conscious of my surroundings, and was standing by a long table, upon which was a large map of the Southern States. In my hand was a lead pencil." Apparently while spellbound Nettie had drawn specific lines, perhaps Confederate encampments, on the map, which amazed Lincoln and the military officers.

Nettie's last visit with President Lincoln was a somber parting. In the waning days of February 1865 Nettie learned of her father's grave illness. Hastily preparing for the journey home, she had a last, brief visit with Lincoln. It was a cordial encounter until the moment that Nettie cautioned the president that her spiritual guides had prophesied great danger for him. Lincoln listened but dismissed the warning.

The following April, like every other newspaper in America, the *Banner of Light* screamed headlines mourning a "Terrible National Calamity! Murder of President Lincoln!"[55] The *Banner of Light* and its subscribers were especially fond of Lincoln, given their absolute belief in his interest in Spiritualism. At the same time, Lincoln's death raised some potentially troublesome issues for Spiritualism. Perhaps the foremost concern was why the spirits had not intervened.

Mrs. J. H. Conant, the resident seer for the *Banner of Light*, posed such a question to her spirit friends about three months after Lincoln's death. She pointedly asked "if they could not have impressed him [Lincoln], or given warning through some other medium, in such a manner as to have averted the calamity." In a soothing response, with a soft rebuke, the spirits reminded Mrs. Conant that death was merely a transition from a mortal state to a more glorious incorporeal existence. As to why a warning was not issued, the spirits "were not permitted to do so. They were silenced by the great Eternal Power ruling in the universe."[56] The cleverly crafted communiqué conveyed two concepts—one asserting that Lincoln's spirit survived and the other answering the skeptics' damaging claim of inaction.

Lincoln became a fairly regular visitor of the *Banner of Light*'s resident medium. The nagging unanswered question about the late president's belief in Spiritualism was finally laid to rest, at least for the newspaper's faithful readers, during one of Mrs. Conant's later séances. Mr. Lincoln's spirit described an avowedly agnostic position on the matter while alive, but death had apparently tipped the balance, leaving the spirit free to declare, "I am a Spiritualist ... for my own coming demonstrates that fact."[57] As a contrivance, it was artful. The response deftly dodged debate by veering away from the popular president's mortal life and placing the admission in the spirit world, well beyond the reach of critics.

Not much time passed between Lincoln's death and mediums claiming psychic contact with the assassinated president. One of the more improbable came from France, where medium "M. Rul" conversed in his native language with Lincoln's supposed spirit. After establishing contact, the Frenchman asked, "What think you of the actual state of affairs in the United States of America?" Lincoln's spirit acknowledged the heart-wrenching impact of four long years of war but optimistically predicted a swift unification. On the subject of the emancipation of the slaves, the response was more measured, with Lincoln's spirit recognizing that several years must pass before passions and prejudices would subside.[58]

As befit his national reputation and dogged promotion of Spiritualism, Judge John W. Edmonds soon weighed in on Lincoln's death.[59] Edmonds attended a séance hosted by Mrs. W.R. Hayden during which contact was made with Frank Edmonds, a dead brother of the judge. Apparently Frank traveled in high circles and made the acquaintance of the president shortly after his death. For spiritualists, and those leaning in that direction, Frank's remarks comforted and confirmed their convictions.

According to Judge Edmonds' account of the séance with his brother, "When Lincoln woke to consciousness in the spirit-world, he was surprised and somewhat confused; for he had no idea that he was dead.... This condition of bewilderment did not, however, last long.... He found himself surrounded and most cordially welcomed." His thoughts immediately gravitated toward his family but soon gave way to a sober reflection of what he had left behind. Lincoln's spirit expressed great faith in the American people and satisfaction with his successor's stewardship of the country.

Edmonds' séance also touched on one of the most troubling aspects of Lincoln's assassination involving the mystique surrounding John Wilkes Booth.

Apparently saints and sinners coexisted in the world beyond. Such close cohabitation did not immediately soften strong emotions, which seemed to linger when the spirits fled their mortal bodies. Such was the case when Booth met Lincoln: "The first living thing that Booth encountered in the spirit-world was Lincoln; and he met him with a bold and defiant air, as if glorifying in the act he had performed, and ready to fight in defense of it." Lincoln's spirit met his assassin with compassion, but Booth would have none of it and walked angrily away.

Both Lincoln and Booth continued to haunt séances long after their respective deaths. Lincoln remained the kind, concerned politician at every encounter, while his assassin seemed to undergo a metamorphosis. Spiritualists preserved Lincoln's memory, never deviating from a psychic script honoring the man. For Booth, however, it was more complicated. He had, after all, murdered the president, but the spiritualists' view of the afterlife apparently did not include eternal punishment.

The spiritual resurrection of John Wilkes Booth served two purposes. First, his eventual repentance served to show spiritualists and skeptics alike that a benevolent Elysium Fields really existed. A typical example occurred when a large group of spiritualists and curious onlookers met in Brooklyn to hear the oracular words of Mrs. Mary J. Wilcoxson. In describing her, a reporter attending the soirée said, "She is about forty years old, was dressed in a tight-fitting black gown ... has light brown hair ... her eyes look as if they had just come out of a March wind or a prolonged trance."[60] Over the next hour Wilcoxson engaged in an airy address that left the nonplussed reporter scrambling to decipher the content.

At the conclusion of Wilcoxson's trance, members of the audience were invited to form a spiritual circle. Several did so, and it was during this séance that John Wilkes Booth decided to make contact. This time it was a totally rehabilitated assassin that spoke: "He says ... that he has become reconciled to Abraham Lincoln. They walk out daily. He says the assassination was based upon an unfortunate misunderstanding. They are now good friends."[61]

A more practical purpose of Booth's spiritual revival was to rebut persistent doubts about his death.[62] Almost immediately after Lincoln's death, conspiracy theories began forming. In some cases witnesses claimed to have seen the assassin, transcribing the particulars in books that the curious could purchase. Another story suggested that instead of Booth dying, an army deserter was killed, all for a rich reward. The sheer number of theories left suspicions in the minds of many, with spiritualists cynically cultivating the unsettled ground.

Years after Lincoln's death, conspiracy theories waxed and waned. One reporter claimed, "I was the only newspaper man present at the disinterment of the remains of the man who killed Abraham Lincoln. I knew John Wilkes Booth."[63] In telling his story, this unnamed reporter recalled exploiting a chance barroom encounter with a man "who represented himself as chief of the Secret Service Detectives." Seizing what seemed like a golden opportunity to interview a high-ranking official, the unnamed reporter plied the detective with copious amounts of alcohol. The alcohol achieved its intended purpose, and the normally reserved detective indignantly declared, "Don't be a fool. Booth was killed.... He is buried under the floor of the old arsenal, on the Island, in Washington." Thinking he had the story of the century, the reporter approached his newspaper editor, who, after hearing the tale, dismissed it as the ramblings of a drunken man.

The frustrated reporter dropped the matter. It was only revived when he attended a séance many years later. Eleven people sat around a table in Brooklyn and joined hands, summoning the spirit of John Wilkes Booth. Much to the surprise of the participants, a psychic medium was able to conjure the assassin's disembodied voice. Among the early questions posed to Booth was where he was buried. Booth confirmed that his mortal remains rested under the floor of the old arsenal. What excited spiritualists was an admission several months later by "Surgeon General Barnes ... saying that Booth was buried under the floor of the old arsenal."

With a mixture of serendipity and guile, and guided by the revelations at the séance, the newspaper man finagled his way into the armory, acting on information that Booth's body was to be returned to surviving family members. Using bluff and bluster, the reporter gained entrance to the burial site and, when the coffin was opened, instantly recognized the malefactor: "To one who had seen Booth on the stage there could be no doubt of the remains. The dry, sandy quality of the soil had preserved them wonderfully."

Perhaps the most disturbing examples of Spiritualism involved mediums who claimed contact with Lincoln's children. The Lincolns had four children, with only the oldest, Robert, surviving into adulthood. Edward died in 1850 as an infant; William, affectionately called "Willie," died at the White House in 1862; and Thomas ("Tad") died in 1871. These deaths deeply distressed the president and his wife, but for Mrs. Lincoln the murder of her husband and the loss of Tad a few years later were particularly disheartening.[64] Spiritualism offered the grieving widow an alternate reality—a problematic path for an already unsettled mind.

A mere four years after Lincoln's death, the presiding psychic at the *Banner of Light* received a spontaneous message from Willie: "I have come ... to bring a message from my father to my mother. My father wishes me to say, for him

... that we love her and shall watch over her.... I am Willie Lincoln."[65] Perhaps the faithful were moved by the tender transmission, but others not involved with Spiritualism surely saw the cruelty.

A similar and equally disturbing communication came from Tad about one year after his death. Once again the *Banner of Light* newspaper was chosen as the means through which the spirit communicated with the material world. In some respects this message was more odious, coming so soon after Tad's death, and dripping with sentiment. As was their custom, the spirits announced their purpose for crossing the barrier separating the living from the departed. Tad Lincoln began by declaring, "I am here to send a brief message to my beloved mother. I have to say that my father, my brother and myself desire that my mother should settle down where she can be most happy.... She knows that we live.... We love her and are sad when she is unhappy."[66]

Spiritualism eliminated the finality that death inevitably brings. In a country reeling from four brutal years of war, it was most alluring, promising much but delivering little. The fact that so many people, across the entire social spectrum, succumbed to Spiritualism's seduction is best viewed as a measure of despair. By turning toward the new belief, these deeply dispirited individuals were turning their backs on established religion, groping in the darkness of depression for any light they could find. One of Spiritualism's leading beacons, the *Banner of Light*, regularly published messages directed toward grieving survivors, many of whom were still in shock from battlefield deaths.

At a time when reality was so painful for so many, a palliative retreat was quite attractive, but, like a mariner choosing to travel between Scylla and Charybdis, Spiritualism forced believers to navigate a perilous pathway between delusion and deception.

Four

Intemperance

The relationship between alcohol and society is complicated, filled with ambiguity and ambivalence, with opinions ranging from adulation to animosity. During the Civil War era the voices grew louder, amplified by alcohol's role in contributing to mayhem, misery and malevolence. At the same time, alcohol's advocates tried to muffle the voices of discontent, setting the stage for another series of battles, ferociously waged by social warriors battling intemperance. In the postwar years the drumbeat grew louder, single-mindedly stifling critics with calls for prohibition.

What constituted an excessive indulgence in alcohol was often a matter of debate. Complicating the discussion were alcohol's many roles—some virtuous, some vicious. Among the first group was alcohol's medicinal role as a staple ingredient in many pharmaceutical preparations. Alcohol's dark nature most obviously surfaced when it was abused as a recreational diversion. In other cases, alcohol was a convenient self-medication, a soothing soporific and mind-numbing beverage, relieving fatigue and temporarily lifting a troubled person's spirits.

Accurately assessing the full impact of intemperance during the Civil War and in the following decades is nearly impossible. Individual intemperance was often covered by thick blankets of denial, dodging, and endless excuses. Societal sensitivities spared many the ignominious labels and medical diagnosis was imprecise, leaving many alcohol-related disorders uncounted. At the other end of the spectrum, instead of minimizing the problem, abstinence-oriented advocates hysterically demonized alcohol, embellishing the evils of intemperance as they preached from pulpits, issued excoriating editorials, and organized temperance crusades.

Mortality statistics from the Eighth United States Census listed the common causes of death for the year ending June 1, 1860.[1] Infectious diseases such as pneumonia, consumption (tuberculosis), scarlatina, and typhoid fever lead the list. Out of the 394,153 deaths reported during this period, intemperance claimed the lives of 842 men and 89 women. That figure probably represents only the clearest and most uncontestable cases, leaving other likely alcohol-related deaths tabulated elsewhere. Delirium tremens, for example, accounted for the deaths of 518 men and 57 women. Other likely alcohol-related conditions afflicting both genders included liver disease, a common outcome of life-long alcohol abuse that was the cause of death for 2,633 individuals. A similar inclusion of at least some of the 681 deaths from jaundice, 1,019 from gastritis, and 18,090 from various accidents might come closer to providing a more complete picture of the ills of intemperance.

The general death rate in 1880, which accounted for changes in the population, was 15.09 per 1,000 persons, an increase from 12.54 two decades earlier.[2] After carefully analyzing the data, the Tenth United States Census report cautiously concluded that "our mortality rate is not as low as it should be." Part of the explanation probably arose from a higher death rate among males, with "venereal diseases, alcoholism ... diseases of the liver ... accidents of all kinds, and suicides" contributing to the excess.

A confounding variable introduced in the 1880 census was the change in terminology, with intemperance being exchanged for alcoholism; the latter accounted for the deaths of 1,388 men and 254 women.[3] Where similarities existed in the two census reports, gastritis claimed the lives of 2,064, jaundice 1,394, other diseases of the liver 4,762, and accidental deaths of all types another 35,901. (Delirium tremens was absent from the 1880 census.)

Another way to roughly estimate intemperance would be through an examination of brewer's and distiller's production runs, rough calculations based on tax revenues, crops such as corn devoted to production, and records left by manufacturers. Using this approach, Americans consumed 107 million gallons of distilled spirits in 1860, a number that leaped to 470 million barrels in 1871. The steep increase in liquor consumption led one author to derisively conclude that in 1871, "In return for this ... the nation receives: 500 murders, 500 suicides, 100,000 criminals, 200,000 paupers, 60,000 deaths from drunkenness, 600,000 besotted drunkards, [and] 600,000 moderate drinkers."[4]

The difficulty of estimating alcohol production was highlighted by disagreements over which type of beverage contributed to increased consumption. A physician calculated the consumption of alcohol at two time points: in 1876, when per capita use was 8.16 gallons, and a decade later, when use rose to 12.46 gallons.[5] Over the course of these ten years the production of distilled spirits remained fairly steady, leaving the enormous increase entirely due to beer consumption.

During the Civil War intemperance did not take a vacation, but it did take a backseat position. In part this was due to alcohol's recreational role, which many no doubt saw as a reasonable response to the rigors of war. Even so, there were scattered voices of dissent both in the ranks and from outside.

Shortly after the war started, a newspaper correspondent lamented the troops' payday behavior. It seemed that all was well before the soldiers received their pay, with the reporter impressed by their orderliness and military bearing. All of that changed within days after the soldiers were rewarded with a month's wages, leading the newspaper man to complain that "since the fatal payday, drunkenness, accompanied with occasional rioting, has been quite common. Drunken men are now to be met with at every turn, and they are not unfrequently seen lying in the gutters, or on the doorsteps, in a state of beastly intoxication."[6]

The same reporter used the spectacle to advance a proposal, one that he was sure would spare the locals and benefit the soldiers: Instead of paying a month's wages all at once, each month an individual soldier would receive only a small portion of his salary, the remainder to be invested in government bonds. At the end of their enlistment, assuming they survived, a tidy sum would have accumulated, presumably setting the soldier up for a life of ease. Of course the local citizens would feel safer in this scenario, being relieved of barroom brawls and similar exhibitions.

The reporter's plan never gained any traction, slipping on several conflicting interests. Saloon keepers clearly benefited from the windfall, as did the federal government through the alcohol-based tax revenues. In addition, soldiers facing the prospects of war and possible injury or death would hardly be motivated to exchange instant gratification for an uncertain future reward. These opposing views were never reconciled, leaving the problems of military intemperance well recognized but essentially sanctioned as an unfortunate cost of war.

It seemed that no outrage was ever sufficient to firmly and decisively shake the military's malaise. Just a few months before the Union Army would suffer a disastrous defeat at the Second Battle of Manassas, soldiers were killing each other in drunken fights. A newspaper briefly mentioned one example: "At Manassas, one soldier was killed by another, to-day, by shooting. Both were drunk. Four men have been found dead within the last 24 hours, in consequence of drinking whisky, a large quantity of which was captured last night."[7] In a belated response, the whisky peddler was arrested.

All too often a drunken soldier's misconduct came at the expense of an innocent civilian. Early in the war, as military units were forming in New Hampshire, many citizens collectively breathed a sigh of relief when the legions of intoxicated soldiers left. Unfortunately, they did not leave quickly enough to spare the life of a young woman who suffered "a most wanton murder ... committed here to-day, about 10 o'clock, by WILLIAM MURRAY, of Company F, Second New-Hampshire Regiment. The victim was an unfortunate girl named MARY BUTLER.... MURRAY, who was drunk, accosted her in the street, and, after exchanging a few words with her, deliberately shot her with his musket. The ball passed entirely through her body, and caused her death in a few moments."[8]

Murray attacked Butler on July 27, 1861; one week later he was executed following a brief court-martial.[9] Much like the crime itself, newspapers accorded the hanging a mere paragraph, buried among other war-related tidbits. In an obvious and gruesome display designed for deterrence, the gallows were erected on a high edifice at Fort Ellsworth near Alexandria, Virginia. This allowed twenty thousand onlookers to witness Murray's death. Murray met his fate without any outward sign of fear or remorse. Based on the sparse coverage, it seemed unlikely that the spectators knew much about the crime and even less about alcohol's role in it.

Angry citizens upset at soldiers' carousals sometimes expressed their concerns through a sort of helpless indignation. Northern states were expected to recruit sufficient numbers of soldiers to swell the ranks of regiments destined to head south, a pressure keenly felt by local bureaucrats. In one example, federal officials' insistent pursuit of numbers prompted grumbling from state officials in New York that "several of the principal cities and towns have declared that they have done more than was required of them in procuring volunteers for the army."

What particularly irked the state officials was the high desertion rate among new recruits, numbers that federal officials apparently subtracted from the state's quota. Enraged state officials argued that "the Government was responsible for the short comings of the soldier after he had successfully passed through the mustering-in ordeal ... he became the military property of the nation and the nation, accordingly, was bound to take care of him, and see that he did not destroy his value as a soldier, either by unnecessary exposure or by intemperance or that he did not take to his heels and skedaddle to parts unknown." Once again the specter of spirits haunted the army.

One of the more infamous incidents sullied a celebratory sendoff of the newly constituted 63rd Infantry Regiment of the Third Regiment Irish Brigade.[10] The 63rd responded to the patriotic call for recruits and, starting in September 1861, mustered sufficient troops to populate the newly formed regiment by late November.[11] Most of the new troops hailed from New York City, but some came from Boston and Albany. Eventually the 63rd joined the Army of the Potomac, steadily developing a hard-won reputation for bravery on the battlefield. None of this would have been predicted based on the regiment's troubled embarkation.

The 63rd Infantry Regiment arrived en masse on an early Thursday morning in late November 1861. With fanfare and flourish the regiment made a gallant display as the men marched down New York City's famous Broadway Street on their way to the wharf where their transport ship was docked. Three companies passed the gates without incident, but the tranquil scene deteriorated rapidly when several women following the men were denied entry. Murmurs of discontent soon gave way to angry protests as several men broke ranks. Guards and commanders vainly attempted to quell the burgeoning riot but completely lost control. Frustrated troops attacked the guards securing the wharf while some soldiers clambered over the restraining gates and fell into the water, with at least one drowning as a consequence. As the melee continued, some of the regimental officers resorted to force, striking the rioters with knives and bayonets and, in least in one case, inflicting mortal wounds.

Many of the soldiers managed to escape the confrontation and, along with friends and family, soon swelled the local saloons. A contemporary observer complained, "Soldiers, who a short time before were orderly and obedient, were now either raving with passion, or so stupidly intoxicated as to be unable to walk." Even more sadly, John Gautley, a private in Company C, and Dennis Reagan, a private in Company B, both died as a result of their drunken escapades.

Increased concerns about alcoholism surfaced soon after the Civil War began. Some of these early efforts were led by men of the clergy, making thunderous demands while denouncing dissipation. Such a gathering took place in New York City's Madison Square, with a coterie of clergymen convincing a large audience to join them in proposing a set of sobriety resolutions aimed at the military.[12] Among the resolutions were suggestions to censure families who secretly hid alcohol among other items mailed to the soldiers, to ban the sale of liquor to soldiers in garrison, and to punish through dismissal any officer drunk while on duty. The meeting concluded with a solicitation, the proceeds of which would furnish the funds to disseminate temperance pamphlets among the soldiers.

In the years preceding the Civil War various sects espousing sobriety fought an uphill battle in a skeptical nation. Perhaps chief among these groups was the American Temperance Union, which traced its origins to 1826.[13] Aside from conferences attended by the ardent advocates of abstinence, groups such as the American Temperance Union preached to the public through pamphlets, journals, and books, some of which surely made their way into army camps once the war got under way.

An example of this propaganda was a short article published in the *Journal of the American Temperance Union* slyly titled "The Sick Soldier—Thoughts of Home." Readers expecting a sentimental tale were partially rewarded, but the obvious subtext promoted a sobering and not so subtle warning about the evils of alcohol. Using an inspirational theme, the story began with what was probably a fairly common scene at the time. A tired, dejected, distraught soldier moaned piteously, "Oh this dreadful exhaustion; this want of strength! Shall I ever regain health?" Turning toward a fellow soldier, later heroically revealed as a teetotaling role model, the sick soldier pleaded, "Pour me out some brandy from this bottle in my haversack ... it raises one's spirits in these dismal times." Although the sober soldier initially honored this request, before handing over the brandy he began to sermonize. An appeal was made to consider the consequences of imbibing, with its negative impact on both military duty and home life. The feel-good story ended on a bright note, with the sick soldier submitting to the sermon and exchanging the brandy for fresh air and warm sunshine.[14]

Efforts to promote abstinence in the army were often greeted with derision, surely by the soldiers but occasionally by newspaper editorials as well.[15] In commenting on temperance campaigners' tactics, one newspaper wryly noted that "a pile of tracts as big as a small house has been sent on to convince the army of the dangers of everything from lager up." This was no exaggeration, as the temperance societies collectively boasted of distributing upward of 100,000 such propaganda booklets. Judged by the ills that alcohol wrought, their efforts seemed more valiant than valuable.

Politicians took ineffective potshots at alcohol. In 1861 President Lincoln signed what was probably the least enforced law of the land, forbidding "selling or giving intoxicating drinks to soldiers."[16] Of course rank had its privileges, and the law did not extend to officers, even though several senior officers attempted to quash the beverage through a spirit of equanimity. A curious quirk of the law allowed roughly half of a cup of "whiskey to each man in the navy in case of excessive fatigue and exposure." Unfortunately, politicians apparently concluded that soldiers' long, tiring marches across snake-infested swamps or dense forests were not sufficiently fatiguing to warrant a similar benefit.

Lawmakers and military commanders viewed liquor and beer differently. Liquor such as whiskey was considered off limits for soldiers while beer and ale were not. As might then be imagined, soldiers took full advantage of the distinction, drinking copious amounts of beer. It was not long before concerned citizens connected an excessive indulgence in this beverage with an increasing number of deaths. Among several New York regiments a spike in deaths was attributed solely to beer drinking.[17]

When military commanders issued orders restricting or preventing the use of alcohol, some newspapers roundly applauded the decision. With a disparaging opinion of the common soldier, one high-toned editorial argued that "the placing of temptation ... beyond his reach, is not only a necessity in preserving discipline, but a real blessing to the soldier himself."[18] According to this editorial, immoderate drinking was a scourge afflicting every soldier, only spared through the benevolence of obligatory abstinence.

A more reasoned opinion came from the U.S. Sanitary Commission, the charter of which focused on all matters affecting soldiers' health and hygiene.[19] Commission members knew that poor field conditions felled more soldiers than the enemy could ever hope to remove. A large influx of soldiers in the earliest days of the war was accompanied by grand visions of glory that neglected such basic needs as food, housing, healthcare, and even recreational activities. Into this void strode disease and indolence, which, with brutal efficiency. thinned the ranks of many regiments. Through determined prodding, the commission slowly convinced military leaders of the pressing need to address these concerns, adopting prevention as the key.

It was not long before the Sanitary Commission trained its sights on alcohol, but the image was at best fuzzy. Part of the distortion was due to alcohol's medicinal role, which clearly fell within the province of the commission's mandate to ensure that soldiers received appropriate healthcare. However, the commission recognized that the immoderate use of alcohol erased all medicinal benefits, leaving in place a more reasonable and less zealous policy.

An example of the Sanitary Commission's prudent planning of alcohol use surfaced early in the war when troop commanders struggled to contain battlefield diseases such as malaria.[20] In the first year of the war military surgeons, with the full support of the commission, prescribed a prophylactic tonic of quinine mixed with about half a cup of whiskey. Soldiers in malaria-ridden regions received the cocktail twice a day, with the whiskey provided through commission resources. After a few months' trial, the Union Medical Department climbed on board, bringing a welcome relief to a much larger swath of the army. The practice soon fell out of favor, no doubt due to a growing proclivity by some surgeons to omit the bitter-tasting quinine. Nonetheless, the medicinal role of alcohol continued to find favor among surgeons, and the commission stood ready to support their practice.

In rationalizing the medicinal use of whiskey, the Sanitary Commission examined the matter rather evenly. It recognized that the cost, transportation, and storage of alcohol came at the expense of more wholesome foods and medicines. Coffee was preferred as a mild stimulant for tired, worn-out soldiers, particularly those who were otherwise healthy. At other times, "when the troops are exposed to fatiguing duties, such as heavy marches and labors in trenches, or in the construction of fortifications ... a daily issue of whiskey in moderate quantities exercises the most beneficial influence."

Infectious diseases were often remedied through the liberal use of spirits. Wine, whiskey and brandy were often chosen for their stimulant effects, with the latter prized for service members suffering from high fevers. Not surprisingly, there was little mention of alcohol improving a soldier's mood, promoting sleep, or banishing (at least momentarily) the harsh realities of war. Whatever the reason, surgeons liberally prescribed alcohol, and the U.S. Sanitary Commission supplied the product.

The commission provided urgently needed medical assistance after the fighting stopped at Gettysburg and the wounded lay on the battlefield while others crowded every available building converted to a makeshift field hospital.[21] More than sixty tons of supplies strained local storage capacity, which would have burst except that "each morning the supply wagons of the Division and Corps Hospitals were before the door, and each day they went away laden with such articles as were desired to meet their wants." Among the necessities transported to the troops were 1,250 bottles of brandy, 1,168 bottles of whiskey, 1,148 bottles of wine, 600 gallons of ale, and, for a special treat, 302 jars of brandied peaches.

Although the Sanitary Commission obviously supported the Union Medical Department's use of alcohol, there were voices of dissent.[22] After fifteen months of hard experience working with the federal government in assessing, advising, and outfitting the army, exasperated commission leaders took aim at the Army Medical Department. The objects of their ire were lax medical inspections of new recruits that populated regiments with unfit soldiers. What particularly alarmed and annoyed the commission was the wholly preventable loss of soldiers from hernias, varicose veins, and "constitutions broken by intemperance." As the commission saw it, even the most perfunctory medical exam would have spared these men and the nation their ignominious inability to make it from garrison to battlefield.

While the northern states were struggling to strike a balance between the economic, medical, recreational, and moralistic roles of alcohol, the southern states were fighting parallel battles. According to one eyewitness in 1862, the Confederate capital of Richmond, Virginia, was "crowded with reenlisted soldiers on furlough. A hundred whiskey shops are in operation on Main-street and the side alleys. Drunken men reel out, tumble into the gutters, sprawl over the sidewalks, brandish knives and pistols, and oftentimes indulge in those deadly conflicts which fill our prisons with candidates for the gallows."[23]

While lamenting the deplorable debauchery, the eyewitness to this spectacle was more concerned with the diversion of corn from the farms to the distilleries. Distillers paid top price for their chief ingredient, inflating the cost well beyond the reach of most poor southerners. At the same time, a staple food product was made less available for the army. Only medicinal alcohol escaped the observer's wrath.

Soldiers' letters from the field to loved ones back home often spoke of the privations of war and sometimes of personal skirmishes with alcohol, some won and some lost. Corporal Charles F. Bancroft, 4th Vermont Infantry Regiment, Company H, wrote to his parents on February 2, 1862, that "the Brandy is all right & safe now & I had last week for one or 2 days a diarrhea & went to the Doctor & got some medicine for it & there was so much opium in it that Friday AM (It was Thursday that I took it) I vomited & was so dizzy & weak in the morning that I could not stand up but I have taken some of the Brandy & it has made me all right."[24]

Bancroft's experience with opium was not particularly unusual, since military surgeons used the medication for many ailments, but in this case it was apparently utilized in an effort to stop the diarrhea. It seems the dose was too large for the soldier, resulting in the vomiting and dizziness, but a dose of brandy restored his balance. Unfortunately, despite the medical interventions and Bancroft's brandy, frail health led to his death two months later on April 30, 1862.

Although any liquor may have sufficed, many soldiers had particular favorites, in part based on a belief that such spirits helped ward off all sorts of maladies. Securing their favorites was often no more difficult than asking a sympathetic friend or family member to mail the item. Charles C. Canning, who achieved the rank of first lieutenant in the 2nd Vermont Infantry Regiment, reached out in just such a manner. In a letter to his friend William Hirt Henry, Canning wrote, "I will tell you how you can do me a favor. I do not drink hardly any liquor, but during this warm weather, I would like some *good* Brandy. We cannot get it here without paying fabulous prices. I wish you would send me one gallon of nice Brandy, and a couple pounds of loaf Sugar to go with it, and if the box is large enough you may put me in a gallon of good Gin. Send it by express to the care of Capt. P.P. Pitkin Ass. Qr. M. Smiths Division, Fort Monroe. It will come through all safe, if you pack it right."[25]

Soldiers' letters surely upset the recipients when they spoke of regiments drenched in alcohol. Joseph Spafford, an officer with a Vermont infantry regiment, wrote of such a scene to his sister, Mary Jane Spafford: "A New York Regt came from Washington to this camp yesterday. The boys who saw them come in said they were a muddy drunken, tired looking lot of men as they ever saw. They said (our boys) that one of them told them he got drunk and lost his gun coming up, and said he 'who blames me? ... We were as tired as man could well be and every time we got a chance we drank, there were men among us *drunk*, who never *drank* before.' I do not doubt this in the least."[26]

Spafford's letter hints at, but does not elaborate on, his observation that intemperance was infectious, afflicting even previous abstainers. His tone was sympathetic, a sort of unstated soldier's bond full of understanding but short on words. These men were drinking to dull the discomforts and dangers of war, though the beverage barely blunted their bitterness. Letters such as this hint at alcohol's role in dulling the psychological consequences of war.

Whatever aid alcohol brought to some common soldiers was often subtracted through guilt. Alcohol demanded a steep price for a short diversion, often paid in anguish directly due to drunkenness. As was the case in many letters, soldiers in some cases attributed their battlefield reversals to an overreliance on alcohol, a harsh but probably accurate assessment that only deepened their disgust. Andrew F. Davis, an officer with the 15th Indiana Infantry Regiment, wrote to his wife, "I think we owe more to General Alcohol than to any one els[e] for our many disgraceful defeats and our slow progress in the prosecution of the war, but enough of this for the subject is painful for any one to think of."[27]

Some letters dripped with reassurance, trying to convince loved ones that the writers were not succumbing to intemperance's evil spell. Valentine G. Barney, an officer with the 9th Vermont Infantry Regiment, wrote to his wife Maria in the winter of 1863, "You say you hope it is not by drinking that I have become so fleshy. When I was unwell for a few days about a month ago the Doctor advised me to drink ale every day and so I have and I think it keeps me in a better state of health ... it is best for me to use it ... and have no fear of becoming so habituated to it as to be able to quit it any time."[28] Clearly Barney was addressing his wife's concern about his possible descent toward drunkenness, which he brushed aside by emphasizing alcohol's medicinal role. Apparently it did not fully relieve her worries, leading Barney to address the issue again in a subsequent letter:

> It seems you have a great deal of anxiety about me and although you dont express any fears about my getting in a habit of drinking intoxicating Liquors you speak often of its use and warn me against it ... and I am glad I am possessed of such a *good* temperance wife.... Maria one thing is very certain ... had I ever been going to become a drunkard I would have been one before now for very many times have I passed through more trying places.... I dont like to tell you of all the times or *under* circumstances in which I have been placed when I have refused the intoxicating cup ... and only for purposes of health have I taken even ale. [N]ow *dont* be anxious on that point for if you are it is merely trouble borrowed.[29]

Barney spared his spouse any description of the battlefield experiences that led men to drink, a temptation he resisted mostly, it seems, to satisfy a suspicious wife. He clearly recognized his wife's intolerance, which apparently even frowned on alcohol's role in blunting the harsh realities of war. In some respects, this soldier was fighting two battles—one against enemy combatants and the other a campaign to convince his life partner of his continued sobriety. The extent to which the latter was a distraction from the former seems evident from Barney's lengthy letter.

Home folks had no shortage of stories chronicling the bad effects of alcohol on military management, morale, and morality. Add to that the tireless efforts of the abstinence advocates, and alcohol became the chief mischief-maker of the war. Newspapers regularly reported both individual and regimental problems, although the former category was mostly populated by officers. Enlisted soldiers' drunkenness seems to have been taken for granted and worthy of print only when associated with criminal behavior.

Newspapers offered readers an almost daily roll call of military disciplinary actions, with alcohol-related offenses often leading the list. In a typical example, two days after Thanksgiving in 1863, a newspaper perfunctorily reported military misdeeds such as "Assistant Surgeon Simon C. Sanger, Sixth New-York cavalry ... for drunkenness, and grossly insulting a lady.... Second Lieut. Richard O. Neill, troop C, Sixth New-York volunteer cavalry, tried for neglect of duty, drunkenness on duty.... Second Lieut. Michael Mungovan, Seventeenth Indiana Volunteer War, tried for ... drunkenness on duty [and] Col. G. Bondox, Sixty-eighth New-York Volunteers, tried for drunkenness on duty, and conduct prejudicial to good order and military discipline; found guilty, and sentenced 'to be cashiered.'"[30]

Several months later not much had changed, with the daily tally reporting an almost identical list of miscreants dismissed from service: "Among recent court-martial decisions are several cases of New-York officers. Assistant Surgeon John R. McCullough, Eighty-second New-York Volunteers, for drunkenness on duty, is found guilty and cashiered; Second Lieut. Aaron J. Goodrich, One Hundred and Twenty-fifth New-York Volunteers, for drunkenness and anti-military conduct, found guilty and dismissed [from] the service; Capt. J.H. Barker, Veteran Corps, dismissed for drunkenness; the dismissal of Capt. Silas E. Warren, Colored Infantry, is confirmed, he having tendered his resignation while under charge of drunkenness."[31]

Such reports surely contributed to a general uneasiness among newspaper readers, particularly when the affliction seemed to be concentrated among military leaders and surgeons. With the nation's future hinging on clear-headed decision-making, the befuddling effect of alcohol was an easy scapegoat for battlefield reversals. Sometimes complaints were directed at the highest echelons of government, with one example bitterly attacking General Ulysses S.

Grant's immoderation: "The massacre at Shiloh, wherein 8,000 Union soldiers were lost through Grant's drunkenness, or incompetency, or both, is a severe commentary on the thoughtless enthusiasm which nominates Grant for a Major-General."[32]

Soldiers' letters to loved ones also complained about the insoluble mixture of liquor and leadership. One example of pointed criticism came in a letter from Joseph Rutherford, a surgeon with the 17th Infantry Regiment Vermont, to his wife Hannah. As a medical doctor, more merit might be placed on his observations, one of which speculated that "the real cause of Hookers removal was *drunkeness*. A man told me who saw him at the last Frederickburgh fight that he (Hooker) was so drunk he that was unable to stand, and Dr. Childes wife told me that he dined at the same table with her at Poolville after our Regt, left them, and he got beastly drunk on the Dr. Whisky, this was only a day or too before his removal from the army. It is many such cases as these that has brought so much disgrace upon our arms."[33]

Drunkenness among doctors was doubly dispiriting, corroding confidence among soldiers and worried families. A mostly unspoken expectation among both groups relied on the sober assessment and reasonable provision of medical assistance for ill or injured soldiers. The bond of trust was broken when a shaky hand reached for a surgical saw and the strong odor of alcohol wafted over the patient. Once again newspapers drily recorded what were probably only the most egregious examples of such professional misconduct: "A General Court-Martial, convened at headquarters, First brigade, Third division, Sixth corps, Army of the Potomac, Jan. 12, 1863, tried Surgeon Luther Thomas, Twenty-sixth New-Jersey Volunteers, on charges of being 'drunk on duty,' and 'conduct to the prejudice of good order and military discipline.' He was tried on several specifications, on some of which he was found guilty, and sentenced to be cashiered."[34] Despite the conviction, President Lincoln restored the soldier to duty.

Confederate soldiers were just as susceptible to the wiles of alcohol as their northern foes. A few months after Virginia joined the southern war effort, the Richmond police court began seeing soldiers such as Zachariah Burnett, who assaulted a civilian and was subsequently handed over to his commanding officer. Another inebriated southern soldier by the name of Frederick Dornin fared better, being released by the police court after drawing his bayonet and threatening a city watchman.[35]

It seems reasonable to speculate that the sheer number of drunk and disorderly soldiers defied any newspaper's efforts to chronicle every episode, leaving only notable cases worthy of a reader's attention, such as that of James Creilley, "a member of the 3d company Washington Artillery." Perhaps it was the storied history of the Washington Artillery, Louisiana's oldest military unit, with campaigns stretching from the First Battle at Bull Run, Antietam, Gettysburg, and eventually ending at Appomattox,[36] that led the reporter to memorialize Creilley's behavior. Of course, it might also have been Creilley's violence—ferociously resisting arrest and remaining unsubdued even after being dragged to jail by civilian authorities. All night long the soldier kept his guards on edge. Creilley's bail was set at $300, an amount that guaranteed his incarceration until his military commander came calling.[37]

Military law, buttressed by religion, patriotism, and a culture emphasizing bravery, integrity, and personal honor, left soldiers few pathways for expressing, much less exhibiting, emotional responses to war. Grousing, gambling, and getting letters from home were some stock siphons, but when these failed an untold number of soldiers turned to desertion, drinking, and poor discipline.

As the war progressed and the public's attitude toward drinking hardened, alcohol use was further demonized, limiting any consideration of alcohol's (admittedly deleterious) role in softening the psychological consequences of combat. Shaping the public's perceptions were seemingly endless accounts of immoderation flowing from the battlefield and a shadow army of militant crusaders relentlessly monitoring and censuring alcohol's use. Connecting consumption with emotional escapism was not part of their battle plan, in part due to a lack of awareness and sensitivity, which, when fused with strongly held moral convictions condemning alcohol use, resulted in an almost delusional denouncement of drinking. This approach promoted an increasingly intolerant and self-righteous campaign with the lofty aim of reengineering America.

Temperance advocates were blunt voices in the years preceding the Civil War, resorting to rhetoric that increasingly fused the morality of religion with the nascent rise of science. As more was learned about the chemistry of alcohol, including its physiological effects on the human body, the newfound knowledge was appropriated by the alcohol abolitionists.

In a tortuous pseudo-scientific and philosophical argument aimed at young people, the author of the *Textbook of Temperance* rejected the notion that alcohol was a product of nature. This seemingly inconsequential assertion was actually an essential plank supporting the temperance movement, so much so that the author of the *Textbook of Temperance* insisted, "It must, by this time, be plain to the meanest capacity, that no blunder can be greater than to rank Alcohol amongst the productions of Nature.... It is, to all intents ... the work of ... man's device ... using and abusing the powers and possibilities latent in Nature."[38] Nature was God's creation, and a benevolent deity did not place this temptation on earth. It was only through man's corruption of nature, with the enabling assistance of Satan, that the evils of alcohol were unleashed. Casting alcohol out of nature was a clever allusion to the original sin, when Adam succumbed to the Devil's temptations.

Just about every church embraced the temperance movement, with sermons momentarily muted by the Civil War. Even Cora Hatch, the famous trance medium, weighed in. It seemed the only spirits shunned by this spiritualist were those among the intoxicating class. A few years before the Civil War began, Hatch was entertaining a large crowd in New York City, and through the course of her ninety-minute transcendental state she touched on the miserable fate awaiting the intemperate soul: "The drunkard, whose idea of pleasure is the orgie ... is quite as degraded hereafter as here. His spirit ... is a worm crawling about upon the city's paving stones; the lowest stage of spiritual life."[39]

Before the war engulfed the nation, the reformers had dreamed of imposing their vision of an alcohol-free society through a constitutional amendment. The guns of war pretty much silenced the movement, even though the most determined members sought to maintain some momentum.

The experience of the Sons of Temperance, one of the earliest and more influential groups in the years before and after the war, was typical of the movement's efforts and the resistance it met. Nearly two decades before the Civil War began, sixteen men pledged a life of abstinence in New York City in 1842 and subsequently created a set of bylaws to govern the future membership of the society. Membership grew rapidly as the Sons of Temperance seeded subgroups through the northeast. The Sons of Temperance had swelled to roughly 750,000 members just before the start of the war.[40]

Nashville, Tennessee, was chosen as the site for the Sons of Temperance's eighteenth annual meeting in 1861, a location made wholly impractical given the declaration of war, which made travel south far too dangerous. A meeting among the group's leaders led to a postponement of the 1861 convention, with subsequent arrangements made for a national conference the following year in Hamilton, Canada. Roughly ten percent of those initiated at the time, or slightly less than 90,000 members, made the trek north to Canada in 1862 to attend the deferred convention. At the mid-point of the Civil War in 1863, the Sons of Temperance met again in Canada, with an even smaller group of 56,000 making their way to Halifax, Nova Scotia. Attendance at this level remained fairly stable, as the most stalwart gathered in 1864 in Cleveland, Ohio, and in 1865 in New Haven, Connecticut. In the decade following the end of the war attendance climbed back to the prewar numbers, after which an irreversible decline followed.

The Sons of Temperance's success in early recruiting efforts netted many prominent clergymen, businessmen, and even some military men. Perhaps most famous among the latter group was a young Lieutenant Ulysses Grant, newly married and assigned to a remote location at Sacket's Harbor, New York, in 1848.[41] At the time Grant was remembered as quiet and sociable and admired for his lack of pretentions. His main passion aside from his job was riding fine horses, to the extent that his meager salary and home life permitted.

Life at Sacket's Harbor moved at a very slow pace, which Grant filled during off-duty hours by attending church, riding, playing checkers, and spending time with his wife. Perhaps it was the boredom of the place combined with church sermons and a new marriage that led Grant to conclude "that there is no safety from ruin by liquor except by abstaining from it altogether." Or perhaps the young lieutenant sensed an inner tendency or vulnerability that, if given free rein, would destroy his military career and domestic life.

For whatever reason, Grant joined the ranks of the Sons of Temperance while stationed at Sacket's Harbor and soon thereafter invited other men to join a lodge he established. Not much is known of the success of his efforts in recruiting other soldiers, but for a time Grant was an ardent abstainer. His passion seemed to fade after leaving Sacket's Harbor, most notably when his excessive consumption of alcohol during the Civil War was more than a matter of mere speculation.

After leaving Sacket's Harbor, Grant and his wife separated, as duty required his assignment to Fort Humboldt near Eureka, California. It was during this long journey through infested lands and waters that Grant apparently broke his temperance pledge. Fort Humboldt's isolated location and desultory duty seemed to encourage immoderation, and Grant's drinking "grew until it was not to be controlled amid surroundings where every incentive was to indulge his cravings." News of his dissipation eventually reached higher army headquarters, forcing his resignation.[42]

Shortly after rejoining the army at the onset of the Civil War, Grant showed the military characteristics that would define his natural leadership through impressive campaigns in Missouri, Kentucky, and Tennessee. Yet once again insinuations surfaced that Grant was drinking, with the most pointed accusations coming after Union forces suffered heavy losses at Shiloh. Reports reached Washington claiming that Grant was "so drunk as to find it impossible to reach the field until the battle was nearly over."[43] Nonetheless, Grant would eventually prevail against the demon intemperance, his politically inspired competitors, and a determined southern foe.

The Sons of Temperance had significant political clout for a small group and even counted remarks from President Lincoln among their accomplishments.[44] A few weeks before Lincoln's Gettysburg Address, the president responded to a message from the Sons of Temperance that contained, in part, a plea to restrict alcohol use in the army. Lincoln took the occasion to remind the organization that many years before the Sons of Temperance took up their banner of abstinence, he was advocating the same.

Even though Lincoln considered intemperance "one of the greatest, if not the very greatest, of all evils among mankind," he ultimately could not support the Sons of Temperance's broader petition for abstinence. When it came to the army, the president was satisfied that military law proscribed drunkenness and, upon conviction, provided painful punishments for violators. It seems that Lincoln drew a line between responsible drinking and dissipation, leaving the former within the province of individual self-control and the latter for the law when a soldier lost control.

Most of the reform efforts were led by members of the clergy embarking on a fervent crusade against alcohol use in any form for any reason. Their arguments were often laced with dramatic, exaggerated, and untenable claims, with one proponent proclaiming that "about ninety percent of the suffering, pauperism and crime … comes from intemperance."[45] Naturally, alcohol prohibition would eliminate this scourge and usher in a new era of harmony and bliss.

Women also took up arms against intemperance and were among the most ardent advocates promoting abstinence, a clear consequence of their firsthand experiences of suffering from a husband's drunkenness. In the beginning their activities were mostly appendages associated with other social causes championed by established churches. Shortly after the Civil War ended, however, the alcohol abolitionists banded together with newly invigorated zeal and formed the Woman's Christian Temperance Union.

Annie Turner Wittenmyer launched the first crusade in 1873 against alcohol in Hillsboro, Ohio, a battle cry that would be heard across America and formally lead to the birth of the Woman's Christian Temperance Union the following year.[46] In what would become a typical tactic, Wittenmyer would lead a band of women to the dens of inequity (hotels and saloons being favorite battlefields) and engage the patrons and proprietors in prayers and petitions.

As might be imagined, not every merchant appreciated Wittenmyer's women storming their establishments and making demands antithetical to their business interests. In one incident a particularly resistant druggist railed against the women and refused to sign their pledge forsaking the sale of spirits. The druggist went as far as printing circulars and distributing them around town forbidding the women from demonstrating near his store. Undaunted, the moral crusaders defied the druggist and resumed their prayers and protests. At this point the battle was carried into the courts, with the druggist seeking and receiving an injunction barring the women from his premises. As the case proceeded through the judicial system, the druggist won Pyrrhic victories only to be left bankrupt in the end.

No matter who was waging the war, the ammunition used by the crusaders was the same. Enlisting science and faith, the temperance movement fired volley after volley, taking careful aim at alcohol producers, promoters, and patrons. All arguments began with the clear conviction that alcohol was evil, a moral denunciation that by itself was not sufficiently persuasive. But when faith failed, science came to the rescue, and zealous scholars dramatized alcohol's influence on human physiology by concluding that it "is known to paralyze the nervous force, to derange the circulation of the blood, dominate the muscular power, disintegrate the vital organs, drive the heart like a slave ... dethrone reason and turn loose the faculties, emotions and passions."[47]

For every argument supporting its use, the alcohol abolitionists had a forceful counter. Members of the temperance movement dismissed propositions proclaiming alcohol's value as a food, medicine, or vital restorative by pointing out what they believed was the inexorable link to a life of crime and poverty. Only national prohibition, usurping the individual's choice and ultimate access, could cure the affliction.

Not everyone applauded the efforts of the alcohol abolitionists; opponents often pointed out examples of the movement's hypocrisy, challenging their distortions of medical science or accusing them of stretching believability beyond the breaking point. One example of those who strained the boundaries of credulity was S.M. Hewlett, a lecturer who harangued a willing but small audience at the Brooklyn Tabernacle.

Despite blanketing the local area with circulars, Hewlett was probably disappointed by the meager attendance, but without displaying any outward signs of frustration he immediately launched into the night's lecture. The best speakers mixed education and entertainment, hoping to sway their audiences while at the same time earning a reputation that would lead to future speaking engagements. Hewlett did the same, but his unsubstantiated accusations of military intemperance came across as shrill and self-serving.

Hewlett's long lecture dwelled on rum and the rebellion, with dramatic insinuations casting aspersions on battles lost and officers relieved of duty. With nothing more than the force of his words, Hewlett faced the audience and "asked how 175 officers from Farragut's fleet at New Orleans were sent home without wounds, and for no other cause than excessive imbibition. He also boldly charged that the terrible disaster of Bull's Bluff was caused by one bottle of corn whiskey." As he droned on, a reporter attending the lecture rationalized that Hewlett "carries you pleasantly along in an oarless boat upon a waveless surface."[48] As such, it was an entertaining evening that went nowhere.

Hewlett escaped with a mild poetic rebuke, but others were not so fortunate. In a withering broadside a newspaper editorial excoriated "certain misguided women [who] are seizing upon the anti-liquor excitement to win a measure of inglorious notoriety, and Dr. Dio Lewis and other unregenerate reformers are peddling enthusiasm at the rate of $50 a night."[49] Lewis was a well-known social reformer who encouraged young girls to pursue physical fitness, healthy nutrition, and a temperate lifestyle, all of which found favor with members of the Woman's Christian Temperance Union.[50] Where many reformers seemed to eschew any semblance of profiteering, Lewis bucked the trend "and is said to have accumulated a fortune."[51]

One of the principal points of debate among doctors in the early 1860s focused on whether alcohol was a food or a poison.[52] From the pages of *The Lancet*, a highly respected medical journal, spirited arguments laced with equal portions of physiology and philosophy tilted toward alcohol's role as a normal part of the human diet. Even those doctors who defined alcohol as a poison were forced to admit that its rapid absorption and physical stimulation could prove lifesaving.

It was an accepted fact at the time that alcohol's main effects were on the nervous system, readily obvious from its capacity to produce fatigue-fighting exhilaration, mental dissociation, sedation, depression, tremor, unsteady gait, and, in the worst cases, seizures. Another truism of the time accepted the notion that all mental and nervous action physically depleted the nerve cells, and only nourishment and rest repaired and rejuvenated the worn-out cells.

For the weary soldier, a cup of beer or a glass of sherry provided an invigorating reprieve. No one denied that alcohol caused such a salutary effect, but definite differences arose regarding the reason. The minority view held that alcohol "does not, restore nervous matter, but that it only stimulates the wasted and jaded brain and nerves to further efforts ... it acts upon them as the whip or spur does upon the jaded horse, making it work at the expense of still further wear and tear."

The majority of doctors considered alcohol an important nutritional supplement that did indeed restore and revitalize brain tissue exhausted by every thought and emotion that the organ generated. What confused the naysayers was a failure to understand that alcohol "is one of that large class of agents whose influence varies ... according to the quantity administered ... so that the effects of a large dose will be ... of a totally different character." By not taking the dose into account, the teetotalers made a fundamental mistake that condemned moderate consumption and its benefits.

The debate continued in the medical journals, with partisans staking out increasingly rigid positions in favor of or opposed to alcohol's status as a food.

It was more than an esoteric discussion, and many interested groups sought shelter from their critics through the cover that science offered. If alcohol was proclaimed a nutrient, it would leave the alcohol abolitionists in the untenable position of acknowledging moderation and abandoning prohibition.

In the politest rebuke possible, a reader in *The Lancet* took issue with any characterization of alcohol as a food product.[53] Struggling mightily to sustain a coherent argument, the letter writer sought to convince readers that alcohol was not a food. Among the reasons cited was alcohol's inability to satiate the appetite, giving way to the common observation that inebriates seemed to lose all control over consumption, which, according to the writer, differed from food, which did not lend itself to such excesses: "There is a limit to the quantity of beef, bread, etc., as well as of jam tarts, which we can consume." The journal readers were probably mystified by this comparison, most likely having seen obese individuals lacking such limits.

The tit-for-tat battle was carried on in *The Lancet* a year later, in 1862, when a physician once again raised the question of whether alcohol was food.[54] In this case, the author was decidedly in favor of classifying alcohol as a nutrient, premised in part on his observation that teetotalers exchanged alcohol consumption for other foods. With a nod to Aristotle, the author resorted to a syllogism to drive his point home: "if a glass of ale was equal to a slice of mutton in its satisfying effect, and the mutton was food, it must follow that ale is food." The writer bolstered his claim by noting that alcohol relieves hunger and by itself can sustain life for extended periods of time.

Three years later Dr. Edward Smith, writing in *The Lancet*, took the pulse of the medical profession and concluded "that the physician possesses no more powerful or valuable agent when administered in fitting doses."[55] Smith recommended alcohol based on its ability to physiologically stimulate the body's organs, with particular emphasis on strengthening the muscular activity of the heart.

The ink was hardly dry on Smith's article before Francis Anstie published a stinging rebuttal in *The Lancet*, accusing the former writer of grossly misrepresenting the scientific evidence and audaciously asserting a position for the profession.[56] Anstie's complaint was twofold, first objecting to Smith's sloppy scientific analysis, and then rebuking his accusation that medicinal alcohol was misused. Subtracting both doctors' mutual antagonism actually left little disagreement between the pair, since neither advocated abstinence.

While the debate about alcohol's nutritional role raged on, another battle was brewing between competing theories of alcoholism, with a medical model quietly challenging the moral view. In the late nineteenth century drunkenness was condemned as a personal failure resulting from a lack of self-control, weak religious conviction, and willful capitulation to a hedonistic life. Moralists maintained that no one was forced to drink alcohol, and the only hope of escape for those caught in the web of chronic inebriation lay in abstinence, a course of action entirely contingent on the person's choice.

The moral model of alcoholism melded well with the dogmatic and combative stance of the temperance movement. For groups such as the Sons of Temperance and the Woman's Christian Temperance Union, the descent to drunkenness was thought to be the result of a person's choices, albeit poor ones. With a sort of circular reasoning, the alcohol abolitionists could point to their members' voluntary sobriety pledges, along with temperance speakers packing auditoriums with adoring audiences, patronizing politicians and weak-kneed saloon keepers, as evidence of their persuasive success. What they failed to change was the real rate of alcoholism, an inconvenient and ignored reality.

While members of the temperance movements were praying and plotting for prohibition and congratulating their collective efforts in closing saloons, the real problem continued unabated. The seemingly obsessive pursuit of alcohol increasingly attracted the attention of psychologically minded doctors. Aiding these doctors' study was the explosion of insane asylums built in America in the latter half of the nineteenth century, which became warehouses for the mentally ill, resembling in outward appearances great industrial factories producing social control, treatment, and research.

The mindless consumption of alcohol at the expense of everything a person held near and dear had all the hallmarks of an irresistible impulse, which was an essential component of a controversial concept called moral insanity.[57] Moral insanity admitted all manner of vices to be reclassified as a special type of insanity, with each behavior having in common the apparent inability to control its expression. A dispassionate description of those suffering from the disorder noted "that their moral sentiments being perverted, and having no longer to control them, they abandon themselves without reserve to all their impulses, and pay no regard to custom, nor decency, nor forms of society."

As might well be imagined, advocates of moral insanity ran headlong into the conventional thinking of the time, which considered such behaviors as public lewdness, fire setting, shoplifting, and drunkenness volitional acts subject to criminal prosecution, not treatment in an insane asylum. Even among the insane asylum superintendents as the trend setters for the mental health profession, there were vitriolic debates about moral insanity and labels such as erotomania, pyromania, kleptomania, and dipsomania, which shielded bad behavior from its expected social consequences. Despite the disagreements, these diagnoses began to fill and slowly swell the insane asylums. In one telling example, the superintendent of the Kings County Lunatic Asylum located in

Flatbush, New York, reported that inebriation was the leading cause of insanity.[58]

A conservative estimate placed the number of alcohol-related admissions to America's insane asylums at ten percent in 1862, with the caveat "that the actual number greatly exceeds this proportion can not be doubted."[59] However, yoking inebriety with an irresistible impulse to drink alcohol did not deter the critics of moral insanity. As they rightly pointed out, it was a fool's errand to figure out when the impulse became irresistible—after the first drink, after many months, or maybe even after years?

While the asylum superintendents were tying themselves in knots trying to unravel the relationship between alcohol and insanity, the number of hospital admissions continued to climb. Although never stated so bluntly, the superintendents were dependent on the public coffers and good will of politicians to maintain their growing empires, and treating victims of intemperance was not popular. Among the latter was "a class of young inebriates found in asylums. Some of these have never known and felt the wholesome, restraining influence of home life.... They become passionate, profane, licentious ... and dangerous."

One of the crowning achievements of the temperance movement was the creation of the short-lived and problem-plagued New York State Inebriate Asylum in Binghamton, New York.[60] Through the unflagging determination of Dr. J. Edward Turner, a multiyear fundraising effort succeeded in building an imposing gothic structure devoted to the care of inebriates. In 1864 the partially constructed asylum opened its doors and began admitting patients. Turner was a strict disciplinarian and extended this approach to the treatment of his patients. With military-style approaches permeating the program, patients were expected to remain at the asylum for a year, confined at night and closely monitored throughout the day as they engaged in Turkish baths and various sports. Family and friends bitterly attacked the prison-like restraints, eventually forcing reforms that allowed patients more liberal movement. Turner was eventually made to resign as superintendent following contentious and chronic battles with the asylum's trustees.

Patients and their families rejoiced at the newfound freedom espoused by Dr. Albert Day, who replaced Turner as superintendent in 1867. The new superintendent's less restrictive program helped propel the asylum's popularity, and by 1869 its census counted 230 patients. The program continued to grow, reaching its highest number of 334 patients in 1872. A mere six years later, following a string of superintendents and ongoing controversies, the population had dwindled to 39 patients, prompting New York's governor to declare the asylum a disastrous failure.[61]

There were several reasons for the asylum's failure. Squabbling among the various stakeholders over financing and treatment philosophies led to fragmented leadership. Members of the public still clung to sentiments that "to tell the drunkard that he is unfortunate rather than criminal, is to promote drunkenness by making it less disreputable" and were probably disgruntled by the "ample, comfortable, even sumptuous appointments."[62]

Perhaps the greatest cause for concern was the unpredictable and, at times, dangerous behavior of the asylum patients.[63] Affording the patients more freedom of movement struck a compassionate note but left the citizens of Binghamton exposed to endless drunken escapades, leading to fines, incarceration, and a growing distrust of the asylum. Suicides and assaults, including an attack on the hapless Dr. Day, surely jarred the local people's nerves. All this led to a growing sense that inebriates were far sicker—in fact, insane—and needed the structure and greater control that an insane asylum provided.

The debate about alcohol entered a new phase when doctors diagnosed dipsomania, a medical diagnosis that equated the excesses of inebriation with insanity.[64] Dipsomania was a befuddling term, but it was tailor made for excusing criminal behavior, and soon the enabling diagnosis became a favorite of defendants. Even though some doctors supported the diagnosis, concerns about misuse of dipsomania as a legal defense eventually led to its demise.

Alcohol was often implicated in criminal misconduct, but unraveling its influence was even more twisted if the defendant had a history of preexisting insanity. Merely excusing any crime committed under the influence of alcohol would totally subvert the moral basis of the law, but the elastic definition of dipsomania came perilously close to doing just that. In an effort to ostensibly help jury members wade through the evidence and lawyers' arguments, Andrew McFarland, the superintendent at the Illinois State Asylum for the Insane, proposed that judges issue a mind-numbing set of instructions: "Care should be taken not [to] confound passions excited by liquor with those which are the natural effects of insanity. For if insanity existed, but would not have manifested itself ... if it had not been stimulated by ... liquor, then the act is not excusable on the ground of insanity. But if the jury can reconcile the evidence tending to prove drunkenness, with a conviction ... from the evidence that the act was one of insanity ... it is their duty ... to acquit."[65]

As a type of insanity, a diagnosis of dipsomania meant that individuals could expect treatment, not punishment. Its insidious onset and invidious course made it particularly challenging to treat, as the usual prescriptions of nutrition, exercise, and moral instruction left the cravings for liquor untouched. Creative merchants of medicines seized the opportunity and were soon promoting various bottled dipsomania treatments.

The cinchona rubra cure was the invention of Dr. Robert D'Unger, a formula guaranteed to eliminate dipsomania. Testimonials from satisfied customers around the country agreed with an anonymous user in Sacramento, California, who proclaimed that "it very quickly eradicated the effects of over-potations, removed the desire for strong drink, and left me completely master of myself in this regard. It did not create any repugnance to the taste of liquor, but simply left me indifferent to it."[66]

Robert D'Unger received his medical degree from the Eclectic Medical College in Philadelphia in 1859, after which he returned to Maryland. At the time D'Unger was more interested in politics than medicine, and at the outbreak of the Civil War his southern sympathies, and the hostile reaction they provoked, forced the young physician to flee to Europe. Toward the end of the war he returned to Maryland and resumed his medical career.[67]

Sometime during this period D'Unger reportedly stumbled upon the cure for dipsomania through a chance encounter. A chronic alcoholic by the name of Bill Stevens sought the services of Dr. D'Unger for a troubling fever. It was a difficult case, and more out of desperation than inspiration, D'Unger prescribed Peruvian red bark instead of the more typical remedy of quinine. The doctor's tonic proved successful in quelling the fever, but it also curiously eliminated Stevens' desire to drink.[68]

Joseph Medill, the editor of the *Chicago Tribune*, actively promoted the cinchona rubra cure and published a fawning interview with the doctor.[69] According to D'Unger, in his first year in Chicago he cured 963 cases of dipsomania. In fourteen cases a relapse occurred, which the doctor attributed to the patients not taking the medicine as prescribed. The interview also offered D'Unger the opportunity to address his critics, the harshest being a chemist who had analyzed the doctor's dipsomania cure and claimed that it "contained 22 to 24 per cent of absolute alcohol, the rest of the mixture being water with a trace of some bitter alkaloid." Naturally, D'Unger disputed these results and trusted that the public would instead accept the thousands of testimonials from those who claimed the cinchona rubra cure was effective.

Dipsomania was a contentious diagnosis. A scathing newspaper editorial sarcastically observed that "formerly most persons looked with contempt and indignation upon the man who squandered his money in drink … we now know that such a man is not deserving of the slightest blame, but rather deserves our earnest sympathy … the drunkard is merely suffering from a disease more painful than small-pox or cholera."[70]

Influential doctors also disagreed with the diagnosis. John Ordronaux, a Civil War army surgeon and prolific author on medical legal issues, filled reams of paper with medical and philosophical arguments contending that "the problem of self-abasement or self-redemption is entirely within [the patient's] control."[71] Ordronaux considered both the malady and the cure a result of a person's voluntary restraint.

Ordronaux's views were by no means radical in the nineteenth century, but a trend toward the medicalization of chronic inebriation was still taking root. The seeds were sown by doctors fertilizing morality with physical rejuvenation. According to N.S. Davis, a physician at the Washingtonian Home of Chicago, "one of the largest and most important public asylums for the reform of inebriates in this country," there came a point when chronic consumption damaged the body's organs to such an extent that willpower was insufficient deterrence.[72] As the brain was perpetually bathed in alcohol, it, too, changed, leaving Davis and like-minded doctors convinced that the alcoholic's downward spiral, neglecting family, friends, and work, had all the hallmarks of insanity. Only a lengthy period of forced abstinence behind the walls of a benevolent asylum could alter the course of this condition. Asylum doctors encouraged healthy activity and proper nutrition to reverse alcohol's ravages.

During the Civil War and the decades that followed, alcohol was increasingly vilified as the chief culprit responsible for society's ills. Temperance groups sought prohibition and doctors demanded more asylums to treat the victims, while at the same time druggists flooded the country with tonics, clever lawyers argued for exculpation, military commanders rewarded troops with potent libations, and the federal government raked in revenues. Embryonic efforts substituting medical treatment for the moral denunciation of alcoholism took root slowly during the Civil War era, a humanizing trend that would replace condemnation with compassion.

Five

Carnival of Crime

Both sides in the great conflict that divided the nation reconciled the accompanying death and destruction in terms of fighting a just war but were left aghast at the wanton wickedness that subsequently stalked society. Bitterness bred by battles lingered long after the war's end, and the victor's domination and the loser's defiance made for a rocky reunification. War had cheapened life by enshrining violence, with bullets ending debates and swords silencing opposition. Adding to the culture of cruelty was a festering, unrelenting intolerance boosting groups that harbored radical, racial, and religious prejudices. Making matters worse were privation and poverty, a legacy of the war that left many people disillusioned and disheartened, with some desperate souls sinking into thievery to survive. Largely missing in the postwar period were contemporary commentaries that connected the psychological traumas of war with the subsequent dystopia—not surprising given the embryonic interest in the individual's suffering.

Journalists started wringing their hands and shaking their heads as a tidal wave of violence flooded America almost immediately after the war ended. In terms of sheer brutality, few decades in American history could match the depths of depravity plumbed in the postwar period. Adding to the mayhem and misery were countless rapes, robberies, swindles, and slaughters, many of which were never solved, leaving perpetrators free, citizens frightened, and justice unrequited. Deepening despair accompanied a loss of faith in public institutions as police and politicians struggled to find solutions.

Less than eight months after Robert E. Lee surrendered and the battlefields lay quiet, any thoughts of peace and tranquility were dashed when voices of alarm declared that "it would really seem that the very Pandora's Box of crime had been opened in the land." From every part of the country a black plague of crime infected cities large and small, an epidemic that led to calls for extreme remedies such as vigilante justice. When the sun set and darkness fell, the dangers multiplied, and only the foolhardy or fully armed ventured forth. Making matters worse, "garroters and robbers hang about the corners and for every one that is arrested a dozen escape."[1]

With the war's end soldiers started streaming back home.[2] Union forces tried to cope with the massive demobilization in an orderly fashion by assigning troops to strategically located rendezvous points to serve the dual purpose of positioning those men for potential postwar reconstruction duties or sending them home. A number of factors conspired to undermine the Union Army's plans, including the slow bureaucratic process and the men's obvious goal of going home, all of which led to wholesale desertion. For the defeated forces in the Confederacy, the demobilization was not accompanied by any structure except an oath forswearing further hostilities against the now united country, a pledge that many ignored as they slowly returned home.

Peace was no antidote to virulent violence, with some of the best evidence coming from the dramatic postwar spike in crime. Arrests in New York were typical of the nation, with 12,592 in the three months beginning in February 1865, a period that witnessed the end of the Civil War. In the first three full months after this period, the alarmed citizens of New York must have reeled as a 60 percent surge in arrests brought the quarterly tally to 20,467. In a sense of charity that would dissipate over the coming months and years, the root cause of the violence was initially attributed to the "social demoralization caused by the war, the evils of which it will take centuries to eradicate."[3]

Drawing a direct line between the men returning home from the battle-fields and the crime spree that simultaneously sprang up cannot be explained by a simple linear relationship. The ensuing antisocial behaviors were simply too broad based, affecting as they did nearly every social segment, both genders, all ages, rich and poor alike. A better explanation might be that an already frac-tured society's pent-up passions, no longer focused on or distracted by the war, were increasingly expressed through brazen and brutal behaviors.

A reluctance to connect demobilization with crime might be inferred from sympathetic newspaper stories deciding that "these crimes have as yet in very few instances been traced to returned soldiers. They, poor fellows, seem, in a great many instances, to have found their wives not of the patient, Penelope type, if forty divorce suits, instituted in a single county by returned soldiers, mean anything."[4]

From the pulpit, pastors proclaimed that "the return to peace was accom-panied by evils of no small magnitude. Immorality, luxury, extravagance, spec-ulation, intemperance, and crime became so frequent and so violent that the periodicals ... referred to these conditions as the Carnival of Crime."[5] The phrase "carnival of crime" was not coined during the Civil War, but its near universal application in newspapers and magazines of the era as a colorful and somewhat sinister symbol enshrined the term for generations.

Although the southern states were not spared, the more populous northern states, flush with victory over their Confederate foes, seemed particularly vulnerable to the avalanche of law-breaking. A Vermont newspaper complained that "highway robberies are frequent; burglaries have become so alarming that in some parts of the country it is dangerous to walk the streets." The normally staid, bucolic state was fast losing faith in its police, prompting a call that "the people must take the matter into their own hands. Vigilance Committees throughout the country will be ... necessary if this carnival of crime should increase or continue."[6]

In some cases a particularly heinous act forced an investigation, as in the case of Martha Grinder, otherwise known as the Pittsburgh Poisoner. Early accounts of the nefarious deeds started trickling out in newspapers across the northeast with mention made of "the poisoning of seven persons by a Mrs. Grinder."[7]

Martha Grinder, her husband, and an infant daughter moved to the environs of Pittsburgh around 1859, creating no particular interest at first, as their poverty blended well with the neighborhood.[8] Eyebrows were first raised a few months after their arrival when the family shed the trappings of poverty, moving into a more spacious home, dressing fashionably, and socializing with members of higher society. Naturally curious, and perhaps suspicious, neighbors wondered about the transformation, but Martha Grinder had a ready explanation, claiming a wealthy relative had left her a sizeable sum. By itself this story may have satisfied the neighbors, but lingering doubts fused with other mysterious goings-on at the Grinders' home.

With the clarity of hindsight, a seemingly insignificant string of food poisonings eventually pointed toward malevolence. A multitude of victims, some of whom died and others who survived, seemed to have one thing in common—they all dined on Martha's food. Among the victims were Martha's next-door neighbor Mary Caruthers, a young servant girl, and two soldiers who were her husband's brothers.[9]

Among the better documented allegations for which Martha Grinder was never charged was the death of Jane R. Buchanan, a young housemaid employed in a nearby home.[10] After four years of steady work, Jane apparently left her Pittsburgh job with the intention of joining a family member in Philadelphia. In preparing for the journey, Jane packed her small cache of possessions, mostly clothes, in a trunk and withdrew about forty dollars from the bank. For unknown reasons, Jane delayed her trip and, in a fatal decision, accepted a position in the Grinder family home on February 24, 1864.

Jane's first night in the Grinder home was miserable, as she suddenly fell ill, beset by violent vomiting and spasms of pain. Over the next few days her condition worsened until the formerly healthy girl died on February 28, 1864, at which time Mrs. Grinder notified Jane's former employer. As news of the death spread and arrangements were being made for the funeral, suspicion once again swirled around Martha when Jane's trunk was opened. It was nearly empty, the clothing, jewelry, and money all missing. In an apparent act of charity Martha reached into her own closet, clothing the young girl's lifeless body for the last time.

Martha's ostensible benevolence did not douse calls for an investigation. A coroner's jury was hastily convened to investigate the death, but an autopsy was not performed and Mrs. Grinder was surely instrumental in helping the jury conclude that Jane died from natural causes. No doubt emboldened by her performance, Martha set her sights elsewhere.

Martha Grinder's fate was sealed with the death of her neighbor, Mary C. Caruthers. Mary was "a young woman—a bride, just commencing a happy life under the most genial circumstances; beautiful to such a degree that she caused … universal admiration."[11] She was by no means rich, but what apparently attracted Martha's attention and ultimately led to her prosecution for murder "was that the deceased (Mrs. CARUTHERS) had been authorized by her father to purchase some property, a fact well known to the defendant, from her intimacy with the family."[12]

During Martha's weeklong trial the revelations shocked the nation as newspapers trumpeted the courtroom drama. Publicity prior to the trial complicated the jury selection, with many potential members already convinced that the accused poisoner was guilty.

Mary Caruthers died on the first day of August 1865, after an illness marked by "vomiting, purging, affection in her throat, burning sensation in the stomach, pain in the breast, and dizziness," which suddenly overtook the young woman on June 27, 1865. During the weeklong trial the prosecutor implicated Mrs. Grinder by noting that all members of the Caruthers family initially took ill in a similar manner when they consumed their neighbor's food. As Mary's plight worsened, Mrs. Grinder became a steady attendant, ostensibly offering daily comfort to the ailing woman. After examining Mary, a physician, no doubt mystified but surely alarmed, urged the family to temporarily vacate their house and retreat to the healthy countryside. This advice was adopted, and their brief sojourn in the country restored Mary's health.

Welcoming Mary home was Martha Grinder, laden was beneficence and poisoned food. Once again Mary fell desperately ill, experiencing the same symptoms as before. Her downward drift toward death brought a worried mother to her bedside, who also fell ill after eating Martha's food. The distraught and sickened mother could do little but watch as her daughter finally died. Mary was laid to rest a short time later, but her body was exhumed on August 30, 1865, after which an autopsy revealed copious quantities of arsenic and antimony.

Mrs. Grinder was only charged with the murder of Mary Caruthers even though the prosecutor presented evidence implicating her in other poisonings. Particular mention was made of "evidence showing that Mrs. Grinder had poisoned the family of Marguerite Smith ... by a bowl of soup ... all who eat were immediately taken sick—one, a child dying."[13]

A number of factors made Martha Grinder's crimes sensational. As a female serial killer, Grinder was certainly unique, but her selfish, ruthless, and emotionless pursuit of poisoning for profit was also shocking. Even for a country just removed from all the horrors of war and seemingly immune to trauma, Grinder still proved upsetting. Her victims were young women and probably children, heartlessly killed by the "American Borgia."

Throughout her trial Martha Grinder remained distant, detached, and disinterested, all of which added to her mystique. At the conclusion of the evidentiary phase of the trial, the jury retired to decide her fate. Hours passed without a decision, and it was not until the next day that Mrs. Grinder stood before the judge and jury to receive, with her trademark stoicism, a guilty verdict. Even when the sentence (death by hanging) was announced, not a flicker of emotion could be seen on the woman's face as she resolutely strode from the courtroom protesting "her innocence, and say[ing] she is the victim of a conspiracy."

The prospect of hanging a woman, coupled with her odd demeanor, provided an opportunity to throw the convicted woman a final lifeline, and so a sanity commission was hastily assembled to examine Mrs. Grinder. Popular sentiment favored labeling her a homicidal monomaniac, a condition that, if established by the sanity commission, would spare her the hangman's noose. Three physicians agreed to examine Mrs. Grinder and, along with the district attorney, made a surreptitious visit to the convicted woman's jail cell. At no time did any member of the commission explain the real purpose for their visit, instead opting for subterfuge, during which the doctors conducted a two-hour interrogation. Mrs. Grinder was open and honest throughout the ordeal, and for her efforts she was pronounced sane by the doctors. "The unhappy woman was purposely kept in ignorance of the object for which the commission visited ... when they informed her who they were, the purpose of the visit, and the conclusion ... she was much affected ... and wept bitterly."

About 100 spectators were assembled around the Pittsburgh courthouse awaiting the arrival of the convicted woman on the afternoon of Friday, January 19, 1866.[14] As the solemn procession wound its way toward the scaffold, a reporter described the scene: "Mrs. Grinder was dressed in a brown alpaca dress, trimmed around the neck and down the front with white lace, lightly made kid slippers, and white stockings. She took a seat provided for her on the scaffold, and remained entirely unmoved." She even smiled at the crowd.

Not a word was uttered as the noose was placed around her neck. An instant later the trap opened and Martha fell through the opening. To the horror of the onlookers, the hangman's noose malfunctioned, leaving her struggling violently for upward of twenty minutes before death intervened. In a final bit of drama, the dead woman's "face wore exactly the same placid, cheerful, smiling expression which characterized it on the scaffold," totally unnerving the spectators.

Mrs. Grinder did not escape the consequences of her poisonings, which may have claimed as many as seven victims and an untold number who survived, even though she ultimately was held accountable for only one. This proved to be the exception as the carnival of crime rolled across the country, overwhelming local police and leaving in its wake a public frustrated by lawlessness. Adding to the exasperation was a growing sense that, even when arrested, a criminal could sidestep justice through a combination of fainthearted, compassionate jurors, unscrupulous lawyers, and medical experts subsuming all manner of deviant behavior under the banner of insanity.

Sometimes the lax legal process led to a comical outcome—amusing, perhaps, but still reinforcing the public's growing lack of faith. One such example took place in Washington, D.C., when a man was hauled into court charged with horse stealing.[15] After the incriminating evidence was presented, the jury left the courtroom as usual. While discussing the defendant's destiny, a loud auction bell interrupted their deliberations, and, recognizing the signal as the start of a bank sale, everyone, including the prisoner, hastened forth. The horse thief made his escape, never to be heard from again.

It seemed that no sector of the nation was spared the twin torments of lawlessness and police inaction. In Cleveland, Ohio, just two years after the Civil War, "rowdies and highway robbers, of the lowest order, are on the increase in our city, fearfully ominous of a high carnival of crime."[16] No street seemed safe, particularly when the darkness of night cloaked the crimes. In the mildest examples an unsuspecting person strolling a major downtown avenue would be knocked insensible and everything of value stolen an instant later. Adding insult to injury were the police, who seemed "to allow the thieves ... to hold a carnival of crime."

Persuasive pundits occasionally drew a straight line between the carnage of war and the burgeoning crime wave. In an article written by an anonymous reporter, a Memphis, Tennessee, newspaper blamed the burst of crime on the human "spirit that, having once been drunken on blood, reels still from the fumes of the long debauch." The reporter's exhortation was grounded in a belief that the air could only be cleared from the pulpit, with clergymen collectively condemning the corruption caused by the conflict and at the same time proclaiming the virtues of a moral life.[17]

Despite the public's faltering faith in government authorities' ability to curb the crime wave, prisons were besieged by an avalanche of new inmates. One of America's oldest and most respected prisons, Eastern State Penitentiary, located in Philadelphia, Pennsylvania, opened for business in 1829 sporting radical prison architecture that supported a philosophy favoring reform over punishment.[18] During the first year of operation the prison housed nine inmates. Throughout the first full year of the Civil War in 1861, the prison admitted 181 new inmates; that number rose to 257 by the end of the armed conflict in 1865. At the end of the decade in 1870, the prison walls were full to bursting when an additional 315 inmates were added.

Informed onlookers in the press touted the rapid rate of incarceration as further confirmation of a carnival of crime.[19] It was just two years after the Civil War, in 1867, that a Philadelphia judge surveying the scene from the bench commented that "for the first time in its history, the Eastern penitentiary is so crowded that it has become necessary to place two prisoners in some of the cells." From its inception Eastern State Penitentiary prided itself on a reformed, modern, more humane treatment of the inmates, which included solitary cells. The overcrowded conditions surely struck a blow to the pride of the facility in having to abandon one of its core principles.

Not surprisingly, lingering animosity between the victorious northern states and their defeated rivals in the south colored the news presented to readers. A Nashville newspaper could scarcely contain its contempt when gloating about the crime wave: "This increase is perhaps the more remarkable because of the boasted higher civilization of that section of the country."[20] The Nashville newspaper bolstered its argument by presenting statistics gathered and reported by a Massachusetts newspaper, drily noting that the Massachusetts State Prison in 1868 had "the largest average numbers ever known," mirroring a trend seen at other detention facilities.

Adding to the misery accompanying the mayhem was a creeping nihilism, a growing futility cultivated by a sense of helplessness. Lengthy prison terms, public executions, passionate pleas from the pulpit, and posturing politicians did not dent the depravity. After bemoaning the fact that "murders of the most horrible description, robberies, outrages and suicides are of daily occurrence," an anonymous reporter figuratively threw his hands in the air in exasperation, wondering "what is there to account for the lapse into barbarity?"[21]

In St. Louis, Missouri, just one year after the war ended, the carnival of crime descended.[22] November alone counted twenty murders, with lesser crimes even more common. Concerned citizens variously prodded and lampooned the police, who finally responded by cracking down "upon some three hundred dens of infamy." No doubt expecting the police action to be short lived and inconsequential, some leading citizens recommended licensing the bordellos, perhaps hoping to exert some control over the apparent chaos while at the same time generating city revenues.

As the prison populations soared, with seemingly no meaningful impact on the rampant crime wave, a closer scrutiny of the inmates revealed a disturbing trend: the vast majority of the newly incarcerated prisoners were former soldiers, part of the vast demobilization at the war's end. For the most part, the revelations connecting the military veterans with the burgeoning jail population was limited to annual reports prepared by prison officials. In some cases scholarly publications noted the findings and discussed their implications, but newspapers, the main portal to the public, seemed curiously uninterested.

Prison officials noted that the trickle that turned into a flood coincided almost perfectly with the war's end and the men's return home.[23] Throughout 1866, at least two-thirds of all inmates newly incarcerated in New England's many prisons were soldiers or sailors. Pennsylvania's Western Penitentiary reported 49 new inmates during the six-month period ending April 1, 1865, a figure that grew to 217 one year later. Roughly sixty percent of those 217 new inmates were veterans. A similar pattern unfolded at the Auburn, New York, prison, with 91 new inmates in the first time period and 440 a year later in 1866.

The spectacle of veterans, some of whom were hobbled by war wounds, languishing in America's jails provoked some predictable pleas. For the adamantly anti-war crowd who never reconciled the conflict with their pacifism, the filling of prisons with veterans was another affirmation of their philosophy. For others, it was the corruption of youth brought about through an immoral military lifestyle. Confirmation of this viewpoint was assured when casual conversations with the inmates left the interviewers concluding "that the moral hedge has been weakened by the army associations and practices; through the frailty of our common nature, and the want of moral courage, they have fallen." Thus some prison officials urged an increase in moral instruction to repair the damage and return rehabilitated soldiers to society.

Not everyone agreed with the kinder, gentler approach. Speaking from the bench, Judge Ludlow addressed members of the grand jury, castigating critics who publicly denounced harsh sentences given to convicted felons. Comparing his role to that of a ship's captain, buffeted by winds and seas threatening to overturn the vessel, Ludlow believed that only a stern hand could steady the ship: "I mean to punish crime, and I hope the passengers who sail with us will at least remain quiet while we direct the course of the ship through the storm."[24]

Legions of followers surely nodded in silent approval on reading Ludlow's thundering remarks. Perhaps not surprisingly, the Massachusetts Board of State Charities took a different view of the situation.[25] While bowing to the realities of a significant increase in soldiers and sailors populating Massachusetts jails, which had doubled from 14.5 percent in the six months before the war ended to 28 percent in the six months following, the members of the board were not eager to blame military service for the change. In fact, the members reasoned that military service simply displaced crime from the streets of Massachusetts to the battlefields and camps where the men were stationed. Although they had no evidence supporting this conclusion, it did clear the path to assert their conviction that crime was universally the result of "poverty, indolence, want of moral training," all of which coincidentally meshed with the Massachusetts Board of State Charities' charter. A year later, the board revisited the issue and, while still recognizing the influx of veterans, conceded that "the majority had been good soldiers and several of them bear honorable wounds."[26]

Tracing the crime wave to the psychologically traumatic consequences of war, although less common than citing moral corruption, was sometimes discussed. Even then, however, it was generally a footnote to a broader discussion, such as when Andrew J. Palm roundly rebuked the lack of humane prison practices in America.[27] Palm wrote that "the country passed through the demoralizing influences of a civil war, and war is a school for crime that turns out its graduates with unfailing certainty." After swerving ever so briefly into the emotional lane, Palm returned to an impassioned plea arguing against punitive prison practices based on their historical failure in deterring crime.

Another discernable trend was the rate of female incarcerations. During the war years of 1861–1865, most prisons had a precipitous decline in their overall population, in the midst of which the number of female prisoners greatly increased.[28] A physician at the Indiana State Prison made a similar observation just before the war began, highlighting the rise in female offenders that would fall just as dramatically when the war was over.[29]

Female felons always seemed to incite a great deal of curiosity, defying as they did the fanciful and romantic notions of nineteenth-century femininity. Just as the increase in female offenders during the Civil War attracted interest, so did any foul deed committed by a woman. Such was the case with Bridget Durgan, charged with the brutal murder of Mary Ellen Coriell in 1867, the wife of a prominent physician in Newmarket, New Jersey.[30] Among the many factors that made the crime a national sensation, aside from the alleged female perpetrator, was the utterly stark contrast that newspaper reporters drew between the common, coarse, and disagreeable features of Bridget and the victim's beauty, compassion, and social position.

Mrs. Coriell was murdered on a cold, blustery night on February 25, 1867. Two days later the public's first knowledge of the dreadful deed was reported with mostly suppositions and suspicions. According to Bridget, a young Irish servant girl who lived with the doctor, his wife and their two-year-old daughter, the night's tragedy began when two strangers inquired about the doctor's whereabouts. Learning that the doctor was not at home, the two strangers left without stating their purpose. Doctor Coriell returned later in the evening, ate a hasty dinner, and then was off again to attend to a neighbor's illness. As he bid his wife good night around 10 p.m., he predicted that his business would most likely force him to spend the night at his patient's home.

Mrs. Coriell, resigned to her husband's absence, retired for the night. Bridget later claimed she heard noises from her employer's room and, suspecting prowlers, was making her way stealthily to investigate when gunshots broke the night's quiet. Acting with a surprising presence of mind, the young servant girl scooped up the couple's baby and fled the house, making her way to a nearby home. Once the alarm was raised, Bridget breathlessly declared that two men had entered the house and murdered Mrs. Coriell. The news spread quickly throughout the small community, and almost immediately a group made its way to the Coriell home. Upon entering the house, dense smoke coming from the bedroom made it almost impossible to see anything, leading one man to crawl about on the floor, his efforts gruesomely rewarded with the discovery of Mrs. Coriell's dead body.

Almost from the outset suspicions swirled around Bridget, in part driven by the inconsistencies in her story that would develop over time, but stemming more from the results of the autopsy. Mrs. Coriell was battered and hacked to death, suffering at least ten distinct knife wounds and a severe bite injury to the neck. It was the latter that led to Bridget's arrest, after the doctor who performed the autopsy matched the neck wound on the victim to the servant girl's teeth.

Bridget Durgan was indicted for the murder of Mrs. Coriell on May 20, 1867, with Charles M. Herbert, the district attorney, solemnly advising the jury "that this was no common case of homicide.... A lovely woman, adorned with all the virtues of a wife and mother, in her own house is butchered by a fiend." As the jury members looked across the room, they presumably agreed with the contrasting vision created by the defendant, described by a reporter as "an ordinary looking Irish girl, with plain features, that are not very expressive. She was plainly clad."[31]

One of the first witnesses called by the prosecution was William Coriell, the husband of the murdered woman. Everyone in the packed courtroom surely listened attentively and sympathetically as Coriell fondly reminisced about his petite, 31-year-old wife, who "weighed about one hundred and ten pounds; was slender, and about five feet four inches in stature." Nine years of marriage, punctuated by the doctor's service in the Civil War, came to an abrupt end with his wife's tragic death.

Coriell's testimony recalled Bridget's arrival on October 22, 1866, and her pending dismissal, but before expanding on that subject he was silenced by the defense counsel's objection. After resuming his testimony, what followed was a tedious description of the house, including where valuables were located, and finally Coriell's close questioning of the defendant. Over the course of several interviews with Coriell, Bridget's inconsistencies, hesitations, and confusion emboldened the doctor, who pointedly asked the woman if she had murdered his wife. Bridget was silent for a moment, no doubt pondering the gravity of her answer, before declaring her innocence but at the same time mysteriously suggesting that she knew more.

Coriell continued to press Bridget over the course of the next several days. At one point, the servant girl seemed to capitulate by declaring that a man named Hunt and another known as Barney Doyle were the culprits, but despite prying further, Coriell could get no more from her. A day later, with no prodding, Bridget accused a girl named Ann Linen, known to Doyle and Hunt, as the real perpetrator. It was not a particularly convincing story, lacking as it did any motive for the murder.

Garnett B. Adrian and William H. Leupp, two experienced attorneys, represented the poor Irish girl at no cost, listening, objecting, and interrogating witnesses as the prosecution ground through the first six days of the trial. Nathan Vars, the local justice of the peace, had presided over the coroner's inquest and was now a central witness in the prosecution's case. Vars had been quite thorough, and much of the evidence unearthed during the inquest surfaced again at the criminal trial. Witnesses testified regarding Bridget's reluctance to have her teeth examined and the force required to obtain a wax impression, her inability to recognize Doyle and Hunt in the courtroom, and her direct accusation of Ann Linen, who fainted in response, leaving Bridget visibly smirking.[32]

Some of the more inflammatory testimony came from another servant girl, Mary Gilroy, who worked at a nearby house in Newmarket. Mary knew the defendant from previous casual conversations and in fact had been invited by Bridget to the doctor's house on the night of the murder. Later that night, Mary, feeling sick, had retired early and was tossing and turning, trying to fall asleep, when she vaguely heard a noise from the nearby house: "I heard Mrs. Coriell say to spare her life for the baby's sake: this I heard before the words 'Keep away from me.'"

The alarming words drifting across the street produced no anxiety or concern, as Mary ignored the threat, rolled over, and went to sleep. A short time later, Mary was awakened again, this time by frantic neighbors desperately dousing the flames from the doctor's house. Once again, most curiously, the nonplussed girl briefly watched the drama and went back to sleep. In the coming days her testimony would come back to haunt her.

In due course the trio whom Bridget had accused—Barney Doyle, Michael Hunt, and Ann Linen—all testified, protesting their innocence and establishing convincing alibis. As might be expected in such a small community, everyone seemed to know each other. Ann and Michael had a romantic relationship, Barney knew the doctor, and Mary hovered around them all. As a material witness and suspect, Ann was dejectedly languishing in jail, an injustice made worse by Mary joining forces with Bridget in a very public defamation denouncing Ann as the chief culprit. No doubt believing they were ending with a dramatic flourish, the prosecutors concluded their case with Mary's testimony.

It was now Mr. Adrian's turn to address the jury, and he began by pointing out an inescapable flaw in the prosecution's case—at no time during six days of evidence and scores of witnesses was a motive for the crime produced. With that bombshell now exploded, Adrian began calling forth witnesses, presumably assembled to burnish the young girl's image. While many did so, several witnesses confounded the picture by painting a less flattering portrait of a girl given to petty thefts and sullenly grumbling and grieving alleged affronts.

One of the more interesting revelations was Bridget's history of having fits, attended to on many occasions by Doctor Coriell, during which "she was stiff as a board and unconscious; her eyes seemed affected; blood would come out of her mouth." As would later become evident, Bridget attached a good deal of importance to the doctor's comforting, compassionate ministrations.

In summing up the case against Bridget, Mr. Leupp turned to the jury and began a long monologue carefully dissecting the prosecution's case.[33] In reviewing the graphic nature of the crime, the attorney reminded the jury members that Mrs. Coriell's body was found with her blouse partially opened and bruises on her arms and legs, darkly suggesting that she was "violated," supporting Bridget's claim of two male robbers. Leupp also scrutinized the timeline, believing it impossible for his client to have uttered the words heard by a neighbor more than 100 feet away, savagely kill Mrs. Coriell, dispose of her own blood-drenched garments, redress in fresh clothes, torch the bedroom, fetch the couple's young daughter and alarm the nearby neighbors of the murder all in the calculated space of ten minutes. Leupp dismissed the prosecution's contention that the wax imprint forcibly taken from Bridget was consequential, commenting that no witness had conclusively proved the connection.

According to her defense attorney, Bridget was "a weak, uncultivated girl—an innocent, taciturn, retiring, modest girl" besieged by accusers exercising their prejudices. At no time did Bridget attempt to flee, nor were any blood-soaked clothes of hers found; it was also doubtful whether she had the strength necessary to carry out the bludgeoning of the victim. Bridget was firmly fastened in a web of conjecture.

Speaking for the prosecution, George M. Robeson summed up the case against Bridget Durgan, recognizing while doing so the inferential evidence but reassuring the jury "that almost all evidence was circumstantial, more or less, differing only in degree."[34] In a tit-for-tat exchange with the defense counsel, Robeson refuted every statement made by Leupp even while acknowledging that "there were circumstances surrounding this case that perhaps seemed to indicate that other persons besides the prisoner were engaged in the murder. He [k]new not. It mattered not." At the conclusion of Robeson's lengthy monologue, a raucous round of applause shook the courtroom.

After a noon recess Judge Vredenburgh returned to a packed courtroom and, taking center stage, proceeded to review the prosecution's case in detail; addressing what must have been a lingering doubt, he advised the jury members that "where circumstances existed it was as safe to convict on circumstances as on direct evidence." Following roughly two hours of instructions from the judge, the jury left the courtroom for deliberations, returned one hour later, and announced its verdict: guilty of first-degree murder.

Bridget was trundled off to jail immediately following her conviction, and in the following days she attracted many sympathizers.[35] As the visitors greeted the 22-year-old girl, they probably silently noted that "she is by no means attractive.... Her head is large, her forehead broad and low, her face full and not expressive ... she is of medium height and rather fleshy." Each came to see the notorious female murderer, still shrouded in mystery. Sitting in her sparse jail cell, Bridget freely told her story, still professing her innocence but now offering details that proved tantalizing. When asked if Mary Gilroy, locked up in a nearby jail cell with a dark cloud of suspicion hanging over her as a possible accomplice, was involved in the murder, Bridget smiled and coyly replied, "You all think Mary Gilroy had something to do with it, don't you?"

Members of a grand jury listened to several witnesses, including Mary

Gilroy, in an effort to determine the other woman's complicity.[36] Once again, stories shifted as witnesses who had previously testified during Bridget's trial offered conflicting evidence. Delia Coyne, who slept in the same bed with the suspect, added a new twist, recalling that "Mary called me when she heard the cry of fire; she was sitting up by the window … she asked me to come and raise the window … while we were at the window, Mary said, 'I think that Bridget has murdered Mrs. Coriell'; at that time it was not known." The 43-year-old Irish woman, twice married and living in America for 30 years, steadfastly proclaimed her innocence.

Bridget's day of reckoning was fast approaching, and on June 17, 1867, she stood before Judge Vredenburgh anxiously awaiting her sentence. Ominously, the judge recounted the evidence, denied a defense motion for a new trial and, after receiving no response from Bridget when she was asked for any final comments, gravely condemned her to be hanged. The shocked woman started "rocking herself to and fro and uttering screams that could be heard far beyond the Court-house. After some delay she was removed, still screaming."[37]

There were more surprises to follow. Now condemned to death, Bridget sat in her solitary cell consumed by thoughts of her fate, alternately crying and screaming, while at other times she appeared unconcerned, laughing and joking with her jailors. During her final days she exonerated Mary Gilroy, surely relieving that unfortunate woman from further suspicion. She also obliquely hinted at a full confession that had been entrusted to a close confidante, who would reveal the truth after her death.[38]

On the morning of her execution Bridget ate a hearty breakfast; visited briefly with Mary Gilroy, now vindicated and free; and, in the company of the sheriff and the Reverend Brendan, slowly ascended the gallows. Hundreds of onlookers crowded the scene, leering, sneering, and teasing the woman until it became clear to everyone that the fateful moment was at hand. As a hush descended over the audience, the sheriff quickly launched Bridget on her final journey.

Not too long after Bridget died, the Reverend Brendan, who had piously walked the path to the gallows with her, published her supposed confession. Readers who had closely followed the trial might have wondered why Bridget, despite endless entreaties and facing eternity, chose to wait until death to reveal her story. Another oddity was Bridget's written confession, allegedly penned by the woman and given to the Reverend Brendan with instructions to reveal its contents after her death. For an uneducated woman with a colorful Irish brogue, it was remarkably well written, an erudite and earnest exposé.

The Reverend Brendan wrote the preamble to the *Life, Crimes, and Confession of Bridget Durgan* with all the dramatic flourish that tabloid readers of any period would expect.[39] Despite being the closest confidante in Bridget's life, as evidenced in her decision to place the confession in his hands, the reverend believed that "throughout all the annals of crime, there has never been recorded a more revolting, wicked deed, than that for which the wretched perpetrator, Bridget Durgan, paid the forfeit of her life."

As she sat in her jail cell awaiting death, the illiterate girl began her confession with a somber, poetic, introspective note: "I am sitting all alone tonight. Alone, did I say? no! no! not alone! Not alone! For all round me flit spectres of darkness and woe. They shake their shadowy fingers in my face.... Now, dear Mr. Brendan, with my dying, solemn voice I will write."

As she reminisced about her life, her thoughts gravitated first to Ireland, where she was born in 1843. According to Bridget's memoir, her employment as a servant began at the age of 12; in a life-changing event three years later, after she had succumbed to the ardent attentions of her employer's son, "I found what had become of me, [and] I resolved to leave Ireland." With a strong sense of shame and little else, Bridget traveled to America and soon thereafter was employed as a housemaid. All was well for a few months, but Bridget had a touch of larceny in her heart, and she was discharged for stealing a trivial trinket. As she wrote in her memoirs, "from that moment I began to hate everybody; but most of all mistresses; and I resolved to kill some one if the chance only came in my way."

Bridget's behavior continued to irk her employers. A particularly vicious exchange with a Mrs. Horning came about because "she and I did not agree very well, and one day she ordered me to leave; and called me a devilish, infernal slut." Almost immediately Bridget's thoughts turned toward killing the woman. Moving from fantasizing about stabbing the woman to looking for an opportunity consumed Bridget for months as she stalked her former employer. However, her plans were foiled when nature intervened and Mrs. Horning died a natural death.

The itinerant Irish woman eventually made her way to Newmarket, New Jersey, and employment with the Coriell family. Bridget readily admitted that Mrs. Coriell was a very good woman, but her real fancy was Dr. Coriell. Clearly Bridget confused the doctor's compassion with a romantic gesture, fostering an intense but imagined attachment with only his wife standing between them. As her desires intensified, Bridget began flirting with the idea of murdering Mrs. Coriell, imagining that the doctor would turn to her for solace. Seeking a pretext, it only took an angry, minor exchange with Mrs. Coriell for Bridget to put her murderous plan into action. And so it was that the young Irish servant girl, singlehandedly and with passionate premeditation, savagely stabbed her employer with a sharp kitchen knife and, armed with a stick in her other hand, battered and bruised Mrs. Coriell. Throughout the assault the Coriells' two-year-old daughter was sitting nearby, prompting the mother, in the midst of the mayhem, to piteously ask for a moment with her child. Bridget granted the request, resuming her attack following the tender moment, finally killing Mrs. Coriell.

While readers surely shook their heads as day after day the newspapers trumpeted news of the Coriell murder and the accompanying trial, the carnival of crime continued, with less celebrated cases clogging the courts. In Nashville, Tennessee, "the Banner last Saturday contains accounts of one suicide, a woman assaulted with an ax, two bloody fights between soldiers and citizens, an attempted rape, a soldier robbed and beaten, a desperate affray between soldiers at a house of ill-fame, in which one was badly wounded by a pistol shot and another stabbed to death." A host of other offenses, too numerous to mention, were simply listed as minor crimes.[40]

In a strange coincidence, almost exactly one month after Bridget Durgan killed Mrs. Coriell, another shocking crime took place in Virginia on the Drinker Farm, around February 28, 1867. It grabbed national attention, having many of the same features of the Durgan case, involving the mysterious death of another young woman.

It seemed unlikely that Virginia, the epicenter of so much of the fighting in the Civil War, would become the center of national attention for a murder. A reporter attending the trial was convinced that the Drinker Farm murder "has excited more interest and feeling in the State of Virginia than any other trial of a similar character that has ever taken place."[41] Hyperbole aside, the facts of the case surely shocked the citizens of the southern state.

Toward the end of February 1867, David Drinker was casually surveying his farm, which was a few miles outside Richmond, Virginia, when a grisly discovery interrupted his walk. Lying on the ground only partially concealed in a grove of pine trees was the body of a young woman, face down, with one hand still gripping some beads. She was wearing handmade clothes and, aside from this rustic note, was judged a pretty woman. Her death at first seemed to have resulted from a gunshot wound to her head, but a closer inspection revealed that the bullet had struck a glancing blow. Throttle marks on her neck led investigators to conclude that she had been strangled to death.

An immediate effort to identify the body was undertaken, and as word of the discovery spread throughout the local area, many people came forward, but none recognized the young woman. Three months passed with investigators patiently collecting clues, which collectively seemed to point toward one man: James Jeter Phillips. Phillips was then working on the nearby Turner farm, along with a brother who was married to one of Turner's daughters. The infatuation with the farmer's daughters extended to James, who was rumored to be engaged to another one. It was no doubt considered a good match by both families, particularly since James was counted among Virginia's scions.

For all of his alleged fealty, James Phillips evidently had a roving eye and a southern dandy charm that seemed to attract the attention of women. A reporter, with faint flattery, described him as follows: "his age is about 25 years, he is of medium stature, slimly built, blue eyes that constantly stare, a puckered mouth, angular chin, sharp nose, good forehead, and glossy chestnut hair." Perhaps even more attractive than his appearance was his reputation as a fearless former Confederate soldier with the "Ninth Virginia Regiment."

The treacherous tale began shortly after Phillips laid down his arms at Appomattox and began wandering home in the company of a fellow soldier, Frank Pitts. On the way, the pair stopped at Pitts' home, and it was here that the fate of Emily Pitts was sealed. Phillips apparently fell in love with Emily, captivating and capturing the country girl's heart in a whirlwind courtship that culminated in a well-attended wedding. Unfortunately, everything changed a few short weeks later.

Tired of Emily's devotion, Phillips fled to Richmond, leaving his wife behind, comforted by a concocted story that soothed the gullible girl. After arriving in the big city, the reprobate romancer resumed his life in the fast lane, interrupted by the war, and once again began orbiting in Richmond's higher social circles. It was a joyous, dazzling experience, courting lovely women, dancing, drinking, and, most important, denying Emily's existence. To all outward appearances, carefully crafted by the scheming scoundrel, he was a rich, eligible bachelor.

Phillips eventually proposed to another young lady, apparently assuming that his poor country wife posed no threat to his bigamous plan. In what turned out to be a miscalculation on Phillips' part, leading to a dreadful intervention by Emily, the news of the pending marriage somehow came to her attention. Emily sent a letter to the other woman claiming her privilege, which the recipient shared with a protesting Phillips. Caught off guard, his footloose fantasies fractured, Phillips was left with only one option: return home and sever the shackles forever.

Emily apparently never suspected her husband's malevolence—just his fidelity. Her calculating, scheming spouse returned to her open arms around Christmastime in 1866. This blissful reunion was made even happier when Phillips invited Emily to join him in Richmond. After making the short journey, the pair spent the next few nights in Richmond, with nothing unusual occurring until February 17, 1867, when both were witnessed together for the last time. Emily's body was discovered ten days later on Drinker's farm.

Phillips was arrested on June 13, 1867, after detectives had pieced together the puzzle. When first accosted, he vehemently denied the murder and, with mounting indignation, proclaimed that he was not married.[42] A quick search of his room at the Turner farm produced a trunk filled with various female garments, a book containing an incriminating inscription to "Miss Emma," and a revolver with only three bullets remaining in the six-cylinder handgun. As each item was revealed, the stolid suspect was unmoved, retaining an aloofness and indifference that seemed to support his claim of innocence.

After his arrest, Phillips was taken to jail, and in the following days, taking advantage of his high social position, he enlisted the services of four eminent local attorneys. Some of the evidence against the accused former soldier started leaking out, including letters from a minister and Frank Pitts confirming the marriage of James Phillips and Emily Pitts on July 13, 1865. Phillips added to the growing suspicion when Frank and his sister Roxana visited him in jail. It was a poignant but fruitless effort by a brother and sister seeking closure. At several points, Roxana pointedly asked Phillips if he had murdered Emily, receiving in turn a cold "I refer you to my counsel for an answer to that."

A grand jury, assembled to determine whether the evidence was sufficient for a criminal trial, commenced work on June 19, 1867, with the prosecution bringing forth a parade of witnesses. Frank Pitts testified early, confirming the marriage, the subsequent absence of the husband, and his infrequent letters to Emily. Among the latter was the last message sent from James Phillips to Emily's family after the pair had seemingly reunited and relocated to Richmond. It was an ominous letter excusing Emily for not writing more often because "she would have written again, but has been suffering with a very sore finger.... I do not know what it is; it is dreadful. She takes morphine and laudanum to compose her. The doctor is very fearful she will have the lockjaw." As would become apparent later, this last letter was a ruse, sowing the seeds of a future cause of death, as Phillips methodically and mercilessly plotted Emily's death.

Phillips' defense strategy attacked the prosecution along two lines: first by producing witnesses who professed knowledge of the defendant's whereabouts during the time alleged for the murder, and by vigorously pounding and rebutting the testimony of opposing witnesses. Throughout the succeeding days, hot and miserable days in July, the trial dragged on with the defendant curiously cool, even amiable with those in the courtroom; when not occupied in social conversation, Phillips was seen deeply engrossed in reading the daily newspaper.

Wrapping up their case, the defense attorneys peremptorily demanded their client be released, which, after a few moments' reflection, was denied by the court. Phillips was returned to jail to await his criminal trial.

Standing hale and hearty before the trial court judge, James Phillips resolutely entered a "not guilty" plea on October 30, 1867. Over the next eighteen days much of the same ground plowed with the grand jury was again unearthed. The defense team sharpened its attacks, no doubt learning from the grand jury experience where to inflict the most damage, and a cavalcade of character witnesses burnished the accused's image.

At the conclusion of the trial, both defense and prosecution made one last plea to the jury. While the prosecutor trod familiar ground by resurrecting the facts, many of which might have grown stale after eighteen days, the defense took a slightly more ingenious tack. With Phillips looking on, the defense admitted the obvious: he had indeed "contracted the marriage when a boy, scarcely twenty-one. There was no beauty to attract him, nor wealth ... when he married this woman, ten years his senior."

In order to establish reasonable doubt in the minds of the jurors, the defense attorneys needed an alternate story, consistent with the facts and plausible. Gathering together the threads of evidence, the shrewd lawyers spun a different scenario. In their version, Phillips left his wife in Richmond after an argument and from that time forward never saw her again. The prosecution could never fix the exact time of death, leaving too wide a gap to be traversed with circumstantial evidence. Emily's body was also badly scratched and bruised, perhaps, as the defense contended, in a vain effort to ward off a rape. Add to all that the prisoner's behavior after her death, never running away and remaining coolly indifferent, and the resulting calculation could only be innocence.

Following lengthy instructions from the judge, the jury was discharged to decide Phillips' fate. Ten jurors voted guilty while the remaining two, later suspected of corruption, remained steadfast in their opposition, leaving the verdict hopelessly unresolved.

A second trial took place on June 15, 1868, although it took five days to assemble a jury. This time the jury members were unwavering in their conviction of Phillips, and the judge compassionately but resolutely sentenced the prisoner to death. A series of appeals followed, with each succeeding in only delaying the sentence.

An unruly, ugly crowd gathered in the jail courtyard to witness James Phillips' belated hanging on July 22, 1870, not quite three and a half years after Emily's death.[43] Awakening at 5 a.m., "he washed, trimmed his mustache, and gave special attention to his curls." Shortly after noon, a delegation of officers accompanied the condemned prisoner to the scaffold, from which the Reverend Dickinson read a short, handwritten statement to the assembled rowdies. Phillips confessed all, forgave everyone, and awaited his ultimate judgment. His wait was short.

The murders of Emily Phillips and Mary Coriell unfolded against the backdrop of a society unraveling at the seams, with traditions upended and faith floundering. In the case of Emily Phillips, artful advocates postponed her husband's day of reckoning for three and a half years, nearly severing a critical link between crime and punishment in the public's mind. Both cases took place shortly after the war ended and dramatized the developing lack of trust that should have precluded such outcomes. As time wore on, crimes and schemes of every imaginable sort increased, and in some cases the sheer brutality was shocking.

With prison populations soaring through increasingly harsh punishment, the hand-wringers looked across the land and, seeing an unabated carnival of crime, were left wondering, "what is there to account for the lapse into barbarity?"[44] A southern newspaper, in commenting on the spiral of violence in the northern states, attributed the cause to "evils resulting from the war."[45]

The crime wave spread in all directions as it blanketed the country, suggesting a common cause. One obvious clue was the war's end, which brought men home from the battlefields, with all their scars, physical and psychological. Four years of war had also drenched America in death, debasing human life.

Such was the case in Indiana, where citizens must have reeled from two months of rampaging violence beginning around Christmas 1868, in a trend mirroring what was happening in the rest of America. Making matters worse was an abject failure to apprehend the felons. Among the many criminals were arsonists, who nearly destroyed a town to hide a murder; the murderers of a railroad conductor who had been wantonly and brazenly killed; a woman suspected of killing a man and his wife; "Sanderson, the fiend who murdered nearly the whole Woodward family.... [and] Vanaman, who has recently confessed that, at his own wedding banquet, he tried to poison all the guests on account of the resistance which a few of them had offered" to his marriage. With the exception of Vanaman, who sickened many and killed a sister-in-law, none of the miscreants were taken into custody. In a nihilistic note concerning Vanaman, the reporter's bitterness was palpable: "it is thought [Vanaman] will hardly be convicted under our present criminal laws."[46]

Violence continued to grip the state of Indiana in the following months. In September 1869 Jacob and Nancy Young were murdered while riding in their carriage.[47] Suspicion soon grew that Nancy E. Clem was the chief culprit, perhaps aided by her brother and another man. It was a particularly vicious assault, and an eyewitness spotted a woman "attired in a dark dress, bearing a remarkable resemblance to Mrs. Clem ... emerging from the fatal spot." A recent rain shower had left the ground moist, and an imprint in the soft earth perfectly matched Clem's shoe. Robbery seemed to be the motive, as Jacob

Young had just withdrawn a large sum of money from the bank, which was missing from the crime scene.

Evidence pointing to Mrs. Clem's complicity continued to accumulate. She was brought to trial, with many no doubt thinking it would be a short affair ending in a just conviction, which did indeed happen. However, what followed totally upended the pursuit of swift justice and surely left numerous people shaking their heads in disbelief. It also affirmed the growing lack of faith in the judicial process.

Nancy Clem successfully appealed the verdict, and in 1869 another trial was held, which resulted in a second guilty verdict followed by another appeal ordering a new trial. Having exhausted the local pool of jurors, the third trial was convened in an adjoining county, with that trial again ending with a conviction. Indefatigable defense attorneys successfully appealed once more in what was becoming a farce. Time was marching on, and in 1873 a fourth trial traveled the same path: another conviction and appeal overturning the verdict. Tired and broke, county officials pled poverty, and with no funds forthcoming for another nonsensical trial, the presiding judge was forced to free Mrs. Clem, convicted of murder in four previous trials.[48]

Mayhem and malevolence continued to stalk the country, surely emboldened by weak law enforcement and strong arguments from defense attorneys when, and if, a suspect was ever brought to trial. Grisly crime scenes also shocked citizens, seemingly impossible given the carnage from the Civil War, but newspapers exercised few restraints and brought the unvarnished facts to their readers. Often presented rather nonchalantly, a typical example in North Carolina involved a man "murdered in his house ... and his body cut in halves and hung in the room in which he slept. No arrests have been made."[49]

Searching for answers led some to conclude "that the devil has literally been turned loose and that he has instituted a carnival of crime."[50] It seemed that every moral boundary was breached—incest, rape, murder, robbery, and endless get-rich-quick schemes. In the midst of this chaos, a natural focus of the public's ire was lax law enforcement.

With riots and out-of-control crime plaguing the city, an intrepid reporter interviewed the mayor of Philadelphia, Daniel Fox. If the reporter expected a defensive politician, racked by accusations of police incompetence, he soon discovered otherwise, as the feisty Fox shook off the complaints. With an equivocating response the mayor acknowledged "the duty of the police, as far as possible, to prevent crime; but they cannot alter the iniquity of men's hearts, nor prevent sudden ebullitions of passion."[51] It was a clever answer, but it probably left the readers wondering what prevented the police from apprehending the felons after the fact.

Terrible murders became the theme of endless articles, large and small, gracing the pages of newspapers. There seemed to be little relationship between the crimes and their coverage except perhaps for well-known or well-heeled victims. It could also have been a reflection of the numbing of society that led some more horrendous crimes to be tucked away below the fold. An example of such nonchalance was a trunk murder that earned a small column in a Philadelphia newspaper. The dreadful story took place in Buffalo, New York, in late January 1869, when "about a week ago a trunk was received at one of the express offices in this city, marked 'to be called for.' Owing to the fact that a very disagreeable smell was emitted from the box, and no one having called for it, it was opened yesterday, and found to contain the body of a woman, badly mutilated."[52] The decomposing body showed evidence of a stab wound near the victim's heart, but little else could be determined, and so another mysterious crime was left for beleaguered police officers to figure out.

It did not take long for the temperance crowd to connect the dots between alcohol consumption and crime. In Philadelphia all thirty-seven known murders in 1868 were attributed to the evils of alcohol.[53] Had it not been for this pernicious influence, a newspaper reporter assured his readers, all of the victims would yet be alive.

Saving some compassion for the alcoholic, the same reporter dwelled at length on mania-a-potu, a medical label affixed to those individuals otherwise known to be suffering from alcohol withdrawal delirium. The name conjured up visions of insanity for the better-informed readers, and for the less literate it severed the obvious link to alcohol abuse. The reporter's description of the disorder was probably designed to scare readers into forsaking the immoral path. Walking through the prison's mania-a-potu ward, "the scenes in this ward are frightful to look upon; the pale face, the cold sweat oozing from him, the raging fever, the pupils of the eye distorted, flashing fire ... writhings, occasioned by excruciating pain ... confined with handcuffs and strapped down to the floor."

It probably never occurred to the temperance zealots that the abundance of alcoholics in prison had another cause. An alternative to the alcohol-causes-crime bromide was a far simpler explanation that actually was consistent with consumption of the mind-altering chemical. Instead of alcohol causing crime, the real correlation between arrest and alcohol abuse was the ease of apprehension, with overindulgence impairing the mobility and planning required to make a successful escape. The police, also knowing full well that alcohol contributed to crime, were more likely to keep an eye on businesses that served liquor, perhaps again accounting for the disproportionate number of intemperate inmates. More cunning and alcohol-free villains were not hobbled by these factors, which made detection more difficult, leading the police to look inept. All of this may have played a role in the public's well-founded concern about crime and the lack of punishment.

One veteran of the Civil War, hobbled by war wounds and the untimely deaths of his wife and child, did not escape justice. Josiah L. Pike was twenty-four years old when he enlisted as a private in Company B with the 40th Regiment, New York Volunteers, otherwise known as the Mozart Regiment.[54] The 40th Regiment had the dubious distinction of claiming one of the highest casualty rates of any New York unit, which came to include Pike in 1862 during the intense fighting around Williamsburg, Virginia. He suffered a grievous wound that that led to an extended convalescence and ultimately a medical discharge from the army.

After recuperating from his wound, Pike joined the navy and participated in the Battle at Mobile Bay in 1864.[55] Throughout his military career the soldier turned sailor also battled with alcohol, usually losing and suffering the consequences. When the war ended, Pike's drinking and thieving proved a poor mix, eventually leading to a two-year stint in prison. Now destitute, he traveled to New Hampshire, leaving his home state of Massachusetts and the prison there behind. Pike found employment in Hampton Falls, a small rural town near the state's capital, with the well-to-do elderly farmer Thomas Brown and his wife, both of whom treated the new farmhand with kindness. It was not reciprocated.

Timothy Leary was another farmhand working on the Browns' farm, and on May 7, 1868, he went to the main farmhouse early in the morning as usual to receive instructions for the day's work. Leary rapped on the door several times but received no reply—this was unusual, as the owner typically arose quite early. Leary's persistence finally was rewarded and the door slowly opened, revealing the elderly farmer drenched in blood from a severe laceration to his forehead. Retaining his presence of mind, Leary cautiously entered the house and made his way to the kitchen, where he found Brown's wife lying in a pool of blood from a fatal head wound. Thomas Brown lingered a week longer before succumbing to the dreadful assault.

Almost immediately after discovering the crime, suspicion centered on Pike, who was subsequently arrested and, following several days in jail with irate citizens threatening vigilante justice, confessed to the murders. The accused man offered few details at the time and failed to define a motive, leaving a mysterious cloud hanging over the assaults.

Pike's trial for the double murders consumed much of the trial court's October term in 1868.[56] Armed with a confession and playing to an enraged public, the prosecutor's task was fairly simple. Pike's defense was left scrambling but played the only card they had by focusing on his intemperance. Witnesses came forth and offered testimony intending to show that in the days preceding the murders Pike was highly intoxicated, erratic, irritable, and confused. With this evidence, Pike was laying the groundwork for an insanity defense arising from dipsomania. In a reversal undermining Pike's argument, the trial court judge refused to admit the opinion testimony of witnesses who believed the prisoner insane. The jury's verdict was not really in doubt when, after a short deliberation, it found him guilty of first-degree murder.

Despite a well-crafted appeal based on the exclusion of important non-expert evidence, and a vigorous, lengthy dissenting opinion, the Supreme Judicial Court of New Hampshire upheld the conviction, paving the way to the gallows.[57] Pike, now without recourse, was sent to prison to await his execution; he was "about five feet eight inches in height, with black hair and eyes and black moustache.... His appearance was decidedly in his favor, and he looked by no means a vicious man." Until the end Pike placed the blame for his predicament squarely on liquor.[58]

Despite the savage murder of the elderly couple, "Pike's last days were … ushered out of life with a surge of sentimental gush that scandalized the state.... Women were allowed to make a fool of Pike. They prayed and sung with him, and held his hands, and patted his cheeks … until Pike … imagined himself a saintly hero."[59] Ascending the gallows after bidding his adoring admirers adieu, Pike complacently accepted the noose about his neck. In a scene that played out all too often, the hangman's ineptitude was on display: due to the rope being too long, Pike's feet loudly smacked the ground, leaving him dazed but not dead. The hangman hastily hauled the insensible inmate back up, ensuring that he would slowly strangle and fulfill the law's mandate.

In New York City an influential newspaper editorial demanded a spirit-free Sabbath, which required the enforcement of existing laws forbidding such commerce.[60] Eliminating the "Sunday carnival of crime and deviltry" would at least give citizens one day of respite from the onslaught. Rallying public sentiment was not successful, nor were politicians seemingly disposed to order the police to crack down. There seemed to be no bar to liquor on Sunday, a visible failure as "wholly drunken wretches staggered out from noon till midnight."

It seemed unlikely that George D. Campbell's death was alcohol related. He survived his stint as a Confederate soldier only to be felled by an act of infamy in Kansas City, Missouri, during the summer of 1870.[61] An unknown assailant killed the 25-year-old man, who hailed from Tennessee, and then, apparently not satisfied with the result, placed the body across a set of railroad tracks. Papers from the mangled body identified the victim but left behind no clues unraveling the mystery of his death.

The carnival of crime smothered society, snuffing out every attempt to explain or control it. A dark dysphoria descended, creating, "in short, a season of demoralization ... affecting alike the Pulpit, the Press, and the Bar." In a broad attack against rampaging immorality, a newspaper editorial deplored the lack of moral leadership, citing the sacrifice of temperance and moderation for indulgence and debauchery. As a result, "the thirst for notoriety and self aggrandisement ... extravagance and foolish display" became the focus of social life and the source of all malevolence, but, according to the writer, there was a solution.

Salvation required a return to antebellum times because "in an evil hour came the dread scourge of internecine War, brother rose against brother.... Youths ... were thrown upon the tide of horror and ruined in the debaucheries of camp life." Soldiers maimed and scarred from the war were visible reminders of the great conflict, but the psychological consequences were expressed in less visible ways.

Many claimed that sagacity was the shield protecting society from evildoers; however, the proponents of this theory probably never met Edward H. Ruloff. By most measures Ruloff was an erudite individual, a learned man of letters, independent and scholarly, all of which harmoniously coexisted with a twisted turn of mind. His lifelong pedantic penchant fostered a gentility that disguised a dark and sinister sociopath, responsible for murdering at least eight people.[62]

Ruloff was born in Canada in 1819 and, in a storybook childhood, passed his youth quietly, voraciously reading anything he could lay his hands on. This singular obsession was turned to his advantage when he opted to study law and, with remarkable rapidity, soon embarked on a successful, albeit brief, legal practice. Ruloff's psychopathic personality blossomed at this point, sabotaging a potentially promising profession with a pointless theft from his employer. His sympathetically inclined employer offered to resolve the matter without legal recourse, but Ruloff arrogantly dismissed the offer. Perhaps Ruloff believed that his legal skills and social position would insulate him; if so, it was a severe miscalculation. After a short trial, he was sentenced to two years in prison.

Bitter but free, Ruloff left Canada, and, after a short, unproductive stay in New York City, he moved about 200 miles north to Dryden, New York. This small rural community initially warmed to the brilliance of the newcomer, but they would soon be burned. Ruloff was industrious and cultivated, captivating enough to secure a position as a high school teacher and win the heart of Harriet Schutt, a totally smitten sixteen-year-old student.

Some indefinable attribute spooked Schutt's parents, who alternately protested and coaxed the young girl to reconsider Ruloff's marriage proposal. It was all in vain, and the parents, no doubt sensing that pressing the case further might rupture their relationship, reluctantly granted their daughter's wish. Harriet should have listened to her parents, whose intuition was more insightful than hers. Almost immediately after the wedding, Ruloff became embroiled in a series of thefts, which, while revealing his true nature, also brought shame on his new wife. As a husband, Ruloff was stern and controlling, preventing his wife from visiting family and friends. With his bad behavior contributing to a growing alienation and isolation, the pair fled to a small city near Ithaca, New York.

Always an ardent student, and looking to exploit the public's fascination with herb doctors, Ruloff took up this practice and was soon a respected member of his new community. Given Ruloff's undeniable sociopathic proclivities, his turn toward medicine may have been nefariously undertaken—after all, what better way to learn about natural poisons and safely, secretly administer them than from behind the cover of respectability that his medical career provided?

In retrospect, perhaps in retaliation for opposing his marriage, the twenty-six-year-old Ruloff was probably responsible for the poisoning deaths of W.H. Schutt's wife and baby. If vengeance was not the principal motive, then Ruloff may have been rehearsing for the main performance: killing his wife and child. In a carefully crafted prelude, Ruloff invited a neighbor to his house; shortly after her arrival a murderous argument broke out between the husband and wife. After some fireworks, both combatants patched things up and the neighbor left.

The next morning Ruloff borrowed a horse and wagon from a nearby neighbor, explaining that his wife and daughter had left with a family member, insinuating the uncle's intention of rescuing the wife following the previous night's heated argument. In their haste to leave, a large trunk had been left behind, and Ruloff felt obliged to transport it to his wife, necessitating the need for the wagon. The neighbor, amiable and accommodating, even helped Ruloff load the heavy box, after which he then departed down the road whistling a merry tune.

Family members were suspicious and soon demanded answers. The unruffled Ruloff insisted that his wife was in Ohio, but when pressed for more information, he fled the area. After a brief sojourn he was arrested and eventually sentenced to prison for ten years following his conviction for kidnapping. Since the bodies of his wife and child were never found, the murder charge floundered. There were two lines of speculation concerning this situation. Initially people believed that Ruloff had dumped the trunk in a nearby lake, but determined dredging produced no results. A more likely theory suggested that the herb doctor, trading on his reputation, had donated the bodies to a local medical school.

In prison Ruloff returned to his books and was a model prisoner, finally released in 1856. Despite the passage of ten years, passions had not subsided among the local citizens, who firmly believed Ruloff guilty of murder, and an effort to convict him on that charge was instituted. It failed, but a new charge for murdering his child succeeded, with the miscreant sentenced to hang. Instead of pondering his fate, Ruloff started scheming. Carefully cultivating a relationship with a gullible young man, Charles Jarvis, and his mother, the prisoner came to have an almost hypnotic influence over both, leading them to engineer his escape. For about two years he wandered around northern Pennsylvania, pilfering what he needed to survive. Tiring of his itinerant life, Ruloff returned to face his fate and, after another trial, successfully outmaneuvered his tormentors and left a free man.

Through the Civil War and in the years until his next arrest in 1870, Ruloff alternately practiced law and studied languages, the latter leading to an academic appointment in philology. Much of this time was spent perfecting his grand opus, *Method in the Formation of Language*, which Ruloff fancied was a sort of literary Rosetta Stone. In 1869 Ruloff, assuming the nom de plume of E. Lenrio, unveiled his work in a grandiose letter to the Philological Convention proclaiming the discovery of "the mystery of modern languages." The author was willing to part with the manuscript for the princely sum of $500,000 and looked forward to meeting with the esteemed membership at a gathering in Poughkeepsie, New York, to discuss the matter. His arrival was greeted politely, but the manuscript was received with less enthusiasm, with both the author and his work adroitly dismissed on account of the Philological Convention's professed weak finances and Ruloff's costly offer.

Finding philological profits elusive, Ruloff returned to the more expedient path of crime. Part of his motivation stemmed from a demand from Mrs. Jarvis and her son, both of whom Ruloff had finagled into helping him escape from jail and, now finding themselves destitute, needed money to survive.[63] With pangs of conscience, and perhaps a touch of compassion that seemed totally out of character, Ruloff devised a scheme that would settle the debt.

Joining forces with Ruloff, Charles Jarvis and another man, William Dexter, plotted the burglary of a store in Binghamton, New York.[64] With all the preparations made, the threesome broke into the store on the night of August 17, 1870. It seemed that the master thief and murderer would be successful yet again, and he probably would have been but for the unforeseen complication arising from two store employees who were sleeping in the store. Both awakened as the robbers were preparing to leave, burdened with stolen goods. A scuffle followed, with the store clerks getting the upper hand over one of the robbers; defying the popular notion that there is no honor among thieves, the other two returned to help. One of the robbers, probably Ruloff, pulled a pistol from his pocket and killed one of the store clerks, after which the trio fled.

The next day two bodies floating in the river were identified as the culprits, presumably victims of drowning in the deep water. In the meantime, Ruloff attempted to escape on foot and was only apprehended by chance. Alert citizens were on the lookout for any suspicious persons, and while an elderly man somewhat fashionably dressed walking along the railroad tracks might not have aroused concern under normal circumstances, he was arrested out of an abundance of caution. Ever the master manipulator, Ruloff was on the verge of being released when, through sheer serendipity, he was recognized as the infamous wife kidnapper.

The courtroom was filled to capacity, with many turned away, as Ruloff's trial began on January 5, 1871, in Binghamton.[65] Even though Ruloff was represented by two defense attorneys, he constantly took the reins, either by leading his attorneys or by posing questions directly to prosecution witnesses. A reporter described the prisoner as a "man of small stature, heavy frame, broad projecting brow, heavy eyebrows, hazel eyes, sallow complexion and large head squarely and firmly set upon his shoulders by a short, stout neck." The Neanderthal-like picture conjured up by this depiction fascinated the public, particularly his large head, which, as would be learned later, contained an equally large brain.

If Ruloff had any hope of dodging justice again, the prosecution's case surely dashed it. An unusual shoe imprint left at the crime scene belonging to an individual with a deformed foot precisely matched a deformity that the defendant possessed. Through meticulous police work, Ruloff was inarguably associated with the other two burglars. This time he would not thwart the court.

Ruloff was convicted and sentenced to hang. Appeals failed and the governor of New York would not intervene. In the court of public opinion, Ruloff's pending execution prompted an impassioned plea from a vocal minority to spare his life, predicated solely on his scholarly attributes. Even Mark Twain joined the chorus, writing that "a man in this disordered state of mind is dangerous to the public peace ... but nothing is to be gained by killing him. He should be treated like any other violent madman, and confined under close and merciful surveillance. With his great power of application and method, he might be made of great use in the administration of a prison or an asylum ... and ... to develop his scheme of philology."[66]

Despite the famous author's suggestion, Ruloff was executed. At no time throughout his long life was there any suggestion that Ruloff was insane— quite the contrary, as he used his intellect to plot crime and continually escape. Ruloff's actions effectively upset the argument that erudition and evil could never be partners.

Ruloff was the exception to the rule, even allowing the decades it took for justice to prevail. A far more common outcome provoked an editorial rebuke after "a drunken rowdy insults a woman, a bystander interferes for her protection, and is instantly stabbed to death" in New York City.[67] It was a blatant assault in broad daylight in a heavily populated area, and none of the witnesses, perhaps shocked by the attack, pursued the perpetrator. While deploring this lack of a civic-minded response, the newspaper editorial could not restrain its contemptuous complaints that "in almost every important crime committed in this City within the last four years ... our imbecile Police would fail to find them." As a consequence of this widely publicized police incompetence and a court system riddled with delays, clever legal defenses and endless appeals, criminals flourished while citizens quailed.

Few crimes could compete in 1871 with Ruloff's escapades, but the public's fascination with the nineteenth-century version of a femme fatale was exploited by newspapers for its subliminal, seductive storyline, and the case of Lydia Sherman was tailor made for such use. Sherman was not particularly attractive, but she was clever, much like a black widow spinning a web and snaring its prey, which in this case meant three men.

Lydia Sherman was arrested on June 30, 1871, in New Brunswick, New Jersey, and charged with the murder of her husband and his two children from a previous marriage.[68] She appeared baffled by the arrest, a curious response noted by the detectives, who attributed her surprise to artful acting, believing as they did that the evidence against her was overwhelming.

Following her arrest Lydia was transported to Connecticut to stand trial for the death of her husband, Nelson Sherman, and two of his four children.[69] Lydia's third marriage was a hastily consummated affair that left little time to discover her husband's intemperance before vows were exchanged. The pair was united on September 30, 1870, setting in motion a chain of events that would eventually lead to the woman's arrest. Two months after the marriage, Nelson's infant boy died, followed six weeks later on New Year's Eve by his fifteen-year-old daughter. As might be imagined, the loss of the children weighed heavily on Nelson, who further descended into depression-driven dissipation. Five months later the husband joined his children in death, shrouded by suspicions that Lydia had poisoned him, earning her the salacious sobriquet of "the Connecticut Borgia."

Far from sullen as she awaited her trial, Lydia was remarkably cool and composed, Perhaps she was comforted by the musings of legal pundits who openly faulted the circumstantial evidence that implicated, but did not corroborate, her guilt. A reporter traveling from New York City to visit the woman in her Connecticut jail cell was not surprised by her protestations of innocence but was unnerved when "she would laugh very heartily at any remark that amused her, but in the next instant a cold gloom came over her face which made one's blood turn cold."

As she sat in jail, newspaper reports of her deadly deeds spread across the country, adding more new details with each edition. It became clear that three deaths in such close succession had aroused the suspicions of Nelson's friends, who urged authorities to launch an investigation, eventually leading to the exhumation of the bodies.[70] Local doctors conducted the autopsies and submitted relevant specimens for chemical analysis, which after several weeks confirmed the presence of lethal amounts of arsenic in each victim. Armed with this knowledge, the detectives soon confirmed that Lydia had purchased arsenic from a nearby merchant.

Lydia's marriage to Nelson Sherman was her third, which, given the manner of his presumptive poisoning death, naturally led detectives to ponder the demises of her previous mates. Her first husband had died under mysterious conditions, which excited local suspicions at the time, but nothing was proven, leaving Lydia free to marry an elderly but well-to-do gentleman. He, too, died rather suddenly following an acute illness, which left Lydia heir to a sizeable estate.[71]

National fascination fueled an intense interest in learning more about the fiendish female, and newspapers across the land obligingly provided details.[72] Lydia was around 48 years old when arrested, with readers soon discovering the primary events of her life. She was born in New Jersey, suffered the loss of her mother shortly thereafter, and was raised by an uncle. Around the age of sixteen Lydia began working as a housekeeper, while at the same time honing her skills as a seamstress.

Lydia met her first husband, Edward Struck, at church, and over the next eighteen years the couple had seven children. When first married Edward was a blacksmith but later became a policeman, a promising choice that ended tragically. While on foot patrol, word came to Edward that a detective had been murdered at a hotel, "and Struck, who went to secure the murderer, had not the spirit to do it, and was discharged from the police force." Humiliated by the label of cowardice he bore, the disgraced policeman sank into a deep depression and, unresponsive to work or pleasure, retreated to the safety of a bedridden life. Now useless to Lydia, the scheming wife resolved to poison her husband and, after acquiring arsenic, soon eliminated her burden. This left her with six children (one dying a natural death shortly after birth) to care for. A few months later, it must have dawned on her that caring for six children was also a burden, and so two of the youngest were poisoned, a six-year-old girl and a four-year-old boy, in the same manner as her husband.

Lydia was just getting started. About a month after the deaths of the two young children, the beleaguered woman was confronted by her fourteen-year-old son's illness, which not only added to her burdensome life but also prevented him from working. A bit of tea laced with arsenic cured that problem, leaving Lydia free to set her malevolent sights on another young daughter, who, after four days of agony, also succumbed. Her oldest daughter died next after a prolonged but presumably natural sickness, although, given the mother's proclivities, poisoning could never be ruled out.

Freed of all obligations, Lydia resumed her former role as a housekeeper and, in this capacity, became acquainted with Dennis Hurlbut, a respectable, hardworking old man who had managed to accumulate a fair fortune. Lydia accepted his proposal of marriage and over the next fourteen months was a dutiful wife, a relationship suddenly terminated by her husband's acute arsenic-like illness. A short time later she married Nelson Sherman, yet again relying on arsenic to cure her ills.

Lydia Sherman was brought to trial on April 16, 1872, in New Haven, Connecticut, charged with the premeditated murder of her husband.[73] Prosecutors were convinced that the circumstantial evidence was more than sufficient to warrant a first-degree murder charge. As the court convened on the first day, all eyes naturally gravitated toward the prisoner, reserved, composed, and conservatively dressed "in a neat black alpaca dress, trimmed with silk velvet, a mixed black and white woollen shawl, white straw hat ... from which drooped over her face a thin lace veil, through which her features were plainly marked."

With the courtroom now packed with visitors and Lydia's two attorneys, the trial commenced with a reading of the lengthy indictment, at the start of which her chivalrous counsel requested permission for her to sit down. Lydia refused and, with the faintest of smiles, listened attentively but stoically to the prosecution's indictment, at the end of which she pled not guilty.

The first prosecution witness was Dr. Beardsley, the Sherman family physician, who had responded to an anxious wife seemingly concerned about her husband's rapidly progressive decline in health. Beardsley knew Nelson Sherman was an alcoholic and no doubt assumed this was the reason for his ill health, but upon examination the doctor's conviction gave way to other concerns. Nelson "had a parched mouth, great thirst, sharp pain in stomach, racking pain in bowels, hot, dry skin, quick pulse and some faintness," none of which was consistent with a drunken episode. Over the next four days the doctor pre-scribed various nostrums, none of which altered the deadly trajectory of the illness, deepening Beardsley's belief that his patient had been poisoned. After Nelson's death Beardsley insisted on an autopsy, from which various specimens were collected for chemical analysis.

Over the course of the eight-day trial Lydia listened impassively as damn-ing testimony came from her mother-in-law, her husband's son, a druggist who had "poured out three-quarters or one ounce" of arsenic at her behest, and the mind-numbing, meticulous evidence from George F. Barker, who performed the chemical analysis on specimens provided from Beardsley's autopsy.

Lydia's defense occupied the sixth day of the trial, during which five wit-nesses collectively commented on Lydia's faithful devotion to a dissipated hus-band. Portraying Lydia as a victim, tirelessly and selflessly propping up a worthless spouse, was a legal tactic to remove any obvious motivation for mur-der. Her lawyers also adroitly undermined the druggist's testimony by acknowl-edging that Lydia had purchased arsenic, but merely to rid her house of rats. A third prong of her defense cast doubt on the doctors' testimony, offering instead a seemingly plausible alcohol-related cause of death.

Lydia Sherman was convicted of second-degree murder, the jury appar-ently convinced of her guilt by the strength of the circumstantial evidence, but, lacking an eyewitness proving that she had concocted and administered the deadly potions, they settled on a verdict that spared her life. Facing the prospect of spending the rest of her life in prison, and with legal appeals fading, Lydia's conscience forced a confession. With varying degrees of ambiguity, she admit-ted poisoning all of her victims, with the exception of Dennis Hurlbut, a doubt-ful declaration given autopsy results revealing fatal traces of arsenic.[74]

Lydia was eventually sent to the Connecticut State Prison in Hartford, from which she managed to escape in 1877, an effort rewarded by only a few days of freedom, quickly terminated by her swift apprehension. A scathing arti-cle described her as "a strange character, full of deceit and cunning under the cover of a smooth tongue.... There has hardly been one like her in the criminal history of this country—one so utterly depraved, with no moral sense what-ever."[75] Closely guarded to prevent another escape, and in declining health, Lydia died rather ignominiously a short time later in 1878.[76]

The Rev. W.C. Steel, preaching from the pulpit of the Methodist Episcopal Church in New York City, dwelled on the murders, suicides, frauds, thefts and other moral depravities destroying the city.[77] Even more disturbing was a deep vein of liberal socialism that alternately romanticized criminals, painting them as victims worthy of the public's sympathy, which removed punishment from the body of justice. Turning to the legal system next, Steel ridiculed "the threadbare plea of insanity for almost every murderer, and the fact that astuteness, craft and cunning are the chief qualifications of a great criminal lawyer ... murderers often escape by a mere quibble." Ending with a plea and a prayer, the reverend urged his flock to petition city leaders for reforms, restoring the antebellum sense of social justice.

For discerning parishioners, a mere week later an affirmation of Steel's biting commentary could be found in a short, one-paragraph news story concerning a murder trial in nearby Philadelphia. William Oskins had murdered his wife and was duly brought before the court to answer for his alleged malfeasance. Like so many other defendants, Oskins resorted to the insanity defense, claiming his intemperance rendered his conduct excusable, an argument accepted by the jury. Had it ended there, the story probably would not have received any notice, being yet another example of what was considered commonplace in 1872, but Oskins' attorney demanded more; "since said acquittal he has recovered his reason, and is now of sound mind, and is detained in custody without just cause."[78]

The collapse in criminal accountability left reporters with plenty of opportunities to write cutting stories. A man named Scannell apparently had a persistent, smoldering thirst for vengeance against another man he stalked for years. An unsuccessful assassination attempt a few years earlier had left his victim wounded, but this outcome was totally unsatisfying. Throwing all caution to the wind, Scannell shot his victim multiple times while a group of nonplussed onlookers stood by.[79] With an abundance of sarcasm, a reporter predicted that "when he is tried, a number of doctors will be brought up to swear that ... Scannell is and always was insane, and then two or three women will be brought into Court and testify that in all relations of life Scannell is a pink of propriety. The counsel for poor Scannell will take an onion into Court and squeeze out a few tears.... Let the poor man go at once."[80]

At one point there came a complaint and call for reforming the insanity defense—albeit from a curious quarter. Henry L. Clinton was a famous attorney, a reputation earned through criminal trials and civil cases such as his work in sustaining the will of tycoon Cornelius Vanderbilt, for which he received a handsome fee.[81] It seemed out of character for an attorney of his stature, familiar with legal strategies, to seek a restriction on the use of the insanity defense. However, in spite of the seeming contradiction, Clinton wrote a lengthy opinion piece directed to the editor of the *New York Times*.[82]

Clinton took particular exception to the use of the insanity defense in serious felony cases such as murder. Perhaps part of Clinton's pique stemmed from the deference given to expert witnesses, who seemed to usurp the jury's decision-making through adamant, authoritarian opinions that left little room for debate. According to the attorney's critique, "the views of many physicians who figure as witnesses for the defense, in these cases, are so broad … that people are beginning to be alarmed lest there be not sane persons left to try criminals…. Strange as it may seem, the modern tendency is in favor of the idea that the commission of crime—especially capital crime—is proof of insanity."

Restoring balance to a seriously askew legal system required, as advocated by Clinton, a minimum fifteen-year period of confinement in an insane asylum following successful acquittal. According to the attorney, adoption of this commonsense approach would promote public safety and at the same time prevent artful lawyers from riding the carnival of crime merry-go–round, which simply returned dangerous felons to the streets. Clinton also hoped that restrictions on the insanity defense would rein in those "physicians and medical writers [who] have surrendered their judgment to wild theory, and bidden farewell to their common sense."

Civility was a major casualty of the rampant wave of crime, with horrific offenses so prodigious that many violations earned little more than a few paragraphs. Another "trunk mystery" baffled the police when a woman's body, missing her arms and legs, was discovered in a box shipped to Quebec, Canada. It took a careful reader to find the few lines sandwiched in between more prosaic political news.[83]

A similar but more sensationalized story dubbed the "Charles River Mystery" took place in Boston in 1872 when "an unknown man was found floating in Charles River, one-half of his body in one barrel and one half in another." What particularly struck the reporter as consequential was an expensive gold watch left among the remains of a thoroughly dismembered corpse. In an attempt to identify the victim, local authorities made the remains available for public viewing, which attracted thousands of apparently civic-minded visitors, none of whom, unfortunately, could unravel the mystery.[84]

Big cities were not the only areas infected with crime; rural communities suffered their share as well, but, given their isolation, such stories rarely grabbed a newspaper's attention. Only the most dramatic, sordid stories made it to the front pages of large northern newspapers, a feat accomplished by the serial exploits of the Kansas-based Bender family.

Silver Creek was a small community in 1871 located in southern Indiana and named for a nearby stream. Farms dotted the region and attracted itinerant workers such as the Bender family, a close-knit group of two men and two women. Were it not for what followed eighteen months later, the Bender family's brief stay in Silver Creek would never have attracted much attention. In any event, when a man named Bandle and his wife were murdered, and their bodies engulfed in a house fire, no one ever suspected the Benders, who, whether from coincidence or connivance, quickly left the area and moved 600 miles west to Cherryvale, Kansas.[85]

Taking advantage of a railroad land claim, the Bender family moved a few miles north of Cherryvale on a barren plain and built a small wooden shack with a nearby barn roughly hewn from sod. A few surrounding acres of perpetually plowed ground, trees, and scraggly crops surrounded the little homestead. An older man and woman were joined by a younger man and woman, by various accounts either children or a married couple. Word soon spread throughout the sparsely populated area that the newcomers were inhospitable and odd, and they somehow radiated a darkness that drove people away.[86]

The Bender family homestead was a sort of prairie oasis conveniently located on a lonely stretch of land frequented by travelers who warmed to the sight of the small building with the word "grocery" boldly lettered on a sign. On entering the small frame house, the unpretentious interior was revealed: a space roughly 14 by 16 feet with a curtain unevenly dividing the space. In the front area a wooden counter and a few groceries offered the promise of a meal while two beds behind the curtain suggested overnight accommodations.

Visitors were probably first greeted by the women, both of whom were remarkable in appearance and behavior.[87] Katie Bender was the younger of the two women, sometimes described as an attractive redhead, though others were less impressed by the "red-faced, unprepossessing young woman.... It was generally believed that she terrorized over all the other portion of the family, and few ever cared to be associated with her." Mrs. Bender, the oldest of the pair, was described in more malignant terms as "about forty-two years old, with iron gray hair ... hard and sinister-looking ... and repulsive features." The patriarch, John Bender, was a brutish figure, while the younger man, also named John, boasted a more wholesome appearance.

Weary travelers probably overlooked their hosts' fearsome-looking appearance, hoping for no more than a decent meal and perhaps a quiet night's sleep. In this isolated stretch of Kansas, journeys were long and lonely, and few travelers kept to strict timetables, so extended absences excited no particular concern, which perfectly suited the Bender family. Even so, whispers, innuendo, and a creeping terror soon replaced this nonchalance as the number of mysteriously missing travelers mounted. With no obvious culprits, local citizens variously blamed roving bandits and a nearby Indian tribe.

Mrs. Bender and the younger Katie reportedly dabbled in the dark arts, with the older woman drawn to brewing potions. Katie was more conventional, proclaiming psychic powers that "can heal all sorts of diseases: can cure Blindness, Fits, Deafness." Her small newspaper advertisements alerted potential prospects and surely induced suffering souls to travel to the Bender family shanty, increasing the traffic flow to this forlorn, forbidding location.

Katie was the public face of the family, with the other three hiding in the shadows while the twenty-year-old woman sought local stages to extoll Spiritualism. Her youth and gender drew audiences, but her supposedly psychic-inspired philosophy shaped the image of a scandalous woman. When possessed by the spirits, Katie could become ecstatic, a frenzy that added a measure of credibility to her contacts with denizens of the afterlife but, when combined with the content of her declarations, cast a decidedly demonic tone. Standing on a stage alone, the inspired spiritualist shocked her audience by embracing free love, incest, and murder: "What if the scoffers do accuse us of free love, is that not as our Heavenly Father intended it? ... Even though it should be a brother's passion for his own sister, I say it should not be smothered, for it is a god-given impulse ... murder—though my assertion may startle, may shock, may horrify you—is not the great crime that your laws would make it.... You ask me how I dare to make so bold an assertion? My answer is that I have often held converse with spirits ... and they know nothing but gratitude for those who had so benefitted them."[88]

Katie's comments could be considered part confession and part exculpation. Her relationship with the young John Bender was never fully understood, and it is an open question as to whether they were siblings or joined through marriage (although the spirits' endorsement of incest hints at the former). By breaking another moral taboo that prohibited murder, the spiritualist was seemingly left free to slaughter innocent victims, secure in the conviction that the dead would welcome the transition.

One of the first hints that the Bender family hostel was a devil's den followed the disappearance of William York, a physician and brother of a well-known Kansas state senator.[89] Toward the end of April 1873, after spending some time visiting with family, William began his return journey to Fort Scott, Kansas, a small town bordering Missouri and roughly ninety miles northeast of Cherryvale, Kansas. Along the route lay the Bender family's inn, an inviting waypoint breaking the boredom of a long journey home. By the time William was passing along this stretch, it was well known among the locals that travelers had a habit of disappearing, a fate that soon became the doctor's as well.

Senator York had the means and motivation to search for his missing brother and, with the help of friends, started scouring the countryside. The conveniently located Bender family inn beckoned the search party to stop for a brief respite, during which the conversation naturally turned toward the fate of William York. The younger John feigned concern and even offered to help the search party. When Katie joined the conversation, she innocently and demurely admitted that William had indeed passed a few moments at the inn but had departed for parts unknown. Taking the senator aside, she suggested a séance, but the search party left, taking with them a nagging suspicion.

Disappointed but determined, Senator York enlisted the services of Thomas Beers, a detective, and implored the man to leave no stone unturned. Beers did just that, patiently tracing William's presumed path, gathering clues along the way that inexorably pointed to the Bender family home. As Beers approached the property, it became obvious that the place was deserted; it was too quiet except for a mangy dog chained nearby and some livestock near death from starvation.

Clearly alarmed by Senator York's determination, and perhaps learning of Beers' efforts, the entire Bender family had made a hasty exit, taking little with them, as evidenced by scattered clothing on the floor and canned goods and various tools left behind, including a collection of hammers. As Beers scanned the room, his attention was drawn to the back area, where the canvas curtain that divided the space had formerly been located. At this point the detective discovered a small trapdoor that he cautiously opened, from which emanated the foulest odor imaginable. The small group of men with Beers explored the pit, which was about six feet deep and through which a crudely cut shaft led outside. A sticky residue saturated the ground in the pit; a closer inspection confirmed that it was congealed blood.

As the group moved outside and surveyed the plowed land, a series of depressions hinted at the awful secrets underground. One of the men got a long metal rod, and with this instrument Beers began the gruesome task of poking at the earth. After pulling the rod from one of the suspicious areas, a piece of cloth clung to the metal, leading Beers to summon shovels. After digging down about four feet, a partially decomposed body was unearthed. Their worst fears were confirmed when the unmistakable features of Dr. York were identified.

For the remainder of that day and the next, the bodies of more victims were unearthed and laid beside their open graves. By the time night fell, eleven bodies had been found, all with their throats cut and bearing evidence of blunt trauma to the base of the skull, with the exception of a young girl, maybe two years old, who had been either strangled or buried alive. Determining the exact number of murders was a futile task, partly because strong speculation suggested that during their two-year residence in Kansas the Bender family may have disposed of many bodies in a nearby river. Apparently the last victim, judging by the body's condition, was a young, attractive, unknown woman who might have sought Katie Bender's help for an abortion.[90]

Given the manner of the victims' brutal deaths, it was not hard to reconstruct the events that led to the murders.[91] Travelers would stop at the Bender family inn, enticed by the thought of a brief respite, and, while entertained and enchanted by Katie's flirting, would be invited to sit at a table in front of the canvas curtain. A candle on the table provided the perfect backlight and ensured that when one of the Bender men struck the visitor's skull while concealed behind the curtain, their aim would be accurate. After dropping the body through the trapdoor, another family member, most likely Katie, would then cut the victim's throat, ensuring death.

As news of the atrocities spread, would-be victims came forward with personal narratives of harrowing escapes from the murderous clutches of the Bender family.[92] One of the earliest accounts came from Mrs. Hesler, an elderly woman interested in Spiritualism who had sought a meeting with Katie. Hesler was an odd, eccentric woman, dismissed by the locals, and so when she described a frightening encounter with the Bender family, no one took it seriously. According to the old woman, when night fell the Benders began drawing pictures of men, stabbing them with knives, and laughing uproariously. Katie began chanting that the spirits often told her to kill people, all the while edging ever closer to Mrs. Hesler, who, despite her reputation, had enough common sense to flee the house.

Father Paul Ponziglione was well aware of the dangers as he journeyed along the trail where so many people had mysteriously disappeared, but as a menacing storm approached, his main concern was finding shelter, and the priest probably considered the Bender family inn a godsend—at first. Instead of a warm reception, "it was like being in the company of some wild animals, tense, alert, and malevolent, waiting to spring." Taking a seat at the table, Ponziglione patiently awaited his dinner, while Katie only managed to serve up a mindless, frenzied banter that dulled the priest's appetite but heightened his anxiety. A quick glance at the curtain revealed the hulking shape of a man with a hammer, totally unnerving the visitor, and, with fear propelling his steps, he beat a hasty retreat.

Fear of capture also motivated the Bender family to hastily leave their home, and with several weeks' head start before the murdering fields were uncovered, they successfully eluded the authorities. Despite an intense dragnet and sizeable rewards, the Benders were never brought to justice. Rumors of their demise or capture were all matters of speculation, but newspapers provided a receptive audience with every titillating tidbit.[93] The sighting in Salt Lake City of a grizzled old man bearing a resemblance to John Bender was sufficient for a New York reporter to travel west and interview the suspect. Another story, told with the greatest confidence, claimed that the Benders had been killed by vigilantes.[94]

Years afterward stories continued to surface accounting for the Bender family's whereabouts. One of the more interesting involved the arrest of two women who were charged with the murder of Dr. York. In a fully litigated trial, during which the older woman allegedly confessed to the prosecuting attorney, all signs pointed to a conviction until evidence surfaced that proved the older woman had been in prison during the period when the Benders were killing their victims. Both women were subsequently released, leaving the fate of the Bender family forever unknown.[95]

Against the backdrop of sensational cases that grabbed headlines and riveted readers, a more pernicious and pervasive assault on society was unfolding, with the unabated crime wave measured in terms of "homicides, fratricides, parricides, infanticides, suicides ... and probably the half is not told." Like a ship free of its moorings, with no crew left on board to steer, the aimless social drift prompted yearnings for a safe moral anchorage where "men must be brought to see clearly the old and everlasting distinction between right and wrong."[96] Four years of a brutal civil war had blurred the moral boundaries and released a swelling tide of scoundrels.

Seemingly inconsequential slights were often deemed sufficient reason to settle any matter with violence.[97] Almost daily, newspapers treated their readers to such stories. One example involved two men competing for the attention of a coquettish young girl, all of whom resided together at the same boarding house. The two men, Magruder and Lockwood, were well educated and fashionable, worked for local newspapers, and were both infatuated with Annie Brown. For whatever reason, Annie and Lockwood quarreled one day, leading the young girl to banish her suitor. This was an opportunity for Magruder, who immediately filled the void, much to the annoyance of Lockwood.

Annie recanted a few days later and was soon on friendly terms again with Lockwood, who could not resist pointing out his change in fortune to Magruder. This led to heated words, and soon the two men were locked in a struggle, eventually separated by a more cool-headed boarder. As Lockwood left the area, he ominously threatened to return the following day, "for I'll shoot you like a dog."

True to his word, Lockwood, fortified by ample amounts of alcohol, staggered down to the boarding house basement the following night and, while the others were enjoying their dinner, inquired as to the whereabouts of Magruder. Annie, perhaps sensing trouble, replied that Magruder had left the house. Lockwood was not convinced and, suspecting that his rival was in his room, ran upstairs, threw the door open, saw his victim, and fired two shots, mortally wounding the other man. His deed now done, Lockwood calmly returned to the basement for his dinner, quipping that his coffee was cold. Lockwood's sense of righteousness, possibly grounded in a conviction that justice would favor his actions, continued his meal as a policeman, summoned by the alarmed residents, stood idly by.

Every big city seemed to be reeling as audacious criminals threw caution to the wind, swindling, thieving, and murdering without restraint. In the spring of 1874 New Orleans was laid to waste as a carnival of crime spread throughout the city. During an emblematic six-week period, a local newspaper was left aghast at the "daring, unscrupulous and unchecked crime ... blood is shed upon the most frequent thoroughfares ... houses filled with sleeping people are set on fire by burglars ... gentleman and ladies, too are seized on the street and violently robbed."[98] Given the sheer volume, it was impossible to catalog the daily offenses, leaving an untold number of crimes unreported.

Even the Lone Star State could not escape the scourge. One Texas newspaper lamented that "the whole State seems to be under the malign influence of some evil spirit."[99] The reporter sounded a more somber note when pondering the consequences of an unchecked crime spree that was socially destabilizing and destructive. Roving bands of outlaws only added to the misery, with honest citizens left pleading for law and order.

From a perch overlooking the nation's capital, the vast panorama of crime enveloping the country was visible: kidnappings, wanton assassinations, malicious destruction of railroad equipment, and scandalous accusations lobbed at the famous, while the infamous were celebrated. The topsy-turvy state of affairs led one reporter to speculate that "imps of evil ... walk the earth and kick up all manner of deviltry on this globe of ours."[100]

If not imps, then more scientific conjecture considered the hot, steamy summer weather a contributing factor to the carnival of crime, as both irritability and inebriation seemed to peak. With that speculation in mind, an Ohio reporter, writing with an abundance of sarcasm, noted that even a casual glance at "the morning papers ... afforded cheerful reading ... the killing of a rough by a bartender, the beating of a wife's brains out by a drunken carman, three children were found starved, two bodies were dragged out of the East River, besides which there were cutting, stabbing and shooting without number."[101]

A more generous opinion concluded that "the hard times, the dullness of business, and the scarcity of employment ... are the cause of the present carnival of crime all over New England."[102] During such times, the temptation to steal increased, or so the reporter reasoned, though he seemingly contradicted this argument a paragraph later by admitting that farm work was plentiful and paid well. The reporter suggested that the discrepancy was real enough and that too many men without means were apparently above soiling their hands as common laborers.

In an odd short story, Mark Twain's wit was shown to full advantage in "The Facts Concerning the Recent Carnival of Crime in Connecticut."[103] Reflecting the time period's obsession with crime, Twain's satire relied on a kernel of truth, draped in humor and a bit of irony, to posit the cause of such widespread wickedness.

The story began with a moment's self-reflection as the author lit a cigar, all the while quietly and happily acknowledging that in doing so he was defying the conventional wisdom frowning on the habit. Only his aunt seemed to have any residual influence on this subject, but even there the author had overcome her strident protests, replacing any guilt with a giddy sense of triumph. As the author mused about his aunt, a knock at the door disturbed his reverie. Opening the door revealed a wizened man, scarcely two feet tall, who imperiously entered the house, took a seat, demanded a pipe, and generally exhibited a most obnoxious, demanding attitude.

Twain's visitor seemed to know a great deal about his personal life, castigating the author for various acts of neglect, rudeness, dishonesty, and even vengeful thoughts, never spoken aloud but instead animating colorful daydreams. It was the visitor's awareness of the latter, his intimate knowledge of Twain's innermost mind, that piqued the author, who then demanded the man's name. To his surprise, the man revealed that he was Twain's conscience.

Once revealed, the author sought to kill his conscience, a burdensome bully who incessantly insisted on following a proper course of action. With a herculean effort Twain attacked his conscience, and the pair struggled as the author slowly but surely gained the upper hand over his diminutive prey, who finally succumbed to the onslaught. It was a jubilant victory, leaving the author entirely free of his pesky conscience: "Since that day my life is all bliss.... Nothing in all the world could persuade me to have a conscience again. I settled all my old outstanding scores.... I killed thirty-eight persons during the first two weeks.... I burned a dwelling that interrupted my view.... I swindled a widow ... and have enjoyed my work exceedingly."

Mark Twain's story contained a nub of truth, laying bare the soulless, sociopathic nature of crime, particularly appropriate for the wanton wickedness afflicting postwar America. Even so, it did not explain the marked uptick in crime following the Civil War, nor did it propose any remedies, leaving readers of "The Facts Concerning the Recent Carnival of Crime in Connecticut" amused but not enlightened.

A more traditional view of the postwar era of crime was often preached from the pulpit, and Jacob M. Manning, who briefly served as the chaplain for the

43rd Regiment, Massachusetts Infantry, conveyed the thoughts of many. Speaking to his congregation as pastor of the Old South Church in Boston, Massachusetts,[104] on June 6, 1875, Manning addressed the crime wave roiling America.[105] He took careful aim at a society where crime flourished, perpetrators scoffed at the police and courts, newspapers glorified their feats while hiding behind a fallacious claim of serving the public's interest and reaping the benefits from an increased circulation, and lawyers served up creative strategies to defeat efforts to punish wrongdoers through tactics such as abusing the insanity defense.

As to the root cause of crime, Manning took note of a prevailing scientific theory that dispassionately blamed nature. No doubt stridently emphasizing his disapproval, the pastor noted that, according to this enlightened scientific opinion, "periods of crime such as we are now passing through ... are due to natural causes at work in society.... The prowling miscreant cannot be expected to feel very guilty for his crimes, if he has believed that they are a part of the fixed course of Nature."

In some respects, Mark Twain's conscience-killing story and Manning's sermon lamenting the loss of a moral sense of guilt are not that far apart. Both describe criminals untethered from society, unconcerned with the consequences of their behavior, reveling in the freedom of solely satisfying their desires, and certain that justice will never thwart their aims.

Tension between the nascent ascendancy of science and the decline of religion as forces influencing society was stoked by the carnival of crime. It was an obvious conflict that led one observer, in Pollyanna-ish exasperation, to proclaim that "if religion and science would cease to regard one another as enemies, it might be a little better for the interest of all concerned."[106] How religion, which relied on unquestioning faith, could ever be reconciled with science, where skepticism ruled supreme, seemed to escape the writer. So, both proceeded along parallel paths, mostly maintaining a respectful distance, rarely collaborating, and even more rarely openly criticizing one another.

Using its tools of collecting and analyzing data, science seemed to be on the verge of a coup in explaining the overwhelming rise of crime. Part of the motivation driving the scientific inquiry grew out of a general dissatisfaction with the penal system, seemingly resistant to the trend of prison practices that favored a convict's reform over punishment. On the front-page edition of *The Sun* for February 22, 1877, intermingled among the crimes of the day, was a curious piece about "The Genealogy of Crime."[107] Before launching into that subject, however, the reporter betrayed a notable bias by boasting "that the most inveterate offender has some rights which society must respect." At a time when public confidence in the legal system was dwindling, such a proclamation probably left some readers less than amused.

In any event, "The Genealogy of Crime" referred to a study examining the people who came to be known as the Jukes, a multigenerational family of criminals. For those individuals influenced by science, the Jukes seemed to confirm that heredity and crime were inextricably interlinked, and perhaps even more compelling was the assertion that this family represented merely the tip of a genetic iceberg.

The Jukes, a fictitious name, were given prominence by Richard L. Dugdale's study of the family's history over the course of seven generations, during which time he traced "seven hundred and nine criminals, paupers, and harlots."[108] Dugdale studied records reaching back to the early 1700s, beginning with a man named Max, who passed a rather dissolute existence in a hovel in central New York State. Living to a ripe old age, Max left behind a large brood of illegitimate children, which Dugdale discovered was propagated through succeeding generations. It was an important finding for Dugdale as he dug further and found that "the illegitimate males were mainly criminals and their sisters were for the most part prostitutes."

Richard L. Dugdale was born in Paris, France, later moving to New York; however, after a few years of public education, Dugdale experienced a serious illness that led the family to relocate to Indiana, hoping the change would improve his health.[109] It did not, and for the remainder of his short life Dugdale was a frail person who pursued more academic interests, gravitating toward sociology. His appointment as a member of the Executive Committee of the Prison Association of New York in 1868 was the defining moment in his life, merging as it did the Prison Association's interest in reforming the penal system and Dugdale's systematic, scientific study of society. Six years later, in 1874, the Prison Association formalized the relationship by asking Dugdale to study patterns of wrongdoing, leading to his concentration on the remarkable criminal consistency of the Jukes family.

Dugdale published the results of his study in 1877, based on a painstaking investigation of census data and personal interviews guided by visits to New York jails and prisons, home to many members of the extended Jukes family.[110] After collecting and collating the material, Dugdale subjected the data to statistical analysis, which provided further insights. The net result was a book laden with numbers, tables, and individual descriptions of succeeding members of the Jukes family replete with criminal behavior running the gamut from rape to robbery.

A superficial glance at Dugdale's work might have left a reader with the inaccurate impression that the author was solely swayed by the genetic transmission of immoral behavior, where in reality "the objective point is to determine how much of each results from heredity, how much from environment.

The answer to these determines the limits of possibility in amending vicious lives." On one point there was little doubt—the Jukes bred immorality and criminality to such an extent that neighbors over the years used the family name as a shorthand term for decadence and depravity.

Sifting and sorting through all of his data, Dugdale developed a theory that sexual promiscuity, not uncommonly incest, was the root cause of either crime or poverty, the two differing by physiologically determined activity levels. Criminals inherited an energetic trait while those destined to be poor had the opposite character. These genetic factors invariably led to behavioral replication through the generations, but Dugdale discovered a sliver of sunshine in the fact that not every family member was a reprobate. It was for this reason that "Jukes" was adopted as a pseudonym to protect the upstanding members of the clan.

According to Dugdale's research, environmental factors, such as differences in education and living conditions, separated the troublemakers from their respectable counterparts, a possibility seized upon as an argument for social and prison reform.[111] Since these factors were obviously modifiable, the study offered a glimmer of hope that crime and immorality could be reduced by improving a person's lot in life. Translated to prison reform, it meant that hard work, education, occupational training, and religion could modify hereditary tendencies that, if left unchecked, would again lead to crime.

As might be imagined, Dugdale's research was greeted with a mixture of praise and reproach. Readers daily regaled by newspaper reports on the carnival of crime were probably skeptical, finding punishment, whether through execution or incarceration, a more appropriate social response. Advocates of this approach were probably disheartened but soothed through validation when a five-year analysis of the 281 homicides in New York City between 1870 and 1875 provided stark evidence that "out of all of this appalling number of man-killers, the perpetrators who suffered death were only seven. Only twenty-four were sent to prison for life. And, reviewing the dreadful list, we discover that more than one-fourth ... were never brought to trial."[112]

Digging deeper into the deaths during that five-year period seemed to confirm New York City's reputation as a "murderers' paradise."[113] Dramatizing the point with clarity, all 281 homicides were carefully tabulated, listing the perpetrators when known, the victims, and the outcomes, beginning with the January 2, 1870, murder of Annie Almes by George Bauman, who then committed suicide. On the same date a year later, Mary Jones died at the hands of her husband, who escaped, never to be heard from again. On and on the list went, perfunctorily cataloging in a few sentences the crimes and punishments, or lack thereof, probably leaving many readers reeling from the injustice.

Vigilante justice flourished in this environment when sentiment trumped sagacity and many were convinced that the legal system was broken beyond repair. Examples of summary executions cropped up frequently, with the perpetrators sanctimoniously assured that their undertaking was justified.

More than a decade had passed since the end of the Civil War when a mob of self-righteous citizens raucously congregated outside the jail in Barboursville, West Virginia, and demanded the release of Edward Williams.[114] His paramour, Mrs. Manning, was located in the same jail; they were awaiting trial for the murder of her husband. Convinced of the pair's guilt, and apparently lacking faith in the legal system, the mob, comforted and blessed by a preacher's prayers, overwhelmed the jailor and dragged Edward outside. With a rope pulled snugly around his neck while he perched precariously on a barrel, the mob taunted its victim, demanding a confession. The condemned man obliged, perhaps hoping such a declaration would spare his life. It was not to be, and after confessing to killing Mrs. Manning's husband, a well-placed kick by someone sent the barrel rolling.

With her dead lover swinging from a tree, the mob turned its attention to Mrs. Manning. Threatened by the spectacle and fearing the same fate, she readily admitted unsuccessfully trying for months to poison her husband. Edward was more successful, splitting her husband's head with an ax while he slept and cutting his throat for good measure. Upon hearing the dreadful details, the mob democratically took a vote and unanimously sentenced Mrs. Manning to death, but they could find no man willing to carry out the deed, leaving the weeping woman to be escorted back to jail.

Murder was not the only motive that inflamed people enough to take justice into their own hands, as evidenced by the events that unfolded in 1872 at the ironically named Gun City in Cass County, a tiny railroad station roughly fifty miles southeast of Kansas City, Missouri.[115] Citizens of the sparsely populated county were incensed and still reeling from a fraudulent bond deal that had enriched several leading citizens of the area while saddling the rest with an oppressive tax burden. County judge J.C. Stephenson and attorney James C. Cline were indicted, but this did not cool the hot heads.

Stephenson and Cline were among a group of about thirty passengers on an eastbound train, halted by a pile of debris deliberately placed on the track at Gun City. The frantic crew desperately brought the train to a stop, barely avoiding a collision, after which a group of eighty masked men bombarded the engine and cars with a shower of bullets. With the train immobilized and the passengers trapped, the mob angrily screamed out Cline's name; when he ventured forth, he was instantly assassinated. Meanwhile, a roving band of thugs moved through the railroad cars intent on finding Stephenson and, succeeding, perfunctorily killed him. Having satisfied their need for vengeance, the vigilantes departed, never to be captured.

Justice delayed was sometimes justice denied, or at least the great pause between crime and punishment encouraged the development of ingenious legal defenses. Such was the case with Pryor N. Coleman, a Union soldier condemned by a military court-martial to death for murdering a woman in 1865.[116] Initial accounts of the curious case reported that "for some reason which does not appear in the record, the sentence was never carried into execution." Nine years later, in 1874, the long arm of the law caught up with Coleman, and a Tennessee state court resurrected the indictment and subsequently reconvicted and resentenced him to death. Using a double jeopardy argument, Coleman's counsel argued that his prior court-martial conviction precluded a second trial in Tennessee, a novel legal theory that eventually attracted the attention of the U.S. Supreme Court.

Coleman was a cavalry soldier belonging to a unit of volunteers organized in Tennessee.[117] Along with a man named Chambliss, the pair raided a whiskey still deep in the surrounding hills, perhaps after scouting the area intent on uncovering some locally manufactured moonshine. Their quest was successful, much to the chagrin of a man named Bell, who helplessly stood by as the soldiers drank his brew. Now fully affected by the potent drink, the two intoxicated soldiers demanded that Bell hand over his money. Bell resisted, earning a merciless beating. It was all witnessed by Mourning Ann, his daughter, who came to her father's rescue and was promptly shot dead. Somehow authorities learned of the atrocity and, after cornering the pair, killed Chambliss and took Coleman prisoner, leading to his subsequent court-martial conviction. He escaped to nearby Kentucky and, after the passage of nine years, mistakenly calculated that his return to Tennessee would excite no interest.

Coleman was apprehended in Tennessee after his return to the state in 1874 and found guilty of murder despite his legal argument that a prior court-martial conviction precluded any further judicial intervention.[118] All appeals failed, setting the stage for the U.S. Supreme Court to render the final opinion, heavily influenced by matters of legal jurisdiction affected by the War Between the States. As the Court reasoned, "The offense having been committed by a soldier ... in the enemy's country ... had no jurisdiction over the army of invasion." Even with that in mind, the Court did not excuse Coleman's actions, the opinion instead directing military authorities to arrest the former soldier.[119]

With nine years of freedom now a memory, a dejected Coleman was seized by military officials and held in confinement in Atlanta, Georgia, awaiting his fate.[120] Although twice sentenced to be hanged, Coleman once again escaped that fate when a presidential decree substituted the threat of death with a lifelong prison sentence.

The unchecked crime wave was mostly an affliction plaguing the northern states, which did not go unnoticed south of the Mason-Dixon line. Viewing the situation from afar, a southern newspaper took smug delight in contrasting the south's rural gentility with the north's tarnished pretensions.[121] In another instance an intrepid reporter defending Texas from similar charges took the time to visit a jail and discovered that only one prisoner hailed from the Lone Star State, leading to a triumphant conclusion that "a large majority of the 'Texas desperadoes' are from other states."[122]

Nearly fifteen years had passed since the Civil War ended with no relief for the victims of criminals running rampant. A disheartening assessment from 1879 noted that "the epidemic of crime is at its height. Murder, arson, rape, burglary, robbery ... [are] now running on full time night and day, and turning out a terribly full harvest of blood-curdling wickedness."[123]

As the pathos played out, there were no shortage of scapegoats, with police, juries, attorneys, politicians, and preachers all receiving heaping doses of blame. The end of America's Civil War ushered in an uncivil war, described at the time as a carnival of crime.

Six

Pretentious Panaceas

Patent medicines were popular in the nineteenth century, and while many were proprietary mixtures, they all shared one essential ingredient: the buyer's belief in the product. Cultivating the public's trust and confidence required extensive advertising adorned with impressive testimonials and scientific sophisms. Preparations made from plants seemed natural and safe, and when exotic botanicals were used, it added an enigmatic element, as did any label bearing the word "Indian."

Joining the manufacturers of patent medicines was an eclectic mix of pretentious "physicians" promoting panaceas through every imaginable philosophy. Their ranks swelled during the Civil War and grew exponentially after the conflict ended, a trajectory propelled by a fundamental loss of faith in traditional medical practice. Clever charlatans exploited this rift, playing on their patrons' passions, offering at best a benign placebo, but in too many cases they provided poisonous concoctions.

The understanding of human psychology was evolving in the nineteenth century but was mostly limited to extreme examples of mental illness, contributing to the burgeoning growth of insane asylums.[1] Some physicians were beginning to explore the relationship between mind and body, a trend that accelerated during the Civil War as cases of homesickness and nostalgia demanded attention. Even so, the prevailing picture of mental illness among physicians and the populace was insanity, a fearsome portrayal that prejudiced most people's disclosure of any significant emotional discomfort. Although the numbers can never be accurately ascertained, peddlers of the pretentious panaceas offered an alternative by targeting symptoms such as nervousness, lassitude, sleeplessness, headaches, and dyspepsia—the somatic and socially acceptable side of the psychological consequences of war.

America inherited its fascination with patent medicines from England.[2]

Colonists sailing to the New World may have packed some pills for the long journey, but newspaper advertisements touting the products did not become commonplace until at least 1750. Revolutionary fervor and subsequent warfare disrupted druggists' importation of English patent medicines, giving rise to home-grown manufacturing. In some cases enterprising American apothecaries answered the demand for the popular Stoughton's and Daffy's Elixirs by preparing the mixtures based on published accounts of their ingredients and using empty stockpiled bottles. As the decades passed, imitation English patent medicines became the norm, rapidly gravitating toward a distinctly American stamp.

In the years immediately preceding the Civil War, Americans could buy a number of proprietary prescriptions, with a few dominating druggists' shelves. Among the more colorful and prominent products were various preparations featuring an American Indian motif, with Dr. Morse's Indian Root Pills serving as a typical example of patent medicines of the era.

Andrew B. Moore developed and manufactured his patent medicine as early as 1854.[3] The following year Moore entered into a contractual agreement with the Comstock Patent Medicine Business for the distribution of his product. Despite intractable legal battles, Comstock succeeded in mass marketing what came to be known as Dr. Morse's Indian Root Pills.

Part of the allure of Comstock's nostrums was based on attractive packaging along with deft and (in the case of Dr. Morse's Indian Root Pills) disingenuous advertising. The fiction began with building an intriguing, imaginary story laced with tender emotional touches. Of course, "Dr. Morse" only existed in the minds of his Comstock creators.

Every bottle of the Indian Root Pills, along with prominent newspaper advertisements, reminded readers that the famous Dr. Morse,

> after completing his education in medical science, traveled widely in Asia, Africa, Europe, and North America, and spent three years among the Indians of our western country, where he discovered the secret of the Indian Root Pills. Returning from one of these journeys after a long absence, he found his father apparently on his death bed.... The Doctor, surprised to see his father so nearly gone, immediately went to his coach, taking there from various plants and roots, which he had learned from the Red Men of the forest as being good for all diseases, and gave them to his father, and in about two hours afterwards he was much relieved.

As the story concluded, readers might well have sighed with relief as Morse's elderly father blossomed with renewed vigor.

After supposedly traveling the world and establishing his credentials through study, the fictitious physician came to the conclusion that all disease arose from impurities of the blood.[4] Dr. Morse's Indian Root Pills solved that problem by opening "the natural passages for the disease to be cast out," a feat accomplished through a combination of herbs that the manufacturer claimed stimulated diuresis, expectoration, catharsis, and an opening of the skin's pores.

Clearing the body's natural passages was a central theme adopted by Dr. Morse's Indian Root Pills because "a large quantity of food and other matter is lodged, and the stomach and intestines literally overflowing with the corrupted mass, thus undergoing disagreeable fermentation, constantly mixing with the blood." The poisonous mess led to all manner of distress, and only Dr. Morse's Indian Root Pills could cleanse the body.[5]

The success of Dr. Morse's Indian Root Pills spawned numerous imitators. A Nashville, Tennessee, drugstore offered a complete line of Indian Doctor patent medicines. Customers could peruse the labels and learn that the Indian Doctor's Forest Syrup would cure coughs, colds and consumption, and that "children cry for it after getting one taste." The Indian Doctor's Blood Purifier cured dyspepsia, rheumatism, and all types of festering blisters, while women could take advantage of the Indian Doctor's Invigorating Cordial "for the cure of female complaints."[6] Customers in North Carolina could procure Wright's Indian Vegetable Pills, guaranteed to purify the blood and cure "fevers and colds, so common in the South."[7] Farmers in rural Ohio could reach for Barrel's Indian anti-parasitic compound or a soothing liniment by the same name, while bald-headed users could restore their youthful appearance with Stafford's Celebrated Indian Hair Tonic.[8] Stafford, whether a real person or not, challenged the doubters to give "a fair trial for the TONIC and he fears not the result."

Indian herb recipes were all the rage, and many contenders entered the crowded field. Dr. W.R. Merwin's Cherokee Medicines, "compounded from roots, barks and leaves," promised to cure users of all sorts of ills. Prospective customers could choose among several different formulations depending on what they hoped to fix. Those afflicted with kidney ailments would order the Cherokee Cure, but more difficult diseases like gonorrhea required an injection. One elixir was touted as a mental restorative and with "three bottles [could] cure the worst case of Impotency."[9]

For an inveterate entrepreneur with a medical inclination, the lure of an Indian medicine practice was probably quite compelling, particularly given the potential for profits. Joining the patent medicine purveyors exploiting the fashion was a group of self-proclaimed doctors who not only prepared the pills but also built successful clinics ministering to the needs of their faithful followers. By word of mouth and through newspaper advertisements, readers learned about miraculous medical cures from Indian herb doctors. Joining the cavalcade of charlatans was Francis Tumblety, a doctor of questionable character and training, peddling patent medicines and false hopes as early as 1857.[10]

Francis Tumblety, a man of many names, was probably of Irish descent.[11]

He lived for many years in Rochester, New York, with his mother and other nearby family members. Even at this early stage of his life Tumblety had managed to draw attention to himself "as a peddler of books upon the cars," a thinly disguised allusion to works of literature probably more salacious than salutary.

Perhaps finding little profit as a bookseller, Tumblety turned his attention toward healthcare and, unveiling a fresh name as Philip Sternberg, launched his new career. At some point he apparently made the acquaintance of, and possibly worked with, Rudolph J. Lyons, a celebrated Indian herb doctor with a conveniently located Rochester office.

Although Lyons was based in Rochester, his excursions around the state brought relief to sufferers unable to make a long journey. His arrival was announced in newspapers with a bold headline: "Important Medical Notice! I have come your prostrate heart to lift, your bleeding wounds to cure, and with the treasure of NATURE'S GIFT, relieve the rich and poor."[12] "Nature's gift" was a tagline conveying to the reader the doctor's reliance on medicines derived from plants, thus tapping into a deep vein of discontent with traditional medical practice. Lyons seemed to understand that mining discontent required additional support, and in an effort to shore up his credibility, he bolstered his reputation with the endorsements of prominent Rochester citizens.

As an added inducement, Lyons mentioned his worldwide travels, dropping hints for his readers regarding the origins of his mysterious, miraculous medicinal formulations.[13] He appealed to those who had given up hope, declaring through "his word and honer ... [to] directly or indirectly induce or cause any invalid ... the strongest probability of a cure." Potential patrons were presumably reassured by the doctor's offer of a free consultation.

Tumblety, probably taking a cue from his mentor, secured (possibly through duplicity) the affidavits of some of Rochester's leading citizens and, armed with these testimonials, headed north to Canada.[14] Tumblety had no sooner begun operations in Montreal when complaints about his presence in the Canadian city surfaced, questioning his medical credentials and obliquely urging patients to voice concerns about his supposedly noxious medications.[15]

By the summer of 1861 Tumblety was again advertising his wares in periodicals, this time in the venerable *Harper's Weekly*. Along with a picture of a man's pock-marked face, a bold banner, "To Be Good Looking," attracted the reader's attention.[16] From a fashionable street address on Broadway in New York City, readers requesting the remedy received one bottle of the miracle lotion in exchange for one dollar, users of which "may obtain a handsome complexion, exempt from pimples, blotches, Etc." Slightly different advertisements continued monthly through September 1861.[17,18]

The pimple business may not have been very profitable, perhaps motivating the so-called doctor to relocate to Washington, D.C. Tumblety consulted with patients in his downtown office in the Washington Building on Pennsylvania Avenue. Testimonials prominently placed in a local newspaper in May 1862 from dozens of Washington citizens purportedly praised Tumblety's unparalleled success in curing cancer, consumption, and scurvy. Typical examples included Mrs. McDowell, who claimed "that I have been blind for two years, and by the aid of Dr. Tumblety's treatment I can walk all over Washington without a guide," an outcome only slightly more astonishing than that of "James King, G Street, Washington D.C., [who] had a large tumor of a cancerous nature removed from his head without resort to the barbarous practice of cutting with a knife."[19]

Tumblety continued to publish testimonials through 1864. John Johnson, a ship's master, "accidently saw one of the Indian herb Doctor's cards. I visited him at his office and obtained medicines from him which completely" cured consumption. Another woman, Mrs. Hutchison, had her sight restored after two years and "can walk all over Brooklyn, without a guide."[20] The list of cures grew so long that some advertisements simply listed the person's name and their cure for problems as varied as consumption, seizures, rheumatism, and tapeworms.[21]

Meanwhile, Tumblety's mentor, Rudolph Lyons, continued to travel across the country peddling his wares. In an 1863 newspaper advertisement the Indian herb doctor detailed his office visits throughout Michigan, Indiana, and Ohio. The same notice reminded readers that Lyons "discerns diseases by the Eyes; he, therefore, asks no questions, neither does he require patients to explain symptoms."[22]

Lyons' cursory examination was a clever marketing ploy. Prospective patients with embarrassing symptoms, particularly those of a sexual or psychological nature, could avoid the discomfort of describing their dilemma. Bolstering that assumption were testimonials, devoid of details but full of praise. A woman's supposed letter to the doctor hinted at her depression in declaring that "four months ago I was very miserable, so much so that my husband and friends despaired of my recovery ... and to your skillful management, I am now well."

The Indian herb doctor trade was simply too lucrative not to attract copycats. In Baltimore, Maryland, Robert Delaney received accolades from a ship's crew after supposedly squelching a nasty outbreak of cholera and other "ship fevers." Delaney invited the public to visit his office and, through his professional care (and the purchase of his "No. 1 and Magic Pain Killer"), either prevent or cure "all Agues."[23]

After failing successively as a saloon keeper, entertainer, cigar dealer, and esoteric lecturer, Louis Drucker set his sights on the Indian herb doctor business, achieving some reassuring recognition for his efforts in St. Louis, Missouri. In spite of his seeming success, the burden of his past was too heavy, and a disconsolate Drucker committed suicide.[24]

In Cincinnati, Ohio, a grateful patient relieved of a chronic eye disease after a month's treatment recommended that other sufferers consult Dr. Van Buren.[25] Next door in Indiana, an ostentatious newspaper advertisement bragged that Dr. Ralphgrame, an Indian herb doctor, "can show more certificates of cures, sworn to by patients, than any other physician in America." In addition to curing the usual assortment of infectious diseases, Ralphgrame offered special help to male and female "victims of secret habit, self abuse" (a readily understood sexual innuendo).[26]

In another interesting trend, the public's escalating use of tonics and bitters seemed to mirror the ascendancy of the temperance movement. Since most makers of so-called patent medicines, which in fact were rarely patented, did not list ingredients, an accurate assessment of the alcohol content was nearly impossible to determine. One of the most popular and heavily marketed was Lydia Pinkham's Vegetable Compound, an innocent-sounding formula containing up to 20 percent alcohol.[27] Pinkham's widely publicized rags-to-riches story, heavily infused with feminist appeal, made her mixture a favorite among women and Pinkham a millionaire.[28]

A typical advertisement for Lydia Pinkham's Vegetable Compound emphasized that "it is suicidal to go day after day with that dull, constant pain in the region of the womb." Left untended, an inflamed womb could lead to cancer, but the daily use of the compound would avert that dreaded outcome. A grateful user of the product, who previously found only transitory relief with morphine, recovered completely with Lydia Pinkham's forty-proof alcohol-laced patent medicine after eight months of daily use.[29]

For obvious reasons, most patent medicine peddlers refrained from emphasizing the alcohol content of their preparations. Dr. S.O. Richardson's Sherry Wine Bitters was an exception, the use of which promised "a sure remedy for the many diseases and debilities that man is subjected to."[30] Perhaps it struck a more refined note, as preparations boasting of wine were more common. Dr. Solomon's Indian Wine Bitters promised cures for erysipelas, indigestion, and all manner of kidney and liver diseases, and if none of those ailed the user, it would also restore a weak appetite.[31] There were many other choices for a discriminating customer, such as Dow's Sherry Wine Bitters, Restorative Wine Bitters, and Dr. Richardson's Sherry Wine Bitters.[32] All of these products found a ready market since no one would argue with a family keeping a tonic, elixir, or bitters around for exigencies, nor would they criticize a man's daily use of the same—for purely medicinal purposes, of course.

Patent medicines were not restricted to adults. One of the most popular remedies for children was advertised by "Mrs. Winslow, an experienced Nurse and Female Physician, [who] presents to the attention of mothers, her Soothing Syrup." Mrs. Winslow's Soothing Syrup was specifically marketed to eradicate the pain and discomfort of a toddler's teething, prompting mothers to "depend upon it ... it will give rest to you and relief and health to your infants."[33]

Typical testimonials for Mrs. Winslow's Soothing Syrup highlighted the medicine's tranquilizing effect on infants, which allowed the family to pass the night in peace. A satisfied mother wrote, "Having a little boy suffering greatly from teething, who could not rest, and at night by his cries would not permit any of the family to do so, I purchased a bottle of the SOOTHING SYRUP ... its effect upon him was like magic; he soon went to sleep, and all pain and nervousness disappeared. We have had no trouble with him since."[34]

Families demanding a night's respite from a fussy baby had other choices as well. Dr. Eaton's Infantile Cordial promised a botanical solution to quell the misery of teething. Advertisements proclaimed the medicine entirely safe, "the very roots from which it is distilled being dug from the forests under the direction of Dr. Eaton, many of them by his own hands." Eaton's cordial was versatile, offering parents a one-bottle remedy for colds, colic, and croup along with almost anything else.[35]

Dr. Eaton's advertisements criticized competitors, taking an oblique swipe at Mrs. Winslow's Soothing Syrup, by boldly declaring that his preparation was free of paregoric and opium.[36] The charge was accurate, as chemical analyses confirmed that Mrs. Winslow's teething formula was packed with morphine.[37] However, Dr. Eaton's medicine was probably little better, since the acknowledged distillation process and the name "Infantile Cordial" gave every indication of an alcohol-based treatment.

Antebellum faith in patent medicines was put to the test during the Civil War, during which medical care was brought directly to the fighting men, an ambitious operation the scale and scope of which strained both Union and Confederate resources. A combination of factors, such as antiquated medical practices, unsanitary camps, relentless illnesses and injuries, and inconsistently vetted doctors, deepened many soldiers' distrust in traditional medicine. As an alternative, soldiers could turn to readily available and medicinally justified alcohol use as a self-prescribed anxiolytic, soporific, restorative, and general cure-all. For those seeking a supposedly less intoxicating choice, a patent medicine was another option, with proprietors priming their preparations with heaping doses of fear and fraud.

One of the remedies exploiting Civil War soldiers' sensibilities was Brandreth's Pills. Just before hostilities broke out, Brandreth's Pills claimed annual sales in the millions for these little boxes of a remedy that cured colds and fevers. Even with those impressive numbers, however, an advertisement lamented that thousands still died from those conditions, an obviously obstinate option given the pill's unrivaled relief.[38]

The brisk pace of sales continued through 1861, as druggists dispensed another one million boxes of Brandreth's Pills, and with the Civil War bringing a new market, the company reminded soldiers that "sutlers supplied [the pills] by the dozen."[39] As a preventive measure, Brandreth's Pills were "important to those living in fever and ague districts," banishing measles, whooping cough, and the headaches of daily life.[40]

Always attentive to plans promoting its product, Brandreth's Pills launched an advertisement in *Harper's Weekly* in 1863 under the bold heading of "Surgeon-General Hammond, by ordering calomel and destructive Minerals from the supply tables, has conferred a blessing on our sick soldiers."[41]

For many Civil War physicians, calomel was an essential medicine, even though its routine use was becoming increasingly controversial, leading to Surgeon-General William Hammond's ham-fisted order banning its widespread use.[42] Through this directive, the surgeon–general waded into deep political waters, provoking the ire of military doctors aggravated by his encroachment on their practice. It also served the interests of his boss, Secretary of War Edwin M. Stanton, furthering a feud between the pair that Hammond would eventually lose.

Calomel, more properly known as mercurous chloride, had a long and storied use in American medicine dating back to the country's earliest days.[43] Benjamin Rush, the eminent colonial politician and physician, had nothing but praise for mercury's medicinal prowess, proclaiming its use, along with blood-letting, indispensable. Rush's enthusiastic endorsement influenced clinical practice for generations, placing Hammond in the contentious position of deposing a venerable luminary.

Even before Hammond's dramatic directive removing calomel, its popularity was wavering under the weight of its poisonous side. In small doses "the first noticeable effect following the administration of mercury ... is seen in an increased activity of the secretions, especially those of the intestines." Mercury's profound impact led physicians to prescribe ever larger doses, a dangerous decision since "it becomes apparent that we are dealing with a destructive agent ... recently healed wounds open afresh; the body becomes emaciated, the face pallid, the whole system becomes particularly susceptible to irritating or depressing influences." Pushed to this level, a soldier produced buckets of saliva, considered a clinically convenient cathartic ridding the body of disease.

Hammond defended his decision as the onslaught of criticism grew. In one instance the besieged surgeon-general showed "the President a photograph of a soldier in the hospital whose nose, left cheek, and upper jaw had been eaten away by gangrene, produced by dosing with calomel."[44] Fortunately, Hammond did have supporters, particularly among enlightened doctors advocating less drastic interventions such as improved camp hygiene and nutrition, aimed more at preventing, not curing, illness.

The makers of Brandreth's Pills had another answer.[45] Touting their supposedly entirely botanical formula, the pills offered a safe, effective alternative to mercury in curing the dysentery and diarrhea that plagued army encampments. Military testimonials buttressed these claims. Roscoe K. Watson, a private with Company F, 17th Regiment, New York Volunteers, claimed that many in his unit were incapacitated with diarrhea and "the army surgeon did not cure us, and I was reduced to skin and bone. Among the company were quite a number of members who had worked in your laboratory at Sing Sing. They were not sick, because they used Brandreth's Pills." Following this fortuitous discovery, Watson and others allegedly became converts, finding health in Brandreth's Pills and, unsurprisingly, by avoiding the military doctor.

Botanical medicines took root, fertilized by soldiers' blind faith and distrust in established medicine. The makers of Brandreth's Pills tilled the ground even more, selfishly sowing seeds of suspicion. According to one self-serving advertisement, "If adopted by Medical Authority in the Army of the United States, a clear saving of FIFTY MILLIONS of DOLLARS would be made, by securing the health and lives of our brave soldiers."[46] It was a clever argument appealing to the reader's patriotism and frugality while indirectly accusing medical authorities of withholding a valuable treatment.

The same advertisement added the testimonials of nineteen members of Private Watson's unit, including the company commander, all of whom unanimously castigated military surgeons. Grateful soldiers drew a stark contrast between their health, restored by a single treatment with Brandreth's Pills, and those "who appeared to be sick in no respect different to us, but who used the remedies prescribed by the regimental surgeon, [and] either died or were sick for weeks in the hospital." It was a harsh, purposeful indictment of military medicine shamelessly promoting Brandreth's Pills.

Brandreth's Pills' ploys may not have been successful, but the indomitable determination of the company once again surfaced in an 1864 marketing campaign unfurled under the following banner: "United States Sanitary Commission.... Is it using all the means Providence has placed within its reach, or is it stiff-necked, and determined that so GREAT a REMEDY as Brandreth's Pills shall not be used to economize the life and health of our soldiers?" Testimonials from the men of Company F, 17th Regiment, New York Volunteers, now swollen to sixty appreciative soldiers, gave credit to Brandreth's Pills for two years of army life unblemished by illness incurred "by the necessary hardships and privations of a soldier's life in the field."[47]

An anonymous testimonial in the *Banner of Light* under the heading "Attention, Soldiers!" announced that "Dr. Dresser ... introduced a medicine for the cure of Chronic Diarrhea with marked success. It was my fortune to witness its effects on a number of patients in the soldiers' hospitals." Having proven its value in saving countless soldiers' lives, the nameless author recommended the treatment's widespread adoption by the public at large.[48]

Patent medicines specifically targeting psychological symptoms were far less common than the innumerable physical cure-alls. Instead of directly addressing mental health issues, entrepreneurs opted for palatable euphemisms such as headaches, lassitude, and irritability. As an early sign of social acceptance, and perhaps an indication of the frequency of such problems, advertisements for Laurie's Chinese Life Pills' appealed directly to this group of symptoms. In learning of a "certain cure for nervous debility," readers of *Harper's Weekly* in 1862 were told that Dr. Adam Laurie, while residing in Hong Kong, had discovered a wonderful medicine brewed from a mysterious plant growing in the Chinese tea fields.[49]

Laurie's Chinese Life Pills exerted their beneficent effects on the user's nervous system and, in so doing, rapidly and safely relieved "Languor, Lassitude, Depression of Spirits, Nervous Headache, Irritability, Excitement, Excessive Use of Tobacco, and all diseases from Impure blood or nervous derangement."[50] Several months later, perhaps in response to poor sales, a demonstrably slimmer advertisement addressed "To the Nervous" simply provided readers with a mailing address, bypassing the usual hyperbole and testimonials. For the price of one dollar a customer would receive one box of Laurie's Chinese Life Pills.[51]

Henry T. Helmbold, showman, druggist extraordinaire, and famous patent medicine man, made and lost fortunes promoting his name and nostrums. In a pseudo-scientific newspaper essay Helmbold extolled the virtues of sarsaparilla, a blood-purifying agent with no equal, particularly given the druggist's self-confessed meticulous preparation of the extract. As a further endorsement of his product, Helmbold claimed that "10,121 were treated for diseases arising from excesses: Habits of Dissipation ... Weak Nerves, Dimness of Vision, Night Sweats, Pallid Countenance, great Mobility, Restlessness, Horror of Society, no Earnestness of Manner. These symptoms, if allowed to continue, would undoubtedly result in Epileptic Fits, Insanity."[52] In an ironic twist, the ostentatious druggist died in an insane asylum, perhaps a consequence of the doctor not taking his own medicine.[53]

During the Civil War patent medicine makers advertised heavily, although not always directly to soldiers. Reluctance to criticize the military while promoting their remedies probably dissuaded most providers from engaging in broader outreach. There were bold exceptions to this approach, however, with Holloway's Pills and Ointment, among others, unabashedly bashing military healthcare.

In 1863, as bloody battles raged across America, a small advertisement in *Harper's Weekly* warned, "Soldier's, see to your own Health, do not trust to the Army supplies.... Holloway's Pills and Ointment should be in every man's knapsack."[54] Another advertisement predicted nothing but misery for soldiers since "young men, rushing into the exposures and dangers of a Soldier's life, [were unprepared] for fatal fevers," which fortunately a few doses of Holloway's Pills would entirely prevent.[55] A few months later an even more dramatic announcement appeared with a woodcut engraving portraying a group of suffering, sick souls, including a partially clad woman, under which the advertisement cautioned that "measles are prostrating the Volunteers by the hundreds; the hospitals are crowded with them, Soldiers be warned in time. Holloway's Pills are positively infallible in the cure of this disease."[56]

Advertisements for Hostetter's Celebrated Stomach Bitters pulled no punches in knocking the army's intransigence in not supplying the troops with this famous remedy. Hostetter's no doubt touched a nerve among soldiers and their families by noting that "sickness destroys more soldiers than cannon, rifles, and bayonets. Our brave boys are now suffering more severely from the terrible epidemics." Aggravating matters even more was the sultry, southern weather, a breeding ground for infectious fevers. The makers of Hostetter's Celebrated Stomach Bitters pleaded with army medical authorities, urging the use of their medicine by cleverly pointing out that "vast quantities of the ordinary alcoholic liquor ... are used for hospital purposes.... Their effect is murderous and it is amazing that they should be resorted to."[57]

The advertisements for patent medicines can be viewed as the producers' best efforts to understand and appeal to a soldier's deepest worries. As such, they represented an indirect measure of the misery from which soldiers sought relief—insights that patent medicine purveyors exploited for propaganda and profits. As with all patent medicines, fluff, fraud, and fear were the principal ingredients that drove sales, revealing, as the intensity of the war escalated, a subtle shift in marketing strategies targeting the psychological consequences of combat.

Hostetter's Celebrated Stomach Bitters provided an example of a slight trend moving toward alleviating the emotional distresses of war with a clever campaign against the "grand army of dyspeptics," an allusion to combat's stomach-churning stimulus. Soldiers ostensibly taking the tonic to overcome the ills of indigestion from a poor diet would also benefit from the fact that it "renews the appetite, cheers the spirits, braces the nerves."[58]

Nineteenth-century medical practice considered diseases of the digestive system, commonly diagnosed as dyspepsia, one of the foremost problems plaguing people. Doctors diagnosed dyspepsia from a broad range of physical symptoms that included such disparate disturbances as bloating, belching, dizziness, headaches, nausea, stomachaches, sleeplessness, and weakness. Physicians linked dyspepsia with its emotional symptoms through its negative nutritional impact on the brain and nervous system. As a consequence, for dyspeptics, "there were diseases of the mind, not the less distressful being denominated nervous for all suffering is nervous, all feeling is nervous—that is, in the nerves." Again the constellation of symptoms was broad and included depression, irritability, anxiety, and confusion.[59]

Dyspepsia's frequency, fusion of physical and nervous symptoms, and resistance to relief was an invitation for exploitation. At a time when human understanding of psychology was in its infancy, and stoicism prized, Hostetter's Celebrated Stomach Bitters offered a morally palatable preparation, packaged to relieve a soldier's wartime heartburn.

The supposed connections between diet, digestion, and disease encouraged some patent medicine makers to market various nerve foods. Individuals seeking relief from chronic headaches, dizziness, and other nervous disorders could rely on E.R. Still's plainly named "nerve food," with each ingredient specifically designed to nourish starving nerves.[60]

There were other markets available besides soldiers and their nerves. In blaming nineteenth-century social trends that restricted a woman's activities, diet, and dress, one writer claimed that "probably no country furnishes such multitudes of peevish, fretful, nervous women as the United States ... and only keeps herself up by stimulants."[61] Enlightened physicians acknowledged the problem and its cause, proposing nutritional, environmental and social solutions. Patent medicine makers had other ideas.

Advertisements for patent medicines pivoted following the war's end. With demobilization looming, Brandreth's Pills swapped soldiers for women. In pitching their pills to women, the trend of relieving both physical and emotional symptoms was evident: "For Females the Brandreth's Pills can not be too highly spoken of. They remove all obstructions, give energy and strength, cure the distressing headache unfortunately so prevalent with the sex, depression of spirits ... nervous affections."[62] Several months later, perhaps recognizing that an exclusive focus on women was limiting sales, Brandreth's Pills were promoted as a cosmetic improving the "good looks" of both men and women while still guaranteeing "cheerfulness and vigor."[63]

Advertisements for Holloway's Pills also changed with the war's end. Forced to find new anxieties, the makers of Holloway's Pills stoked fears about growing urbanization, a trend exacerbated by men returning home from distant battlefields. As a result of "crowded cities malaria and fogs are breathed over and over again ... hence the sluggishness of mind and body, the weariness and irritability of many persons."[64]

Not all patent medicines reformulated their marketing strategies. Some, such as E. Dexter Loveridge's Wahoo Bitters, resisted the trend, relying instead on the same tried and true recipes featuring Indian-inspired restoratives. Promoted as "The Great Indian Beverage," Wahoo Bitters dispelled dyspepsia through a secret combination of barks, herbs, and roots. As an added bonus, Loveridge mixed the dry ingredients with "Pure Rye Whiskey," giving teetotalers an undisguised medicinal pathway for alcohol consumption.[65]

The supposed connections between diet, digestion, and disease encouraged other patent medicine makers to move into a new market promoting nerve nutrition and supposedly safe sedatives. In a possible reflection of a nation struggling with the psychological aftermath of war, a veritable explosion in these purported anxiolytics greeted America's dawn of peace.

Among the wares widely advertised during the Civil War era was Dodd's Nervine, peddled as an opium-free sedative that "calms the agitated mind."[66] Nervine accomplished that feat by means of its "nutritive principle. It has affinity for the Nervous Fibres."[67] Ayer's sarsaparilla relieved nervousness by removing harmful impurities from the blood.[68]

Advertisements for Winchester's Hypophosphites claimed to provide cures for "all derangements of the Nervous and Blood Systems."[69] An 1867 advertisement for Winchester's Hypophosphites boldly titled "Important to Invalids" could have been an indirect message to Civil War veterans, many of whom were still suffering from the lingering wounds of war. With "promptness and certainty," Winchester's Hypophosphites promised cures for all types of physical problems and "all whose Vital Forces are depressed, rendering necessary a Nervous Tonic and Invigorator."[70]

For thrifty-minded consumers, Turner's Universal Neuralgia Pill cured all nervous diseases, sometimes after only one day's use.[71] John Lord, a supposedly grateful patent medicine customer, claimed that after four years of suffering from chronic dyspepsia and insomnia, all of his symptoms vanished thanks to Dr. Quain's Magic Condition Pills.[72] Willis Sawens, a physician with a penchant for patent medicines, sold popular products such as the alcohol-filled Dr. Sawens' Life Invigorating Bitters; for those specifically afflicted with anxiety, Dr. Sawens' Magic Nervine Pills soothed frayed nerves.[73]

Patent medicine makers crafted their formulas using a mixture of scientific proofs, pompous proclamations, and endless endorsements, all in an effort to bolster a belief-based business. With the growth of medical knowledge and public education, the pretentious prescribers of the period adjusted, incorporating the new discoveries into more sophisticated campaigns.

Few problems inspired more fear and foreboding at this time than mental disorders, heavily shrouded in suspicion and shame. In what was a laudable, if indirect and mostly unintended, effect, the panaceas packaged by these practitioners emphasized the physiological etiology of mental illness, minimizing the moral stigma.

In a dramatic example, a newspaper reader's attention surely must have gravitated toward the eye-catching headline "He Committed Suicide!" Further on, the reader would learn that "his case was a sad one, but no worse than that of any other nervous sufferer.... The same or similar consequences are likely to result to anyone who has any of these advance symptoms to an awful end." Fortunately, by avoiding worthless remedies and fraudulent physicians and taking Dr. Miles' Restorative Nervine, that fateful outcome was avoidable.[74]

As a self-proclaimed expert on nervous disorders, Dr. Franklin Miles criticized clinicians who clung to old-fashioned theories. According to him, all physical problems, including dyspepsia, stemmed from nerve dysfunction. Using an analogy of the time, Miles explained that a mysterious nervous force moved "to every part of the body, just as electric current is conveyed along the telegraph wires to every station, large or small." In his theory, dyspepsia was the direct result of irritated nerves enervating the stomach.[75]

Dr. Miles advertised across the country. Testimonials played an important role in promoting his products, and a full-page advertisement in 1894 prominently publicized "Dr. Miles' Restorative Nervine—The Only Remedy for Nervous Diseases Admitted to the World's Fair." Two dozen solemn faces surrounded the page, a caption beneath each a declaration of the medicine's prowess in conquering brain fatigue, headaches, chronic nervousness, insomnia, and melancholy.[76]

In a more focused advertisement, Dr. Miles reached out to Confederate veterans. A picture of a serious-looking man was accompanied by a somber story. Driven to despair by nervousness, forgetfulness, insomnia, confusion, and depression, the man had mournfully concluded that "I was no good on earth." However, what might have ended in tragedy was averted through the use of six bottles of Dr. Miles' Restorative Nervine.[77]

Informative pamphlets often supplemented newspaper advertisements. These publications provided more details for discerning readers, and Dr. Miles gratified them with "New and Startling Facts for Those Afflicted with Nervous Diseases."[78] Miles stuffed his little treatise with a product catalog, his medical theories, and the obligatory testimonials, as well as an autobiography.

According to Dr. Miles, he began his medical work after the Civil War ended, and through continuous study and research he became one of America's "leading physicians, whose reputation and practice as a specialist extends throughout the United States." After moving to Chicago, the celebrated doctor began his patent medicine business with a complete line of products such as Restorative Tonic, Restorative Nervine, and Restorative Nerve Pills. Every disorder that his products would cure received a detailed description, including such topics as delirium tremens, insanity, nervous dyspepsia, and hysteria. For the "blues, melancholy," Miles reminded readers that those conditions "are not imaginary complaints as some uncharitable and not well posted people believe…. They are the result of an irritable and exhausted condition of the brain." Complete relief followed the faithful use of Dr. Miles' restorative remedies.

The ingenuity of the pretentious panaceas closely paralleled the social and scientific trends of the time. Two mysterious forces shaping society during the nineteenth century, neither of which were new but which, as a result of scientific inquiry and industrialization, were becoming more commonplace, were electricity and magnetism.

Medical uses of electricity required a practical means of creating and storing the energy. The development of the Leyden jar in 1745 and the subsequent invention of galvanic cells decades later spurred medical research that associated electricity with human neuromuscular activity. Physicians conducted a broad range of experiments, hoping to reverse muscle paralysis, the loss of vision, deafness, and other neurological afflictions.[79]

The Civil War era cemented certain medical uses of electricity. William A. Hammond, the controversial surgeon-general of the U.S. Army, devoted his post-military career to neurology. In 1869 Hammond published his translated version of Moritz Meyer's German textbook, *Electricity in Its Relations to Practical Medicine*. Meyer's book provided physicians with a detailed explanation of the electrical equipment, physiological theories, and clinical applications for the diagnosis and management of many forms of pain and paralysis.[80]

Various scientific experiments demonstrated that electric currents caused muscle contractions, including the muscles surrounding blood vessels. One of the leading theories of insanity at the time ascribed the morbid development of the mental disorder to "cerebral congestion," a term suggesting excessive blood in the brain. A respected medical journal noted that "certain forms of delirium and cerebral excitement, and also many hallucinations of the different senses are of this nature, and are completely cured by the application of the electric current to the head," a result understood to be a direct consequence of blood vessel constriction.[81]

In spite of scientific understanding, most people considered electricity a mysterious force, a devastating power unleashed when lightning struck the earth, shattering trees and killing unsuspecting animals and people. Spiritualists saw similarities between the imperceptible nature of electricity and the invisible spirit world, arguing for the reality of the latter through the certainty of the former. Electric doctors and electric patent medicines exploited the burgeoning medical knowledge by foisting fresh frauds on an unsuspecting public.

Once it became a matter of faith that "a medium possesses a peculiar quality of magnetism and electricity," psychic healers opened shop.[82] Dr. J.T. Gilman Pike was a believer, and from his office in Boston he promised patients a beneficial blend of two invisible healing forces, spiritual and electric.[83] Dr. I.G. Atwood provided a similar service in New York City.[84] Dr. Fitzgibbon, accompanied by Miss Ella Vanwie, a pretty young medium, lectured to large audiences in Washington, D.C., on human electricity.[85] In central New Jersey, patients could take advantage of the "healthy healing effect of the purest kind of electricity, emanating from the human battery of Dr. Van Etten."[86]

Nellie Craib-Beighle was another self-proclaimed doctor known for possessing an electric hand. As part of a spectral circuit, Nellie conducted the energy provided by a group of ghosts, resulting in electricity traveling down her right shoulder to her fingers. The energized woman spent long hours every day delivering the therapeutic current to throngs of suffering patients. At the end of a day's work, she retreated to the sanctity of her home and the company of her spirit guides.[87]

Dr. Larue took no chances and advertised his skills as both an Indian doctor and an electrical physician. Like many other quacks, Larue traveled extensively, and in 1872 he took up temporary residence in New York City, having completed a tour through Ohio and Indiana. Larue immodestly claimed unrivaled success treating chronic diseases.[88]

Electricity sparked a similar trend among patent medicine makers energized by the potential profits. One of the first was Professor De Grath's Electric Oil, a formulation for the treatment of rheumatism, neuralgia, fevers, and deafness. As part of a clever marketing scheme, the professor offered the mayor of Philadelphia one hundred dollars for his favorite charity if the electric oil failed to cure any disease.[89]

Professor De Grath unabashedly declared that the "oil acts on the system with electricity ... all organic derangement of the animal system is the effect of an obstruction of the physio-electric fluid in the organ diseased." As might be expected, his preparation removed that barrier.[90] For the impatient, Professor De Grath's Electric Oil cured a stomachache in five minutes, a headache in fifteen minutes, and nervous disorders in one or two days, but for the hard of hearing it might take a full four days to overcome deafness.[91]

In a pious and pompous faith-based advertisement, Professor De Grath equated his miraculous medicine with the biblical cures achieved by anointing the sick with oil.[92] During the Civil War Professor De Grath's Electric Oil continued to advertise, but the focus shifted to emphasizing the "chemical and electrical principles" responsible for the medicine's relief of deafness, headaches, and just about every other imaginable problem.[93]

The success of Professor De Grath's Electric Oil bred imitations. Golden Electric Oil promised a cure for diphtheria.[94] Roger's Electro-Magnetic Oil upped the ante and would cure any pain, including a nervous headache, in five minutes. Resolving dyspepsia and "weakness peculiar to females" took a bit longer but always led to a successful outcome.[95]

Dr. Smith's Electric Oil was a guaranteed cure for headaches and deafness; if not suffering from those conditions, the oil was promoted as an antiseptic, a gentle alternative to pouring alcohol over fresh wounds.[96] Twenty minutes after swallowing a dose of Dr. Galutia B. Smith's miraculous medicine, "color appears on the pallid cheek, the eyes begin to brighten up, and cheerfulness takes the place of abject misery."[97] A year later, in 1871, the marketing focus changed, still promoting a cure for rheumatism, neuralgia and deafness, but now boldly emphasizing a new indication for "nerve power ... a real sedative without opium."[98]

The awkwardly named Crook's Electric Oil from Pine Hill, Kentucky, promised relief from all sorts of pain faster than any other preparation.[99] Dr. Thomas' Electric Oil was "worth its weight in gold," curing chronic back pain, asthma, rheumatism, wounds, and, as always, diphtheria.[100] In a testament to the vanity of the day, Dr. Leon's Electric Hair Renewer was touted as a cure for baldness and gray hair and lauded for restoring a youthful appearance to a woman's tresses.[101]

A few months before the Civil War ended, the *Banner of Light* featured an array of announcements such as "Dr. A. P. Pierce, Clairvoyant, Magnetic, and Electric Physician, attends to diseases of Body and Mind."[102] In a competing notice, Dr. White was said to cure all diseases through electricity by laying his hands on the sufferer, presumably transmitting his therapeutic energy in the process.[103] For a one-dollar admission price, the curious could attend a series of five lectures presented by Mary Lucas "instructing ladies in the Use of Electricity, Mesmerism, and all remedies proper for the Cure of All Diseases."[104]

Rivaling the mystery of electricity was magnetism, another enigmatic force that was the subject of scientific study. Physicians were studying magnets almost a century before the Civil War, but Franz Mesmer essentially hijacked the field with his theories and practice of animal magnetism. Mesmer believed that all humans, in varying degrees, had innate magnetic energy, and those pos-

sessed with an abundance of this energy could heal those with less by trans-
ferring the curative force through simply touching them. His controversial
magnetic theory attracted both condemnation and confirmation, with advocates and antagonists attacking each other.[105]

Mesmer's concept of health through animal magnetism was ripe for
exploitation. During the Civil War era prospective patients could visit magnetic
doctors, many of whom were also spiritualists, and procure magnetic medicines
from nearby druggists.

The citizens of Urbana, Ohio, enthusiastically greeted the "magnetic doctor" in November 1865, filling a local venue for a weekend and earning the
doctor $1,200, leading a local newspaper to sarcastically note that "this is very
profitable magnetism."[106] In New York City, Dr. James A. Neal set up shop as
a self-styled magnetic doctor and cured diseases by rubbing his hands over the
sources of his patients' afflictions. Neal admitted that he lacked a medical
diploma, offering in its place "not a written one, but an unwritten one from
Almighty."[107] Elsewhere Dr. and Mrs. Gallion offered their services as magnetic
and clairvoyant physicians, taking up residence in a central Missouri location
and promising to cure stubborn medical problems considered hopeless by
other doctors.[108] Dr. James Porter challenged skeptics to visit his office in Memphis, Tennessee, and witness a free public demonstration of his magnetic healing.[109]

In a lengthy front-page notice in a local Vermont newspaper, Dr. Merriam
promised cures through his "magnetic operations," thus avoiding noxious medicines and surgery. Without further explanation, the traveling healer assured
his readers that in ten out of twelve cases stubborn diseases would yield to his
treatment. Merriam provided a long list of physical ailments responsive to his
treatments, such as consumption, dyspepsia, diarrhea, gout, and swollen joints,
while also promising relief to individuals suffering from mental depression,
nervous depression, bad appetite, stuttering, and wakefulness.[110]

Magnetic doctors attracted desperate clients by offering them hope hyped
through testimonials, made all the more convincing when attributed to well-
known people. Alert readers of a southern newspaper might have noticed a
short insert announcing the marriage of Mark Twain in Elmira, New York, "to
Miss Olivia Langdon, of that city, a spirituelle young lady, who for years was
confined to a sick room, from which she was released by the manipulations of
a magnetic doctor."[111]

Dr. J.E Briggs, a magnetic healer with a New York City office, offered his
patients the deal of "No Cure, No Pay."[112] A few miles away, Madame Clifford,
a clairvoyant and healer, provided magnetic baths.[113] Dr. D.A. Smith specialized
in psychological disorders and, after years of study and research, discovered

that nervousness, hysteria, nervous prostration, and "female weakness" resulted from a person's dwindling magnetic potential, which his treatment restored.[114] Without fanfare or elaboration, Dr. Fanyou, yet another magnetic healing physician with an office in New York City, cured all nervous diseases.[115]

Dr. James Chesley was a psychic medium who combined magnetism and electricity, curing hopeless cases as he traveled throughout Massachusetts.[116] His business boomed, and the charitable doctor responded by renting a large building in Boston and outfitting his Durham Medical Institute with medicated baths and other modern conveniences.[117]

Patients in Philadelphia could visit J. H. Rhodes, MD, "a regular graduate of the Medical School" who added clairvoyance and magnetic healing to his therapeutic regimen. For those unable to make an office visit, upon receipt of two dollars and the person's address, age and marital status, Rhodes would arrange a medical examination with a spirit doctor. How and when the spirit would conduct the examination was left to the patient's imagination, but upon receiving the results of the consultation, Rhodes would send by mail the spirit-prescribed magnetic treatments.[118]

Rhodes adopted the use of magnetized paper in his clinical practice, a convenient mail-order item that customers could procure for a nominal cost of one dollar.[119] Magnetized paper was gaining some popularity as a treatment for nervous disorders, with other practitioners such as Dr. A.S. Hayward joining Rhodes in its use.[120] From his office in Milwaukee, Wisconsin Dr. Freeman likewise prescribed magnetized paper for all "nervous difficulties."[121]

Patent medicine makers offered an alternative for those unable or unwilling to visit a "doctor" with proprietary magnetic formulations. Perhaps the most popular was Dr. Trask's Magnetic Ointment, adorned with an impressive-looking mechanical contraption on the label, presumably conveying a scientific source for the medicine.[122]

Dr. Trask's Magnetic Ointment advertised widely, perhaps justifying its claim "as the most popular Ointment in the United States." Applying the compound would treat everything from rheumatism to wounds, with an incredible added benefit as "no doubt the best known remedy" for diphtheria.[123]

As with most patent medicines, an intriguing tale explained the magnetic ointment's discovery. After laboring for twenty years concocting various plant-based remedies, the seventy-year-old Dr. Trask settled on a "combination of these powerful Vegetable Extracts with Electricity or Magnetism in the form of an Ointment." Once applied, the salve supposedly permeated every cell in the body, ensuring that "no patient ever need die" from some dreaded disease. Dr. Trask's Magnetic Ointment would also cure all nervous afflictions.[124]

Nothing breeds replication more than success, and the widespread appeal of Dr. Trask's Magnetic Ointment encouraged imitation. Haley's Magnetic Oil treated the typical ailments for "man or beast," an economic inducement avoiding the need for separate liniments.[125] Roger's Magnetic Oil offered users the option of applying the lotion externally or swallowing the compound, with either choice relieving pain in mere minutes.[126] Some discerning customers of magnetic remedies might have wondered about the professed powers of Lyon's Magnetic Insect Powder, guaranteed to eliminate cockroaches, ants, and bedbugs.[127]

Positioned immediately below a newspaper appeal for medical school graduates to apply for positions as military surgeons was Professor Reed's Magnetic Oil, a surefire cure for sore joints, frostbite, and "nervous affections," the very tonic worn-out soldiers might have enjoyed.[128] Pennsylvania patrons could also purchase Dr. Russell's Magnetic Oil, magnanimously labeled as "the Great, the Grand, the Only reliable remedy" for rheumatism and various scrapes and sprains.[129]

Makers of Hull and Chamberlain's Magnetic and Electric Powders touted their product as a "great nervine regulator" and an all-around remedy for female diseases. Despite its name, the powders were nonmetallic and entirely vegetable.[130] Dr. William Clark's Spirit Magnetic Vegetable Remedies invoked supernatural credibility. Speaking from beyond the grave through Jeannie Waterman Danforth, a psychic medium and magnetic healer, Clark guided his host in the formulation of products to cure diseases and strengthen frayed and tired nerves.[131] In yet another example, a very simple two-sentence advertisement offered the public "spiritual pills as a certain cure for the Fevers and Ague."[132]

Kunkel's Bitter Wine of Iron added citrate of magnetic oxide and yellow Peruvian bark to complement the alcohol-based tonic designed to cure indigestion, acid stomach, and nervousness. More specifically, Kunkel's product targeted symptoms of emotional distress, infusing the user with a warm glow of well-being while improving sleep, appetite, and energy.[133]

Dr. H.B. Storer's Female Restorative was another spirit-channeled patent medicine for the relief of female weakness. Storer's compound increased a woman's "Vital Magnetism" and, as a sedative, soothed jangled nerves. In an odd appeal, Storer promised that "this medicine lends no assistance to child-murder,"[134] which may have been an oblique reference to the disinhibiting effect of alcohol, a common ingredient in many patent medicines. Subsequent advertisements highlighted Storer's nostrum as a spirit-free nutritive mixture, emphasizing that alcohol "is an element of discord and death, and [one should] avoid it, when in sickness or health."[135]

Testimonials from grateful patients supplemented Dr. Storer's advertisements. A woman from Indiana wrote that "your medicine has wrought a great change in me," which included warmer hands and feet and an improved complexion. Another customer from Connecticut welcomed the medicine's "pleasant effect on my nervous system." An anonymous user thanked Dr. Storer and the spirits on behalf of "suffering womanhood."[136]

As knowledge of magnetism and electricity became more common, panacea producers exploited this information by proposing an imbalance between a person's intrinsic positive and negative energy as the basis of their treatments. One of the most heavily promoted products adopting this theory was Mrs. Spence's Positive and Negative Powders.

Two years after the Civil War ended, an ostentatious advertisement promoted Mrs. Spence's Positive and Negative Powders "for the Healing of the Nation! The Great Spiritual Remedy!" The allusion to binding the wounds of war was obvious, and grateful customers offered a glimpse of those troubles, such as Libbie G. Barrett, who extolled the patent medicine for relieving her chronic headaches.[137]

In another reference to the war's conclusion, one advertisement for Mrs. Spence's Positive and Negative Powders highlighted the "Irresistible Army of Witnesses to the Supremacy of the Great Spiritual Remedy." Astute readers of this newspaper may have wondered about Mrs. Spence, since her contribution to the medication seemed obscure, with Professor Payton Spence taking full credit for the discovery and formulation of the spiritual remedy.[138]

Readers were no doubt mystified by the opening lines of another advertisement announcing the presence of "the Secret Army of Invisible Workers silently and without show or parade, an immense army annually spreads all over the United States." These ominous-sounding invaders were actually delivering messages around the country praising Mrs. Spence's Positive and Negative Powders. A tabulation of 38,808 testimonials grouped by diseases cured revealed dyspepsia, neuralgia, fever, sleeplessness, nervousness, and various respiratory disorders as the chief conditions from which patients sought relief.[139]

Claiming that magnetism held revolutionary healing power, Mrs. Spence's preparations offered customers a choice between the magnetically polarized positive and negative powders, broadly touted as treating all nervous diseases and female ailments. More specifically, the positive powders relieved pain, female weakness, and inflammation, while the negative powders were reserved for nervous disorders and "low fevers" such as typhoid.[140]

Customers not interested in the claims of patent medicines could choose a medical device that supposedly achieved equally miraculous results. An 1867 advertisement for Dr. Hall's Voltaic Armor or Magnetic Bands and Soles relied on this same pseudo-scientific sophistry of magnetic polarization to promote its product as a cure-all, particularly for nervous disorders. The impressive-sounding Voltaic Armor Association manufactured the magnetic bands for specific areas of the body. Customers could order head bands for three dollars, presumably for the relief of chronic headaches. Magnetic bands for the waist, perhaps meant to cure dyspepsia, cost five dollars, as did breast bands, seemingly designed for heartache, anxiety, or other "female" problems.[141]

William Wilson was the creator (and chief promoter) of the "Wilsonia magnetic garments … the marvel of the world … dumbfounding the scientists and physicians, and making glad the hearts of the people."[142] Wilson sewed tiny magnetic studs into his patented underwear and shoe soles to prevent the "endless ills that flesh is heir to."[143]

In the years immediately following the Civil War, most patent medicine providers marketed their wares by emphasizing physical disorders such as dyspepsia. Medicines promoting the relief of psychological problems were less common, mainly due to the stigma attached to mental disorders. Dyspepsia straddled the moral gulf, cloaking the expression and potential treatment of emotional distress behind an acceptable façade. This state of affairs began to change over subsequent decades, as the advertising for patent medicines pivoted toward the relief of psychological problems.

Advertisements for Carter's Little Nerve Pills linked nervousness with dyspepsia, unambiguously suggesting that these conditions were synonymous. Carter's Little Nerve Pills were "specially [made] for those who suffer from Nervousness, Sleeplessness, Nervous and Sick Headache, Weak Stomach, Dyspepsia, Indigestion, etc."[144] The producer of the pills was confident, guaranteeing not just relief but also a complete cure from sick headaches, and would oblige the skeptic with hundreds of testimonials.[145]

For those who wanted more than a pill and would never countenance liquor, Malt Bitters "quiets the nerves, perfects digestion, cheers the mind."[146] Hop Bitters took a more personal route, advising that "if you are a man of business weakened by the strain of your duties avoid stimulation use Hop Bitters. If you are a man of letters toiling over midnight work, to restore brain nerve and waste, use Hop Bitters." Perhaps hinting at suicide, the patent medicine offered hope to the weak and depressed, assuring users that Hop Bitters saved many lives.[147]

Dr. J.B. Simpson's Specific Medicine treated the anxious, depressed, and irritable consumer, and it even proved effective for insanity. Two contrasting illustrations dramatized the medicine's impact—one portrayed the haggard face of an elderly woman before using Dr. J.B Simpson's Specific Medicine, while a smiling, younger woman showed the results.[148] Two years later an almost identically worded advertisement illustrated with before-and-after figures of men promoted Gray's Specific Medicine.[149]

In addition to mental illness, patent medicines exploited concerns regarding alcoholism, a burgeoning social problem motivating the temperance movement. Dr. S.B. Collins dismissed moral weakness as the cause of alcoholism, instead arguing that the disease resulted from an alcohol-induced physiological change in the body, a condition that his Liquor Antidote would completely reverse.[150] The supposedly non-intoxicating, botanically based Parker's Ginger Tonic was another perfect remedy for nervousness, insomnia, and drunkenness.[151]

The marketing of patent medicines, as conveyed in newspaper advertisements and product labels, provides indirect evidence of the ills that concerned postwar Americans. While faith was the chief ingredient of all patent medicines, the purposes for which they were formulated suggest that emotional disorders progressively became primary targets for treatment, bringing into focus the psychological consequences of war.

Seven

Return of Reason

Emotional turmoil resulting from four years of civil war contributed to decades of mayhem, misery, and malevolence on a scale unprecedented in America's short history. Subsequent social fissures created chasms filled with the doubters, desperate, disconnected, discontented, depressed, dishonest, and drained, and each group sought an outlet. A loss of faith in traditional religion and hopes for a reunion with lost loved ones led to the growth of Spiritualism. Others sought relief in alcohol, patent medicines, and suicide, while desperation, deceit, and derision gave rise to a carnival of crime.

Like any detour, the socially circuitous diversion eventually redirected many of the travelers back to the main path. Some, such as suicide victims and criminals, never rejoined society, leaving behind a permanent legacy of the war's impact. For society as a whole, the return to reason was slow, with disillusionment and distrust hampering recovery, an enduring psychological consequence of the Civil War.

The rough road to recovery required a concerted effort to deconstruct the delusions foisted on the public for fame and fortune. In a paradoxical way, the efforts that paved the way for the return to reason also built new pathways that guided a healthier society in the coming generations.

Medical practice had lost its luster during the Civil War and sought to restore the sheen through science, ushering in a renaissance of professional integrity. The lack of trust in medical practitioners opened the door for deception, ushering in a wave of charlatans who exploited every imaginable innovation and ideology. Pushing back against them were serious clinicians steeped in scientific study, determined to close the door on deception.

George M. Beard was a physician specializing in nervous disorders and the practice of the newly emerging field of electrical medicine.[1] After serving as an assistant surgeon in the Union Navy, Beard published many articles on the role of electricity in both explaining and treating mental and neurological disorders. Beard prized the methodical process of scientific inquiry and abhorred those who hijacked its credibility in an effort to dupe a gullible public. He took particular aim at Spiritualism, admonishing the pseudo-scientific practitioners as phony peddlers.

Speaking before a rapt audience at the Long Island Historical Society, Dr. Beard began his attack on Spiritualism by noting the enabling influence of the Civil War: "Since the war, and as a result in part of the demoralization of the war, there has been ... social corruption."[2] His audience, comprising mostly women and well-known men of medicine, listened as Beard connected the dots between the recently concluded conflict, the lingering social discontent, the loss of faith in established institutions, and a hope-driven search for deliverance from dysphoria. It was the perfect set of circumstances in which dealers in delusion could flourish.

Not content with lecturing, the doctor inveigled an invitation from the reclusive Eddy family of New York and set about studying the manifestations that were the talk of the country. Based on his observations, Beard came to the conclusion that the Eddy family's exploits were all tricks, many of which he easily reproduced.[3]

During a séance when the various materializations came forth, the room was exceedingly dark and the Eddy family made sure that no one came within ten feet of the ghosts. Beard gained permission to test the spirits with an electric battery, hoping to deliver a jolt that would send the phony phantoms screaming from the séance. The always cautious Eddy family allowed the experiment with the stipulation that one of them would operate the battery. As might be expected, the ploy failed, leaving Beard to muse that if "some man of muscle should seize ... the materialized shape, there is no doubt that the personator would give him the best evidence of materiality."[4]

Beard considered Spiritualism totally antithetical to a world struggling to rise above superstitious beliefs. His was a plea for rationality, replacing the false hope of Spiritualism with the promise and credibility of scientific inquiry. The doctor was particularly troubled by charlatans, clairvoyants, and other dealers in deceit who presented their products in popular scientific terms, noting that "at the present time electricity is the city of refuge to which all forms of delusion run."

Having spent his professional life studying medicine and electricity, Beard urged the members of his audience to either ignore Spiritualism or subject the practitioners to scientific investigation. Beard was convinced that an understanding of human physiology, psychology, and the physics of electricity and magnetism would always expose the fraudulent spiritualist.

Beard became a showman of sorts, traveling to scientific, medical, and historical conferences debunking psychic mediums as "nothing mysterious ... all persons are liable to trance under extremes of emotional tension, circumstances of terror, or reaction to nervous shock." To further support his argument, the doctor assertively noted the precise anatomic location in the brain responsible for the altered state of consciousness.[5]

As a man steeped in the scientific method, Beard tested his hypothesis that trance states were normal physiological reactions and easily reproduced by conducting a series of experiments.[6] To prove his point, Beard invited a group of eminent doctors to his New York City office to witness the results of his research. The small assemblage waited as Beard prepared to demonstrate induced trance-like states in four young men, trained over a period of several weeks to quickly descend into an insensible mental state following a whiff of ether. Beard then waved his hand over their eyes in a short downward motion, instantly sending each man into a dreamlike state, totally oblivious to their surroundings.

To prove that each man was entranced, Beard poked and prodded his subjects. A brilliant light that would have left a normal person blinking, flinching, and in tears produced no response from the hypnotized men. Touching an eye, placing pepper in the mouth, and screaming loudly in their ears likewise produced no discernable response. Perhaps the most interesting test followed the doctor's command that one of the men stare at the ceiling, followed by a suggestion that a band of angels would soon emerge. The man did as directed, his eyes moving excitedly as he followed his imagination around the room.

A few days later Beard took his show on the road, presenting his case to an audience at the New York Academy of Sciences.[7] While most attendees were sensible men of science, a few scalawags, looking for a night's entertainment, periodically punctuated Beard's lecture on the science of trance-like states with snickers and irreverent laughter. The undaunted doctor carried on, amazing the more respectful members of his audience with demonstrations of induced trances. One man was paralyzed stiff as a board and carted around the stage in a perfect state of rigidity. Another was insensitive to pins pricking his face, and, in a dramatic closing act, Beard discharged a pistol loaded with blanks near a man's ear, startling the attendees but leaving the man unfazed.

Despite his sober attempts to discourage a gullible public's belief in Spiritualism, Beard fell short of his goal, failing in part by adopting the same theatrics used by prominent spiritualists. While Beard's explanation of trance-like states differed from what the spiritualists offered, his equally entertaining experiments eroded some of his credibility.

Joining Beard in deconstructing Spiritualism was William Hammond, a fellow physician respected for his insightful, scientific observations. Hammond was well known in America, beginning with his controversial service as surgeon-general in the Civil War and extending to his decree leading to the publication of *The Medical and Surgical History of the War of the Rebellion*.[8] After the war, Hammond rose to prominence as a neurologist testifying as an expert witness in famous criminal trials and through a dizzying array of publications.[9]

One of Hammond's lesser-known treatises, *Physics and Physiology of Spiritualism*, represented his effort to provide a medical explanation for the fashionable faith. A reporter reviewing the book admitted that many mysteries of life defy rational understanding, but when it came to Spiritualism the whole humbug was traceable to a person's nervous system.[10]

Hammond first published a short version of *Physics and Physiology of Spiritualism* in the *North American Review*, and in the opening pages he pulled no punches in declaring that "there [have] always been ... individuals whose love for the marvelous is so great, and whose logical powers are so small, as to render them susceptible of entertaining any belief."[11] With this entrée, Hammond took direct aim at spiritualists and their followers, sparing no vitriol in dismissing the whole lot as ignorant. In a further rebuke, the author brushed aside claims made by psychic mediums that they had harnessed mysterious magnetic or electrical forces.

Flush with praise for his work, Hammond expanded the topic and published a book with the same title.[12] In accounting for the spiritualistic manifestations, he accused some psychic mediums of being nothing more than talented magicians, experts at sleight of hand and other feats of legerdemain. Even while criticizing their fraud, Hammond clearly admired the spiritualists' skill as masters of deception.

In an interesting broadside, Hammond took his battle with Spiritualism directly to the readers of the *Banner of Light*, attacking the faith on the spiritualists' turf. In a letter to the newspaper's editor in 1876, Hammond's animosity was palpable, complaining that "I am sick unto death of the childish and irrational manner in which men of science, theologians ... allow your beliefs to go unchecked.... They content themselves with blank denials and silly suggestions, and foolishly hope" that reason will prevail.[13]

As might be imagined, the *Banner of Light* published Hammond's tirade, using the attack as an opportunity to play a pious victim role while simultaneously refuting the charges. In a biting rebuttal, Hammond was dismissed along with "his worthless book entitled 'Spiritualism and Nervous Disorders' ... his object is to show that our facts are all chimerical and that such phenomena as levitation, independent writing, lifted chairs or tables, etc., are impossible."[14] Portraying Hammond as one of Spiritualism's implacable, dogmatic adversaries, the *Banner of Light* spared no ink in attacking its foe, "whose ignorance in respect to the actual facts of Spiritualism seems to be equaled only by his arrogance and temerity."[15]

Hammond infuriated spiritualists by exposing the tricks of their trade, an offense made worse by his proposition that nervous disorders, not psychic phenomena, explained a medium's fundamental ability to enter into a trance. At a time when Spiritualism was flourishing and could count as many as four million adherents, Hammond's critique initially received a cool, impartial response from reviewers. Aside from outright fraud and trickery, Hammond considered spiritualists' peculiar manifestations the result of mental disease.[16]

Based on methodical clinical analyses, Hammond described the neurological basis for self-induced entrancement that emulated a medium's trances. Chief among these neurological conditions was somnambulism, otherwise known as sleepwalking, which had piqued the interest of many nineteenth-century physicians, with Hammond devoting considerable study to this phenomenon. From his observations, Hammond concluded that somnambulism could be summoned in "persons of impressionable nervous systems ... and readily be induced by artificial means."[17]

Somnambulism was a naturally occurring trance-like state that, according to Hammond, persons of a nervous temperament were prone to experience. Hysteria was another mental condition, and "in all persons affected ... the occurrence of symptoms which simulate organic diseases" was the key feature.[18] The hysterical patient could simulate every imaginable condition, including paralysis, loss of vision, seizures, hallucinations, mania, and sundry other physical problems. Hammond attributed the mysterious machinations of the medium to these mental conditions, along with more frankly fraudulent tricks.

The recognition that Spiritualism was a religion, clung to by many people, left Hammond conceding that "to reason ... would be a waste of words, just as much as would be the attempt to persuade a madman out of his delusion."[19] Conquering Spiritualism required more than science, which only offered cold realities, a poor substitute for the yearnings of the faithful to reunite with their lost loved ones.

Instead of relying on medical theories, Washington Irving Bishop, godson of the famous author Washington Irving, exposed spiritualists such as Katie King, Anna Fey, and the Eddy family through old-fashioned study and training.[20] He then replicated their mysteries in surprising theatrical performances.

An impressive group of spectators, including judges, politicians, and other prominent individuals, patiently awaited the performance of Washington Bishop, advertised as an exposé of Spiritualism.[21] In the moments before his arrival the audience had the opportunity to study the stage, the most noticeable object being a large pole firmly attached to the floor, which could be hidden from view by a curtain. A piano, a small table, and several chairs completed the simple ensemble.

Bishop was joined on stage by an assistant who introduced the night's entertainment with a long-winded speech that tried the patience of the spectators. After concluding his preamble, Bishop's assistant asked for volunteers from the audience to join the pair on stage; after some prodding, two esteemed gentleman agreed to come up.

With the preliminaries now concluded, the assistant passed a rope through a stout iron ring attached to the pole and asked the volunteers to securely bind Bishop's hands together. Bishop now took a seat with his back resting against the pole. A ligature was placed around his head and the pole, his feet tied, and silver dollars placed on his feet. It was seemingly impossible for the man to move, and if he did so, the silver dollars would betray his movements. The assistant then placed a tambourine, silver bells, and a pistol on the pinioned man's knees and closed the curtain.

In mere seconds, the pistol was fired, followed by the cacophony of the bells and tambourine, after which all were unceremoniously tossed over the curtain. When the exhibition was over, the assistant opened the curtain to reveal the bound man with the silver dollars still place. Bishop followed this act with other supposedly spiritual manifestations such as slate writing and various materializations.

Bishop was not finished. His goal was exposure, and during the next part of the presentation he did just that by asserting "all spiritualistic performers had long hands, thin wrists and waists, and flexible bodies. Through peculiar physical conformation, and by acquired strength … he had been enabled to perform the tricks." To prove his point, Bishop reenacted the same feats in full view of the audience, quickly slipping his hands free from restraints sufficient to fire a pistol and write mysterious messages on a slate.

Beard, Bishop and Hammond confronted Spiritualism indirectly, emulating the mediums' tricks through replication, removing the mystique, and exposing the deception. Others were less restrained in their efforts and directly challenged the imposters.

A successful séance required passive, compliant attendees. Spiritualists set the rules and did their best to weed out troublemakers. Sometimes they failed, with spectacular results. A man named Chaplin, well schooled in the art of mediumship by the Eddy family, left his mentors and started conducting séances in a nearby Vermont town. Three men, suspecting chicanery, wheedled their way into Chaplin's dark séance. As the lights dimmed and the securely cinched psychic's cabinet closed, the sounds of bells, tambourines, and a violin's shrill notes broke the silence. A moment later a small, hunched figure appeared and started moving slowly around the cabinet. One of the three men sprang across the room and seized the supposed spirit while another illuminated the area, revealing a chagrined Chaplin.[22]

In a similar scenario, an unexpected embarrassment descended on Dr. H.C. Gordon, a fashionable medium with an elegant and mystical office in New York City.[23] Visitors entering Gordon's inner sanctum marveled at a large, ostentatious dais conveniently situated next to the séance table. Candles, medicine bottles, and a revised version of the New Testament received from the spirit world added to the room's supernatural aura.

At the appointed time, Gordon channeled the spirit of Bishop White, who arose near the dais like a ghost from its sepulcher. A disembodied head materialized in the same area, which Bishop grasped in a showy display, but the night's most incredible act came next. Four men pretending interest in the séance, but really out to expose Gordon's scam, gained entrance to the event. When Bishop White appeared with the floating head, one of the men vaulted onto the dais, a struggle ensued, and the "spirit" fled.

The fleet-footed Bishop ran from the room with his assailant in hot pursuit. He was eventually cornered, and a closer examination revealed a sheepish Dr. Gordon clad in a white frock. The newcomers searched the area and discovered eight stuffed masks, all recognizable as Gordon's materialized spirits. Fearing the worst, the disgraced medium swore he would hold no more public functions.

Emboldened skeptics increasingly challenged Spiritualism's legitimacy, leading a newspaper editorial in 1876 to proclaim that "the exposure of spiritual humbugs has been so complete this year that there ought to be no doubt in the minds of the public regarding the utter humbuggery and fraud of the whole bunch of mediums."[24] The declaration's tone of finality was a bit premature, but the forces of reason were gaining ground.

Adding to the public's loss of faith were scammers, schemers, and swindlers. In St. Louis, spectators looked forward to a night's entertainment revealing the secrets of Spiritualism. With the audience seated and patiently waiting, the only magic that night was the disappearance of the performer, along with $200 in ticket sales.[25]

Among all the schemes, spirit photography was arguably the most destructive and deceitful, in every case an imposture exploiting the misery of family members desperately seeking tangible reminders of a lost loved one. The virulent growth of such phony photographers was a blight on the social landscape, encouraging a determined group of disbelievers to prune the field.

One way to thin the crop of con artists was through ridicule. A sarcastic editorial questioned why ghosts, "refusing to be captured like ordinary mortals, have consented to allow themselves to be photographed." It was a reasonable question, and one that led to further musing about the proliferation of such willing spirits and their obliging photographers. Mincing no words, the editorial condemned "such piteous folly on one side and arrant deception on the other."[26]

Careful observation exposed certain photographs. One photographer in Memphis, Tennessee, repeatedly used the same photographic plate when developing his spirit images. As a consequence of this discovery, the flaw was just like a fingerprint, positively pointing out the double exposure deception.[27]

The most definite and damaging indictments came from reputable photographers annoyed by the scam. Charles Moore, a Boston photographer, specialized in exposing such fraud and claimed many notable successes.[28] One of the first involved a man named Evans, a spiritualist with an enchanted camera that mysteriously summoned ghosts. Evans would greet customers in his dimly lit studio, determine the deceased person they wanted a picture of, engage in some theatrical hocus pocus with the camera, and then develop the spirit image in his darkroom.

Moore figured out the trick using his knowledge of photography and some classic detective work. Evans had created a series of photographic plates with filmy images and would select the one that best matched the customer's choice, such as a child, man, or woman. To avoid detection, Evans kept the plates in his coat pocket and only developed the pictures once safely inside the darkroom. The customer's wistful imagination embellished the misty, indistinct images into actual people, completing the sad swindle.

George W. Kitchell operated a respectable photography studio in New York City. His reputation apparently attracted the attention of Jay J. Hartman, an itinerant construction worker from Ohio interested in building a spirit photography business. Almost immediately upon his arrival in New York City, Hartman approached Kitchell with that proposition, hoping to cement the alliance. As later became known, Kitchell recognized his erstwhile partner's deceitful designs, but, in an effort to spoil the scheme, he accepted the offer.[29]

A few days later Hartman procured a pair of photographic plates, one with six heads eerily floating around and another with a vague image of an elderly woman. Armed with the instruments of deception, Hartman briefed Kitchell on the details. It was a simple plan adopted by many phony photographers: An eager customer would arrange an appointment at Kitchell's studio with the express purpose of obtaining a spirit photo, take a seat in front of the camera, and await divine intervention. The first snapshot always failed to produce a ghost image, a situation Hartman explained as a result of disconnected psychic forces. With a few incantations and another pose by the customer, the photographer disappeared into the darkroom and, using one of the phony plates, developed and delivered the fraud.

Spirit photography spread across the country, producing ripples of disbelief. Out west, "the 'spirit photograph' business has been successfully executed in Los Angeles," with the reporter subsequently cautioning readers about the artifice.[30] In Chicago, a group of spiritualists marveling at a series of spirit photos and declaring the images proof of their beliefs were upset when a reporter exposed the fraud.[31] Horatio Eddy, never one to miss an opportunity, strained credulity by offering visitors spirit photographs in total darkness and without the expense or bother of a camera.[32]

From the epicenter of American Spiritualism in Rochester, New York, a chance discovery uncovered another case of fraud. Two determined women, suspecting chicanery, took their doubts to a local spirit photographer. Both women requested a sitting, subsequently receiving two spirit photographs. The pictures included distinct images of young, fashionably dressed ladies hovering in the background. After paying for the pictures, they went home and carefully studied the ghostly images, both women sensing some vague recognition of the floating figures. A glance at a stack of nearby ladies' magazines prodded their memory, and thumbing through the pages revealed the exact "ghostly" pictures reproduced in their spirit photographs.[33]

A reputable photographer by the name of P.P. Pence exposed the tricks of the trade as practiced by Mrs. Annie Stewart, a Terre Haute, Indiana, medium through an affidavit "being duly sworn upon his oath."[34] In a concerted effort to win the confidence of the spiritualist, Pence had suggested she consider bolstering her business with spirit photography, an offer that included his coaching. After a day's reflection, Stewart accepted the proposal.

Pence set the hoax in motion by producing photographic plates purporting to show Mrs. Stewart's twenty spirit guides amiably arrayed around her visage. Inspiration for the copied images came from magazines and old photos. Stewart used this photograph as the promotional gimmick announcing her new psychic endeavor.

Customers flocked to Mrs. Stewart's spiritual emporium. To ensure an adequate number of phony photographic plates, Pence created hundreds of negatives, guaranteeing an almost endless parade of ghosts. Mrs. Stewart's role in the fraud was limited to waving her hand over the camera in a dignified display and selecting the phony plate that best matched the customer's expectations. Throughout the entire process, with the exception of entering the darkroom, Pence invited the scrutinizing gaze of skeptics, none of whom discovered the deft sleight of hand that exchanged the blank photographic plate with the phony negative.

202 Psychological Consequences of the American Civil War
Pence eventually retired from the spirit photography business, ceding the enterprise to Mrs. Stewart. The relationship between the two continued on a friendly basis, an intimacy facilitating disclosure of the spiritualist's "fear of being exposed.... I suppose they would give me a coat of tar and feathers."

By 1880 spirit photography was fading as a flash-in-the-pan phenomenon, succumbing to reason and derision. One photographer produced a picture of a woman's dead husband surrounded by angels in heavenly repose, provoking the patron, who "sued him for false pretenses. She knew the location better than that."[35]

Nothing undermined Spiritualism more than a medium's confession. Mrs. Collier, a psychic medium in Springfield, New York, perhaps inconveniently located too near Rochester, abandoned the business, finding it impossible "to be strictly honest and get adequate remuneration for the time and trouble expended."[36]

Daniel Dunglas Home, one of the most celebrated and accomplished mediums, performed an amazing array of supposedly spirit-inspired feats, many of which his competitors could never duplicate. From this vaunted position Home both criticized and revealed the crude tricks employed by fake mediums, only partially preserving their identity. It was a clever maneuver that left Home exposing others while enhancing his credibility as a genuine mystic.

Home published his tell-all book, *Lights and Shadows of Spiritualism*, in 1877. His goal was a principled one: enshrining Spiritualism by removing the taint of fraud. Home generously identified three types of deceit: "the first is made up of persons who, while really possessing medial gifts, will, when much tempted, resort to fraud.... The second section consists also of mediums ... being utterly unprincipled, rather prefer to cheat.... In the third class I place charlatans."[37]

Home devoted two chapters in his book to exposing the tricks of dishonest mediums, a romp that included detailed descriptions of phony materializations, the production of fruit and flowers, playing musical instruments, spirit writing, and even spirit photography. *Lights and Shadows of Spiritualism* did little to burnish the increasingly tarnished view of Spiritualism, creating instead a growing cynicism.

Without a doubt, the most grievous assault on Spiritualism came from the original promoters: Margaret and Catherine Fox.[38] Both sisters profited poorly from Spiritualism, with poverty and despondency being their primary wages, and in a stunning admission, the sisters affixed their approving signatures to a tell-all book appropriately titled *The Death-blow to Spiritualism*. Nothing epitomized Spiritualism more than the mysterious rappings, a trick that Margaret conceded involved "the manner in which the joints of the foot can be used without lifting it from the floor."

Those returning to reason in America in the years following the Civil War slowly took aim at another false belief: the promises of patent medicines. Like Spiritualism, a one-two punch delivered by scientific scrutiny and responsible public exposures left the makers on the ropes, struggling to remain relevant.

Patent medicine makers prospered through deeply entrenched dealings. Newspapers counted on the advertising revenues, druggists filled their shelves and registers, and quack doctors prescribed and promoted the pretentious panaceas. Efforts to unravel the cozy dealings were met with fierce resistance.

Orange Judd entered the ring determined to deliver a knockout blow to patent medicines. Judd had all the requisite bona fides to enter the fray. During the Civil War he had worked with the United States Sanitary Commission, and afterward he devoted his efforts to farm science, earning a reputation as a scientist and promoting his opinions as publisher of the *American Agriculturist*.[39]

From the pages of his publication, Judd announced his opposition to patent medicine advertisements, a policy change that precluded their subsequent appearance in the magazine.[40] In doing so, Judd struck out broadly against the worthless, damaging claims of patent medicines, reserving particular contempt for Dr. Byrn, the maker and distributor of the Great Japanese Pho-kota. Dr. Byrn did not take the criticism kindly, responding with a libel lawsuit.[41]

In a case positioned as attacking "the liberty of the press," the defendant Orange Judd rebutted Byrn's claim of defamation by asserting the truth of his opinion. Presiding Judge Brady, in responding to a plea by the plaintiff to strike the more inflammatory language from Judd's statement, hinted at the court's position: "This world is not composed of Solomons, and even men of good judgement, and large experience, especially when the wish is wedded to the hope, are sometimes easily trapped. Drugs should be dispensed with great caution, and the laws which are designed to protect the people … cannot be too stringent."

Orange Judd prevailed; however, his victory was a technical one, given the plaintiff's refusal to submit his patent medicine for chemical analysis, arguing that his secret remedy would suffer irreparable harm through disclosure. Unhappy with the trial court's verdict, the plaintiff appealed and suffered another stinging rebuke from an incredulous judge, marveling "that he can bring an action for libel for injury alleged to be done to his trade in medicines, by denouncing them as arrant quackery, and at the same time protect himself against exposure by claiming them to be valuable secrets, is a proposition that cannot be maintained."[42]

Medical journals noted the connection between advertising and patent medicines, creating a direct link to profits. National advertising pumped up profits, followed by a precipitous decline if the patent medicine maker reduced these expenditures.[43] A more traditional approach probably adopted as the rationale for accepting the lucrative trade mused that "it is easy, of course, to turn away all advertisements of patent medicines, if we adopt the theory of doctors that they are all frauds. But it would be equally just to say that the doctors are all frauds, because some undoubtedly are."[44] Missing in this self-serving sophistry was the publication's monetary incentive to maintain the profitable status quo.

The occasional exposé of a particularly troublesome practice alerted newspaper readers to the perils of patent medicines. Dr. D.M. Lindsay, a middle-aged man with a rough complexion and clad in the garb of a Mexican rancher, ostentatiously paraded through the downtown streets of Philadelphia advertising his Bueno Medicina. Lindsay enlisted an impressive sales force of at least one hundred men to peddle his patent medicine. As they traveled throughout the northeastern states, Lindsay and his recruits provided free samples of Bueno Medicina, a potent concoction mostly composed of alcohol. Customers loved the brew and ordered thousands of bottles of Bueno Medicina (costing one dollar each) through the mail. In return, the customer received an attractive package with an Indian motif and an extensive list of ailments that the medicine supposedly cured. Opening the package, however, revealed nothing more than a block of wood.[45]

Decent doctors had to contend with a fundamental reality: many patients really had no physical ailments, suffering instead from emotional and personality problems that defied the best efforts of nineteenth-century doctors. A New York physician described the ethical dilemma: "If you tell them the truth, that they are perfectly well, they will get mad and go to some other doctor who [is] maybe an advertising quack.... Or they will go and buy patent medicines and injure themselves."[46]

The bout between patent medicines and their sycophants, in one corner, and their critics, in the other, needed a referee, a role assumed by science. Chemists and druggists started investigating the ingredients of patent medicines, leading to some startling revelations. Their findings slowly tilted the balance against the patent medicine makers.

It was estimated that in 1883 Americans spent $40 million on patent medicines, a staggering sum given their inexpensive and generally ineffective ingredients.[47] The realization that it "has become quite fashionable for the public in general to believe they are suffering from nervous disorders" compelled the authors' disclosure that the typical ingredients of such preparations included celery, kola, gentian, cinchona, and phosphorous. A popular nerve tea contained valerian root, peppermint, and orange flowers. Electric headache cures were essentially alcohol with a small piece of cotton soaked in mustard oil suspended in the bottle with impressive-looking but useless wires. Dr. Thomas'

Electric Oil was a complicated recipe consisting of ingredients such as one ounce each of sassafras, wintergreen, hemlock and turpentine oils, as well as an ounce of chloroform and one ounce of tincture of opium, all dissolved in 64 ounces of alcohol.

An analysis of Trask's Magnetic Ointment revealed an unattractive mix of lard, raisins, and tobacco, whereas the principal ingredients of Morehead's Magnetic Ointment were equal parts tar and extract of belladonna. Smith's Electric Oil was a more noxious combination of linseed, olive, and sassafras oils mixed with chloroform. The formulation of various bitters invariably included alcohol, in many cases exceeding twenty percent of the patent medicine's contents.[48]

By the end of the nineteenth century patent medicines were losing favor, although they were not yet fully vanquished. However, the next century brought the industry to its knees through sensational public exposés such as Samuel Hopkins Adams' withering attack published in a series of articles in *Collier's Weekly* under the banner "The Great American Fraud."[49] In these articles, Adams elaborated on the dangers of patent medicines, detailing the poisonous doses of chloroform, hydrogen cyanide, sulfuric acid, and acetanilide (the latter a common ingredient in various analgesic and nervous preparations that could permanently relieve the patient's symptoms through death). Adams was especially concerned about patent medicines formulated with addictive ingredients such as opium and alcohol.

Long before Adams published his articles, concerns were surfacing that "proprietary medicinal preparations composed largely of spirits are now, to any effect, used for their stimulating rather than their real medicinal" role. Evidence of abuse came from the New York State Inebriate Asylum, where detailed clinical histories disclosed an increasing number of admissions directly due to a vast array of elixirs, tonics, bitters, and syrups readily obtainable by anyone.[50] For many years, patent medicines mostly escaped the shrill condemnation reserved for saloons, providing a pathway for alcohol use that was deemed morally acceptable since it was supposedly restricted to the aches and pains of life.

Toward the end of the nineteenth century responsible politicians could no longer ignore the evidence of patent medicine fraud and the growing number of habituated users. Lawmakers were increasingly concerned about products such as Peruna, which was nothing more than bottled alcohol disguised as a medicine.[51] Some of the other patent medicines that invited lawmakers' scrutiny included Hood's Sarsaparilla, which was a flavorful remedy containing seventeen percent alcohol; Mrs. Winslow's Soothing Syrup, which calmed irritable, teething infants with morphine or laudanum; and remedies for jittery nerves containing heaping doses of alcohol or bromides, as in the case of Dr. Miles' Restorative Nervine.

Regulatory reforms and legal actions came in quick succession. In one example, a federal attorney prosecuted the felonious claims of Professor De Grath's Electric Oil.[52] A chemical analysis of the patent medicine identified turpentine and cinnamon oils among the ingredients, as well as ammonia and chloroform. The successful prosecution convinced the trial court judge that Professor De Grath's Electric Oil was neither safe nor effective, and the product's label claiming otherwise was both misleading and fraudulent.

A Brooklyn, New York, pharmacist in 1886 gave a glimpse of the business at the turn of the century. Profits were declining due to market saturation, and customers expected deep discounts. Typical drugstore denizens diagnosed themselves, spending countless hours hobnobbing about imaginary ills. In another indication of the emotional distress infecting society, the druggist pejoratively noted that "a drugstore is a great resort for hypochondriacs."[53]

Part of the turn toward patent medicines was undeniably the result of a loss of faith in traditional medical practices. The Civil War wounded the reputation of medicine, although doctors had made demonstrable progress in improving camp sanitation, battlefield care, and surgery, and there was even nascent recognition of the psychological consequences of war. In spite of these successes, the public's negative perception of physicians contributed to the growth of patent medicines and dubious doctors.

Less than ten years after the war was over a satirical story spread across the reunited states. Many readers no doubt chuckled and nodded their heads in agreement as they pondered "An Essay on Doctors." With more than a kernel of truth, the essay ridiculed the endless parade of practitioners: "old school doctors and doctors of the new school, and doctors without any schooling whatever.... There are doctors of laws, and doctors of sons-in-laws ... electric doctors ... cold water doctors ... root doctors ... spiritual doctors and doctors very much out of spirits; magnetic doctors and doctors who haven't any magnetism.... Indian doctors, as they call themselves, know nothing whatever about Indians."[54]

Devious doctors prescribed false promises and, like patent medicines and Spiritualism, offered too much and delivered too little. Curing the ills of the medical profession required the fundamental reform of medical education, professional licensing, clinical practice standards, innovation, and research.

Substantial rumblings of reform started shaking medical education roughly a decade after the Civil War. In 1877 a tally of American medical schools, not counting upstarts like homeopathy and botanical colleges, revealed 65 programs granting the doctor of medicine degree. On closer inspection, only five schools had a three-year curriculum and only two required an entrance examination. This sorry state of education did not go unnoticed, and public pressure, as expressed through popular publications and politicians, provided the impetus for gradual improvement.[55]

As time went on, the renaissance in medical practice began in earnest. In many cases the greatest reformers were Civil War doctors—having seen the worst, they now sought the best. Among this group of visionaries was Andrew Taylor Still, who served as a hospital steward in 1861 with the Cass County Home Guards, subsequently attached to the 9th Kansas Cavalry.[56]

During his brief tenure as a steward, Still learned firsthand the limits of military medicine, observing "that a surgeon's outfit was complete when it contained calomel, quinine, whiskey, opium, rags, and knife." He condemned a military surgeon's excessive use of medicinal alcohol, believing that "in just this manner the love of strong drink is instilled in many a man." Still had similar qualms about calomel, quinine, and opium.[57]

Andrew Taylor Still's wartime experiences, coupled with the tragic deaths of his wife and three children from spinal meningitis, forced a deep, thoughtful reassessment of America's medical practices. At the core of his beliefs was a conviction that doctors relied too much on noxious medications and alcohol, a concern that led to his development of a radical new approach to healthcare called osteopathy.

When asked to define osteopathy, Still explained that "it is scientific knowledge of anatomy and physiology in the hands of a person of intelligence and skill, who can apply that knowledge to the use of man when sick or wounded by strains, shocks, falls, or mechanical derangement of any kind to the body." Still's osteopathy considered the healthy human body a finely tuned instrument, with disease being the result of an imbalance in the machinery, corrected through manipulation that restored the proper anatomical relationships between bone, muscle, and nerves.[58]

As an upstart, osteopathy faced withering resistance from traditional medicine's hegemony. But the new practice succeeded by tapping into a deep-seated distrust of pill-pushing physicians and patent medicine peddlers. Osteopathy was "nature's way to health," an approach that placed a premium on prevention and palliation, emphasizing the body's innate restorative abilities.[59]

Osteopathy was the right tonic at the right time. Its emergence symbolized the progress that would define the next century. Lingering wounds from a great war were fading, but their impact still resonated, shaping society in dramatic, demonstrable ways. As the country returned to reason, Spiritualism and it ghosts were receding, patent medicines were losing their luster, and the cavalcade of quacks was dwindling. Medicine was entering a more scientific era that included a deeper appreciation and understanding of psychological disorders.[60] America was recovering from decades of depression, doubt, and disappointment.

Chapter Notes

Introduction

1. Bowman, S.M., and R.B. Irwin. *Sherman and His Campaigns: A Military Biography*. New York: C. B. Richardson, 1865.

2. Williams, G.F., M.B. Brady, and A. Gardner. *The Memorial War Book: As Drawn from Historical Records and Personal Narratives of the Men Who Served in the Great Struggle*. New York: Lovell Brothers, 1894.

3. Mottelay, P.F., and T. Campbell-Copeland. *Frank Leslie's The Soldier in Our Civil War*. New York: S. Bradley Publishing Company, 1890.

4. "Battle of Antietam Creek." *New York Times*, September 18, 1862.

5. "The Battle of Antietam." *New York Times*, September 21, 1862.

6. "The Army and Navy." *New York Times*, January 6, 1862.

7. "How a Mother Received Her Son Who Had Deserted." *Cincinnati Daily Press*, October 4, 1861.

8. "Dear Brother." *Weekly Perrysburg Journal*, January 16, 1862.

9. Irwin, R.B. "Seeking the Bubble." *United States Service Magazine*, 1865.

10. Spitzka, E.C. *Insanity, Its Classification, Diagnosis, and Treatment: A Manual for Students and Practitioners of Medicine*. New York: Bermingham & Company, 1883.

11. "A Letter Found." *Highland Weekly News*, May 8, 1862.

12. "Nostalgia." *Cleveland Morning Leader*, July 10, 1862.

13. Moore, Frank. *Anecdotes, Poetry, and Incidents of the War: North and South: 1860–1865/ Collected and Arranged by Frank Moore*. Home-sick in the Hospital. New York: Published for the Subscribers, 1866.

14. Mowris, J.A. *A History of the One Hundred and Seventeenth Regiment, N.Y. Volunteers, [Fourth Oneida] from the Date of its Organization. August 1862, Till That of Its Muster Out. June, 1865. by J.A. Mowris, M.D. Regimental Surgeon*. Hartford, CT: Case, Lockwood and Company, 1866.

15. Peters, De Witt C. "Remarks on the Evils of Youthful Enlistments and Nostalgia." *American Medical Times: Being a Weekly Series of the New York Journal of Medicine*, 1863.

16. "Fill Up the Armies." *New York Daily Tribune*, July 19, 1864.

17. Lande, R.G. *Madness, Malingering, and Malfeasance: The Transformation of Psychiatry and the Law in the Civil War Era*. Washington, DC: Brassey's, 2003.

18. "Nostalgia." *Cleveland Morning Leader*, October 16, 1861.

19. Beck, Theodric Romeyn. *Elements of Medical Jurisprudence*. 12th edition. Philadelphia: J. B. Lippincott & Co., 1863.

20. Otis, George A., and J.E. Barnes. *The Medical and Surgical History of the War of the Rebellion (1861–65)*. Vol. 3, *On Certain Diseases Not Heretofore Discussed*. Washington, DC: U.S. Government Printing Office, 1870.

21. Gildersleeve, B.L. *The Creed of the Old South, 1865–1915*. Baltimore, MD: Johns Hopkins Press, 1915.

22. Seddon, James A. *Regulations for the Army of the Confederate States*. Richmond, VA: J. W. Randolph, 1864.

23. "Camp Douglas." *Jeffersonian*, March 16, 1865.

24. H.J.W. "Our Prisoners." *New York Times*, November 26, 1864.

Chapter One

1. H.J.W. "Our Prisoners." *New York Times,* November 26, 1864.

2. "How a Mother Received Her Son Who Had Deserted." *Cincinnati Daily Press,* October 4, 1861.

3. "A Letter Found." *Highland Weekly News,* May 8, 1862.

4. Moore, Frank. *Anecdotes, Poetry, and Incidents of the War: North and South: 1860–1865/Collected and Arranged by Frank Moore. Homesick in the Hospital.* New York: Published for the Subscribers, 1866.

5. "Nostalgia." *Cleveland Morning Leader,* July 10, 1862.

6. "Nostalgia." *Cleveland Morning Leader,* October 16, 1861.

7. Mowris, J.A. *A History of the One Hundred and Seventeenth Regiment, N.Y. Volunteers, [Fourth Oneida] from the Date of its Organization. August 1862, Till That of Its Muster Out. June, 1865. by J.A. Mowris, M.D. Regimental Surgeon.* Hartford, CT: Case, Lockwood and Company, 1866.

8. Beck, T.R. and W. Dunlop. *Elements of Medical Jurisprudence.* London: John Anderson, 1825.

9. Lande, R. G. "Felo De Se: Soldier Suicides in America's Civil War." *Military Medicine* 176(5)(2011):531–36.

10. McBride, J.R. *History of the Thirty-Third Indiana Veteran Volunteer Infantry During the Four Years of Civil War, from Sept. 16, 1861, to July 21, 1865: And Incidentally of Col. John Coburn's Second Brigade, Third Division, Twentieth Army Corps, Including Incidents of the Great Rebellion.* Indianapolis, IN: W.B. Burford, 1900.

11. "Suicide of the Quartermaster of the Second Regiment." *Troy Daily News,* May 29, 1863.

12. "Army of the Potomac." *New York Times,* August 23, 1863.

13. "Inquests by Coroner Wildey." *New York Times,* October 12, 1865.

14. "The Great Rebellion." *New York Times,* October 20, 1861.

15. "Melancholy Case of Suicide." *New York Herald,* November 9, 1862.

16. "Suicide of a Suspected Assassin." *Daily Picayune,* April 27, 1865.

17. Curwen, J., and American Psychiatric Association. *History of the Association of Medical Superintendents of American Institutions for the Insane, from 1844 to 1874, Inclusive.* American Psychiatric Association, 1875.

18. Silkenat, D. *Moments of Despair: Suicide, Divorce, and Debt in Civil War Era North Carolina.* Chapel Hill: University of North Carolina Press, 2011.

19. "Suicide." *Richmond Daily Dispatch,* August 8, 1861.

20. *Ibid.*

21. "Suicide of a Soldier." *Richmond Daily Dispatch,* June 11, 1862.

22. "Suicide." *Richmond Daily Dispatch,* May 13, 1862.

23. "Correspondence of the Richmond Dispatch." *Richmond Daily Dispatch,* December 14, 1861.

24. "Suicide of a South Carolina Volunteer." *Richmond Daily Dispatch,* February 24, 1862.

25. "Probable Suicide." *Richmond Daily Dispatch,* April 18, 1862.

26. "Deplorable Occurrence." *Richmond Daily Dispatch,* May 24, 1861.

27. "Suicide." *Richmond Daily Dispatch,* August 18, 1863.

28. "Suicide at Sea." *Richmond Daily Dispatch,* March 7, 1865.

29. "Robinson." *Richmond Daily Dispatch,* October 1, 1864.

30. "Dentist Shoots Self in Fatal Accident." *Daily Virginian,* January 18, 1862.

31. "A Soldier's Wife Commits Suicide." *New York Times,* February 5, 1864.

32. "Suicide and Murder." *Richmond Daily Dispatch,* June 13, 1862.

33. "Suicide by Poison." *New York Times,* February 5, 1863.

34. "Melancholy Suicide." *Richmond Daily Dispatch,* November 6, 1861.

35. "Suicide of a Husband." *Richmond Daily Dispatch,* October 6, 1863.

36. Livermore, T.L. *Numbers and Losses in the Civil War in America, 1861–1865.* Boston: Houghton, Mifflin, 1900.

37. United States Census Office, J.M. Edmunds, and United States Department of the Interior. *Statistics of the United States: (including Mortality, Property, & C.) in 1860; Compiled from the Original Returns and Being the Final Exhibit of the Eighth Census.* Washington, DC: U.S. Government Printing Office, 1866.

38. United States Census Office and J.C.G. Kennedy. *Preliminary Report on the Eighth Census. 1860.* Washington, DC: U.S. Government Printing Office, 1862.

39. United States Census Office and F.A. Walker. *A Compendium of the Ninth Census (June 1, 1870): Compiled Pursuant to a Concurrent Resolution of Congress, and Under the Direction of the Secretary of the Interior.* Washington, DC: U.S. Government Printing Office, 1872.

40. *Ibid.*

41. "The Registrar and General's Annual Report." *Medical Times and Gazette.* London: J. & A. Churchill, 1873.

42. United States Census Office and F.A. Walker. *A Compendium of the Ninth Census (June 1, 1870): Compiled Pursuant to a Concurrent Resolution of Congress, and under the Direction of the Secretary of the Interior.* Washington, DC: U.S. Government Printing Office, 1872.

43. *Publications of the American Statistical Association.* Boston: W.J. Schofield, 1895.

44. "Extraordinary Suicide." *New York Times,* April 9, 1869.

45. "Abandonment and Suicide of a Young Woman." *New York Times,* February 25, 1868.

46. Kennan, George. "The Problems of Suicide." *McClure's Magazine,* 1908.

47. Otis, G.A. *A Report of Surgical Cases Treated in the Army of the United States from 1865 to 1871.* Washington, DC: U.S. Government Printing Office, 1871.

48. "A Lady Suicide." *Brooklyn Eagle,* December 29, 1865.

49. "A Tragic Affair." *Brooklyn Eagle,* January 11, 1867.

50. "Suicide by an Ex-Navy Officer." *Brooklyn Eagle,* January 28, 1867.

51. "John Rabus, from Gotha." *New York Times,* March 26, 1866.

52. *Ibid.*

53. Niven, J. *Gideon Welles: Lincoln's Secretary of the Navy.* New York: Oxford University Press, 1973.

54. "The Recent Tragedy at Glastonbury, Conn.—Suicide of a Son of Hon. Thaddeus Welles." *New York Times,* December 31, 1866.

55. Welles, G., and E.T. Welles. *Diary.* Boston: Houghton, Mifflin, 1911.

56. Shoaf, Dana B. *The Death of a Regular,* 2013. Accessed March 30, 2013. http://www.sykesregulars.org/dor.php.

57. "Suicide of Lieut. Robert Welles." *New York Times,* December 30, 1866.

58. "Suicide." *Frank Leslie's Illustrated Newspaper,* February 5, 1870.

59. "Suicide in the U.S." *Frank Leslie's Illustrated Newspaper,* November 15, 1873.

60. Silkenat, D. *Moments of Despair: Suicide, Divorce, and Debt in Civil War Era North Carolina.* Chapel Hill: University of North Carolina Press, 2011.

61. Myer, W.G., and United States Supreme Court. *Federal Decisions: Cases Argued and Determined in the Supreme, Circuit and District Courts of the United States.* St. Louis, MO: Gilbert Book Co., 1887.

62. *Life Insurance Company v. Terry,* 82 U.S. 15 Wall. 580 (1872).

63. Palmer, O.H. "Suicide and Life Insurance." *New York Times,* May 1, 1873.

64. "Liability of Insurance Companies for Losses by Suicide." *American Journal of Psychiatry* 30(1873):259–70.

65. *Lincoln Herald* (Lincoln, NE), 1988.

66. Gray, John P. "Suicide." *American Journal of Psychiatry* 35(1878):37–73.

67. Palmer, O. H. "Suicide Not Evidence of Insanity." *American Journal of Psychiatry* 34 (1878):425–61.

68. *Ibid.*

69. MacDonald, Carlos F. "Feigned Insanity, Homicide, Insanity." *American Journal of Insanity* 35(3)(1879):411–32.

70. "Suicide of a Telegraph Operator." *Boston Herald,* July 26, 1865.

71. "Suicide of Two Army Officers." *New York Herald,* July 22, 1865.

72. Fout, F.W. *The Dark Days of the Civil War, 1861 to 1865: The West Virginia Campaign of 1861, the Antietam and Harper's Ferry Campaign of 1862, the East Tennessee Campaign of 1863, the Atlanta Campaign of 1864.* F.A. Wagenfuehr, 1904.

Chapter Two

1. Dewey, D.M. *History of the Strange Sounds or Rappings: Heard in Rochester and Western New-York, and Usually Called the Mysterious Noises! Which Are Supposed by Many to Be Communications from the Spirit World, Together with All the Explanation That Can as Yet Be Given of the Matter.* Rochester, NY: D. M. Dewey, 1850.

2. Spicer, H. *Facts and Fantasies: A Sequel to Sights and Sounds; The Mystery of the Day.* London: T. Bosworth, 1853.

3. Capron, E.W. *Modern Spiritualism: Its Facts and Fanaticisms, Its Consistencies and Contradictions. With an Appendix.* New York: B. Marsh, 1855.

4. *Ibid.*

5. *Ibid.*

6. Spicer, H. *Facts and Fantasies: A Sequel to Sights and Sounds; The Mystery of the Day.* London: T. Bosworth, 1853.

7. *Ibid.*

8. *Ibid.*

9. *Ibid.*

10. Hammond, William A. *Sleep and Its Derangements.* Philadelphia: J.B. Lippincott, 1873.

11. Practical Magnetizer. *The History and Philosophy of Animal Magnetism: With Practical Instructions for the Exercise of This Power.* Boston: J. N. Bradley, 1843.

12. *Ibid.*

13. *Ibid.*

14. Rodgers, W.H. *Facts in Magnetism, Mesmerism, Somnambulism, Fascination, Hypnotism, Sycodonamy, Etherology, Pathetism, &c: Explained and Illustrated.* Auburn, NY: Derby, Miller and Co., 1849.

15. Capern, T. *The Mighty Curative Powers of Mesmerism.* London: H. Baillière, 1851.

16. Table Moving. *Table Moving by Animal Magnetism Demonstrated.* London: John Wesley, 1853.

17. *Ibid.*

18. Barrett, H.D. *Life Work of Mrs. Cora L.V. Richmond.* Chicago: Hack & Anderson, 1895.

19. "Spiritualism in the Tabernacle." *New York Daily Tribune,* April 11, 1857.

20. "Life in New York." *Daily Dispatch,* April 23, 1857.

21. "Another Convert to Spiritualism." *Daily Dispatch,* April 7, 1857.

22. "Miss Cora Hatch, the Eloquent Medium of the Spiritualists." *Frank Leslie's Illustrated Newspaper,* May 9, 1857.

23. Abbott, O., I.E. Davenport, and W.H. Davenport. *The Davenport Brothers. Their History, Travels, and Manifestations. Also the Philosophy of Dark Circles, Ancient and Modern.* New York: Abbott, 1864.

24. "The Davenport Brothers." *New York Herald,* May 5, 1864.

25. "The Davenport Brothers and Coroner Norris." *Brooklyn Eagle,* May 17, 1864.

26. "The Davenport Mystery." *Brooklyn Eagle,* May 13, 1864.

27. de Mandeville, J. *History of the 13th Regiment, N.G., S.N.Y.: Containing Over Forty Illustrations and Many Biographical Sketches.* New York: Press of G.W. Rodgers, 1894.

28. Cotham, E.T. *Battle on the Bay: The Civil War Struggle for Galveston.* Austin: University of Texas Press, 1998.

29. "The Davenport Mystery." *Brooklyn Eagle,* May 13, 1864.

30. Colby, Luther. "The Davenport Outrage." *Banner of Light,* March 18, 1865.

31. Davis, A.J., and W. Fishbough. *The Principles of Nature, Her Divine Revelations, and a Voice to Mankind.* New York: S. S. Lyon & W. Fishbough, 1851.

32. Edmonds, John. "The End and Aim of Spiritual Intercourse." *Spiritual Magazine,* 1860.

33. Horowitz, M. *Occult America: The Secret History of How Mysticism Shaped Our Nation.* New York: Bantam Books, 2009.

34. Berry, William, and Luther Colby. *Banner of Light,* January 7, 1860.

35. Berry, William, and Luther Colby. *Banner of light,* January 14, 1860.

36. Parker, T., and J.W. Day. *Biography of Mrs. J.H. Conant, the World's Medium of the Nineteenth Century: Being a History of Her Mediumship from Childhood to the Present Time: Together with Extracts from the Diary of Her Physician; Selections from Letters Received Verifying Spirit Communications Given Through Her Organism at the Banner of Light Free Circles; Specimen Messages, Essays, and Invocations from Various Intelligences in the Other Life, Etc., Etc., Etc.* Boston: William White & Co., 1873.

37. *Ibid.*

38. Colby, Luther. "Message Department." *Banner of Light,* January 11, 1862.

39. Colby, Luther. "Message Department." *Banner of Light,* May 3, 1862.

40. Hall, J.C. *Stand of the United States Army at Gettysburg.* Bloomington: Indiana University Press, 2003.

41. Colby, Luther. "Message Department." *Banner of Light,* December 5, 1863.

42. *Ibid.*

43. Schmutz, J.F. 2009. *The Battle of the Crater: A Complete History.* Jefferson, NC: McFarland, 2009.

44. Colby, Luther. "Message Department." *Banner of Light,* September 3, 1864.

45. Colby, Luther. "Message Department." *Banner of Light,* May 13, 1865.

46. Goodhue, B.W. *Incidents of the Civil War.* Chicago: J. D. Tallmadge, 1890.

47. Beatty, J. *The Citizen-soldier: The Memoirs of a Civil War Volunteer.* Lincoln: University of Nebraska Press, 1998.

48. Hardinge, E. *Modern American Spiritualism: A Twenty Years' Record of the Communion Between Earth and the World of Spirits, by Emma Hardinge.* New York: E. Hardinge, 1870.

49. *Ibid.*

50. *Ibid.*

51. "The Burnside Expedition." *New York Time,* January 12, 1862.

52. "Fortress Monroe." *New York Times,* June 9, 1862.

53. Murphet, H. *Yankee Beacon of Buddhist Light: Life of Col. Henry S. Olcott.* Wheaton, IL: Theosophical Publishing House, 1988.

54. *Ibid.*

55. Olcott, Henry. "The World of Spirits." *New York Sun,* September 5, 1874.

56. *Ibid.*

57. Olcott, Henry. "Able-Bodied Apparitions." *New York Sun*, November 4, 1874.

58. Olcott, Henry S. *People from the Other World*. Hartford, CT: American Publishing Company, 1875.

59. *Ibid.*

60. W.H.C. "A Visit to the Eddys." *New York Sun*, October 14, 1874.

61. "Up-Town Ghost Business." *New York Sun*, November 30, 1874.

62. Olcott, Henry S. *Theosophy, Religion and Occult Science*. London: George Redway, 1885.

63. Olcott, Henry. "Ghosts That Are Ghosts." *New York Sun*, August 18, 1875.

64. *Ibid.*

65. Nartonis, David K. "The Rise of 19th-Century American Spiritualism, 1854–1873." *Journal for the Scientific Study of Religion* 49 (2)(2010):361–73.

66. Colby, Luther. "Eddy Persecution Fund." *Banner of Light*, February 16, 1867.

67. "Spiritualism Smashed." *New York Times*, July 2, 1866.

68. Lavoie, J.D. *The Theosophical Society: The History of a Spiritualist Movement*. Boca Raton, FL: Brown Walker Press, 2012.

69. Kiddle, Henry. *A Manual of Astronomy and the Use of the Globes: For Schools and Academies*. New York: Ivison, Phinney, Blakeman & Co., 1865.

70. Kiddle, Henry. *How to Teach*. Cincinnati, OH: Van Antwerp, Bragg, & Co., 1877.

71. Kiddle, Henry. *Common-school Teaching: A Lecture Delivered Before the Teachers' Association of the City of Brooklyn, September 28, 1877*. New York: E. Steiger, 1877.

72. Ciriello, M.J., and United States Catholic Conference, Department of Education. *Formation and Development for Catholic School Leaders: The Principal as Spiritual Leader*. Washington, DC: United States Catholic Conference, Department of Education, 1996.

73. Kiddle, H. *Spiritual Communications: Presenting a Revelation of the Future Life, and Illustrating and Confirming the Fundamental Doctrines of the Christian Faith*. New York: Author's Publishing Company, 1879.

74. *Ibid.*

75. "The Real Point in the Kiddle Case." *Brooklyn Eagle*, May 8, 1879.

76. "Is It the Result of Mental or Physical Overstrain?" *Brooklyn Eagle*, May 25, 1879.

77. "Mr. Kiddle on Mediums." *Brooklyn Eagle*, May 15, 1880.

78. Trollope, A. *Thackeray*. London: Macmillan, 1879.

79. Colby, Luther. "Thackeray." *Banner of Light*, January 23, 1864.

80. Davenport, R.B. *The Death-blow to Spiritualism: Being the True Story of the Fox Sisters, as Revealed by Authority of Margaret Fox Kane and Catherine Fox Jencken*. New York: G. W. Dillingham, 1888.

81. Wallace, A.R. *On Miracles and Modern Spiritualism: Three Essays*. London: James Burns, 1875.

82. Thackeray, W.M. *Vanity Fair: A Novel Without a Hero*. London: Bradbury and Evans, 1853.

83. Podmore, F. *Modern Spiritualism: A History and a Criticism*. Cambridge: Cambridge University Press, 2011.

84. Bell, Robert. "Stranger Than Fiction." *Cornhill Magazine* (G. Smith and W.M. Thackeray, eds.), 1860.

85. *Ibid.*

86. Wallace, A.R. *On Miracles and Modern Spiritualism*. London: James Burns, 1875.

87. van Schlun, B. *Science and the Imagination: Mesmerism, Media, and the Mind in Nineteenth-century English and American Literature*. Berlin: Galda + Wilch Verlag, 2007.

88. Dickens, Charles, J. Leech, A. Rackham, and G.A. Williams. *A Christmas Carol: A Ghost Story of Christmas*. Createspace Independent Publishing, 2013.

89. Dickens, Charles, and David Stuart Davies. *Ghost Stories*. London: CRW, 2009.

90. Howitt, W. *The History of the Supernatural in All Ages and Nations: And in All Churches, Christian and Pagan: Demonstrating a Universal Faith*. London: Longman, Green, Longman, Roberts, & Green, 1863.

91. Dickens, Charles. *The Works of Charles Dickens*. London: Chapman and Hall, 1911.

92. Spurgeon, C.H. *The Soul Winner*. Grand Rapids, MI: William B. Eerdmans, 1989.

93. Tomalin, C. *Charles Dickens: A Life*. New York: Penguin Press, 2011.

94. Dickens, Charles, and M. Cardwell. *The Mystery of Edwin Drood*. New York: Oxford University Press, 2009.

95. Cabot, M.R. *Annals of Brattleboro, 1681–1895*. Brattleboro, VT: Press of E. L. Hildreth, 1922.

96. "The Mystery of Edwin Drood." *London: The Spiritual Magazine*, 1873.

97. Dickens, Charles, with T.P. James. *The Mystery of Edwin Drood: Complete*. Brattleboro, VT: T.P. James, 1874.

98. Cox, J.R. *The Dime Novel Companion: A Source Book*. Westport, CT: Greenwood Press, 2000.

Chapter Three

1. Gernsheim, H. *A Concise History of Photography.* New York: Dover, 1986.
2. Stefoff, R. *The Camera.* Tarrytown, NY: Marshall Cavendish Benchmark, 2007.
3. "Spirit Photography." *Spiritual Magazine,* 1862.
4. Carroll, B.E. *Spiritualism in Antebellum America.* Bloomington: Indiana University Press, 1997.
5. "Spirit Photographs." *Spiritual Magazine,* 1863.
6. "A Wonderful Mystery." *The Sun,* February 15, 1869.
7. "Ghosts in Photography." *The Sun,* April 13, 1869.
8. "A Stupendous Fraud." *New York Times,* April 13, 1869.
9. "The Spurious Spirits." *The Sun,* April 14, 1869.
10. "Spiritual Photographs." *New York Times,* April 17, 1869.
11. "Spiritualism in Court." *New York Daily Tribune,* April 22, 1869.
12. "Spiritual Photographs." *New York Times,* April 17, 1869.
13. *Ibid.*
14. "The Fools Not All Dead." *Ottawa Free Trader,* July 24, 1869.
15. "Spiritual Photography." *New York Times,* April 24, 1869.
16. "The Spirit Photographs." *The Sun,* April 29, 1869.
17. *Ibid.*
18. "Spirit Photographs." *New York Times,* April 29, 1869.
19. "Spiritual Photography." *Harper's Weekly,* May 8, 1869.
20. "The Spirit Photographer." *Sunday Appeal,* May 9, 1869.
21. Colby, Luther. "W.H. Mumler, the Spirit Photographer." *Banner of Light,* July 10, 1869.
22. Colby, Luther. "Lecture on Spirit Photography." *Banner of Light,* November 13, 1869.
23. Keith, G.W. "Spirit Photography." *Banner of Light,* November 22, 1870.
24. Baker, Francis. "Spirit-Photography in Los Angeles, Cal." *Banner of Light,* August 12, 1871.
25. Keith, G.W. "Spirit Photography." *Banner of Light,* November 22, 1870.
26. Wheeler, E.J., I.K. Funk, and W.S. Woods. *The Literary Digest,* 1894.
27. Colby, Luther. "Spirit Photographs." *Banner of Light,* January 1, 1870.
28. Colby, Luther. "Mumler!" *Banner of Light,* May 13, 1871.
29. Colby, Luther. n.t. *Banner of Light,* December 5, 1874.
30. Mumler, William. "The Personal Experiences of William Mumler in Sprit Photography." *Banner of Light,* January 9, 1875.
31. Mumler, William. "The Personal Experiences of William Mumler in Sprit Photography." *Banner of Light,* January 30, 1875.
32. Mumler, William. "The Personal Experiences of William Mumler in Sprit Photography." *Banner of Light,* March 27, 1875.
33. *Ibid.*
34. "W.H. Mumler." *Spiritual Magazine,* 1872.
35. Mumler, William. "The Personal Experiences of William Mumler in Sprit Photography." *Banner of Light,* January 30, 1875.
36. "Lincoln Spiritualist." *Brooklyn Eagle,* September 9, 1863.
37. "Is President Lincoln a Victim of Spiritualism?" *Urbana Union,* June 3, 1863.
38. Whitney, John F. "Was Abraham Lincoln a Spiritualist?" *Banner of Light,* October 8, 1892.
39. *Spirit of Democracy* (Woodsfield, OH), February 11, 1873.
40. Sprague, E.W. *A Future Life Demonstrated: Or, Twenty-seven Years a Public Medium.* Detroit, MI: E. W. Sprague, 1908.
41. Hardinge, E. *Modern American Spiritualism: A Twenty Years' Record of the Communion Between Earth and the World of Spirits.* New York: E. Hardinge, 1870.
42. Martin, J., W.J. Birnes, and G. Noory. *The Haunting of America: From the Salem Witch Trials to Harry Houdini.* New York: Tom Doherty Associates, 2011.
43. "Col. Simon P. Kase Dies of Old Age." *The Columbian,* August 30, 1900.
44. "Simon P. Kase Died in Philadelphia." *Montour American,* August 30, 1900.
45. "Spiritualist Encamped." *The Sun,* July 21, 1879.
46. Williams, E. *Abraham Lincoln a Spiritualist: Lecture.* Venice Art Press, 1891.
47. Burr, W.H. "District of Columbia." *Banner of Light,* November 4, 1893.
48. Donovan, J.W. *Modern Jury Trials and Advocates: Containing Condensed Cases with Sketches and Speeches of American Advocates; the Art of Winning Cases and Manner of Counsel Described, with Notes and Rules of Practice.* New York: Banks and Brothers, 1881.
49. Maynard, N.C. *Was Abraham Lincoln a Spiritualist? or, Curious Revelations from the Life of a Trance Medium.* Philadelphia: R. C. Hartranft, 1891.

50. Whitney, John F. "Was Abraham Lincoln a Spiritualist?" *Banner of Light*, October 8, 1891.

51. Maynard, N.C. *Was Abraham Lincoln a Spiritualist? or, Curious Revelations from the Life of a Trance Medium.* Philadelphia: R. C. Hartranft, 1891.

52. Ibid.

53. "The Rebellion." *Urbana Union*, May 14, 1862.

54. Maynard, N.C. *Was Abraham Lincoln a Spiritualist? or, Curious Revelations from the Life of a Trance Medium.* Philadelphia: R. C. Hartranft, 1891.

55. Stanton, Edwin. "Terrible National Calamity." *Banner of Light*, April 22, 1865.

56. Conant, J.H. "Message Department." *Banner of Light*, July 8, 1865.

57. Conant, J.H. "Abraham Lincoln." *Banner of Light*, March 16, 1867.

58. Sterling, J.M. "Evocation of Abraham Lincoln." *Banner of Light*, December 30, 1865.

59. Edmonds, John. "Letter from Judge Edmonds." *Banner of Light*, December 22, 1866.

60. "Spooks That Speak." *Brooklyn Eagle*, September 19, 1870.

61. Ibid.

62. "The Uneasy Ghost Authoritatively Laid to Rest." *Brooklyn Eagle*, January 14, 1877.

63. Insider. "John Wilkes Booth." *Brooklyn Eagle*, February 8, 1885.

64. Neely, M.E., and R.G. McMurtry. *The Insanity File: The Case of Mary Todd Lincoln.* Carbondale: Southern Illinois University Press, 1993.

65. "Willie Lincoln." *Banner of Light*, May 29, 1869.

66. "Tad Lincoln." *Banner of Light*, July 27, 1872.

Chapter Four

1. United States Census Office, J.M. Edmunds, and United States Department of the Interior. *Statistics of the United States: (including Mortality, Property, & C.) in 1860; Compiled from the Original Returns and Being the Final Exhibit of the Eighth Census.* Washington, DC: U.S. Government Printing Office, 1866.

2. United States Census Office and J.S. Billings. *Tenth Census of the United States, 1880: Mortality and Vital Statistics Part 1.* Washington, DC: U.S. Government Printing Office, 1886.

3. United States Census Office, F.A. Walker, C.W. Seaton, and H. Gannett. *Census Reports Tenth Census. June 1, 1880: Mortality and Vital Statistics. Portfolio of Plates and Diagrams.* Washington, DC: U.S. Government Printing Office, 1886.

4. Eddy, R. *Alcohol in History: An Account of Intemperance in All Ages; Together with a History of the Various Methods Employed for Its Removal.* New York: National Temperance Society and Publication House, 1887.

5. Madden, J. *Shall We Drink Wine? A Physician's Study of the Alcohol Question.* Milwaukee, WI: Owen & Weihbrecht Company, 1899.

6. "Payment of the Volunteers." *New York Times*, July 7, 1861.

7. "Soldiers Killing Each Other from Alcohol." *New York Times*, June 28, 1862.

8. "Murder of a Woman—Drunkenness among the Troops." *New York Times*, July 28, 1861.

9. "By Telegraph." *National Republican*, August 3, 1861.

10. "A Riot among the Soldiers of the Third Regiment Irish Brigade." *New York Times*, November 30, 1861.

11. *The Union Army: A History of Military Affairs in the Loyal States 1861–65—Records of the Regiments in the Union Army—Cyclopedia of Battles—Memoirs of Commanders and Soldiers.* Vol. 2, *Cyclopedia of Battles.* Madison, WI: Federal Publishing Company, 1908.

12. "Temperance in the Army." *New York Times*, August 5, 1861.

13. Pickett, D., C.T. Wilson, and E.D. Smith. *The Cyclopedia of Temperance, Prohibition and Public Morals.* New York: Methodist Book Concern, 1917.

14. American Temperance Union. "The Sick Soldier—Thoughts of Home." *Journal of the American Temperance Union: and the New-York Prohibitionist*, July 1863.

15. "Temperance Folks." *Brooklyn Eagle*, August 5, 1861.

16. Cherrington, E.H. *The Evolution of Prohibition in the United States of America: A Chronological History of the Liquor Problem and the Temperance Reform in the United States from the Earliest Settlements to the Consummation of National Prohibition.* Westerville, OH: American Issue Press, 1920.

17. "Mortality from Drinking Beer." *Brooklyn Eagle*, July 10, 1861.

18. "Suppression of Intemperance in the Camps." *New York Times*, August 6, 1861.

19. Stillé, C.J. *History of the United States Sanitary Commission, the General Report of Its Work during the War of the Rebellion.* New York: Hurd & Houghton, 1868.

20. Woodward, J.J., I.M. Rutkow, and United States Army Medical Department. *Outlines of the Chief Camp Diseases of the United States Armies: As Observed During the Present War*. San Francisco: Norman Publishing, 1863.

21. Stillé, C.J. *History of the United States Sanitary Commission, the General Report of Its Work during the War of the Rebellion*. New York: Hurd & Houghton, 1868.

22. H. Bellows, W.H. Van Buren, and C.R. Agnew. "The Sanitary Commission: Letter from the Executive Committee to the President." *New York Times*, July 21, 1862.

23. "Important from Fort Monroe: News from Richmond and Other Points in the Rebel States." *New York Times*, March 6, 1862.

24. Bancroft, Charles F. "Charles F. Bancroft Civil War Letter." Vermont Historical Society Library, 1862.

25. Zeller, P.G. *The Second Vermont Volunteer Infantry Regiment, 1861–1865*. Jefferson, NC: McFarland, 2002.

26. Spafford, Joseph. "Joseph Spafford to Mary Jane Spafford." Vermont Historical Society Library, 1862.

27. Davis, Andrew F. "Andrew F. Davis Papers, 1862." In *Civil War Diaries and Letters*. Iowa City: University of Iowa, Digital Library Services, 2007.

28. Barney, Valentine G. "Valentine G. Barney to Maria Barney." Vermont Historical Society Library, 1863.

29. Barney, Valentine G. "Barney Letter to Wife." Vermont Historical Society Library, 1863.

30. "War Gazette." *New York Times*, November 28, 1863.

31. "News from Washington." *New York Times*, April 12, 1864.

32. "Grant Drunk." *New York Times*, April 22, 1862.

33. Rutherford, Joseph. "Joseph Rutherford to Hannah Rutherford" (1863). In *Vermonters in the Civil War*. Burlington: Special Collections, Bailey-Howe Library, University of Vermont, 2004.

34. "The Case of Surgeon Luther Thomas." *New York Times*, April 9, 1863.

35. "Police Court." *Richmond Daily Dispatch*, July 27, 1861.

36. Owen, W.M. *In Camp and Battle with the Washington Artillery of New Orleans: A Narrative of Events during the Late Civil War from Bull Run to Appomattox and Spanish Fort*. Boston: Ticknor & Company, 1885.

37. "Drunk and Disorderly." *Richmond Daily Dispatch*, September 17, 1863.

38. Lees, F.R. *Textbook of Temperance*. New York: Z. P. Vose & Company, 1869.

39. "Mrs. Cora Hatch on Spirits." *New York Times*, January 23, 1858.

40. Cary, S.F. *Historical Sketch of the Order of the Sons of Temperance: An Address Delivered at the Fortieth Annual Session of the National Division, Held at Halifax, N.S. in July, 1884*. Halifax, Nova Scotia: W. Theakston, 1884.

41. Garland, H. *Ulysses S. Grant: His Life and Character*. New York: Doubleday & McClure, 1898.

42. Van Orden, W.H. *Life of General U.S. Grant: Together with His Military Services*. New York: Albert Sibley and Co., 1885.

43. *Ibid.*

44. Barrett, J.H. *Life of Abraham Lincoln*. Mechanicsburg, PA: Stackpole Books, 1865.

45. Shaw, J. *History of the Great Temperance Reforms of the Nineteenth Century, Exhibiting: The Evils of Intemperance, the Methods of Reform, the Woman's Crusade, and the Coming Conflict on the Temperance Question*. Cincinnati, OH: Hitchcock & Walden, 1875.

46. Wittenmyer, A.T., and F.E. Willard. *History of the Woman's Temperance Crusade: A Complete Official History of the Wonderful Uprising of the Christian Women of the United States Against the Liquor Traffic, which Culminated in the Gospel Temperance Movement*. Philadelphia: Published at the Office of the Christian Woman, 1878.

47. Blair, H.W. *The Temperance Movement: Or, The Conflict Between Man and Alcohol*. Boston: W. E. Smythe Company, 1888.

48. "Rum and Rebellion." *Brooklyn Eagle*, April 15, 1864.

49. "Misguided Efforts." *Brooklyn Eagle*, March 6, 1874.

50. American Institute of Instruction. *Fifty-seventh Annual Meeting of the American Institute of Instruction*. Boston: Willard Small, 1887.

51. Connor, L. "Editorial." *American Lancet*, 1886.

52. Hooper, Daniel. "The Alcohol Question." *The Lancet* 77(1969)(1861):507–9.

53. Johnson, Metcalfe. "The Alcohol Question." *The Lancet* 78(1981)(1861):168–69.

54. Inman, Thomas. "Is Alcohol Food?" *The Lancet* 80(2033)(1862):188–89.

55. Smith, Edward. "On Alcohol." *The Lancet* 86(2198)(1865):426–27.

56. Anstie, Francis. "On the Physiological and Therapeutical Action of Alcohol." *The Lancet* 86(2195)(1865):343–45.

57. Falret, Jules. "On Moral Insanity." *American Journal of Insanity* 24(1867):52–63.

58. "The Insane." *Brooklyn Eagle*, November 29, 1873.

59. Cook, George. "The Relations of Inebriety to Insanity." *American Journal of Insanity* 28(4)(1862):321–49.

60. Crothers, T.D. "America's Inebriate Asylums." *Journal of the American Medical Association* 21(14)(1893).

61. Kimball, Laurie A., Karla M. Eisch and Wesley Haynes. "National Historic Landmark Nomination: New York State Inebriate Asylum." Washington, DC: U.S. Department of the Interior, National Park Service, 1997.

62. "The Inebriates' Home." *Brooklyn Eagle*, May 31, 1872.

63. Turner, J.E. *The History of the First Inebriate Asylum in the World: By Its Founder; An Account of His Indictment, also a Sketch of the Woman's National Hospital, by Its Projector.* New York: J.E. Turner, 1888.

64. McFarland, Andrew. "Insanity and Intemperance." *American Journal of Insanity* 19 (1863):448–70.

65. *Ibid.*

66. "The Cinchona Rubra Cure." *Sacramento Daily Union*, August 30, 1880.

67. Reilly, John E. "Robert D'Unger and His Reminiscences of Edgar Allen Poe in Baltimore." *Maryland Historical Magazine* 88 (1993): 60–72.

68. "Drunkenness Cured." *North Otago Times*, June 23, 1879.

69. "Cinchona Rubra." *Chicago Times*, January 22, 1880.

70. "Kleptomania." *New York Times*, September 5, 1877.

71. Ordronaux, John. "Is Habitual Drunkenness a Disease?" *American Journal of Insanity* 30(1874):430–43.

72. Davis, N.S. "What Is Needed for the Successful Treatment of Inebriates?" *Journal of Nervous & Mental Disease* 3(1)(1876):79–83.

Chapter Five

1. "The Carnival of Crime." *Evening Star*, November 30, 1865.

2. Chambers, J.W., and F. Anderson. *The Oxford Companion to American Military History.* New York: Oxford University Press, 1999.

3. "A Terrible Increase in Crime." *Spirit of Democracy*, September 6, 1865.

4. "Carnival of Crime." *Daily Phoenix*, August 19, 1865.

5. Beardsley, F.G. *A History of American Revivals.* New York: American Tract Society, 1912.

6. "News Summary." *Vermont Transcript*, December 1, 1865.

7. "The Carnival of Crime." *Raftsman's Journal*, September 13, 1865.

8. "Sketch of the Life of Mrs. Grinder: Is She a Professional Poisoner?" *New York Times*, September 3, 1865.

9. Schechter, H. *Psycho USA: Famous American Killers You Never Heard Of.* New York: Ballantine Books, 2012.

10. "Sketch of the Life of Mrs. Grinder: Is She a Professional Poisoner?" *New York Times*, September 3, 1865.

11. "Martha Grinder—The Evil That She Did Lives After Her." *New York Times*, September 23, 1866.

12. "The Pittsburgh Poisoning Case." *New York Times*, October 30, 1865.

13. "The American Borgia." *New York Times*, January 20, 1866.

14. "Execution of Mrs. Grinder." *New York Times*, January 21, 1866.

15. "Carnival of Crime." *Jeffersonian*, July 4, 1867.

16. "Carnival of Crime." *Daily Ohio Statesman*, November 16, 1867.

17. "Infamous." *Public Ledger*, May 23, 1867.

18. Vaux, R. *Brief Sketch of the Origin and History of the State Penitentiary for the Eastern District of Pennsylvania, at Philadelphia.* Philadelphia: McLaughlin Brothers, 1872.

19. "John Brown's Soul." *Clearfield Republican*, March 7, 1867.

20. "Crime, North and South." *Nashville Union and American*, November 7, 1868.

21. "Carnival of Crime." *The Columbian*, January 3, 1868.

22. "Increase of Crime in the City." *New York Times*, February 11, 1866.

23. Lowell, Norton. "American Prisons." *North American Review*, 1866.

24. "Legal Intelligence." *Evening Telegraph*, October 4, 1869.

25. Massachusetts State Board of Charities. *Second Annual Report of the Board of State Charities.* 1866.

26. Massachusetts State Board of Charities. *Third Annual Report of the Board of State Charities of Massachusetts to Which Are Added the Reports of the Secretary, and the General Agent of the Board.* 1867.

27. Pennsylvania Prison Society, *Journal of Prison Discipline and Philanthropy*, 1892.

28. E.C. Wines, and Theodore W. Dwight. *The Nation.* New York: J.H. Richards & Company, 1867.

29. *13th Annual Report of the Officers of the*

Indiana State Prison, Including the Report of the Warden, Moral Instructor, Physician, and Board of Directors for the Year Ending Dec. 15, ... to the Governor. Indianapolis, IN: J.C. Walker, 1860.

30. "Murder at Newmarket, N. J.; The Wife of a Physician Murdered in Her Own House." *New York Times*, February 27, 1867.

31. "The Coriell Murder: Trial of Bridget Durgan at New Brunswick, N. J.—The Indictment." *New York Times*, May 21, 1867.

32. "The Coriell Murder: Trial of Bridget Durgan at New Brunswick, N.J. Fifth and Sixth Day's Proceedings." *New York Times*, May 27, 1867.

33. "Infamous." *Public Ledger*, May 23, 1867.

34. "The Coriell Murder: Bridget Durgan Found Guilty." *New York Times*, June 1, 1867.

35. "The Coriell Murder: A Visit to Bridget Durgan." *New York Times*, June 3, 1867.

36. "The Coriell Murder: Testimony Regarding the Alleged Complicity of Mary Gilroy." *New York Times*, June 6, 1867.

37. "The Coriell Murder: Bridget Durgan to Be Hanged Aug. 30." *New York Times*, June 18, 1867.

38. "Bridget Durgan: The Approaching Execution." *New York Times*, August 28, 1867.

39. Durgan, B. *Life, Crimes, and Confession of Bridget Durgan, the Fiendish Murderess of Mrs. Coriel: Whom She Butchered, Hoping to Take Her Place in the Affections of the Husband of Her Innocent and Lovely Victim.* New York: C.W. Alexander, 1867.

40. "Carnival of Crime." *Clarksville Chronicle*, January 22, 1869.

41. "The Drinker Farm Murder Trial—Peculiarly Atrocious Character of the Crime." *New York Times*, November 20, 1867.

42. Phillips, J.J. *The Drinker's Farm Tragedy: Trial and Conviction of James Jeter Phillips, for the Murder of His Wife.* Richmond: J. Wall Turner, 1868.

43. Ward, H.M. *Public Executions in Richmond, Virginia: A History, 1782–1907.* Jefferson, NC: McFarland, 2012.

44. "Carnival of Crime." *The Columbian*, January 3, 1868.

45. "Crime, North and South." *Nashville Union and American*, November 7, 1868.

46. "Indiana." *New York Times*, February 20, 1869.

47. "Indiana Justice." *New York Times*, March 6, 1874.

48. "Mrs. Clem." *New York Times*, May 4, 1874.

49. "North Carolina." *Athens Post*, February 5, 1869.

50. "Father Seduces His Daughter." *Union Flag*, March 12, 1869.

51. "Mayor Fox His Honor Subject to an Interview." *Evening Telegraph*, October 6, 1869.

52. "From Buffalo Discovery of a Terrible Murder." *Evening Telegraph*, January 26, 1869.

53. "Intemperance." *Evening Telegraph*, March 27, 1869.

54. Floyd, F.C. *History of the Fortieth (Mozart) Regiment, New York Volunteers: Which Was Composed of Four Companies from New York, Four Companies from Massachusetts and Two Companies from Pennsylvania.* Boston: F. H. Gilson Company, 1909.

55. "The New Hampshire Tragedy." *Cincinnati Enquirer*, May 23, 1868.

56. Thompson, I.G., and I. Browne. *The American Reports: Containing All Decisions of General Interest Decided in the Courts of Last Resort of the Several States with Notes and References.* San Francisco: Bancroft-Whitney, 1872.

57. Shirley, John M. *Reports and Cases Argued and Determined in the Supreme Judicial Court of New Hampshire.* Concord, NH: B.W. Sanborn and Co., 1872.

58. "Murderers in the New Hampshire State Prison." *New York Times*, November 3, 1868.

59. Robinson, Henry. "Charles Marseilles." *Granite Monthly: A New Hampshire Magazine*, 1897.

60. "The Sunday Liquor Business." *New York Tribune*, July 12, 1870.

61. "Murder of a Tennessean." *Sweetwater Enterprise*, July 14, 1870.

62. *Life, Trial, and Execution of Edward H. Ruloff: The Perpetrator of Eight Murders, Numerous Burglaries, and Other Crimes: Who Was Recently Hanged at Binghamton, N.Y.* Philadelphia: Barclay & Company, 1871.

63. "The Murderer Ruloff." *New York Times*, April 3, 1871.

64. "Some Notable Trials." *New York Times*, December 15, 1895.

65. "The Ruloff Trial." *New York Times*, January 7, 1871.

66. Twain, M., V. Fischer, M.B. Frank, and L. Salamo. *Mark Twain's Letters, 1870–1871.* Berkeley: University of California Press, 1995.

67. "A Chance for the Detectives." *New York Times*, September 10, 1871.

68. "A Woman of the Period." *Memphis Sunday Appeal*, July 2, 1871.

69. "The Connecticut Borgia." *Nashville Union and American*, July 14, 1871.

70. "More about the Lydia Sherman Case." *Leavenworth Weekly Times*, July 6, 1871.

71. "Extraordinary Crime by Poisoning." *Belmont Chronicle*, July 6, 1871.

72. "Mrs. Sherman's Horrible Confession." *Wyandot County Republican*, January 23, 1873.

73. Sherman, L. *The Poison Fiend! Life, Crimes, and Conviction of Lydia Sherman (the Modern Lucretia Borgia), Recently Tried in New Haven, Conn., for Poisoning Three Husbands and Eight of Her Children: Her Life in Full!, Exciting Account of Her Trial—the Fearful Evidence.* Philadelphia: Barclay & Company, 1872.

74. "A Confession." *Memphis Daily Appeal*, January 14, 1873.

75. "The New Lucretia Borgia." *News and Herald*, June 21, 1877.

76. "Special Dispatch." *The Telegraph*, May 24, 1878.

77. "The Increase in Crime." *New York Times*, February 5, 1872.

78. "An 'Insane' Murderer Suddenly Restored to Reason." *New York Times*, February 11, 1872.

79. "Scannell." *New York Times*, November 4, 1872.

80. "Scannell." *New York Times*, November 5, 1872.

81. "Death of Henry L. Clinton." *New York Times*, June 8, 1899.

82. Clinton, Henry. "Abuse of the Insanity Plea." *New York Times*, March 29, 1873.

83. "Trunk Murder." *Eaton Weekly Democrat*, January 4, 1872.

84. "The Charles River Mystery." *New York Times*, November 8, 1872.

85. "A Bloody Trail." *Weekly Kansas Chief*, June 19, 1873.

86. "A Murderers' Den." *New York Times*, May 12, 1873.

87. "The Kansas Murders." *New York Times*, May 13, 1873.

88. Triplett, F. *History, Romance and Philosophy of Great American Crimes and Criminals...: With Personal Portraits, Biographical Sketches, Legal Notes of Celebrated Trials, and Philosophical Disquisition Concerning the Causes, Prevalence and Prevention of Crime.* New York: N. D. Thompson, 1885.

89. "Human Butchery." *Lincoln County Herald*, May 21, 1873.

90. Triplett, F. *History, Romance and Philosophy of Great American Crimes and Criminals...: With Personal Portraits, Biographical Sketches, Legal Notes of Celebrated Trials, and Philosophical Disquisition Concerning the Causes, Prevalence and Prevention of Crime.* New York: N. D. Thompson, 1885.

91. "Kansas Butchery." *Democratic Press*, May 22, 1873.

92. Lehman, Leola. "The Butchering Benders." *Great West: True Stories of Old Frontier Days*, 1971.

93. "Mysterious Murders." *New York Times*, April 19, 1874.

94. "The Bender Family." *New York Times*, November 30, 1876.

95. McCune, H.L. "A Reminiscence." *Kansas City Bar Monthly*, 1903.

96. "The Prevalence of Crime." *Green-Mountain Freeman*, July 23, 1873.

97. "Carnival of Crime." *Charleston Daily News*, January 28, 1873.

98. "Carnival of Crime." *Daily Phoenix*, May 16, 1874.

99. "Carnival of Crime." *Weekly Democratic Statesman*, July 2, 1874.

100. "An Era of Crime." *National Republican*, July 27, 1874.

101. "The Carnival of Crime." *Ashtabula Telegraph*, August 29, 1874.

102. "Hard Times." *Vermont Farmer*, June 25, 1875.

103. Twain, M. *The Writings of Mark Twain: Tom Sawyer Abroad, Tom Sawyer the Detective, and Other Stories, Etc., Etc.* New York: Harper and Brother, 1899.

104. Hill, H.A. *History of the Old South Church (Third Church) Boston: 1669–1884.* Boston: Houghton, Mifflin, 1889.

105. Manning, J.M. *The Carnival of Crime: A Sermon Preached Sunday Morning, June 6, 1875.* Boston: Lee and Shepard, 1875.

106. "An Era of Crime." *National Republican*, July 27, 1874.

107. "The Genealogy of Crime." *The Sun*, February 22, 1877.

108. "Hereditary Crime." *The Sun*, August 4, 1877.

109. Shepard, E.M. *The Work of a Social Teacher: Being a Memorial of Richard L. Dugdale.* New York: Society for Political Education, 1884.

110. Dugdale, R.L. *"The Jukes": A Study in Crime, Pauperism, Diseases, and Heredity; Also, Further Studies of Criminals.* New York: G. P. Putnam's Sons, 1877.

111. "New Publications—The Jukes." *New York Times*, July 29, 1877.

112. "Killing No Murder." *New York Times*, January 25, 1876.

113. "Murders of Five Years." *New York Times*, January 25, 1876.

114. "Extraordinary Lynching Scene." *New York Times*, January 24, 1876.

115. Switzler, W.F., C.R. Barns, R.A. Campbell, A.J. Conant, and G.C. Swallow. *Switzler's*

Illustrated History of Missouri, from 1541 to 1877. St. Louis, MO: C. R. Barns, 1879.

116. "Twice Sentenced to Be Hanged." *New York Times*, December 7, 1878.

117. "A Decision That Might Have Covered the Marion County Case." *Wheeling Daily Intelligencer*, May 6, 1879.

118. "Pryor N. Coleman's Case." *Memphis Daily Appeal*, April 19, 1879.

119. Sparks, J., E. Everett, J.R. Lowell, and H.C. Lodge. *North American Review*, 1890.

120. "Pryor Coleman's Sentence." *Knoxville Daily Chronicle*, June 28, 1879.

121. "Crime at the North." *New Orleans Daily Democrat*, July 12, 1879.

122. "Texas Crime." *Brenham Weekly Banner*, April 11, 1879.

123. "Crime Epidemic." *Evening Star*, June 19, 1879.

Chapter Six

1. Deutsch, A. *The Mentally Ill in America: A History of Their Care and Treatment from Colonial Times.* New York: Columbia University Press, 1946.

2. Griffenhagen, George B. *Old English Patent Medicines in America.* Washington, DC: Smithsonian Institution, 1959.

3. Shaw, R.B. *History of the Comstock Patent Medicine Business and Dr. Morse's Indian Root Pills.* Washington, DC: Smithsonian Institution Press, 1972.

4. Judson, B.L. "Pills." *Jeffersonian Democrat*, March 9, 1860.

5. "Dr. Morse's Indian Root Pills." *Potter Journal*, December 8, 1859.

6. "Indian Doctor's Remedies." *Nashville Patriot*, September 17, 1859.

7. "Wright's Indian Vegetable Pills." *The Southerner*, April 2, 1859.

8. "Indian Remedies." *Holmes County Farmer*, March 1, 1860.

9. Merwin, W.R. "Cherokee Medicines." *Rochester NY Union & Advertiser*, February 16, 1865.

10. "The Indian Herb Doctor from Canada." *Morning Freeman*, July 5, 1860.

11. "The Alleged Conspirators." *Evening Star*, May 11, 1865.

12. Lyons, R.J. "Important Medical Notice!" *Livingston Republican*, January 1, 1857.

13. Lyons, R.J. "Appointments." *Jeffersonian Democrat*, March 9, 1860.

14. "The Alleged Conspirators." *Evening Star*, May 11, 1865.

15. "To the Editor of the Pilot." *Montreal Pilot*, September 16, 1857.

16. Tumblety, Francis. "To Be Good Looking." *Harper's Weekly*, July 13, 1861.

17. Tumblety, Francis. "Dr. Tumblety's Pimple Banisher." *Harper's Weekly*, August 24, 1861.

18. Tumblety, Francis. "Dr. Tumblety's Pimple Banisher." *Harper's Weekly*, September 7, 1861.

19. "Additional Testimonials." *Evening Star*, May 5, 1862.

20. Hutchison, Mrs. "Blindness Cured." *Brooklyn Eagle*, March 4, 1864.

21. "Engineer at the Harlem Railroad Shop." *Brooklyn Eagle*, April 23, 1864.

22. Lyons, R.J. "Appointments." *Hillsdale Standard*, November 10, 1863.

23. Delaney, Robert. "Important—Yellow Fever and Black Vomit." *Daily Exchange*, September 11, 1858.

24. "Singular Suicide." *Richmond Dispatch*, November 8, 1860.

25. "To the Editors of the Cincinnati Daily Press." *Cincinnati Daily Press*, June 27, 1861.

26. Ralphgrame. "Dr. Ralphgrame." *Indiana State Sentinel*, June 26, 1861.

27. Williams, S.E. "The Use of Beverage Alcohol as Medicine, 1790–1860." *Journal of Studies on Alcohol* 41(5)(1980):559.

28. Hubbard, E., and Roycroft Shop. *Lydia E. Pinkham: Being a Sketch of Her Life and Times.* East Aurora, NY: Roycrofters, 1915.

29. Pinkham, Lydia. "Neglect Is Suicide." *Donahoe's Magazine.*, 1897.

30. Petersen, W.J., and State Historical Society of Iowa. *Pain-killer Almanac: A Facsimile Reproduction, Slightly Enl. of an 1868 Almanac.* Cincinnati, OH: J.N. Harris & Co., 1868.

31. Solomon, J.M. *Indian Wine Bitters & Rheumatic Drops. For Sale by All Druggists.... The Greatest Blood Purifier and Liver and Kidney Cure in the World.... Prepared by Dr. James M. Solomon, Jr., Attleboro, Mass.* Five Points, NY: Donaldson Brothers, 1870.

32. Hanson, D. *Dominicus Hanson's Catalogue of Apothecary, Book and Variety Store.* Rochester, N.H. Dover, NH: Dover Gazette Power-Press, 1854.

33. Winslow. "Mrs. Winslow Soothing Syrup." *Holmes County Farmer*, March 1, 1860.

34. Winslow. "Mrs. Winslow's Soothing Syrup." *New York Times*, December 1, 1860.

35. "Mothers." *Holmes County Farmer*, March 1, 1860.

36. "Mothers." *Daily Intelligencer*, October 11, 1860.

37. Michigan State Board of Health. *Sixth*

Annual Report of the Secretary of the Board of Health. Lansing, MI: W.S. George & Co., 1878.

38. "Warranted Purely Vegetable." *New Orleans Daily Crescent,* October 5, 1860.

39. "Brandreth's Pills." *Evening Star,* March 8, 1862.

40. "Brandreth's Pills." *Cleveland Morning Leader,* September 29, 1862.

41. Brandreth's Pills. "Surgeon-General Hammond." *Harper's Weekly,* August 15, 1863.

42. Gillett, M.C. *The Army Medical Department, 1818–1865.* Washington, DC: U.S. Government Printing Office, 1987.

43. Coulter, H.L. *Science and Ethics in American Medicine, 1800–1914.* Richmond, CA: North Atlantic Books, 1982.

44. Trall, R.T. *Herald of Health.* New York: R.T. Trall Publishers & Co., 1863.

45. Brandreth's Pills. "Surgeon-General Hammond." *Harper's Weekly,* August 15, 1863.

46. Brandreth's Pills. "How the United States Can Save 50,000,000 Dollars per Annum." *Harper's Weekly,* November 14, 1863.

47. Brandreth's Pills. "United States Sanitary Commission." *Harper's Weekly,* February 6, 1864.

48. "Attention, Soldiers!" *Banner of Light,* April 8, 1865.

49. Bulpin, George. "Laurie's Chinese Life Pills." *Harper's Weekly,* March 29, 1862.

50. Ibid.

51. "Laurie's Chinese Life Pills." *Harper's Weekly,* January 31, 1863.

52. Helmbold, Henry T. "To the Public." *New York Times,* October 28, 1863.

53. "H.T. Helmbold Dies in an Insane Asylum." *New York Times,* October 26, 1894.

54. "Soldier's, See to Your Own Health." *Harper's Weekly,* May 9, 1863.

55. "Soldiers, to the Rescue!" *Harper's Weekly,* April 25, 1863.

56. "Measles Are Prostrating the Volunteers." *Harper's Weekly,* July 4, 1863.

57. "Hostetter's Celebrated Stomach Bitters—Health of the Army." *Harper's Weekly,* April 25, 1863.

58. "Hostetter's Celebrated Stomach Bitters." *Harper's Weekly,* March 2, 1864.

59. Hall, W.W. *Dyspepsia and Its Kindred Diseases.* New York: R. Worthington, 1877.

60. Still, E.R. "Nerve Food—A Spiritual Gift." *Banner of Light,* May 7, 1870.

61. Trall, R.T. *Digestion and Dyspepsia: A Complete Explanation of the Physiology of the Digestive Processes.* New York: S.R. Wells, 1874.

62. "Brandreth's Pills." *Harper's Weekly,* March 18, 1865.

63. "The Good Looks of Both Men and Women." *Harper's Weekly,* August 19, 1865.

64. "Holloway's Pills." *Harper's Weekly,* September 23, 1865.

65. Loveridge, E. Dexter. "The Great Indian Beverage." *Evening Argus,* September 9, 1865.

66. Marsh, Bela. "Some Folk's Can't Sleep Nights." *Banner of Light,* January 7, 1865.

67. "Some Folks Can't Sleep Nights." *The Columbian,* October 25, 1867.

68. "Business Matters." *Banner of Light,* June 9, 1866.

69. "Consumption and Nervous Debility!" *Banner of Light,* July 7, 1866.

70. "Important to Invalids." *Banner of Light,* March 16, 1867.

71. "Turner's Universal Neuralgia Pill." *Banner of Light,* February 19, 1870.

72. "Dr. Quain's Magic Condition Pills." *Banner of Light,* December 29, 1877.

73. Landers, Jon J. "W. Sawens and Company." *Bottles Along the Mohawk.* Accessed May 14, 2016. http://www.mohawkvalleybottleclub.com/ArchiveArticles/PDF_Articles/Sawens.pdf.

74. Miles, Franklin. "He Committed Suicide!" *Mower County Transcript,* September 13, 1893.

75. Miles, Franklin. "Surrounded by Mystery." *Kansas Agitator,* May 3, 1894.

76. Miles, Franklin. "Dr. Miles' Restorative Nervine—The Only Remedy for Nervous Diseases Admitted to the World's Fair." *Lawrence Democrat,* March 23, 1894.

77. United Daughters of the Confederacy. *The Confederate Veteran Magazine,* 1895.

78. Miles, Franklin. "New and Startling Facts for Those Afflicted with Nervous Diseases." 1893.

79. Fisher, G.T. *A Practical Treatise on Medical Electricity, Containing a Historical Sketch of Frictional and Voltaic Electricity, as Applied to Medicine: With Plain Instructions for the Use of Electric, Galvanic, Electro-magnetic Instruments, Etc.* London: T & R Willats, 1845.

80. Meyer, M., and W.A. Hammond. *Electricity in Its Relations to Practical Medicine.* New York: D. Appleton, 1869.

81. Papillon, Fernand. "Electricity and Life." *American Journal of Insanity,* 1873.

82. "Q: What Constitutes a Person a Medium." *Banner of Light,* March 7, 1868.

83. Pike, J.T. Gilman. "Dr. J.T. Gilman Pike." *Banner of Light,* November 16, 1867.

84. "I.G. Atwood." *Banner of Light,* February 24, 1866.

85. "Human Electricity." *Banner of Light,* March 17, 1866.

86. "The Vineland Democrat." *Banner of Light,* January 16, 1869.

87. Owen, J.J. *"Our Little Doctor"*: *Helen Craib-Beighle and the Magic Power of Her Electric Hand.* San Francisco: Hicks-Judd, 1893.

88. Larue. "Indian Doctor!! and Electrical Physician." *Eaton Weekly Democrat*, March 21, 1872.

89. De Grath. "$100 Proclamation." *Daily State Sentinel*, October 23, 1856.

90. De Grath. "Discovered at Last!" *Brooklyn Daily Eagle*, April 20, 1858.

91. De Grath. "Prof. De Grath's Electric Oil." *Brooklyn Daily Eagle*, June 21, 1858.

92. De Grath. "Electric Oil." *Daily Morning Post*, November 15, 1859.

93. De Grath. "Professor De Grath's Electric Oil." *Weekly Mariettian*, April 25, 1863.

94. Barr, W. "Diptheria!" *Evening Telegraph*, September 10, 1864.

95. Rogers, S. "Roger's Electro-Magnetic Oil." *Columbia Spy*, June 1, 1867.

96. Frey, Ettinger. "Good News. Electric Oil." *Hancock Jeffersonian*, September 11, 1868.

97. Smith, G. B. "Dr. Smith's Electric Oil." *Leavenworth Weekly Times*, October 27, 1870.

98. Smith, G. B. "New Combination!!" *Evening Gazette*, June 7, 1871.

99. Crooke, C. "Crook's Electric Oil." *Hartford Herald*, October 3, 1877.

100. Richbodt, Louis. "Dr. Thomas' Electric Oil." *Indianapolis Leader*, October 30, 1880.

101. Ziegler, Smith. "Dr. Leon's Celebrated Preparations." *Jeffersonian*, January 3, 1867.

102. Pierce, A.P. "Dr. A. P. Pierce, Clairvoyant, Magnetic, and Electric Physician." *Banner of Light*, January 28, 1865.

103. Mann, Charles. "We Reprint." *Banner of Light*, February 4, 1865.

104. Lucas, Mary. "A Course of Five Lectures." *Banner of Light*, April 1, 1865.

105. Haller, John S. *American Medicine in Transition, 1840–1910.* Urbana: University of Illinois Press, 1981.

106. "The So Called 'Magnetic Doctor.'" *Urbana Union*, November 22, 1865.

107. "Spiritualism in New York Court." *The Star of the North*, February 22, 1865.

108. Gallion. "To the Public." *Holt County Sentinel*, October 26, 1866.

109. Porter, James. "Dr. Jas Porter Late of New Orleans." *Public Ledger*, May 28, 1873.

110. Merriam. "Just Arrived." *Green-Mountain Freeman*, June 3, 1868.

111. "Elmira, NY." *Nashville Union and American*, February 10, 1870.

112. Briggs. "No Cure, No Pay." *Brooklyn Daily Eagle*, December 21, 1872.

113. Clifford, Madame. "Clairvoyants." *Brooklyn Daily Eagle*, October 21, 1872.

114. Smith, D.A. "Catarrh Cured." *Brooklyn Daily Eagle*, September 22, 1874.

115. Fanyou. "Dr. Fanyou." *Brooklyn Daily Eagle*, August 25, 1877.

116. Chesley, James. "Dr. James Canney Chesley." *Banner of Light*, February 19, 1870.

117. Chesley, James. "Durham Medical Institute." *Banner of Light*, April 23, 1870.

118. Rhodes, J. H. "J. H. Rhodes, M.D." *Banner of Light*, March 10, 1877.

119. *Ibid.*

120. Hayward, A.S. "Magnetized Paper." *Banner of Light*, April 21, 1877.

121. Sherwood, John. "I Most Cheerfully Recommend." *Banner of Light*, June 22, 1867.

122. D. Ransom, Son & Co. *Ransom's Family Receipt Book.* Buffalo, NY: Barker, Jones, & Co. Printers, 1892.

123. Meyer. "Trask's Magnetic Ointment." *Lincoln County Herald*, April 23, 1868.

124. Ransom. "Dr. Trask's Magnetic Ointment." *Alpena Weekly Argus*, October 21, 1873.

125. Stewart. "Haley's Magnetic Oil." *Clarksville Chronicle*, November 27, 1869.

126. Rogers. "Roger's Magnetic Oil." *Rock Island Argus*, January 9, 1872.

127. "Lyon's Magnetic Insect Powder." *Brooklyn Daily Eagle*, June 15, 1871.

128. Johnston, Simon. "Professor Reed's Magnetic Oil." *Pittsburgh Daily Gazette and Advertiser*, December 3, 1863.

129. "Dr. Russell's Magnetic Oil." *Reading Eagle*, September 1, 1868.

130. Hull and Chamberlain. "Hull and Chamberlain's Magnetic and Electric Powders." *Banner of Light*, January 16, 1875.

131. Chase, Warren. "Dr. William Clark's Spirit Magnetic Vegetable Remedies." *Banner of Light*, October 10, 1868.

132. Barr, W. "Spiritual Pills." *Evening Telegraph*, September 10, 1864.

133. Hostetter, J.H. "Kunkel's Bitter Wine of Iron." *Pilot*, November 10, 1863.

134. Storer, H.B. "Important Notice to Every Woman, Maiden, Wife or Mother." *Banner of Light*, December 17, 1870.

135. Storer, H.B. "Important Facts Concerning the Use of the New Medicine Dr. Storer's Nutritive Compound." *Banner of Light*, December 31, 1870.

136. Storer, Dr. "Conclusive Testimony, Scientific and Popular, to the Value of the New Medicine Dr. Storer's Nutritive Compound." *Banner of Light*, April 1, 1871.

137. Spence, Payton. "For the Healing of

the Nation! The Great Spiritual Remedy!" *Banner of Light*, April 13, 1868.

138. Spence, Payton. "Irresistible Army of Witnesses to the Supremacy of the Great Spiritual Remedy." *Banner of Light*, August 17, 1867.

139. Spence, Payton. "The Secret Army of Invisible Workers." *Banner of Light*, November 12, 1870.

140. Spence, Payton. "Mrs. Spence's Positive and Negative Powders." *Banner of Light*, January 14, 1865.

141. Voltaic Armor Association. "Dr. Hall's Voltaic Armor or Magnetic Bands and Soles." *Banner of Light*, March 23, 1867.

142. Wilson, William. "Wilsonia." *Brooklyn Daily Eagle*, August 16, 1881.

143. Wilson, William. "Wilsonia Triumphant." *Brooklyn Daily Eagle*, November 29, 1881.

144. Carter Medicine Company. "Carter's Little Nerve Pills." *Medina Tribune*, December 16, 1880.

145. Butler, G.M. "Carter's Little Nerve Pills." *Mexico Independent*, May 18, 1881.

146. Malt Bitters Company. "Malt Bitters." *Evening Gazette*, May 22, 1880.

147. "Hop Bitters Company." *Pulaski Democrat*, February 24, 1881.

148. Richbodt, Louis. "Dr. J.B. Simpson's Specific Medicine." *Westfield Republican*, June 14, 1880.

149. Walker, W.H. "Gray's Specific Medicine." *Westfield Republican*, June 14, 1882.

150. Collins, S.B. "The Habit of Drinking." *Banner of Light*, February 15, 1873.

151. Hiscox. "Parker's Ginger Tonic." *Medina Tribune*, November 10, 1881.

Chapter Seven

1. White, J.T. *The National Cyclopedia of American Biography*. New York: J. T. White Company, 1898.

2. "Spiritualism: The Counterfeits of Science and How to Detect Them." *New York Times*, November 20, 1874.

3. "Spiritualism." *Brooklyn Daily Eagle*, November 3, 1874.

4. *Ibid.*

5. "Mesmerism in Society." *New York Times*, April 3, 1881.

6. "Mesmeric Experiments." *New York Times*, January 7, 1881.

7. "The Science of Trance." *New York Times*, January 11, 1881.

8. Barnes, Joseph K. *The Medical and Surgical History of the War of the Rebellion (1861–*1865) Prepared, in Accordance with the Acts of Congress, Under the Direction of Surgeon General Joseph K. Barnes, United States Army: Part 1*. Washington, DC: U.S. Government Printing Office, 1870.

9. Lande, R.G. *Madness, Malingering, and Malfeasance: The Transformation of Psychiatry and the Law in the Civil War Era*. Washington, DC: Brassey's, 2003.

10. "Is This Spiritualism?" *New Ulm Weekly Review*, June 25, 1879.

11. Hammond, William A. "Physics and Physiology of Spiritualism." *North American Review* 110(227)(1870):233–60.

12. Hammond, William A. *The Physics and Physiology of Spiritualism*. New York: Appleton, 1871.

13. Hammond, W.A. "Spiritualism and Nervous Derangement, by Dr. Hammond." *Banner of Light*, September 16, 1876.

14. "The Secret Out." *Banner of Light*, September 6, 1876.

15. "The Exposers." *Banner of Light*, July 8, 1876.

16. "Spiritualism and Science." *Brooklyn Daily Eagle*, December 15, 1870.

17. Hammond, William A. *The Physics and Physiology of Spiritualism*. New York: Appleton, 1871.

18. *Ibid.*

19. Hammond, William A. *The Physics and Physiology of Spiritualism*. New York: Appleton, 1871.

20. "Entertainment Extraordinary." *Brooklyn Daily Eagle*, June 13, 1876.

21. "Humbug." *Brooklyn Daily Eagle*, June 16, 1876.

22. "The Fraud of the Eddy Materializations Exposed." *The Sun*, March 26, 1875.

23. "Exposing the Jugglers." *The Sun*, March 3, 1873.

24. "Seance Professors Come to Grief." *Brooklyn Daily Eagle*, August 28, 1876.

25. "A Self-Styled Professor." *Brooklyn Daily Eagle*, July 14, 1868.

26. "Photographed 'Spirits.'" *New York Times*, October 29, 1876.

27. "Spirit Photographs." *Public Ledger*, July 10, 1872.

28. "Spirit Photographs." *New York Times*, July 29, 1877.

29. "Spirit Photograph." *Brooklyn Eagle*, October 14, 1877.

30. "Read It." *Weekly Arizona Miner*, July 29, 1871.

31. "Once More." *Essex County Herald*, October 17, 1874.

32. "The Latest Performance of the Eddys." *Rutland Daily Globe*, June 22, 1876.

33. "Spirit Photography." *Public Ledger*, July 3, 1879.

34. Pence, P.P. "Spooks and Goblins." *Leavenworth Weekly Times*, September 25, 1879.

35. "Spirit Photo Ridiculed." *True Northerner*, January 2, 1880.

36. "Spiritual Mediums." *Brooklyn Daily Eagle*, July 20, 1875.

37. Home, D.D. *Lights and Shadows of Spiritualism*. London: Virtue & Company, 1877.

38. Davenport, R.B. *The Death-blow to Spiritualism: Being the True Story of the Fox Sisters, as Revealed by Authority of Margaret Fox Kane and Catherine Fox Jencken*. New York: G.W. Dillingham, 1888.

39. "Orange Judd." *Chicago Tribune*, December 28, 1892.

40. Root, A.I. *Gleanings in Bee Culture*. Medina, OH: A. I. Root Company, 1892.

41. "The Liberty of the Press." *New York Times*, February 13, 1872.

42. "The Liberty of the Press." *New York Times*, February 1, 1874.

43. Shrady, George M. *Some Facts about Patent Medicines*. Vol. 22, *The Medical Record*. New York: William Wood and Company, 1882.

44. Holland, J.G. *Scribner's Monthly*, 1881.

45. "The Latest Swindle." *Pittsburg Dispatch*, September 23, 1889.

46. "Plenty of Inducements." *Brooklyn Daily Eagle*, April 5, 1891.

47. Hiss, A.E. *Thesaurus of Proprietary Preparations and Pharmaceutical Specialties: Including "Patent" Medicines, Proprietary Pharmaceuticals, Open-formula Specialties, Synthetic Remedies, Etc.* Chicago: G.P. Engelhard, 1898.

48. Ebert, A.E. *The Standard Formulary*. Chicago: G.P. Engelhard, 1896.

49. Adams, S.H. "The Great American Fraud." *Collier's Weekly*, 1905.

50. "Reports of a Commission Appointed for a Revision of the Revenue System." *Report of the Special Commissioner of the Revenue*. Washington, DC: U.S. Government Printing Office, 1866.

51. *Nostrums & Patent Medicines*. Fargo: North Dakota Agricultural College, 1916.

52. Service and Regulatory Announcements, United States Department of Agriculture, Bureau of Chemistry. *Notices of Judgment Under the Food and Drugs Act*. Washington, DC: U.S. Government Printing Office, 1918.

53. "Their Own Doctors." *Brooklyn Daily Eagle*, September 5, 1886.

54. Contributor, Fat. "An Essay on Doctors." *Camden Journal*, January 2, 1873.

55. "Reform in Medical Education." *New York Times*, December 8, 1878.

56. Trowbridge, C. *Andrew Taylor Still, 1828–1917*. Kirksville, MO: Truman State University Press, 1991.

57. Still, Andrew Taylor. *Autobiography of Andrew T. Still*. Kirksville, MO: Andrew Taylor, 1897.

58. Still, Andrew Taylor. *The Philosophy and Mechanical Principles of Osteopathy*. Redditch, UK: Read Books, 2015.

59. "Osteopathy." *Houston Daily Post*, August 6, 1899.

60. Lande, R.G. *The Abraham Man: Madness, Malingering and the Development of Medical Testimony*. New York: Algora, 2012.

Bibliography

"Abandonment and Suicide of a Young Woman." *New York Times*, February 25, 1868.

Abbott, O., I.E. Davenport, and W.H. Davenport. *The Davenport Brothers. Their History, Travels, and Manifestations. Also the Philosophy of Dark Circles, Ancient and Modern.* New York: Abbott, 1864.

Adams, S.H. "The Great American Fraud." *Collier's Weekly*, 1905.

"Additional Testimonials." *Evening Star*, May 5, 1862.

"The Alleged Conspirators." *Evening Star*, May 11, 1865.

"The American Borgia." *New York Times*, January 20, 1866.

American Institute of Instruction. *Fifty-seventh Annual Meeting of the American Institute of Instruction.* Boston: Willard Small, 1887.

American Temperance Union. "The Sick Soldier—Thoughts of Home." *Journal of the American Temperance Union: and the New-York Prohibitionist*, July 1862.

"Another Convert to Spiritualism." *Daily Dispatch*, April 7, 1857.

Anstie, Francis. "On the Physiological and Therapeutical Action of Alcohol." *The Lancet* 86 (2195)(1865):343–45.

"The Army and Navy." *New York Times*, January 6, 1862.

"Army of the Potomac." *New York Times*, August 23, 1863.

"Attention, Soldiers!" *Banner of Light*, April 8, 1865.

Baker, Francis. "Spirit-Photography in Los Angeles, Cal." *Banner of Light*, August 12, 1871.

Bancroft, Charles F. "Charles F. Bancroft Civil War Letter." Vermont Historical Society Library, 1862.

Barnes, Joseph K. *The Medical and Surgical History of the War of the Rebellion (1861–65) Prepared, in Accordance with the Acts of Congress, Under the Direction of Surgeon General Joseph K. Barnes, United States Army: Part 1.* Washington, DC: U.S. Government Printing Office, 1870.

Barney, Valentine G. "Barney Letter to Wife." Vermont Historical Society Library, 1863.

———. "Valentine G. Barney to Maria Barney." Vermont Historical Society Library, 1863.

Barr, W. "Diptheria!" *Evening Telegraph*, September 10, 1864.

———. "Spiritual Pills." *Evening Telegraph*, September 10, 1864.

Barrett, H.D. *Life Work of Mrs. Cora L.V. Richmond.* Chicago: Hack & Anderson, 1895.

Barrett, J.H. *Life of Abraham Lincoln.* Mechanicsburg, PA: Stackpole Books, 1865.

"The Battle of Antietam." *New York Times*, September 21, 1862.

"Battle of Antietam Creek." *New York Times*, September 18, 1862.

Beardsley, F.G. *A History of American Revivals.* New York: American Tract Society, 1912.

Beatty, J. *The Citizen-soldier: The Memoirs of a Civil War Volunteer.* Lincoln: University of Nebraska Press, 1998.

Beck, Theodric Romeyn. *Elements of Medical Jurisprudence.* 12th edition. Philadelphia: J. B. Lippincott & Co., 1863.

Beck, T.R., and W. Dunlop. *Elements of Medical Jurisprudence.* London: John Anderson, 1825.

Bell, Robert. "Stranger Than Fiction." *Cornhill Magazine* (G. Smith and W.M. Thackeray, eds.), 1860.

Bellows, H., W.H. Van Buren, and C.R. Agnew. "The Sanitary Commission: Letter from the

Executive Committee to the President." *New York Times,* July 21, 1862.

"The Bender Family." *New York Times,* November 30, 1876.

Berry, William, and Luther Colby. *Banner of Light,* January 7, 1860.

_____ and _____. *Banner of Light,* January 14, 1860.

Blair, H.W. *The Temperance Movement: Or, The Conflict Between Man and Alcohol.* Boston: W. E. Smythe Company, 1888.

"A Bloody Trail." *Weekly Kansas Chief,* June 19, 1873.

Bowman, S.M., and R.B. Irwin. *Sherman and His Campaigns: A Military Biography.* New York: C. B. Richardson, 1865.

"Brandreth's Pills." *Cleveland Morning Leader,* September 29, 1862.

"Brandreth's Pills." *Evening Star,* March 8, 1862.

"Brandreth's Pills." *Harper's Weekly,* March 18, 1865.

Brandreth's Pills. "How the United States Can Save 50,000,000 Dollars per Annum." *Harper's Weekly,* November 14, 1863.

_____. "Surgeon General Hammond." *Harper's Weekly,* August 15, 1863.

_____. "United States Sanitary Commission." *Harper's Weekly,* February 6, 1864.

"Bridget Durgan: The Approaching Execution." *New York Times,* August 28, 1867.

Briggs. "No Cure, No Pay." *Brooklyn Daily Eagle,* December 21, 1872.

Bulpin, George. "Laurie's Chinese Life Pills." *Harper's Weekly,* March 29, 1862.

"The Burnside Expedition." *New York Time,* January 12, 1862.

Burr, W.H. "District of Columbia." *Banner of Light,* November 4, 1893.

"Business Matters." *Banner of Light,* June 9, 1866.

Butler, G.M. "Carter's Little Nerve Pills." *Mexico Independent,* May 18, 1881.

"By Telegraph." *National Republican,* August 3, 1861.

Cabot, M.R. *Annals of Brattleboro, 1681–1895.* Brattleboro, VT: Press of E. L. Hildreth, 1922.

"Camp Douglas." *Jeffersonian,* March 16, 1865.

Capern, T. *The Mighty Curative Powers of Mesmerism.* London: H. Baillière, 1851.

Capron, E.W. *Modern Spiritualism: Its Facts and Fanaticisms, Its Consistencies and Contradictions. With an Appendix.* New York: B. Marsh, 1855.

"Captured Letter." *Highland Weekly News,* May 8, 1862.

"The Carnival of Crime." *Ashtabula Telegraph,* August 29, 1874.

"Carnival of Crime." *Charleston Daily News,* January 28, 1873.

"Carnival of Crime." *Clarksville Chronicle,* January 22, 1869.

"Carnival of Crime." *The Columbian,* January 3, 1868.

"Carnival of Crime." *Daily Ohio Statesman,* November 16, 1867.

"Carnival of Crime." *Daily Phoenix,* August 19, 1865.

"Carnival of Crime." *Daily Phoenix,* May 16, 1874.

"The Carnival of Crime." *Evening Star,* November 30, 1865.

"Carnival of Crime." *Jeffersonian,* July 4, 1867.

"The Carnival of Crime." *Raftsman's Journal,* September 13, 1865.

"Carnival of Crime." *Weekly Democratic Statesman,* July 2, 1874.

Carroll, B.E. *Spiritualism in Antebellum America.* Bloomington: Indiana University Press, 1997.

Carter Medicine Company. "Carter's Little Nerve Pills." *Medina Tribune,* December 16, 1880.

Cary, S.F. *Historical Sketch of the Order of the Sons of Temperance: An Address Delivered at the Fortieth Annual Session of the National Division, Held at Halifax, N.S. in July, 1884.* Halifax, Nova Scotia: W. Theakston, 1884.

Chambers, J.W., and F. Anderson. *The Oxford Companion to American Military History.* New York: Oxford University Press, 1999.

"A Chance for the Detectives." *New York Times,* September 10, 1871.

"The Charles River Mystery." *New York Times,* November 8, 1872.

Chase, Warren. "Dr. William Clark's Spirit Magnetic Vegetable Remedies." *Banner of Light,* October 10, 1868.

Cherrington, E.H. *The Evolution of Prohibition in the United States of America: A Chronological History of the Liquor Problem and the Temperance Reform in the United States from the Earliest Settlements to the Consummation of National Prohibition.* Westerville, OH: American Issue Press, 1920.

Chesley, James. "Dr. James Canney Chesley." *Banner of Light,* February 19, 1870.

_____. "Durham Medical Institute." *Banner of Light,* April 23, 1870.

"Cinchona Rubra." *Chicago Times,* January 22, 1880.

"The Cinchona Rubra Cure." *Sacramento Daily Union,* August 30, 1880.

Ciriello, M.J., and United States Catholic Conference, Department of Education. *Formation and Development for Catholic School Leaders: The Principal as Spiritual Leader.* Washington,

DC: United States Catholic Conference, Department of Education, 1996.

Clifford, Madame. "Clairvoyants." *Brooklyn Daily Eagle*, October 21, 1872.

Clinton, Henry. "Abuse of the Insanity Plea." *New York Times*, March 29, 1873.

"Col. Simon P. Kase Dies of Old Age." *The Columbian*, August 30, 1900.

Colby, Luther. "The Davenport Outrage." *Banner of Light*, March 18, 1865.

_____. "Eddy Persecution Fund." *Banner of Light*, February 16, 1867.

_____. "Lecture on Spirit Photography." *Banner of Light*, November 13, 1869.

_____. "Message Department." *Banner of Light*, January 11, 1862.

_____. "Message Department." *Banner of Light*, May 3, 1862.

_____. "Message Department." *Banner of Light*, December 5, 1863.

_____. "Message Department." *Banner of Light*, September 3, 1864.

_____. "Message Department." *Banner of Light*, May 13, 1865.

_____. "Mumler!" *Banner of Light*, May 13, 1871.

_____. "Spirit Photographs." *Banner of Light*, January 1, 1870.

_____. "Thackeray." *Banner of Light*, January 23, 1864.

_____. "W.H. Mumler, the Spirit Photographer." *Banner of Light*, July 10, 1869.

_____. n.t. *Banner of Light*, December 5, 1874.

Collins, S.B. "The Habit of Drinking." *Banner of Light*, February 15, 1873.

Conant, J.H. "Abraham Lincoln." *Banner of Light*, March 16, 1867.

_____. "Message Department." *Banner of Light*, July 8, 1865.

"A Confession." *Memphis Daily Appeal*, January 14, 1873.

"The Connecticut Borgia." *Nashville Union and American*, July 14, 1871.

Connor, L. "Editorial." *American Lancet*, 1886.

"Consumption and Nervous Debility!" *Banner of Light*, July 7, 1866.

Contributor, Fat. "An Essay on Doctors." *Camden Journal*, January 2, 1873.

Cook, George. "The Relations of Inebriety to Insanity." *American Journal of Insanity* 28(4)(1862):321–49.

"The Coriell Murder: A Visit to Bridget Durgan." *New York Times*, June 3, 1867.

"The Coriell Murder: Bridget Durgan Found Guilty." *New York Times*, June 1, 1867.

"The Coriell Murder: Bridget Durgan to Be Hanged Aug. 30." *New York Times*, June 18, 1867.

"The Coriell Murder: Testimony Regarding the Alleged Complicity of Mary Gilroy." *New York Times*, June 6, 1867.

"The Coriell Murder: Trial of Bridget Durgan at New Brunswick, N. J.—The Indictment." *New York Times*, May 21, 1867.

"The Coriell Murder: Trial of Bridget Durgan at New Brunswick, N.J. Fifth and Sixth Day's Proceedings." *New York Times*, May 27, 1867.

Cotham, E.T. *Battle on the Bay: The Civil War Struggle for Galveston*. Austin: University of Texas Press, 1998.

Coulter, H.L. *Science and Ethics in American Medicine, 1800–1914*. Richmond, CA: North Atlantic Books, 1982.

Cox, J.R. *The Dime Novel Companion: A Source Book*. Westport, CT: Greenwood Press, 2000.

"Crime, North and South." *Nashville Union and American*, November 7, 1868.

"Crime at the North." *New Orleans Daily Democrat*, July 12, 1879.

"Crime Epidemic." *Evening Star*, June 19, 1879.

Crooke, C. "Crook's Electric Oil." *Hartford Herald*, October 3, 1877.

Crothers, T.D. "America's Inebriate Asylums." *Journal of the American Medical Association* 21(14)(1893).

Curwen, J., and American Psychiatric Association. *History of the Association of Medical Superintendents of American Institutions for the Insane, from 1844 to 1874, Inclusive*. American Psychiatric Association, 1875.

D. Ransom, Son & Co. *Ransom's Family Receipt Book*. Buffalo, NY: Barker, Jones, & Co. Printers, 1892.

Davenport, R.B. *The Death-blow to Spiritualism: Being the True Story of the Fox Sisters, as Revealed by Authority of Margaret Fox Kane and Catherine Fox Jencken*. New York: G. W. Dillingham, 1888.

"The Davenport Brothers." *New York Herald*, May 5, 1864.

"The Davenport Brothers and Coroner Norris." *Brooklyn Eagle*, May 17, 1864.

"The Davenport Mystery." *Brooklyn Eagle*, May 13, 1864.

Davis, A.J., and W. Fishbough. *The Principles of Nature, Her Divine Revelations, and a Voice to Mankind*. New York: S. S. Lyon & W. Fishbough, 1851.

Davis, Andrew F. "Andrew F. Davis Papers, 1862." In *Civil War Diaries and Letters*. Iowa City: University of Iowa, Digital Library Services, 2007.

Davis, N.S. "What Is Needed for the Successful Treatment of Inebriates?" *Journal of Nervous & Mental Disease* 3(1)(1876):79–83.

"Dear Brother." *Weekly Perrysburg Journal*, January 16, 1862.

"Death of Henry L. Clinton." *New York Times*, June 8, 1899.

"A Decision That Might Have Covered the Marion County Case." *Wheeling Daily Intelligencer*, May 6, 1879.

De Grath. "Discovered at Last!" *Brooklyn Daily Eagle*, April 20, 1858.

_____. "Electric Oil." *Daily Morning Post*, November 15, 1859.

_____. "$100 Proclamation." *Daily State Sentinel*, October 23, 1856.

_____. "Prof. De Grath's Electric Oil." *Brooklyn Daily Eagle*, June 21, 1858.

_____. "Professor De Grath's Electric Oil." *Weekly Mariettian*, April 25, 1863.

Delaney, Robert. "Important—Yellow Fever and Black Vomit." *Daily Exchange*, September 11, 1858.

de Mandeville, J. *History of the 13th Regiment, N.G., S.N.Y.: Containing Over Forty Illustrations and Many Biographical Sketches.* New York: Press of G.W. Rodgers, 1894.

"Dentist Shoots Self in Fatal Accident." *Daily Virginian*, January 18, 1862.

"Deplorable Occurrence." *Richmond Daily Dispatch*, May 24, 1861.

Deutsch, A. *The Mentally Ill in America: A History of Their Care and Treatment from Colonial Times.* New York: Columbia University Press, 1946.

Dewey, D.M. *History of the Strange Sounds or Rappings: Heard in Rochester and Western New-York, and Usually Called the Mysterious Noises! Which Are Supposed by Many to Be Communications from the Spirit World, Together with All the Explanation That Can as Yet Be Given of the Matter.* Rochester, NY: D. M. Dewey, 1850.

Dickens, Charles. *The Works of Charles Dickens.* London: Chapman and Hall, 1911.

Dickens, Charles, and M. Cardwell. *The Mystery of Edwin Drood.* New York: Oxford University Press, 2009.

Dickens, Charles, and David Stuart Davies. *Ghost Stories.* London: CRW, 2009.

Dickens, Charles, with T.P. James. *The Mystery of Edwin Drood: Complete.* Brattleboro, VT: T.P. James, 1874.

Dickens, Charles, J. Leech, A. Rackham, and G.A. Williams. *A Christmas Carol: A Ghost Story of Christmas.* Createspace Independent Publishing, 2013.

"Dr. Morse's Indian Root Pills." *Potter Journal*, December 8, 1859.

"Dr. Quain's Magic Condition Pills." *Banner of Light*, December 29, 1877.

"Dr. Russell's Magnetic Oil." *Reading Eagle*, September 1, 1868.

Donovan, J.W. *Modern Jury Trials and Advocates: Containing Condensed Cases with Sketches and Speeches of American Advocates; the Art of Winning Cases and Manner of Counsel Described, with Notes and Rules of Practice.* New York: Banks & Brothers, 1881.

"The Drinker Farm Murder Trial—Peculiarly Atrocious Character of the Crime." *New York Times*, November 20, 1867.

"Drunk and Disorderly." *Richmond Daily Dispatch*, September 17, 1863.

"Drunkenness Cured." *North Otago Times*, June 23, 1879.

Dugdale, R.L. *"The Jukes": A Study in Crime, Pauperism, Diseases, and Heredity; Also, Further Studies of Criminals.* New York: G. P. Putnam's Sons, 1877.

Durgan, B. *Life, Crimes, and Confession of Bridget Durgan, the Fiendish Murderess of Mrs. Coriel: Whom She Butchered, Hoping to Take Her Place in the Affections of the Husband of Her Innocent and Lovely Victim.* New York: C.W. Alexander, 1867.

Ebert, A.E. *The Standard Formulary.* Chicago: G.P. Engelhard, 1896.

Eddy, R. *Alcohol in History: An Account of Intemperance in All Ages; Together with a History of the Various Methods Employed for Its Removal.* New York: National Temperance Society and Publication House, 1887.

Edmonds, John. "The End and Aim of Spiritual Intercourse." *Spiritual Magazine*, 1860.

_____. "Letter from Judge Edmonds." *Banner of Light*, December 22, 1866.

"Elmira, NY." *Nashville Union and American*, February 10, 1870.

"Engineer at the Harlem Railroad Shop." *Brooklyn Eagle*, April 23, 1864.

"Entertainment Extraordinary." *Brooklyn Daily Eagle*, June 13, 1876.

"An Era of Crime." *National Republican*, July 27, 1874.

"Execution of Mrs. Grinder." *New York Times*, January 21, 1866.

"The Exposers." *Banner of Light*, July 8, 1876.

"Exposing the Jugglers." *The Sun*, March 3, 1873.

"Extraordinary Crime by Poisoning." *Belmont Chronicle*, July 6, 1871.

"Extraordinary Lynching Scene." *New York Times*, January 24, 1876.

"Extraordinary Suicide." *New York Times*, April 9, 1869.

Falret, Jules. "On Moral Insanity." *American Journal of Insanity* 24(1867):52–63.

Fanyou. "Dr. Fanyou." *Brooklyn Daily Eagle*, August 25, 1877.

"Father Seduces His Daughter." *Union Flag*, March 12, 1869.

"Fill Up the Armies." *New York Daily Tribune*, July 19, 1864.

Fisher, G.T. *A Practical Treatise on Medical Electricity, Containing a Historical Sketch of Frictional and Voltaic Electricity, as Applied to Medicine: With Plain Instructions for the Use of Electric, Galvanic, Electro-magnetic Instruments, Etc.* London: T & R Willats, 1845.

Floyd, F.C. *History of the Fortieth (Mozart) Regiment, New York Volunteers: Which Was Composed of Four Companies from New York, Four Companies from Massachusetts and Two Companies from Pennsylvania*. Boston: F. H. Gilson Company, 1909.

"The Fools Not All Dead." *Ottawa Free Trader*, July 24, 1869.

"Fortress Monroe." *New York Times*, June 9, 1862.

Fout, F.W. *The Dark Days of the Civil War, 1861 to 1865: The West Virginia Campaign of 1861, the Antietam and Harper's Ferry Campaign of 1862, the East Tennessee Campaign of 1863, the Atlanta Campaign of 1864*. F.A. Wagenfuehr, 1904.

"The Fraud of the Eddy Materializations Exposed." *The Sun*, March 26, 1875.

Frey, Ettinger. "Good News. Electric Oil." *Hancock Jeffersonian*, September 11, 1868.

"From Buffalo Discovery of a Terrible Murder." *Evening Telegraph*, January 26, 1869.

Gallion. "To the Public." *Holt County Sentinel*, October 26, 1866.

Garland, H. *Ulysses S. Grant: His Life and Character*. New York: Doubleday & McClure, 1898.

"The Genealogy of Crime." *The Sun*, February 22, 1877.

Gernsheim, H. *A Concise History of Photography*. New York: Dover, 1986.

"Ghosts in Photography." *The Sun*, April 13, 1869.

Gildersleeve, B.L. *The Creed of the Old South, 1865-1915*. Baltimore, MD: Johns Hopkins Press, 1915.

Gillett, M.C. *The Army Medical Department, 1818-1865*. Washington, DC: U.S. Government Printing Office, 1987.

Goodhue, B.W. *Incidents of the Civil War*. Chicago: J. D. Tallmadge, 1890.

"The Good Looks of Both Men and Women." *Harper's Weekly*, August 19, 1865.

"Grant Drunk." *New York Times*, April 22, 1862.

Gray, John P. "Suicide." *American Journal of Psychiatry* 35(1878):37-73.

"The Great Rebellion." *New York Times*, October 20, 1861.

Griffenhagen, George B. *Old English Patent Medicines in America*. Washington, DC: Smithsonian Institution, 1959.

Hall, J.C. *Stand of the United States Army at Gettysburg*. Bloomington: Indiana University Press, 2003.

Hall, W.W. *Dyspepsia and Its Kindred Diseases*. New York: R. Worthington, 1877.

Haller, John S. *American Medicine in Transition, 1840-1910*. Urbana: University of Illinois Press, 1981.

Hammond, William A. *On Certain Conditions of Nervous Derangement, Somnambulism—Hypnotism—Hysteria—Hysteriod Affections, Etc.* New York: G.P. Putnam's Sons, 1881.

_____. "Physics and Physiology of Spiritualism." *North American Review* 110(227)(1870): 233-60.

_____. *The Physics and Physiology of Spiritualism*. New York: Appleton, 1871.

_____. *Sleep and Its Derangements*. Philadelphia: J.B. Lippincott, 1873.

_____. "Spiritualism and Nervous Derangement, by Dr. Hammond." *Banner of Light*, September 16, 1876.

Hanson, D. *Dominicus Hanson's Catalogue of Apothecary, Book and Variety Store. Rochester, N.H.* Dover, NH: Dover Gazette Power-Press, 1854.

Hardinge, E. *Modern American Spiritualism: A Twenty Years' Record of the Communion Between Earth and the World of Spirits*. New York: E. Hardinge, 1870.

"Hard Times." *Vermont Farmer*, June 25, 1875.

Hayward, A.S. "Magnetized Paper." *Banner of Light*, April 21, 1877.

Helmbold, Henry T. "To the Public." *New York Times*, October 28, 1863.

"Hereditary Crime." *The Sun*, August 4, 1877.

Hill, H.A. *History of the Old South Church (Third Church) Boston: 1669-1884*. Boston: Houghton, Mifflin, 1889.

Hiscox. "Parker's Ginger Tonic." *Medina Tribune*, November 10, 1881.

Hiss, A.E. *Thesaurus of Proprietary Preparations and Pharmaceutical Specialties: Including "Patent" Medicines, Proprietary Pharmaceuticals, Open-formula Specialties, Synthetic Remedies, Etc.* Chicago: G.P. Engelhard, 1898.

H.J.W. "Our Prisoners." *New York Times*, November 26, 1864.

Holland, J.G. *Scribner's Monthly*, 1881.

"Holloway's Pills." *Harper's Weekly*, September 23, 1865.

Home, D.D. *Lights and Shadows of Spiritualism.* London: Virtue & Company, 1877.

Hooper, Daniel. "The Alcohol Question." *The Lancet* 77(1969)(1861):507–9.

Horowitz, M. *Occult America: The Secret History of How Mysticism Shaped Our Nation.* New York: Bantam Books, 2009.

Hostetter, J.H. "Kunkel's Bitter Wine of Iron." *Pilot,* November 10, 1863.

"Hostetter's Celebrated Stomach Bitters." *Harper's Weekly,* March 2, 1864.

"Hostetter's Celebrated Stomach Bitters— Health of the Army." *Harper's Weekly,* April 25, 1863.

"How a Mother Received Her Son Who Had Deserted." *Cincinnati Daily Press,* October 4, 1861.

Howitt, W. *The History of the Supernatural in All Ages and Nations: And in All Churches, Christian and Pagan: Demonstrating a Universal Faith.* London: Longman, Green, Longman, Roberts, & Green, 1863.

"H.T. Helmbold Dies in an Insane Asylum." *New York Times,* October 26, 1894.

Hubbard, E., and Roycroft Shop. *Lydia E. Pinkham: Being a Sketch of Her Life and Times.* East Aurora, NY: Roycrofters, 1915.

Hull and Chamberlain. "Hull and Chamberlain's Magnetic and Electric Powders." *Banner of Light,* January 16, 1875.

"Human Butchery." *Lincoln County Herald,* May 21, 1873.

"Human Electricity." *Banner of Light,* March 17, 1866.

"Humbug." *Brooklyn Daily Eagle,* June 16, 1876.

Hutchison, Mrs. "Blindness Cured." *Brooklyn Eagle,* March 4, 1864.

"I.G. Atwood." *Banner of Light,* February 24, 1866.

"Important from Fort Monroe: News from Richmond and Other Points in the Rebel States." *New York Times,* March 6, 1862.

"Important to Invalids." *Banner of Light,* March 16, 1867.

"The Increase in Crime." *New York Times,* February 5, 1872.

"Increase of Crime in the City." *New York Times,* February 11, 1866.

"Indian Doctor's Remedies." *Nashville Patriot,* September 17, 1859.

"The Indian Herb Doctor from Canada." *Morning Freeman,* July 5, 1860.

"Indian Remedies." *Holmes County Farmer,* March 1, 1860.

"Indiana." *New York Times,* February 20, 1869.

"Indiana Justice." *New York Times,* March 6, 1874.

"The Inebriates' Home." *Brooklyn Eagle,* May 31, 1872.

"Infamous." *Public Ledger,* May 23, 1867.

Inman, Thomas. "Is Alcohol Food?" *The Lancet* 80(2033)(1862):188–89.

"Inquests by Coroner Wildey." *New York Times,* October 12, 1865.

"The Insane." *Brooklyn Eagle,* November 29, 1873.

"An 'Insane' Murderer Suddenly Restored to Reason." *New York Times,* February 11, 1872.

Insider. "John Wilkes Booth." *Brooklyn Eagle,* February 8, 1885.

"Intemperance." *Evening Telegraph,* March 27, 1869.

Irwin, R.B. "Seeking the Bubble." *United States Service Magazine,* 1865.

"Is It the Result of Mental or Physical Overstrain?" *Brooklyn Eagle,* May 25, 1879.

"Is President Lincoln a Victim of Spiritualism?" *Urbana Union,* June 3, 1863.

"Is This Spiritualism?" *New Ulm Weekly Review,* June 25, 1879.

"John Brown's Soul." *Clearfield Republican,* March 7, 1867.

"John Rabus, from Gotha." *New York Times,* March 26, 1866.

Johnson, Metcalfe. "The Alcohol Question." *The Lancet* 78(1981)(1861): 168–69.

Johnston, Simon. "Professor Reed's Magnetic Oil." *Pittsburgh Daily Gazette and Advertiser,* December 3, 1863.

Judson, B.L. "Pills." *Jeffersonian Democrat,* March 9, 1860.

"Kansas Butchery." *Democratic Press,* May 22, 1873.

"The Kansas Murders." *New York Times,* May 13, 1873.

Keith, G.W. "Spirit Photography." *Banner of Light,* November 22, 1870.

Kennan, George. "The Problems of Suicide." *McClure's Magazine,* 1908.

Kiddle, Henry. *Common-school Teaching: A Lecture Delivered Before the Teachers' Association of the City of Brooklyn, September 28, 1877.* New York: E. Steiger, 1877.

_____. *How to Teach.* Cincinnati, OH: Van Antwerp, Bragg, & Co., 1877.

_____. *A Manual of Astronomy and the Use of the Globes: For Schools and Academies.* New York: Ivison, Phinney, Blakeman & Co., 1865.

_____. *Spiritual Communications: Presenting a Revelation of the Future Life, and Illustrating and Confirming the Fundamental Doctrines of the Christian Faith.* New York: Author's Publishing Company, 1879.

"Killing No Murder." *New York Times,* January 25, 1876.

Kimball, Laurie A., Karla M. Eisch and Wesley Haynes. "National Historic Landmark Nomination: New York State Inebriate Asylum." Washington, DC: U.S. Department of the Interior, National Park Service, 1997.

"Kleptomania." *New York Times,* September 5, 1877.

"A Lady Suicide." *Brooklyn Eagle,* December 29, 1865.

Lande, R.G. *The Abraham Man: Madness, Malingering and the Development of Medical Testimony.* New York: Algora, 2012.

_____. "Felo De Se: Soldier Suicides in America's Civil War." *Military Medicine* 176(5) (2011):531–36.

_____. *Madness, Malingering, and Malfeasance: The Transformation of Psychiatry and the Law in the Civil War Era.* Washington, DC: Brassey's, 2003.

Landers, Jon J. "W. Sawens and Company." *Bottles Along the Mohawk.* Accessed May 14, 2016. https://mohawkvalleybottleclub.com/ArchiveArticles/PDF_Articles/SAWENS.pdf.

Larue. "Indian Doctor!! and Electrical Physician." *Eaton Weekly Democrat,* March 21, 1872.

"The Latest Performance of the Eddys." *Rutland Daily Globe,* June 22, 1876.

"The Latest Swindle." *Pittsburg Dispatch,* September 23, 1889.

"Laurie's Chinese Life Pills." *Harper's Weekly,* January 31, 1863.

Lavoie, J.D. *The Theosophical Society: The History of a Spiritualist Movement.* Boca Raton, FL: Brown Walker Press, 2012.

Lees, F.R. *Textbook of Temperance.* New York: Z. P. Vose & Company, 1869.

"Legal Intelligence." *Evening Telegraph,* October 4, 1869.

Lehman, Leola. "The Butchering Benders." *Great West: True Stories of Old Frontier Days,* 1971.

"A Letter Found." *Highland Weekly News,* May 8, 1862.

"Liability of Insurance Companies for Losses by Suicide." *American Journal of Psychiatry* 30(1873):259–70.

"The Liberty of the Press." *New York Times,* February 13, 1872.

"The Liberty of the Press." *New York Times,* February 1, 1874.

Life, Trial, and Execution of Edward H. Ruloff: The Perpetrator of Eight Murders, Numerous Burglaries, and Other Crimes: Who Was Recently Hanged at Binghamton, N.Y. Philadelphia: Barclay & Company, 1871.

"Life in New York." *Daily Dispatch,* April 23, 1857.

Life Insurance Company v. Terry, 82 U.S. 15 Wall. 580 (1872).

Lincoln Herald (Lincoln, NE), 1988.

"Lincoln Spiritualist." *Brooklyn Eagle,* September 9, 1863.

Livermore, T.L. *Numbers and Losses in the Civil War in America, 1861–1865.* Boston: Houghton, Mifflin, 1900.

Loveridge, E. Dexter. "The Great Indian Beverage." *Evening Argus,* September 9, 1865.

Lowell, Norton. "American Prisons." *North American Review,* 1866.

Lucas, Mary. "A Course of Five Lectures." *Banner of Light,* April 1, 1865.

Lyons, R.J. "Appointments." *Hillsdale Standard,* November 10, 1863.

_____. "Appointments." *Jeffersonian Democrat,* March 9, 1860.

_____. "Important Medical Notice!" *Livingston Republican,* January 1, 1857.

"Lyon's Magnetic Insect Powder." *Brooklyn Daily Eagle,* June 15, 1871.

MacDonald, Carlos F. "Feigned Insanity, Homicide, Insanity." *American Journal of Insanity* 35(3)(1879):411–32.

Madden, J. *Shall We Drink Wine? A Physician's Study of the Alcohol Question.* Milwaukee, WI: Owen & Weihbrecht Company, 1899.

Malt Bitters Company. "Malt Bitters." *Evening Gazette,* May 22, 1880.

Mann, Charles. "We Reprint." *Banner of Light,* February 4, 1865.

Manning, J.M. *The Carnival of Crime: A Sermon Preached Sunday Morning, June 6, 1875.* Boston: Lee and Shepard, 1875.

Marsh, Bela. "Some Folk's Can't Sleep Nights." *Banner of Light,* January 7, 1865.

"Martha Grinder—The Evil That She Did Lives After Her." *New York Times,* September 23, 1866.

Martin, J., W.J. Birnes, and G. Noory. *The Haunting of America: From the Salem Witch Trials to Harry Houdini.* New York: Tom Doherty Associates, 2011.

Massachusetts State Board of Charities. *Second Annual Report of the Board of State Charities, Crime.* 1866.

_____. *Third Annual Report of the Board of State Charities of Massachusetts to Which are Added the Reports of the Secretary, and the General Agent of the Board.* 1867.

Maynard, N.C. *Was Abraham Lincoln a Spiritualist? or, Curious Revelations from the Life of a*

Trance Medium. Philadelphia: R. C. Hartranft, 1891.

"Mayor Fox His Honor Subject to an Interview." *Evening Telegraph*, October 6, 1869.

McBride, J.R. *History of the Thirty-Third Indiana Veteran Volunteer Infantry during the Four Years of Civil War, from Sept. 16, 1861, to July 21, 1865: And Incidentally of Col. John Coburn's Second Brigade, Third Division, Twentieth Army Corps, Including Incidents of the Great Rebellion.* Indianapolis, IN: W.B. Burford, 1900.

McCune, H.L. "A Reminiscence." *Kansas City Bar Monthly*, 1903.

McFarland, Andrew. "Insanity and Intemperance." *American Journal of Insanity* 19(1863): 448–70.

"Measles Are Prostrating the Volunteers." *Harper's Weekly*, July 4, 1863.

"Melancholy Case of Suicide." *New York Herald*, November 9, 1862.

"Melancholy Suicide." *Richmond Daily Dispatch*, November 6, 1861.

Merriam. "Just Arrived." *Green-Mountain Freeman*, June 3, 1868.

Merwin, W.R. "Cherokee Medicines." *Rochester NY Union & Advertiser*, February 16, 1865.

"Mesmeric Experiments." *New York Times*, January 7, 1881.

"Mesmerism in Society." *New York Times*, April 3, 1881.

Meyer. "Trask's Magnetic Ointment." *Lincoln County Herald*, April 23, 1868.

Meyer, M., and W.A. Hammond. *Electricity in Its Relations to Practical Medicine.* New York: D. Appleton, 1869.

Michigan State Board of Health. *Sixth Annual Report of the Secretary of the Board of Health.* Lansing, MI: W.S. George & Co., 1878.

Miles, Franklin. "Dr. Miles' Restorative Nervine—The Only Remedy for Nervous Diseases Admitted to the World's Fair." *Lawrence Democrat*, March 23, 1894.

_____. "He Committed Suicide!" *Mower County Transcript*, September 13, 1893.

_____. "New and Startling Facts for Those Afflicted with Nervous Diseases." 1893.

_____. "Surrounded by Mystery." *Kansas Agitator*, May 3, 1894.

"Misguided Efforts." *Brooklyn Eagle*, March 6, 1874.

"Mr. Kiddle on Mediums." *Brooklyn Eagle*, May 15, 1880.

Moore, Frank. *Anecdotes, Poetry, and Incidents of the War: North and South: 1860–1865/Collected and Arranged by Frank Moore. Homesick in the Hospital.* New York: Published for the Subscribers, 1866.

"More about the Lydia Sherman Case." *Leavenworth Weekly Times*, July 6, 1871.

"Mortality from Drinking Beer." *Brooklyn Eagle*, July 10, 1861.

"Mothers." *Daily Intelligencer*, October 11, 1860.

"Mothers." *Holmes County Farmer*, March 1, 1860.

Mottelay, P.F., and T. Campbell-Copeland. *Frank Leslie's The Soldier in Our Civil War.* New York: S. Bradley Publishing Company, 1890.

Mowris, J.A. *A History of the One Hundred and Seventeenth Regiment, N.Y. Volunteers, [Fourth Oneida] from the Date of its Organization. August 1862, Till That of Its Muster Out. June, 1865. by J.A. Mowris, M.D. Regimental Surgeon.* Hartford, CT: Case, Lockwood and Company, 1866.

"Mrs. Clem." *New York Times*, May 4, 1874.

"Mrs. Cora Hatch on Spirits." *New York Times*, January 23, 1858.

"Mrs. Sherman's Horrible Confession." *Wyandot County Republican*, January 23, 1873.

Mumler, William. "The Personal Experiences of William Mumler in Spirit Photography." *Banner of Light*, January 9, 1875.

_____. "The Personal Experiences of William Mumler in Spirit Photography." *Banner of Light*, January 30, 1875.

_____. "The Personal Experiences of William Mumler in Spirit Photography." *Banner of Light*, March 27, 1875.

"Murder at Newmarket, N. J.; The Wife of a Physician Murdered in Her Own House." *New York Times*, February 27, 1867.

"Murder of a Tennessean." *Sweetwater Enterprise*, July 14, 1870.

"Murder of a Woman—Drunkenness among the Troops." *New York Times*, July 28, 1861.

"The Murderer Ruloff." *New York Times*, April 3, 1871.

"A Murderers' Den." *New York Times*, May 12, 1873.

"Murderers in the New Hampshire State Prison." *New York Times*, November 3, 1868.

"Murders of Five Years." *New York Times*, January 25, 1876.

Murphet, H. *Yankee Beacon of Buddhist Light: Life of Col. Henry S. Olcott.* Wheaton, IL: Theosophical Publishing House, 1988.

Myer, W.G., and United States Supreme Court. *Federal Decisions: Cases Argued and Determined in the Supreme, Circuit and District Courts of the United States.* St. Louis, MO: Gilbert Book Co., 1887.

"Mysterious Murders." *New York Times*, April 19, 1874.

"The Mystery of Edwin Drood." *London: The Spiritual Magazine*, 1873.

Nartonis, David K. "The Rise of 19th-Century American Spiritualism, 1854–1873." *Journal for the Scientific Study of Religion* 49(2) (2010):361–73.

Neely, M.E., and R.G. McMurtry. *The Insanity File: The Case of Mary Todd Lincoln*. Carbondale: Southern Illinois University Press, 1993.

New Hampshire Supreme Court and J. Parker. *The New Hampshire Reports*. Concord, NH: Capital Offset Company, 1872.

"The New Hampshire Tragedy." *Cincinnati Enquirer*, May 23, 1868.

"The New Lucretia Borgia." *News and Herald*, June 21, 1877.

"New Publications—The Jukes." *New York Times*, July 29, 1877.

"News from Washington." *New York Times*, April 12, 1864.

"News Summary." *Vermont Transcript*, December 1, 1865.

Niven, J. *Gideon Welles: Lincoln's Secretary of the Navy*. New York: Oxford University Press, 1973.

"North Carolina." *Athens Post*, February 5, 1869.

"Nostalgia." *Cleveland Morning Leader*, October 16, 1861.

"Nostalgia." *Cleveland Morning Leader*, November 16, 1861.

"Nostalgia." *Cleveland Morning Leader*, 1862.

"Nostalgia." *Cleveland Morning Leader*, July 10, 1862.

Nostrums & Patent Medicines. Fargo: North Dakota Agricultural College, 1916.

Olcott, Henry. "Able-Bodied Apparitions." *New York Sun*, November 4, 1874.

_____. "Ghosts That Are Ghosts." *New York Sun*, August 18, 1875.

_____. *People from the Other World*. Hartford, CN: American Publishing Company, 1875.

_____. *Theosophy, Religion and Occult Science*. London: George Redway, 1885.

_____. "The World of Spirits." *New York Sun*, September 5, 1874.

"Once More." *Essex County Herald*, October 17, 1874.

"Orange Judd." *Chicago Tribune*, December 28, 1892.

Ordronaux, John. "Is Habitual Drunkenness a Disease?" *American Journal of Insanity* 30 (1874):430–43.

"Osteopathy." *Houston Daily Post*, August 6, 1899.

Otis, G.A. *A Report of Surgical Cases Treated in the Army of the United States from 1865 to 1871*. Washington, DC: U.S. Government Printing Office, 1871.

Otis, George A., and J.E. Barnes. *The Medical and Surgical History of the War of the Rebellion (1861–65)*. Vol. 3, *On Certain Diseases Not Heretofore Discussed*. Washington, DC: U.S. Government Printing Office, 1870.

Owen, J.J. *"Our Little Doctor": Helen Craib-Beighle and the Magic Power of Her Electric Hand*. San Francisco: Hicks-Judd, 1893.

Owen, W.M. *In Camp and Battle with the Washington Artillery of New Orleans: A Narrative of Events during the Late Civil War from Bull Run to Appomattox and Spanish Fort*. Boston: Ticknor & Company, 1885.

Palmer, O.H. "Suicide and Life Insurance." *New York Times*, May 1, 1873.

_____. "Suicide Not Evidence of Insanity." *American Journal of Psychiatry* 34(1878): 425–61.

Papillon, Fernand. "Electricity and Life." *American Journal of Insanity*, 1873.

Parker, T., and J.W. Day. *Biography of Mrs. J.H. Conant, the World's Medium of the Nineteenth Century: Being a History of Her Mediumship from Childhood to the Present Time: Together with Extracts from the Diary of Her Physician; Selections from Letters Received Verifying Spirit Communications Given Through Her Organism at the Banner of Light Free Circles; Specimen Messages, Essays, and Invocations from Various Intelligences in the Other Life, Etc., Etc., Etc.* Boston: William White & Co., 1873.

"Payment of the Volunteers." *New York Times*, July 7, 1861.

Pence, P.P. "Spooks and Goblins." *Leavenworth Weekly Times*, September 25, 1879.

Pennsylvania Prison Society. *Journal of Prison Discipline and Philanthropy*, 1892.

Peters, De Witt C. "Remarks on the Evils of Youthful Enlistments and Nostalgia." *American Medical Times: Being a Weekly Series of the New York Journal of Medicine*, 1863.

Petersen, W.J., and State Historical Society of Iowa. *Pain-killer Almanac: A Facsimile Reproduction, Slightly Enl. of an 1868 Almanac*. Cincinnati, OH: J.N. Harris & Co., 1868.

Phillips, J.J. *The Drinker's Farm Tragedy: Trial and Conviction of James Jeter Phillips, for the Murder of His Wife*. Richmond: J. Wall Turner, 1868.

"Photographed 'Spirits.'" *New York Times*, October 29, 1876.

Pickett, D., C.T. Wilson, and E.D. Smith. *The Cyclopedia of Temperance, Prohibition and Public Morals*. New York: Methodist Book Concern, 1917.

Pierce, A.P. "Dr. A. P. Pierce, Clairvoyant, Magnetic, and Electric Physician." *Banner of Light,* January 28, 1865.

Pike, J.T. Gilman. "Dr. J.T. Gilman Pike." *Banner of Light,* November 16, 1867.

Pinkham, Lydia. "Neglect Is Suicide." *Donahoe's Magazine,* 1897.

"The Pittsburgh Poisoning Case." *New York Times,* October 30, 1865.

"Plenty of Inducements." *Brooklyn Daily Eagle,* April 5, 1891.

Podmore, F. *Modern Spiritualism: A History and a Criticism.* Cambridge: Cambridge University Press, 2011.

"Police Court." *Richmond Daily Dispatch,* July 27, 1861.

Porter, James. "Dr. Jas Porter Late of New Orleans." *Public Ledger,* May 28, 1873.

Practical Magnetizer. The History and Philosophy of Animal Magnetism: With Practical Instructions for the Exercise of This Power. Boston: J. N. Bradley, 1843.

"The Prevalence of Crime." *Green-Mountain Freeman,* July 23, 1873.

"Probable Suicide." *Richmond Daily Dispatch,* April 18, 1862.

"Pryor Coleman's Sentence." *Knoxville Daily Chronicle,* June 28, 1879.

"Pryor N. Coleman's Case." *Memphis Daily Appeal,* April 19, 1879.

Publications of the American Statistical Association. Boston: W. J. Schofield, 1895.

"Q: What Constitutes a Person a Medium." *Banner of Light,* March 7, 1868.

Ralphgrame. "Dr. Ralphgrame." *Indiana State Sentinel,* June 26, 1861.

Ransom. "Dr. Trask's Magnetic Ointment." *Alpena Weekly Argus,* October 21, 1873.

"Read It." *Weekly Arizona Miner,* July 29, 1871.

"The Real Point in the Kiddle Case." *Brooklyn Eagle,* May 8, 1879.

"The Rebellion." *Urbana Union,* May 14, 1862.

"The Recent Tragedy at Glastonbury, Conn.— Suicide of a Son of Hon. Thaddeus Welles." *New York Times,* December 31, 1866.

"Reform in Medical Education." *New York Times,* December 8, 1878.

"The Registrar and General's Annual Report." *Medical Times and Gazette.* London: J. & A. Churchill, 1873.

Reilly, John E. "Robert D'Unger and His Reminiscences of Edgar Allen Poe in Baltimore." *Maryland Historical Magazine* 88(1993):60–72.

"Reports of a Commission Appointed for a Revision of the Revenue System." *Report of the Special Commissioner of the Revenue.* Washington, DC: U.S. Government Printing Office, 1866.

Rhodes, J. H. "J. H. Rhodes, M.D." *Banner of Light,* March 10, 1877.

Richbodt, Louis. "Dr. J.B. Simpson's Specific Medicine." *Westfield Republican,* June 14, 1880.

_____. "Dr. Thomas' Electric Oil." *Indianapolis Leader,* October 30, 1880.

"A Riot Among the Soldiers of the Third Regiment Irish Brigade." *New York Times,* November 30, 1861.

"Robinson." *Richmond Daily Dispatch,* October 1, 1864.

Robinson, Henry. "Charles Marseilles." *Granite Monthly: A New Hampshire Magazine,* 1897.

Rodgers, W.H. *Facts in Magnetism, Mesmerism, Somnambulism, Fascination, Hypnotism, Sycodonamy, Etherology, Pathetism, &c: Explained and Illustrated.* Auburn, NY: Derby, Miller, & Co., 1849.

Rogers. "Roger's Magnetic Oil." *Rock Island Argus,* January 9, 1872.

Rogers, S. "Roger's Electro-Magnetic Oil." *Columbia Spy,* June 1, 1867.

Root, A.I. *Gleanings in Bee Culture.* Medina, OH: A. I. Root Company, 1892.

"The Ruloff Trial." *New York Times,* January 7, 1871.

"Rum and Rebellion." *Brooklyn Eagle,* April 15, 1864.

Rutherford, Joseph. "Joseph Rutherford to Hannah Rutherford" (1863). In *Vermonters in the Civil War.* Burlington: Special Collections, Bailey-Howe Library, University of Vermont, 2004.

"Scannell." *New York Times,* November 4, 1872.

"Scannell." *New York Times,* November 5, 1872.

Schechter, H. *Psycho USA: Famous American Killers You Never Heard Of.* New York: Ballantine Books, 2012.

Schmutz, J.F. *The Battle of the Crater: A Complete History.* Jefferson, NC: McFarland, 2009.

"The Science of Trance." *New York Times,* January 11, 1881.

"Séance Professors Come to Grief." *Brooklyn Daily Eagle,* August 28, 1876.

"The Secret Out." *Banner of Light,* September 6, 1876.

Seddon, James A. *Regulations for the Army of the Confederate States.* Richmond, VA: J. W. Randolph, 1864.

"A Self-Styled Professor." *Brooklyn Daily Eagle,* July 14, 1868.

Service and Regulatory Announcements, United States Department of Agriculture, Bureau of Chemistry. *Notices of Judgement* under the Food and Drugs Act. Washington, DC: U.S. Government Printing Office, 1918.

Shaw, J. *History of the Great Temperance Reforms of the Nineteenth Century, Exhibiting: The Evils of Intemperance, the Methods of Reform, the Woman's Crusade, and the Coming Conflict on the Temperance Question*. Cincinnati, OH: Hitchcock & Walden, 1875.

Shaw, R.B. *History of the Comstock Patent Medicine Business and Dr. Morse's Indian Root Pills*. Washington, DC: Smithsonian Institution Press, 1972.

Shepard, E.M. *The Work of a Social Teacher: Being a Memorial of Richard L. Dugdale*. New York: Society for Political Education, 1884.

Sherman, L. *The Poison Fiend! Life, Crimes, and Conviction of Lydia Sherman (the Modern Lucretia Borgia), Recently Tried in New Haven, Conn., for Poisoning Three Husbands and Eight of Her Children: Her Life in Full!, Exciting Account of Her Trial—the Fearful Evidence*. Philadelphia: Barclay & Company, 1872.

Sherwood, John. "I Most Cheerfully Recommend." *Banner of Light*, June 22, 1867.

Shirley, John M. *Reports and Cases Argued and Determined in the Supreme Judicial Court of New Hampshire*. Concord, NH: B. W. Sanborn & Co., 1872.

Shoaf, Dana B. *The Death of a Regular*, 2013. Accessed March 30, 2013. http://www.sykes regulars.org/dor.php.

Shrady, George M. *Some Facts about Patent Medicines*. Vol. 22, *The Medical Record*. New York: William Wood and Company, 1882.

Silkenat, D. *Moments of Despair: Suicide, Divorce, and Debt in Civil War Era North Carolina*. Chapel Hill: University of North Carolina Press, 2011.

"Simon P. Kase Died in Philadelphia." *Montour American*, August 30, 1900.

"Singular Suicide." *Richmond Dispatch*, November 8, 1860.

"Sketch of the Life of Mrs. Grinder: Is She a Professional Poisoner?" *New York Times*, September 3, 1865.

Smith, D.A. "Catarrh Cured." *Brooklyn Daily Eagle*, September 22, 1874.

Smith, Edward. "On Alcohol." *The Lancet* 86 (2198)(1865):426–27.

Smith, G. B. "Dr. Smith's Electric Oil." *Leavenworth Weekly Times*, October 27, 1870.

_____. "New Combination!!" *Evening Gazette*, June 7, 1871.

"The So Called 'Magnetic Doctor.'" *Urbana Union*, November 22, 1865.

"Soldiers Killing Each Other from Alcohol." *New York Times*, June 28, 1862.

"Soldier's, See to Your Own Health." *Harper's Weekly*, May 9, 1863.

"Soldiers, to the Rescue!" *Harper's Weekly*, April 25, 1863.

"A Soldier's Wife Commits Suicide." *New York Times*, February 5, 1864.

Solomon, J.M. *Indian Wine Bitters & Rheumatic Drops. For Sale by All Druggists.... The Greatest Blood Purifier and Liver and Kidney Cure in the World.... Prepared by Dr. James M. Solomon, Jr., Attleboro, Mass*. Five Points, NY: Donaldson Brothers, 1870.

"Some Folks Can't Sleep Nights." *The Columbian*, October 25, 1867.

"Some Notable Trials." *New York Times*, December 15, 1895.

Spafford, Joseph. "Joseph Spafford to Mary Jane Spafford." Vermont Historical Society Library, 1862.

Sparks, J., E. Everett, J.R. Lowell, and H.C. Lodge. *North American Review*, 1890.

"Special Dispatch." *The Telegraph*, May 24, 1878.

Spence, Payton. "For the Healing of the Nation! The Great Spiritual Remedy!" *Banner of Light*, April 13, 1868.

_____. "Irresistible Army of Witnesses to the Supremacy of the Great Spiritual Remedy." *Banner of Light*, August 17, 1867.

_____. "Mrs. Spence's Positive and Negative Powders." *Banner of Light*, January 14, 1865.

_____. "The Secret Army of Invisible Workers." *Banner of Light*, November 12, 1870.

Spicer, H. *Facts and Fantasies: A Sequel to Sights and Sounds; The Mystery of the Day*. London: T. Bosworth, 1853.

Spirit of Democracy (Woodsfield, OH), February 11, 1873.

"Spirit Photo Ridiculed." *True Northerner*, January 2, 1880.

"Spirit Photograph." *Brooklyn Eagle*, October 14, 1877.

"The Spirit Photographer." *Sunday Appeal*, May 9, 1869.

"Spirit Photographs." *New York Times*, April 29, 1869.

"Spirit Photographs." *New York Times*, July 29, 1877.

"Spirit Photographs." *Public Ledger*, July 10, 1872.

"Spirit Photographs." *Spiritual Magazine*, 1863.

"The Spirit Photographs." *The Sun*, April 29, 1869.

"Spirit Photography." *Public Ledger*, July 3, 1879.

"Spirit Photography." *Spiritual Magazine*, 1862.

"Spiritual Mediums." *Brooklyn Daily Eagle*, July 20, 1875.

"Spiritual Photographs." *New York Times*, April 17, 1869.

"Spiritual Photography." *Harper's Weekly*, May 8, 1869.

"Spiritual Photography." *New York Times*, April 24, 1869.

"Spiritualism." *Brooklyn Daily Eagle*, November 3, 1874.

"Spiritualism and Science." *Brooklyn Daily Eagle*, December 15, 1870.

"Spiritualism in Court." *New York Daily Tribune*, April 22, 1869.

"Spiritualism in New York Court." *The Star of the North*, February 22, 1865.

"Spiritualism in the Tabernacle." *New York Daily Tribune*, April 11, 1857.

"Spiritualism Smashed." *New York Times*, July 2, 1866.

"Spiritualism: The Counterfeits of Science and How to Detect Them." *New York Times*, November 20, 1874.

"Spiritualist Encamped." *The Sun*, July 21, 1879.

Spitzka, E.C. *Insanity, Its Classification, Diagnosis, and Treatment: A Manual for Students and Practitioners of Medicine*. New York: Bermingham & Company, 1883.

"Spooks That Speak." *Brooklyn Eagle*, September 19, 1870.

Sprague, E.W. *A Future Life Demonstrated: Or, Twenty-seven Years a Public Medium*. Detroit, MI: E. W. Sprague, 1908.

Spurgeon, C.H. *The Soul Winner*. Grand Rapids, MI: William B. Eerdmans, 1989.

"The Spurious Spirits." *The Sun*, April 14, 1869.

Stanton, Edwin. "Terrible National Calamity." *Banner of Light*, April 22, 1865.

Stefoff, R. *The Camera*. Tarrytown, NY: Marshall Cavendish Benchmark, 2007.

Sterling, J.M. "Evocation of Abraham Lincoln." *Banner of Light*, December 30, 1865.

Stewart. "Haley's Magnetic Oil." *Clarksville Chronicle*, November 27, 1869.

Still, Andrew Taylor. *Autobiography of Andrew T. Still*. Kirksville, MO: Andrew Taylor, 1897.

_____. *The Philosophy and Mechanical Principles of Osteopathy*. Redditch, UK: Read Books, 2015.

Still, E.R. "Nerve Food—A Spiritual Gift." *Banner of Light*, May 7, 1870.

Stillé, C.J. *History of the United States Sanitary Commission, the General Report of its Work during the War of the Rebellion*. New York: Hurd & Houghten, 1868.

Storer, Dr. "Conclusive Testimony, Scientific and Popular, to the Value of the New Medicine Dr. Storer's Nutritive Compound." *Banner of Light*, April 1, 1871.

Storer, H.B. "Important Facts Concerning the Use of the New Medicine Dr. Storer's Nutritive Compound." *Banner of Light*, December 31, 1870.

_____. "Important Notice to Every Woman, Maiden, Wife or Mother." *Banner of Light*, December 17, 1870.

"A Stupendous Fraud." *New York Times*, April 13, 1869.

"Suicide." *Frank Leslie's Illustrated Newspaper*, February 5, 1870.

"Suicide." *Richmond Daily Dispatch*, August 8, 1861.

"Suicide." *Richmond Daily Dispatch*, May 13, 1862.

"Suicide." *Richmond Daily Dispatch*, August 18, 1863.

"Suicide and Murder." *Richmond Daily Dispatch*, June 13, 1862.

"Suicide at Sea." *Richmond Daily Dispatch*, March 7, 1865.

"Suicide by an Ex-Navy Officer." *Brooklyn Eagle*, January 28, 1867.

"Suicide by Poison." *New York Times*, February 5, 1863.

"Suicide in the U.S." *Frank Leslie's Illustrated Newspaper*, November 15, 1873.

"Suicide of a Husband." *Richmond Daily Dispatch*, October 6, 1863.

"Suicide of a Soldier." *Richmond Daily Dispatch*, June 11, 1862.

"Suicide of a South Carolina Volunteer." *Richmond Daily Dispatch*, February 24, 1862.

"Suicide of a Suspected Assassin." *Daily Picayune*, April 27, 1865.

"Suicide of a Telegraph Operator." *Boston Herald*, July 26, 1865.

"Suicide of Lieut. Robert Welles." *New York Times*, December 30, 1866.

"Suicide of the Quartermaster of the Second Regiment." *Troy Daily News*, May 29, 1863.

"Suicide of Two Army Officers." *New York Herald*, July 22, 1865.

The Sun, November 30, 1874

"The Sunday Liquor Business." *New York Tribune*, July 12, 1870.

"Suppression of Intemperance in the Camps." *New York Times*, August 6, 1861.

Switzler, W.F., C.R. Barns, R.A. Campbell, A.J. Conant, and G.C. Swallow. *Switzler's Illustrated History of Missouri, from 1541 to 1877*. St. Louis, MO: C. R. Barns, 1879.

Table Moving. *Table Moving by Animal Magnetism Demonstrated*. London: John Wesley, 1853.

"Tad Lincoln." *Banner of Light*, July 27, 1872.

"Temperance Folks." *Brooklyn Eagle*, August 5, 1861.

"Temperance in the Army." *New York Times,* August 5, 1861.

"A Terrible Increase in Crime." *Spirit of Democracy,* September 6, 1865.

"Texas Crime." *Brenham Weekly Banner,* April 11, 1879.

Thackeray, W.M. *Vanity Fair: A Novel Without a Hero.* London: Bradbury and Evans, 1853.

"Their Own Doctors." *Brooklyn Daily Eagle,* September 5, 1886.

13th Annual Report of the Officers of the Indiana State Prison, Including the Report of the Warden, Moral Instructor, Physician, and Board of Directors for the Year Ending Dec. 15, ... to the Governor. Indianapolis, IN: J.C. Walker, 1860.

Thompson, I.G., and I. Browne. *The American Reports: Containing All Decisions of General Interest Decided in the Courts of Last Resort of the Several States with Notes and References.* San Francisco: Bancroft-Whitney, 1872.

"To the Editor of the Pilot." *Montreal Pilot,* September 16, 1857.

"To the Editors of the Cincinnati Daily Press." *Cincinnati Daily Press,* June 27, 1861.

Tomalin, C. *Charles Dickens: A Life.* New York: Penguin Press, 2011.

"A Tragic Affair." *Brooklyn Eagle,* January 11, 1867.

Trall, R.T. *Digestion and Dyspepsia: A Complete Explanation of the Physiology of the Digestive Processes.* New York: S.R. Wells, 1874.

_____. *Herald of Health.* New York: R.T. Trall Publishers & Co., 1863.

Triplett, F. *History, Romance and Philosophy of Great American Crimes and Criminals...: With Personal Portraits, Biographical Sketches, Legal Notes of Celebrated Trials, and Philosophical Disquisition Concerning the Causes, Prevalence and Prevention of Crime.* New York: N. D. Thompson, 1885.

Trollope, A. *Thackeray.* London: Macmillan, 1879.

Trowbridge, C. *Andrew Taylor Still, 1828–1917.* Kirksville, MO: Truman State University Press, 1991.

"Trunk Murder." *Eaton Weekly Democrat,* January 4, 1872.

Tumblety, Francis. "Dr. Tumblety's Pimple Banisher." *Harper's Weekly,* August 24, 1861.

_____. "Dr. Tumblety's Pimple Banisher." *Harper's Weekly,* September 7, 1861.

_____. "To Be Good Looking." *Harper's Weekly,* July 13, 1861.

Turner, J.E. *The History of the First Inebriate Asylum in the World: By Its Founder; An Account of His Indictment, also a Sketch of the Woman's*

National Hospital, by Its Projector. New York: J.E. Turner, 1888.

"Turner's Universal Neuralgia Pill." *Banner of Light,* February 19, 1870.

Twain, Mark. *The Writings of Mark Twain: Tom Sawyer Abroad, Tom Sawyer the Detective, and Other Stories, Etc., Etc.* New York: Harper and Brother, 1899.

Twain, Mark, V. Fischer, M.B. Frank, and L. Salamo. *Mark Twain's Letters, 1870–1871.* Berkley: University of California Press, 1995.

"Twice Sentenced to Be Hanged." *New York Times,* December 7, 1878.

"The Uneasy Ghost Authoritatively Laid to Rest." *Brooklyn Eagle,* January 14, 1877.

The Union Army: A History of Military Affairs in the Loyal States 1861–65—Records of the Regiments in the Union Army—Cyclopedia of Battles—Memoirs of Commanders and Soldiers. Vol. 2, *Cyclopedia of Battles.* Madison, WI: Federal Publishing Company, 1908.

United Daughters of the Confederacy. *The Confederate Veteran Magazine,* 1895.

United States Census Office and J.S. Billings. *Tenth Census of the United States, 1880: Mortality and Vital Statistics Part 1.* Washington, DC: U.S. Government Printing Office, 1886.

United States Census Office, J.M. Edmunds, and United States Department of the Interior. *Statistics of the United States: (including Mortality, Property, & C.) in 1860; Compiled from the Original Returns and Being the Final Exhibit of the Eighth Census.* Washington, DC: U.S. Government Printing Office, 1866.

United States Census Office and J.C.G. Kennedy. *Preliminary Report on the Eighth Census. 1860.* Washington, DC: U.S. Government Printing Office, 1862.

United States Census Office and F.A. Walker. *A Compendium of the Ninth Census (June 1, 1870): Compiled Pursuant to a Concurrent Resolution of Congress, and under the Direction of the Secretary of the Interior.* Washington, DC: U.S. Government Printing Office, 1872.

United States Census Office, F.A. Walker, C.W. Seaton, and H. Gannett. *Census Reports Tenth Census. June 1, 1880: Mortality and Vital Statistics. Portfolio of Plates and Diagrams.* Washington, DC: U.S. Government Printing Office, 1886.

"Up-Town Ghost Business." *New York Sun,* November 30, 1874.

Van Orden, W.H. *Life of General U.S. Grant: Together with His Military Services.* New York: Albert Sibley and Co., 1885.

van Schlun, B. *Science and the Imagination: Mesmerism, Media, and the Mind in Nineteenth-*

century English and American Literature. Berlin: Galda + Wilch Verlag, 2007.

Vaux, R. *Brief Sketch of the Origin and History of the State Penitentiary for the Eastern District of Pennsylvania, at Philadelphia.* Philadelphia: McLaughlin Brothers, 1872.

"The Vineland Democrat." *Banner of Light,* January 16, 1869.

Voltaic Armor Association. "Dr. Hall's Voltaic Armor or Magnetic Bands and Soles." *Banner of Light,* March 23, 1867.

Walker, W.H. "Gray's Specific Medicine." *Westfield Republican,* June 14, 1882.

Wallace, A.R. *On Miracles and Modern Spiritualism: Three Essays.* London: James Burns, 1875.

"War Gazette." *New York Times,* November 28, 1863.

Ward, H.M. *Public Executions in Richmond, Virginia: A History, 1782–1907.* Jefferson, NC: McFarland, 2012.

"Warranted Purely Vegetable." *New Orleans Daily Crescent,* October 5, 1860.

Welles, G., and E.T. Welles. *Diary:* Boston: Houghton, Mifflin, 1911.

"W.H. Mumler." *Spiritual Magazine,* 1872.

W.H.C. "A Visit to the Eddys." *New York Sun,* October 14, 1874.

Wheeler, E.J., I.K. Funk, and W.S. Woods. *The Literary Digest,* 1894.

White, J.T. *The National Cyclopedia of American Biography.* New York: J. T. White Company, 1898.

Whitney, John F. "Was Abraham Lincoln a Spiritualist?" *Banner of Light,* October 8, 1892.

Williams, E. *Abraham Lincoln a Spiritualist: Lecture.* Venice Art Press, 1891.

Williams, G.F., M.B. Brady, and A. Gardner. *The Memorial War Book: As Drawn from Historical Records and Personal Narratives of the* *Men Who Served in the Great Struggle.* New York: Lovell Brothers, 1894.

Williams, S.E. "The Use of Beverage Alcohol as Medicine, 1790–1860." *Journal of Studies on Alcohol* 41(5)(1980):559.

"Willie Lincoln." *Banner of Light,* May 29, 1869.

Wilson, William. "Wilsonia." *Brooklyn Daily Eagle,* August 16, 1881.

_____. "Wilsonia Triumphant." *Brooklyn Daily Eagle,* November 29, 1881.

Wines, E.C., and Theodore W. Dwight. *The Nation.* New York: J.H. Richards & Company, 1867.

Winslow. "Mrs. Winslow's Soothing Syrup." *Holmes County Farmer,* March 1, 1860.

_____. "Mrs. Winslow's Soothing Syrup." *New York Times,* December 1, 1860.

Wittenmyer, A.T., and F.E. Willard. *History of the Woman's Temperance Crusade: A Complete Official History of the Wonderful Uprising of the Christian Women of the United States Against the Liquor Traffic, Which Culminated in the Gospel Temperance Movement.* Philadelphia: Published at the Office of the Christian Woman, 1878.

"A Woman of the Period." *Memphis Sunday Appeal,* July 2, 1871.

"A Wonderful Mystery." *The Sun,* February 15, 1869.

Woodward, J.J., I.M. Rutkow, and United States Army Medical Department. *Outlines of the Chief Camp Diseases of the United States Armies: As Observed during the Present War.* San Francisco: Norman Publishing, 1863.

"Wright's Indian Vegetable Pills." *The Southerner,* April 2, 1859.

Zeller, P.G. *The Second Vermont Volunteer Infantry Regiment, 1861–1865.* Jefferson, NC: McFarland, 2002.

Ziegler, Smith. "Dr. Leon's Celebrated Preparations." *Jeffersonian,* January 3, 1867.

Index

Indian herb doctors 172, 174–75, 185, 206
Indian Root Pills 171
Indian spirits 62
Indiana State Prison 131
inebriation 117, 119–20, 122, 162; chronic 18, 118, 122
infanticides 161
Infantile Cordial 176
insanity 5–7, 25, 34, 122, 155–56; moral 118–20; temporary 91
insanity defense 36, 146, 155, 164
insomnia 25, 182–83, 192
intemperance 10–11, 25, 106, 108, 114, 124; deaths 26; estimate 100; military 101, 115

jail 111, 134–35, 140, 145, 152, 167; population 130
James, Thomas 74–75
Jarvis, Charles 149
Jarvis Hospital 7
jaundice 100
Johnson, John 174
Jones, Mary 166
Journal of Insanity 36
Judd, Orange 203
the Jukes 165–66
jury 33, 154–55, 169; coroner's 126; grand 130, 135, 140–41; members 120, 132, 134–35

Kansas City 146, 167
Kase, Simon P. 89–90
Kaufman, Daniel 29
Kein, Catherine 23
Kerne, George 30
Keyes, Henry 37
Kiddle, Henry 68–69
Kiddleism 69
King, James 174
King, Katie 197
Kings County Lunatic Asylum 118
Kitchell, George W. 200
kleptomania 118
Kunkel's Bitter Wine 189

Langdon, Olivia 187
Large, W.H. 21
Larrantree, Harry 22
Larue, Dr. 185
Laurie, Adam 179
Laurie, Cranston 92–93
Laurie's Chinese Life Pills 179
Leary, Timothy 145
Lee, Robert E. 58, 123
Leon's Electric Hair Renewer 186
Leslie, Frank 32

letters 5, 13, 15, 59, 89–90, 108
Leupp, William H. 133–35
levitation 44, 48, 71, 196
Lewis, Dio 116
Leyden jar 184
life insurance 33, 35
Lincoln, Abraham 34, 69; death 88, 94–97; mediums claiming psychic contact 95; spirit 95–96; spiritualism 87–88, 91–92; widow and spiritualism 86
Lincoln, Edward 97
Lincoln, Tad 98
Lincoln, Willie 98
Lindsay, D.M. 204
Linen, Ann 133–34
liquor antidote 192
liver diseases 100, 175
Lord, John 182
Loveridge, E. Dexter 182
Lowry, Nelson 29
Lucas, Mary 186
Ludlow, Judge 130–31
Lydia Pinkham's Vegetable Compound 175
Lyon's Magnetic Insect Powder 189
Lyons, Rudolph J. 173–74

Madame Clifford 187
Magic Eloquence 45
Magic Pain Killer 174
magnetic baths 187
magnetic doctor 53, 67, 186–87, 189, 206
magnetic healing 187–88
magnetic method 54
magnetic power 47–48
magnetism 45–47, 53–54, 184–86, 190, 194, 206
magnetized paper 63, 188
magnetizers 46–48
malaria 61, 105, 182
malingering 7–9, 16
Malt Bitters 191
mania-a-potu 144
manifestations 43, 66, 72, 194; marvelous 48, 65; melodious 50; spiritual 196, 198; startling 41
Manning, Jacob M. 163–64
marketing, patent medicines 175, 177–78, 180–82, 185–86, 192
Maryland 3, 7, 92, 121, 174
Mason, Oscar 82
Massachusetts Board of State Charities 131
Massachusetts State Prison 129
Maynard, Nettie Colburn 91, 93
McClure's Magazine 29
McCullough, John R. 109
McFarland, Andrew 120
measles 180